IET SECURITY SERIES 09

# Authentication Technologies for Cloud Computing, IoT and Big Data

## Other volumes in this series:

# Authentication Technologies for Cloud Computing, IoT and Big Data

Edited by
Yasser M. Alginahi and Muhammad Nomani Kabir

The Institution of Engineering and Technology

Published by The Institution of Engineering and Technology, London, United Kingdom

The Institution of Engineering and Technology is registered as a Charity in England & Wales (no. 211014) and Scotland (no. SC038698).

First published 2019

The Institution of Engineering and Technology
Michael Faraday House
Six Hills Way, Stevenage
Herts, SG1 2AY, United Kingdom

www.theiet.org

**British Library Cataloguing in Publication Data**
A catalogue record for this product is available from the British Library


**ISBN 978-1-78561-556-6 (hardback)**
**ISBN 978-1-78561-557-3 (PDF)**


Typeset in India by MPS Limited
Printed in the UK by CPI Group (UK) Ltd, Croydon

# Contents

## 11 Cryptographic engines for cloud based on FPGA    273
*Ramasubramanian Natarajan and Manjith Baby Chellam*

## 12 Data protection laws    309
*Hiba Alginahi, Yasser M. Alginahi and Muhammad Nomani Kabir*

# Preface

Authentication is the process of verifying the identity of a user or a process that intends to access a secured system through some valid means, e.g., identification card, driver's license, signature, password, PIN number, iris, or fingerprint. Enforcing authentication process for users or processes is extremely important for information security. Security apprentices, practitioners, and researchers need to have the knowledge of authentication processes and how to use the processes for current and new technologies, e.g., IoT, cloud computing, and big data. To fulfill the need, a new book with title "Authentication Technologies for Cloud Computing, IoT and Big Data" is written on in-depth topics of authentication and it is worthwhile to read this book as it covers fundamentals and advanced topics of authentication technologies.

While there is a lot of current research focusing on various aspects of authentication, we lack strong references on the topic and there are new concerns with technologies such as IoT, big data, and cloud computing. The contributing authors of the book consist of a team of young and senior researchers in the field around the world. The book provides an in-depth discussion on the state-of-the-art research and development in authentication technology, including fundamentals, algorithms, implementation, applications, research challenges, and future trends related to authentication technology in information systems.

In the book, the fundamentals of authentication technologies, i.e., information security, cryptographic algorithms, data authentication algorithms, watermarking, and biometric authentication are presented with comprehensive examples and algorithmic details. The book includes some attractive topics in the era of big data, IoT, cloud computing, i.e., lightweight security algorithms for IoT applications, identification schemes for post-quantum era, authentication for cloud application, cryptographic algorithms on FPGA for cloud application and data protection laws. In addition, the book provides future research directions and open problems related to the evolution of technologies.

The book will be a good reference for researchers (in academic and industry) who are interested in information security. The book contains the fundamental knowledge of authentication technologies which can be an excellent reference for students, teaching staff, and practitioners; and the book furthermore includes advanced topics for security experts, academic, and industrial researchers.

Yasser Alginahi and Muhammad Nomani Kabir

# Chapter 1

# Introduction

*Muhammad Nomani Kabir[1] and Yasser Alginahi[2]*

Authentication is central to any security issue, involving the verification process of the identity of a person or a process to access a secured system. Therefore, authentication is extremely important to guarantee the smooth flow of information without troubles. Authentication process is implemented for data in storage and data in-transit with communication network. Critical systems, e.g., energy, banking and finance, defense, transportation, business process, manufacturing, water system, and emergency services heavily rely on information systems and networks. Authentication has become an integrated part of modern computing and communication technologies, e.g., Internet of Things (IoT), cloud computing, and connected vehicles. This chapter provides an overview of the book, its theme, and purpose by introducing the topics of the book that presents the current technological advances and the new trends in authentication in information security.

This chapter begins with the basic explanation of the terms—authentication and related terminologies. Then, a brief history of authentication breaches is presented, providing a glimpse of the ever-evolving mechanism of authentication hacks over the passage of time. The sophisticated nature of authentication breaches demonstrates the growing necessity of enhanced authentication techniques in the modern life. This is the reason, why a new book is written on the topic and we emphasize that it is worthwhile to study this book as it covers in-depth topics of authentication.

Then the chapter provides the organization of the remaining chapters in the book with a short, but a precise, description of each chapter. The first six chapters cover foundation of authentication technologies, i.e., information security, cryptographic algorithms, data authentication algorithms, watermarking, and biometric authentication with comprehensive examples and algorithmic details. Some attractive topics in the age of big data, IoT, and cloud computing, e.g., lightweight security algorithms for IoT applications, identification schemes for post-quantum era, authentication for cloud application, cryptographic algorithms on field-programmable gate array (FPGA) for cloud application and data protection laws are included in the next six chapters. Each chapter provides an extensive description of the topic with algorithmic

[1]Faculty of Computer Systems & Software Engineering, University Malaysia Pahang, Malaysia
[2]Department of Electrical and Computer Engineering, University of Windsor, Canada

details following the current state-of-the-art research and development. The chapter points out current issues and problems with a critical discussion associated with the topic and at the same time, it refers to possible solutions of those problems. The chapters present research directions and open problems relating to the evolution of technologies in the coming future.

## 1.1    Basic terminologies and motivation

Information systems play an important role in communication, financial management, business processes, manufacturing, and research and development for organizations and individuals. Critical systems (e.g., energy, banking and finance, defense, law enforcement, transportation, water systems, and emergency services) heavily rely on information systems and networks. Therefore, security is very important to guarantee the smooth flow of information without problems. Authentication is known as one of the most important security features, and its role in the domain of network and data storage is extremely important. Authentication is the act of verifying a claim of identity. Specifically, authentication is the verification of a user who endeavors to access a secured system through some valid means, e.g., identification card, driver's license, signature, password, PIN number, iris, or fingerprint. For example, a student S wants to rent some books from a library. S shows his/her identification (ID) number to the library official who identifies S by visually examining the ID photo against S. Upon verification of the identity S, S is authenticated and the official proceeds with the renting process through the book rental system (software) of the library. The official again checks the photograph, identification number in the system before recording the information of the books for S. Thus, after the second round of authentication, the books are handed to S. Again, S can access the book rental system at home to check the information of his/her rented books by entering the correct username and password, which authenticates that S is the person whom the username belongs to. Relating to authentication, there are three terms, confidentiality, integrity, and availability (CIA) which are essential components of information security [1,2].

*Confidentiality* in information security is a component which ensures that any unauthorized person, entity, or process is not able to access the information. Confidentiality makes sure that information is made available to an authorized person or process and hid from those who are not authorized to possess the information. A similar term, privacy implies to protect the information from unauthorized viewers. Confidentiality can be lost by laptop theft, password theft, or sensitive e-mails sent to the wrong individuals.

*Integrity* of information is a component that maintains and ensures the accuracy and completeness of information over its entire lifecycle. This implies that information can only be modified by an authorized person or process and remains at the same state as it has been after the modification. A receiver R of an e-mail (information) must have the same e-mail (information) as the sender T sends R. Referring to the book rental example, the student S wants to check his/her rented book in the system and upon entering the username and password, S must find the correct information of the rented books. Integrity of information can be broken by man-in-the-middle attack, password theft, or insider attack.

*Availability* is a component that ensures the information available to those who are authorized to access them. Availability includes three elements—the computing device to store and process the information; the security mechanism to protect it; the communicating networks to access it—which must work properly to make the information available. Thus, service disruptions due to power outages, hardware failures, and system upgrades cause a system unavailable. Furthermore, a system becomes unavailable due to denial-of-service attacks, which can be activated by a huge number of incoming messages to the system. For example, the student S wants to check the return dates of the rented books; S can make it correctly if the book rental system is available, i.e., communication network, the server and the authentication scheme using username with password properly work. However, S cannot access the system, if a power outage or hardware failure occurs at server side or communication network, or a denial-of-service attack hinders the communication.

Throughout the age of information security, there are numerous data breaches resulting from authentication errors—from the simple information theft of a personal credit card to the retrieval of a confidential state secret. The sophistication of the attack has greatly enhanced with the new computing technologies, and advanced theoretical and computational methods. Here, we just state the few well-known events [3,4] in the past years.

In 2017, River City Media, a company that involves phishing and hacking activities was targeted which resulted in leaking of 1.37 billion e-mails addresses, business logs, employee chats, and accounts to the public. The hackers accessed the information through a faulty backup of the company's information. In 2016, hackers succeeded to transfer $81 million from Bangladesh Bank to Rizal Commercial Banking Corporation in the Philippines and an additional $20 million to Pan Asia Banking through Federal Reserve Bank of New York using SWIFT system. The hackers first sent more than three dozen requests to Federal Reserve Bank of New York to transfer millions of dollars from Bangladesh Bank to bank accounts in the Philippines, Sri Lanka, and other parts of Asia. Due to mis-authentication, $81 million was deposited into four accounts at a Rizal branch. Fortunately, Bangladesh Bank managed to stop the other transactions of $850 million.

In 2014, Sony Pictures, a Hollywood film studio, went through a series of attacks for several months. Hackers called as *Guardians of Peace* broke into the database of the studio in which they retrieved confidential data—personal information of the employees and four then-unreleased movies. Sony Pictures lost an estimated $100 million, suffering from data dump and clean-up after the event.

In 2013–2014, Yahoo underwent two massive data breaches; in that over a billion user accounts including personal information, e.g., full names, birthdays, phone numbers, and their encrypted passwords were hacked. The company first acknowledged the attacks in 2016, and it asked the users to amend their passwords. In 2012, Court Ventures Owned by Experian, a large credit bureau, fell prey to a Vietnamese crime ring, pretending as an American private investigator, and the company sold its clients' private data, e.g., banking information, credit card details, and social security numbers to the crime ring. It was reported that over 200 million records were tricked to deliver to the crime ring.

These attacks demonstrate the sophistication of the techniques which the hackers use to infiltrate the highly secured systems by manipulating authentication process. Enforcing strong authentication processes for vulnerable entry points of the system is extremely important for information security. It is necessary for security apprentices, practitioners, and researchers to have the knowledge of authentication processes and how to use the processes for current and new technologies, e.g., IoT, cloud computing, and big data. To fulfill the need, a new book is written on the in-depth topics of authentication and it is worthwhile to study this book as it covers fundamental and advanced topics of authentication.

## 1.2    Overview of the book chapters

The overview of the book chapters can be presented as follows: Chapter 2 with title "Information Security" written by Baig, Zeadally, and Woodward begins with the description of five fundamental principles of information security: confidentiality, integrity, availability, authenticity, and non-repudiation. Definitions and standards, e.g., X.509, transport layer security, hash, digital signatures, public key infrastructure, and OAuth in information security are presented. Then different threats are classified as spoofing, tampering, repudiation, information disclosure, denial of service, and elevation of privilege, which can be addressed by the security properties authentication, integrity, non-repudiation, confidentiality, availability, and authorization, respectively. Next information or data are classified based on risk level of damage to the national interest, organization, or individuals according to different institutions, e.g., Australian Government security and the NATO. Furthermore, a number of frameworks for IoT applications, e.g., SmartThings from Samsung, HomeKit from Apple, Amazon Web Services (AWS) IoT from Amazon, ARM mbed from ARM, Azure IoT Suite from Microsoft, Brillo/Weave from Google, and Calvin from Ericsson are discussed with an emphasis of security. An IoT framework SmartThings from Samsung facilitates smart services on homes, e.g., controlling the light switch (on/off), or a thermostat (heater, cooler or fan on/off) using OAuth protocols for authentication to connect with remote authorized IoT devices. Similarly, HomeKit, an IoT framework developed by Apple enables management and control of IoT devices in a home where a public key-based encryption standard, ed25519 along with a digital signature is used for authentication. The IoT framework Calvin developed by Ericsson provides management and control service of IoT devices where X.509 standard is used for authentication. Brillo/Weave developed by Google is an IoT framework running on Android platform where authentication of devices and users is performed through an OAuth protocol, in addition to a digital certificate. IoT framework mbed by ARM designed for ARM microcontrollers has a common operating system across all IoT devices, but supports several communication protocols, e.g., MQTT, HTTP, and AMQP. The device-side security functionality uVisor of ARM mbed provides secure communications among mbed IoT devices as well as between the devices and the centralized cloud using mbed TLS. ARM mbed does not include authentication scheme explicitly; however, mbed can incorporate authentication scheme with X.509 standard through a proper configuration. AWS licensed by Amazon is a cloud-based IoT framework that provides the capability of secure device communication and remote control for IoT devices. A device gateway must be deployed in the AWS IoT setup that acts as an intermediary between AWS IoT devices and the AWS cloud server. Authentication is facilitated through X.509. Secure communications are established using SSL/TLS that encrypts and digitally signs all the information.

The authors present the regulation Health Insurance Portability and Accountability Act (HIPAA) that sets the standards, processes, and procedures to access the personal health information. They also discuss National Institute of Standards and Technology (NIST) framework for critical infrastructure cybersecurity to provide a guideline for business drivers to maintain cybersecurity activities sustainable and effective. The chapter ends with future research challenges in the era of IoT, specifically, with heterogamous IoT devices, threats at different operational levels, flawed hardware design, operating environment, third-party applications, and cost of protection.

Chapter 3 with title "Data Authentication Algorithms" written by Al-Shareeda discusses the data authentication algorithms of information security. Data authentication is essential to achieve specific security requirements in communication by ensuring data integrity (data has not been fabricated) that assures that the data senders are authorized users, i.e., certified data originators. The received data is authenticated by authentication algorithms. Simple authentication schemes are the schemes that use passwords and hash functions. With the progression of cryptography, authentication process uses encrypted checksums or Message Authentication Codes (MAC) which are of the symmetric key cryptography in which a secret symmetric key is shared between the sender and the receiver. The asymmetric key cryptographic algorithms or digital signature algorithms which share a public key and a private key between the sender and the receiver are used for more advanced authentication protocols such as the public key infrastructure (PKI). The digital signature algorithms, e.g., Rivest–Shamir–Adleman (RSA), and more advanced elliptic curve digital signature algorithm (ECDSA) are now used to fulfill more security requirements. Biometry-based authentication, e.g., fingerprint, iris, and face recognition play an important role in authentication. Furthermore, authentication can be attained using watermarking and steganography techniques.

This chapter presents a comprehensive overview of the modern authentication algorithms by classifying the methods into the categories, i.e., password, cryptography, biometry, watermarking-, and steganography-based methods. Since biometry and watermarking- and steganography-based methods are the topics of two separate chapters in this book, the author in this chapter focuses on cryptography-based methods in details by elaborating on hashing functions, e.g., secure hash function (SHA), symmetric authentication algorithms, e.g., MAC, and asymmetric authentication algorithms (digital signatures), e.g., RSA, ECDSA with their algorithmic details using some examples. The strengths and weaknesses of the popular algorithms of each category are also discussed. Next, the author concludes the chapter by connecting the presented algorithms in the light of cloud computing, IoT, and big data, with a further outlook on the current research challenges and future trends of research.

Chapter 4 with title "Cryptographic Algorithms" written by Rashidi provides a short, but precise, description of different types of modern cryptographic methods. There are two categories of cryptography—symmetric (private-key) and asymmetric (public-key) cryptography. Symmetric cryptography, e.g., data encryption standard (DES) and advanced encryption standard (AES), use a private key of certain length to encrypt a message from sender's side and decrypt the message at receiver's side. The author describes DES and AES with algorithmic details using examples for message encryption and decryption. Asymmetric cryptography such as RSA, ElGamal public-key encryption, and elliptic curve cryptosystems (ECCs) are discussed in detail. The protocols involving public-key cryptography are also given. Furthermore, the author provides a description on digital signatures, e.g., RSA digital signature, ElGamal signature, Schnorr signature, and elliptic curves digital signature schemes. Hash functions using SHA are also provided. However, two hard problems arise in modern public key cryptosystems: the integer factorization problem (IFP) and discrete logarithm problem (DLP). These two problems are discussed and possible solutions are suggested.

The author further describes the authentication techniques and security for IoT, big data, and cloud computing. Since IoT integrates the Internet to the physical world, it poses new security challenges. To ensure that no untrusted users can get access to the devices, authentication method has to be implemented for identifying devices in a network to restrict access. Security in big data consists of infrastructure security of data, data privacy, data management and integrity, and reactive security. The challenges of detecting and preventing advanced threats and malicious intruders must be solved using big data style analysis. Some of the challenges are associated with the intrinsic characteristics of IoT. The advantages and disadvantages of the cryptographic methods are also included in the chapter. Finally, research challenges and future direction on cryptographic methods are presented.

Chapter 5 with title "Digital Watermarking Algorithms for Multimedia Data" by Islam *et al.* provides watermarking algorithms for multimedia. Watermarking algorithms can be used to authenticate the ownership of multimedia data, e.g., images, audios, and videos. In cryptographic system, a sender transmits a message in an encrypted form to a recipient for preserving the confidentiality of data. However, once the message is decrypted, there is no control to check the illegal redistribution of the decrypted content due to the availability of multimedia manipulation software. Thus, security issues occur in the form of authentication breach, copyright violation, and loss of integrity. To deal with illegal copying and distribution, and unauthorized manipulation of multimedia data, digital watermarking is considered as one of the promising solutions. In a watermarking technique, a watermark is embedded into the original image. The watermarked multimedia is then distributed, transmitted, or published. When the watermarked multimedia needs to be verified for copyright protection, ownership verification or content authentication, the watermark is extracted from watermarked multimedia. Watermarking techniques which address copyright protection use robust watermarking, and which address illegal content manipulation use fragile watermarking approach. Another watermarking called semi-fragile watermarking is a popular method which sustains certain attacks on watermarked multimedia and reinforces the authentication property of multimedia documents.

In this chapter, the authors begin with the basic properties and application areas of watermarking. They classify different types of watermarking based on human perception (visible, invisible), detection process (blind, non-blind), method (robust, fragile, semi-fragile), cover media (image, audio, video), and embedding domain (spatial, transform), and then the watermarking methods, e.g., robust, fragile and semi-fragile are described in the context of principles, algorithms, and related works. Advantages and disadvantages of the watermarking methods are provided. The possible attacks on images are also categorized according to image enhancement, noise addition, geometric manipulation, and compression. The attacks can be simulated on multimedia document to evaluate the strength of a watermarking algorithm. In addition, research challenges such as balancing among the imperceptibility, robustness and embedding capacity of the watermark schemes; designing suitable reversible watermarking techniques for medical, banking, and crime investigation are discussed.

Chapter 6 with title "Biometric Authentication" written by Al-Saggaf and Abdul Majid starts with the fundamental and importance of biometric authentication in the present era. Biometric authentication has become challenging in this technologically connected world with modern smart gadgets. Reliance only on security codes and password keys brings about serious security loopholes, since more sophisticated digital thefts and threats are carried out these days by hackers and imposters, such as duplicating or using counterfeited ID cards. Hence, the science of biometrics plays a critical role to revolutionize the identification, verification, and authentication of digital data using some of the unique human features which have withstood the tests of times. An interesting fact among the human beings is that certain characteristics that make them unique from each other can be utilized to recognize the identity. From the cradle to grave, these characteristics would remain the same, irrespective of how exponentially the human population increases. The authors then discuss different biometric authentication technologies for individuals based on—physical characteristics, such as fingerprint, face, voice, iris, ear, and vein pattern,—and behavioral attributes, such as signature verification, keystroke dynamics, and gesture biometrics. The authentication is performed using different algorithms which are implemented on different hardware. A typical algorithm first extracts the biometric features from the physical or behavioral characteristics (e.g., scanned image or recorded voice) and stores these unique features as templates with identities of users in the database system in order to facilitate identification. Authentication of an individual under inquiry is conducted by comparing the biometric feature in the database with the extracted biometric feature of that individual. Matching in the comparison confirms that the newly collected biometric feature already exists in the database, providing the identity of the individual.

In this chapter, the authors discuss different types of attacks and threats on the biometric systems (e.g., fake identification using artificial face or a finger) and their countermeasures. Despite the robustness and viability of biometrics security, the systems are still considered vulnerable to cyber-physical attacks and they are susceptible to digital threats. The countermeasures—biometric cryptosystem, fuzzy commitment scheme, fuzzy vault scheme, cancelable biometrics are preventive measures against the attacks. Therefore, it is extremely important to thwart the attacks on biometric remote user authentication in which a remote server verifies the legitimacy of a user over a communication channel using the biometric data. The authors conclude the chapter with research challenges of security issues in biometric cloud.

Chapter 7 with title "Lightweight Block Ciphers with Applications in IoT" contributed by Pehlivanoglu *et al.* presents authentication techniques needed to maintain secure communication for resource-constrained IoT systems using lightweight block ciphers. IoT system brings a lot of benefits—at the same time, incurs security risks because of security loopholes associated with IoT devices. Security risks can be prevented by using cryptographic algorithms for the resource-constrained IoT system. A lightweight cryptographic algorithm is required for the resource-constrained IoT system in order to avoid overhead of computational complexity and latency. Lightweight cryptography e.g., block cipher converts plaintext blocks into ciphertext blocks using a cryptographic algorithm with a secret key. Diffusion and confusion schemes used in cryptographic algorithms protect the ciphertext from statistical analysis. A good confusion scheme deters to relate the ciphertext with the key while a good diffusion scheme conceals the statistical distribution property of the plaintext through the ciphertext, i.e., the ciphertext is dramatically influenced by a slight change in the key bits.

The chapter starts with the fundamental of block cipher, i.e., the components and matrices which are required to design a block cipher. The hardware efficiency of the linear algebra-based diffusion matrices was analyzed using the XOR count metric. The existing best-known XOR count results for efficient maximum distance separable (MDS) matrices were compared. Then a comprehensive survey on lightweight block ciphers used to design the resource-constrained IoT system is presented. The authors compare ten lightweight block ciphers in order to evaluate the performance in terms of power and energy consumption, latency, security level, throughput, and efficiency on 8-bit, 16-bit, and 32-bit microcontrollers. Design of lightweight block ciphers with their components is presented in detail, including the diffusion layers, which provides the required diffusion and resistance against the most well-known attacks—linear and differential cryptanalysis. The authors discuss the advantages and disadvantages of the algorithms, clarifying authentication problems and implementation issues for IoT devices. Finally, a guideline is provided to develop lightweight block ciphers for the low-cost Wi-Fi module in IoT systems. The authors also point out the future research directions on this challenging area.

Chapter 8 with title "Identification Schemes in Post-Quantum Era Based on Multivariate Polynomials with Applications in Cloud and IoT" contributed by Akleylek and Soysaldi presents authentication techniques using multivariate polynomials over a finite field in post-quantum era. Identity and access control services carried out using traditional public key cryptosystems, e.g., RSA, DSA, ECDSA, are important areas of research in clouds and IoT. However, these secure crypto-systems will be broken with advent of the new computing device—quantum computer and subsequently, this threatens to breach the authentication security of IoT and cloud. Thus, it is worthwhile to develop new cryptosystems that are quantum-secure and can be efficiently adapted to IoT and cloud systems. The authors found that multivariate polynomials and lattice-based cryptosystems are efficient for IoT and cloud systems in post-quantum world.

In this chapter, the authors present an overview of the secure identity man-agement schemes using multivariate polynomials over a finite field. They begin with the basic definitions related to the structure of identification schemes. Then, the authors provide a short, but precise, discussion of identification schemes based on the multivariate polynomials by considering applications on different platforms. The schemes are demonstrated from the fundamental perspective considering zero knowledge property and the different numbers of passes, e.g., 3-pass and 5-pass. After scrutinizing open problems in the literature, the authors propose a novel identification scheme based on multivariate quadratic polynomials with the objective of achieving a lower computational complexity. Then, they compare the proposed identification scheme with the most prominent schemes in terms of commitment length, memory requirements, and computation time. The chapter is concluded with the discussion on quantum secure identification schemes for cloud, IoT, and big data applications, as well as their research challenges.

Chapter 9 with title "Authentication Issues for Cloud Applications" authored by Rashidi focuses on the authentication technologies in the cloud system. Cloud computing is a technology that shares computing resources and other services to run cloud applications through the Internet. Cloud applications involve security issues as they include multiple systems and technologies such as networks, databases, oper-ating systems, virtualization, resource scheduling, load balancing, concurrency control, parallel computing, and memory management. Therefore, providing secure communications for the systems and technologies is extremely important for secured cloud applications. In cloud computing, authentication, that is, the process of vali-dating and guaranteeing the identity of cloud service subscribers or users, plays an important role. The reliability and security of the cloud computing environment are especially based on authentication. Therefore, this chapter presents security issues for cloud applications by providing authentication technologies in the cloud system.

The chapter begins with the security aspects of the cloud environment, e.g., identity and access management, confidentiality and data encryption, attacks against information in cloud environments and virtualization security. Each of these aspects of security challenges is discussed in detail. Next, detailed authentication technolo-gies for cloud applications are explained, and advantages and disadvantages of authentication methods are also presented. The chapter ends with future research challenges.

Chapter 10 with title "Insider Threat Problem from a Cloud Computing Per-spective," written by Padayachee, presents the security risks with the cloud storage due to insider threats. Cloud computing provides computing resources with a quick, cost-effective, and scalable way for both large and small organizations. Cloud storage security is susceptible to information security risks due to loopholes in the cloud system that needs to be addressed. Insider threat will become particularly sinister with the weakness of cloud computing, since the insider, an individual who has legitimate access to an organization's information technology infrastructure uses the authority granted to him/her for an illegitimate gain. From a cloud computing perspective, the concept of the insider is multi-contextual and consequently propagates more opportunities for malfeasance.

This chapter starts with definitions related to insider threats, e.g., network authentication, authorization, security, reliability, transparency, and scalability. The author discusses various types of insider threats in the cloud-computing domain, and challenges involved in managing the insider threats. Specifically, security issues involving the cloud services, e.g., PaaS, SaaS, and IaaS service models are explained. Possible solutions for the insider threats emanating from cloud service users (CSUs) and cloud service providers (CSPs) are given. Specific techniques proposed for cloud-related insiders, e.g., encryption, detection, prevention, honeypots, authentication, and the related concept of access control are presented. Finally, applications, open questions and future research challenge in the technical, social, and socio-technical domains are presented.

Chapter 11 with title "Cryptographic Engines for Cloud Based on FPGA" written by Ramasubramanian and Manjith provides implementation techniques of four cryptographic algorithms—AES, DES, SHA, and MD5 on FPGA for applications in cloud computing. Cryptographic algorithms are used in the security applications and devices. Encryption and decryption are used in the cloud server for full virtual machine encryption, protection of data at-rest, data in-transit, etc. Execution of cryptographic operations on the processor reduces the efficiency and increases heat production. Integration of cloud data centers with FPGA devices, which are customized hardware circuits designed according to the need, provides the opportunity to implement critical tasks, which in turn improves the performance and reduces heat production.

The chapter describes basic principles of AES, DES, SHA, and MD5, and their implementation techniques on FPGA. Efficiency for each algorithm is computed in terms of throughput, latency, and resource utilization. The implemented security system can be used in embedded systems, IoTs, cloud servers, network security processors, etc. Security system is created using two encryption accelerators: AES, DES, and two authentication accelerators: SHA and MD5. The system uses dynamic partial reconfiguration (DPR) feature to load the accelerator on-demand on FPGA. The authors illustrated how the proposed security system loads the encryption/authentication accelerator on-demand. Thus, static power can be reduced by loading only the necessary modules. Cryptographic algorithms implemented on FPGA are stored as bitstreams which are vulnerable to attacks such as, reverse engineering, cloning and insertion of Trojans. As a future direction of research, the authors emphasize on the logic encryption of the hardware which is made using insertion of logic gates or multiplexers. Encrypted hardware circuits cannot be reverse engineered or insert Trojans without a key.

Chapter 12 with title "Data Protection Laws" by H. Alginahi, Y. Alginahi, and Kabir presents an overview of data protection laws (DPLs) and policies available in different countries and organizations. Data protection is a concern for individuals and organizations which collect, analyze, store, and transmit data. Data can be written on paper or stored on a computer, IoT, or cloud storage or communicated through networks. Information stored in storages or communicated through networks must not fall in the hands of the people who may use it in fraud, abuse or scam. Hence, the systems need to have legislations, policies, guidelines, rules, laws or directives that govern the use, transmission, storage, and processing of information on their premises, systems, and networks to guarantee the protection of information for organizations and individuals. The objective of data protection laws is to provide a balance among protection of data, proper use of data, and data acquisition for forensic or criminal investigation. In this technological era, governments and institutions impose data protection policies upon the organizations and individuals to implement DPLs to govern the usage, transmission, and storage of information. The data exposure statistics are overwhelmingly alarming making it a large responsibility upon governments and organizations to take measures to protect sensitive information.

In this chapter, the authors discuss principles of DPLs, data classification, global cyberlaws, DPLs for social media, EU General Data Protection Regulation (GDPR), challenges of DPLs and cybersecurity, data privacy, and cyber security checklist. The authors started with most perilous data breaches that affected millions of users over the past decade. The principles of DPLs and data classification based on required level of security are discussed. The authors provided some important statistics on global cyberlaw legislations based on United Nations Conference on Trade and Development (UNCTAD) with the following categories: data protection and privacy, online consumer protection, e-transactions, and cybercrime. The authors present a list of countries and their legislation relating to data protection. Cybersecurity challenges relating to DPLs with the issues of cross-border data, new technologies, balancing surveillance and data protection, and unrealistic compliance burdens are elaborated. Finally, recommendations and future direction in this area, e.g., developing and updating a cybersecurity checklist, developing a uniform global data protection policy, training, and educating the people on up-to-date security policies, are included with insightful concluding remarks.

Finally, Chapter 13 summarizes the book with some concluding remarks.

Based on the above discussion on the book chapters, it can be noted that the book contains fundamental knowledge of authentication technologies which can be an excellent reference for students, teaching staff, and practitioners; and the book furthermore includes advanced topics on authentication for security experts, academic, and industrial researchers.

# References

[1]  Stallings W, and Brown L. *Cryptography and network security: Principles and practice*. Seventh edition, Pearson Education Limited, Edinburgh Gate, Essex, England; 2017.

[2] Whitman, ME, and Mattord, HJ. *Principles of information security*. Sixth edition, Cengage Learning, *Boston*, Massachusetts, USA; 2017.

[3] Edwards B, Hofmeyr S, and Forrest S. 'Hype and heavy tails: A closer look at data breaches.' *Journal of Cybersecurity*. 2016; 2(1): 3–14.

[4] Data Breach [Online]. 2018, https://en.wikipedia.org/wiki/Data_breach [accessed 14 Sep 2018].

*Chapter 2*

# Information security

*Zubair Baig[1], Sherali Zeadally[2]*
*and Andrew Woodward[3]*

Information security is a very important component of system and network security. The understanding and implementation of the five pillars of information security, namely, confidentiality, integrity, availability, authenticity, and non-repudiation, is fundamental to the protection of information assets from the omnipotent adversarial cyber threat. The evolving adversary requires a counter active information security program for both small and large organizations. This chapter defines the fundamental elements of information security, and presents the core standards for information security, threat classes, and data classification standards. With the rapid adoption of the Internet of Things (IoT) paradigm, IoT device security has become an important topic, which is addressed in detail in this chapter. Standards associated with information security in health care, as well as the National Institute of Standards and Technology (NIST) framework for cyber security, are also described in detail. The chapter concludes with a discussion on the foreseeable challenges for information security in the IoT era.

## 2.1 Introduction

Security of information is very critical for smooth system functionality and seamless operations in the world of heterogeneous computing. The five commonly known pillars of information security are confidentiality, integrity, availability, authenticity, and non-repudiation, as shown in Figure 2.1. Security of information as a discipline has evolved during the past 30 years from the era of centralized mainframe machines storing information in kilobytes to the current era of information supercomputers that hold terabytes of data at an affordable cost. Rapid advances in computing power, speed of data transfer, and the abilities of the adversary to carry out sophisticated cyber-attacks with relative ease, have encumbered the task of securing information across the heterogeneous computing devices that store and process information. The challenge of securing information has thus

[1]School of Information Technology, Deakin University and CSIRO, Data61, Australia
[2]College of Communication and Information, University of Kentucky, USA
[3]School of Science, Edith Cowan University, Australia

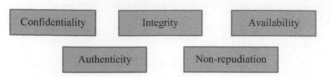

*Figure 2.1    The five pillars of information security*

become increasingly complicated. Legacy computing and communication devices with standard operating systems, including Windows-based systems, pose a set of challenges for information security, that are different from the ones faced by contemporary computing devices of the Internet of Things (IoT). These IoT devices have custom-built operating systems which can be exposed if a vulnerability specific to their set of protocols and standards is discovered. Consequently, the security solution that must be applied for maintaining the five pillars of information security in the world of IoT must be optimal for each category of devices identified.

Cyber threats posed to information assets are ever-evolving, and the rate of evolution of the threat landscape is beyond the abilities of current cybersecurity solutions for containment. Several questions emerge out of the current threat landscape to the information security paradigm. These include: What are the distinct categories of contemporary electronic devices that hold information assets? How best can a cybersecurity solution be planned and implemented so that it is effective in protecting the information assets of a given electronic device? Can the cyber security solution adapt to the evolving threat landscape post deployment? What is the best approach for managing the risk posed to information assets?

In this chapter, we define the key terminology associated with information security and provide a thorough insight into the information security domain as it stands in contemporary times.

## 2.2   Confidentiality

**Confidentiality** of information implies that only authorized personnel are given access to read data, and that the creation, transmission, and storage of information assets is done such that information is not decipherable by unauthorized users [1]. Confidentiality of information can be assured through the planning, deployment, and maintenance of cryptographic methods that can be used for encrypting data for confidentiality purposes. Data that is required to be kept confidential must be encrypted and stored and/or transmitted to the intended destination. Consequently, confidentiality of data can be provided for both data at-rest as well as data in-transit. Transmission of encrypted data is also a key component of network security wherein, the assurance of data privacy can only be provided if a data encryption and decryption scheme is deployed.

A cryptographic key management system is required for establishing and maintaining public and private keys for public-key cryptosystems and shared symmetric keys for symmetric key-based encryption schemes. Key distribution is defined as the task of distributing keys to all entities that will encrypt their data.

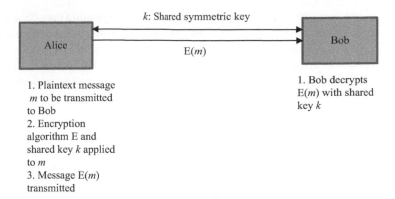

*Figure 2.2    Symmetric key encryption*

## 2.2.1    Symmetric key cryptography

Symmetric key cryptography [2] is based on the principle of a single key shared among all parties willing to communicate with each other securely (as shown in Figure 2.2). The two parties must share a secret key beforehand that will allow them to encrypt and decrypt their messages before transmitting them over an insecure communication channel. The components of a symmetric key-based scheme include a shared secret key $k$, an encryption algorithm $E$, and a decryption algorithm $D$. A message $m$ that is to be encrypted is submitted as input to the encryption algorithm $E$. The algorithm performs a series of operations on the plaintext message $m$, whilst using the shared secret key $k$, in order to produce a cipher text $c$, for transmission over an insecure communication channel to the intended recipient. The recipient applies the decryption algorithm $D$ on cipher text $c$, in order to retrieve the plaintext $m$. In order for the symmetric key encryption and decryption scheme to function correctly, both communicating parties must share the secret key $k$ beforehand. Popular symmetric key encryption schemes include the data encryption standard (DES) and advanced encryption standard (AES).

## 2.2.2    Public key cryptography

*Public key cryptography* includes methods and procedures for the generation of key pairs (public and private), for each user or system, and the definition of methods for use of these key pairs for encryption and decryption of plaintext messages.

Public key cryptography [3] is based on the concept of a key pair, *public* and *private*, for each key owner, where the owner can either be a system or an individual user. The key pair concept was originally developed and proven by Diffie and Hellman in 1976 [4]. They defined the concept of encryption with one key of the pair and decryption with the other key of the same pair. The principle of public key encryption is the one-way trapdoor, wherein the underlying mathematical function for encryption and decryption is not reversible, difficult, or near-to impossible to implement. The concept first proposed by Diffie and Hellman was further expanded upon by Rivest, Shamir, and Adelman, to develop the first public key cryptography system known as RSA [3]. Given that the private key of the key pair must be kept a secret by the key owner, any system can adopt the RSA public key scheme for encrypting a message using the public key of the intended recipient, and having it transmitted across an insecure communication channel, for subsequent decryption by the recipient using her private key.

Compared to symmetric key cryptography, public key-based encryption schemes generally required more processing and storage resources, and are therefore more expensive to implement.

## 2.3   Integrity

Data integrity is the process of confirming the accuracy of data over its life. The integrity of data is a critical component of information security, and mechanisms and processes must be in place for maintaining data integrity. One of the most popular approaches for defining the verification of data is the use of *message digests* or *hashes*. A cryptographic hash function is a sequence of steps that transforms a collection of bits comprising data into a fixed length value known as a hash, which is irreversible. Hash functions can be applied for maintaining data and message integrity through the following 3-step process [5]:

1.   A message is input to a hash function for processing and generating a hash value.
2.   The message is stored in a data repository or transmitted across an insecure communication channel along with its hash value.
3.   To verify the message integrity, the hash value is recomputed for the given message, and the result obtained is compared against the stored or received hash.

Common examples of hash functions include MD-5 and SHA-1.

*Message authentication codes (MACs)* [5] are an extension to the standard hash function. MACs are produced through the application of cryptographic procedures on the hash value of a given message. By encrypting the hash value of a given message using a secret key, an MAC is produced. As the key is a secret known only to the sender and receiver of the message, or to the owner of the data when it is stored, an MAC does verification of both the integrity of the data as well as the authenticity of the entity which computed the MAC.

## 2.4   Availability

Information assets must be available for provisioning of services to legitimate users without ever failing. If an event causes the asset to become unavailable, requestors of service are consequently denied access. A denial of service attack (DoS) [6], attempts to cripple the resources of a victim's computing device, by flooding it with a large volume of network traffic, making it unable to provide the required services to legitimate requestors of the services. In addition, an exploit within the operating system or an application of a computing device, can be tampered with, so as to cause the device to disengage from provisioning of routine services. If the DoS attack is carried out from multiple sources, it is termed a distributed denial of service (DDoS) attack. Such attacks affect the availability of information systems and pose a security threat to them.

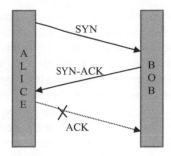

*Figure 2.3   TCP-SYN attack perpetrated by ALICE*

The TCP-SYN attack is a popular DoS attack (as shown in Figure 2.3) that targets a vulnerability of the transmission control protocol (TCP). According to [7], any system running TCP is vulnerable to this attack. The attack is carried out as follows: a legitimate client system attempts to establish a connection with a server by sending it a SYN message. The server responds to this client request through a SYN-ACK message. The client then sends a response to the server's response through an ACK message. In summary, a total of three messages are exchanged between the client and the server in order to establish a communication channel between them.

The three-way handshaking mechanism is exploitable when the adversary may pose as a legitimate client and participate in the three-way TCP handshake albeit by not sending the third message, ACK, back to the server. Consequently, an open connection request remains in the server's memory, in the form of a data structure of pending connections. By repeating this malicious activity several times, the server's finite memory resources are exhausted through too many partial connec-tions. Consequently, the availability of the server is affected.

*Direct DDoS attacks* involve numerous participating attacker machines that are compromised by the adversary for generating a large volume of network traffic for delivery to the victim's machine, in a short span of time. *Reflector DDoS attacks* on the other hand operate as follows: the attacker compromises numerous machines on the Internet, which are effectively triggered to generate numerous fictitious requests with false source addresses to other reflector machines on the Internet. The reflector machines respond to these requests, thereby flooding the victim machine with a large volume of network traffic simultaneously

## 2.5   Authenticity

In everyday life, it is imperative for information systems to identify users by means of authenticating their credentials, before granting them access to the system. Authentication is a key pillar of information security as it provisions security to the system by ensuring that only legitimate users are interacting and carrying out their tasks. Traditional information systems implement usernames and passwords for user authentication. Passwords still remain a key method for authenticating users [8]. With fewer passwords, the tendency of users to remember their passwords is higher, as opposed to remembering a large number of passwords corresponding to the increasing numbers of user accounts per person, as is evident in contemporary times. However, the abilities of password-based authentication systems to reset passwords with relative ease have helped maintain the usability of these systems. Several password-retrieval schemes [8] have also been proposed in the literature for verification of a user's identity by asking non-conventional secret questions that the user has to answer so as to successfully retrieve a forgotten password. One scheme proposed in [8] is to question the user based on his or her location. Examples of such questions include: "Where did you meet your best friend?," "Where was your first party?," and "Where was your saddest moment?"

The performance of password-retrieval systems that were based on location-specific secret questions for the user was found to be better than of those systems that relied on traditional secret questions.

For a long time, biometric technologies have been a strong technology player for information security. According to [9], biometric authentication methods can be grouped into two categories, namely, behavioral-based authentication and physiological-based authentication.

Behavioral-based authentication methods help identify and recognize people through behavioral patterns including signatures, keystrokes/typing, and voice prints. Behavioral patterns are known to have a high degree of variation, which encumbers the authentication tasks. Various factors affect the behavior of a person. These can include stress and illness. However, such systems are found to be cost-effective in the implementation and are readily acceptable by users.

Physiological-based authentication methods verify the identity of a human user through traits such as those obtained from his or her fingerprints, iris maps (blood vessel patterns in the eye), palm geometry, DNA, and facial traits. Such methods are found to be more reliable than behavior-based methods because the stability index of physiological traits is comparatively higher. Unfortunately, due to a variety of reasons, biometric authentication is still not widely implemented, and is yet to fully deliver its potential in order to replace conventional username and password authentication schemes [10].

## 2.6  Non-repudiation

Repudiating one's actions after they have been enacted is defined as non-repudiation. Malicious activities perpetrated against information systems typically leave behind a trail of evidence that can be followed to be led back to the adversary. However, malicious actions of the adversary can be repudiated by him or her, which is a threat to the security of information resources. In the event of a cyber-crime, it is the task of the cybersecurity enforcement team to validate non-repudiation claims through necessary steps taken to preserve evidence [11]. For digital platforms, non-repudiation can be defeated through the application of digital signatures for ascertaining both the origin as well as the validity of data. Repudiation of malicious actions against information can also be defeated through verification of the claims against log files that store information of all transactions for the target system or network associated with a cyber-attack. For the purposes of non-repudiation, it is vital that there is proper maintenance of log files for each information asset enumerated, and for the information systems and networks.

## 2.7    Standards

### 2.7.1    X.509

The X.509 standard, developed by the International Telecommunication Union (ITU), is a collection of frameworks for providing public key-based authentication services. These frameworks are comprised of public key certificates, attribute certificates as well as a range of authentication services. Public keys defined through the standard are assigned to users, systems or services. The standard provisions an underlying foundation based on which certificate issuance, management, revocation, and use services can be implemented. The generic nature of the authentication scheme provided by X.509 allows its easy adoption by a wide range of applications and systems. Public key-based services based on the standard can be utilized to meet the information security requirements of confidentiality of data, as well as the capability to verify information integrity through digital signatures. In addition, the standard facilitates role based access control (RBAC), through its attribute certificate definitions. Two forms of authentication are specified in the standard, namely, username/password based on verifying claimed identity, and strong authentication based on cryptographic (PKI) credentials [12].

### 2.7.2    Transport layer security

Transport layer security (TLS) is a widely adopted protocol comprising cryptographic primitives and services, used by most, if not all, World Wide Web (WWW) secure communications. Applications of TLS, which is a successor to secure sockets layer (SSL), include e-commerce, banking services, and online payment platforms. The TLS protocol is supported by all major web browsers including Mozilla, Internet Explorer, Chrome, Safari, and Opera. TLS provides strong cryptographic implementation for securing client-server sessions, so as to protect information from tampering, deletion, and forgery. TLS client–server connections are anonymous, mutually authenticated, and integrity checked. Mandatory TLS cryptographic implementations include Diffie–Hellman for key agreement and exchange, digital signature standard (DSS) for digital signature generation and verification, and triple-data encryption standard (3DES) for symmetric encryption of information. Extensions to these core TLS implementations include provisioning for advanced encryption standard (AES)-based encryption, elliptic curve cryptography (ECC), and elliptic curve digital signature algorithm (ECDSA) [13].

### 2.7.3    Hashes

A hash is defined as a set of bits that are obtained after applying a mathematical function to an arbitrary length message. Cryptographic hash functions produce fixed length hash outputs regardless of the length of the input message. Hash values allow the receiver of a message to be able to reproduce the hash value and compare it with the received one, for validating the integrity of the message. As the hash function merely produces a string which indicates whether a change has been made to any given data set or not, data confidentiality is not provided [13].

### 2.7.4 Digital signatures

Digital signatures are the most common application of a hash function. Digital signature generation algorithms encrypt the hash value of a given message using the private key of the sender. The receiver of the message accompanied with the digital signature would thus be able to verify both the integrity of the received message, by recomputing the hash value, as well as the authenticity of the sender, whose private key was used to encrypt the hash of the message [13].

### 2.7.5 Public key infrastructure

The public key infrastructure (PKI) is a key management framework that facilitates the generation, distribution, storage, revocation, and the use of public keys as part of a public–private key pair. The framework, also referred to as PKI, can generate public key based certificates, which are comprised of the identity of the owner of the public key, and the public key itself. In addition, PKI binds the public key with the corresponding private key of each owner. User identities must be unique within the PKI framework for it to function correctly. A centralized certification authority (CA) is assigned the tasks of certificate management such as registration of users, binding of public keys to private keys for individual users, and binding of users to attributes (for legacy systems). The PKI manages the revocation lists, which hold identities and certificates of revoked users [13].

### 2.7.6 Public key cryptography

Public key cryptography (PKC) is defined as the set of methods applied to encrypt messages using a key belonging to a public–private key pair, where the knowledge of one key of the pair does not lead to derivation of the other key of the pair. The public key portion can be made public, and the private key, by definition, must be kept secret by the key owner. Common examples of PKC include RSA and ElGamal, while the less popular PKC standards include Goldwasser–Micali, Blum–Goldwasser, Paillier, and Rabin systems. The PKC is comprised of three components, namely, key generation, encryption algorithm, and decryption algorithm. Public keys that are published for use must be certified by a verified CA [13].

### 2.7.7 OAuth

OAuth [14] is an authorization framework that facilitates user access to services based on predefined access policies. Four roles are specified by OAuth, namely, resource owner is the entity with permission to grant access to its protected resources; resource server hosts the protected resources and is capable of accepting and responding to access requests; client is the application or service making the request on behalf of the resource owner; and the authorization server which issues access tokens to clients after successful authentication of resource owners. The sequence of messages exchanged between a service-seeking client and the OAuth system includes the following:

1. The client makes an authorization request to the resource owner, which grants or denies it authorization.
2. The client sends the authorization granted message to the authorization server and receives an access token.
3. The client uses the access token to access the resource through the resource server.

### 2.7.8 Kerberos (RFC 4120)

Kerberos [15] is a network authentication protocol which allows nodes to communicate over an insecure or untrusted network, and is used in Microsoft's active directory service (ADS) to authenticate users who want to access services. It uses symmetric key cryptography, although there are extensions to the protocol which allow for the use of PKI. A typical Kerberos installation is comprised of an authentication server (AS), a key distribution center (KDC), a service server (SS), clients, and principals. Other components include an authenticator, the ticket granting ticket (TGT), and the ticket granting service (TGS). When this system is used for client authentication, the following process occurs:

1. The client sends a clear text message to the AS requesting access to a service.
2. If the client is in the AS user database, it generates a secret key using the password of the validated user along with a TGS session key and a TGT.
3. The client decrypts the TGS session key with its own password. If they do not match, it will not decrypt which further validates, or invalidates the message in the case that the server was not legitimate.
4. The client then sends the TGT to the TGS with the service it wishes to access and an authenticator, which is composed of the client ID and a timestamp.
5. The TGS decrypts the client's session key, and if it matches the originally granted key, then it returns a client to server ticket and a client server session key.
6. The client connects to the SS and sends the client to server ticket (encrypted with the session key) and a new authenticator is generated in the same way, but using the TGS session key.
7. The SS decrypts these messages, and if all of them are validated then the SS responds to the client that it is willing to provide the requested service and starts to do so.

## 2.8 Threat classes

According to [16], threat classes for information systems can be categorized based on two main principles, namely, classification methods based on attack techniques and those based on threat impacts. A threat agent is defined as an actor who poses a threat to an information system or asset, and may belong to one of three classes, namely, human, technological, and force majeure. The motivation of a threat actor

*Table 2.1    Threats and associated information security properties*

| Threat | Information security property |
| --- | --- |
| Spoofing | Authentication |
| Tampering | Integrity |
| Repudiation | Non-repudiation |
| Information disclosure | Confidentiality |
| Denial of service | Availability |
| Elevation of privilege | Authorization |

could either be deliberate or accidental, with the outcomes of both posing a risk to the information system. The origin of a threat may be either external or internal. According to Microsoft's STRIDE model [17], it represents the six popular threats against information systems, namely, spoofing, tampering of data, and repudiation of misuse actions, information disclosure, DoS, and elevation of privilege. The model addresses known threats, which can be categorized according to the goals and motives of attackers. The mapping of the six threats of the STRIDE model to the information system properties are presented in Table 2.1 [17].

*Spoofing* is defined as the impersonation of a legitimate user of an information system, with the intention of stealing information or disrupting services. *Tampering* as a threat involves the modification of information either in transit or at rest. A threat actor may *repudiate* its actions that may have led to a loss to the information system of the organization. For example, a malicious e-mail sent out from a legitimate user's mailbox to a victim information system, which was subsequently repudiated as an action on the part of the sender. *Disclosure* of information refers to the revelation of information to an unauthorized entity. Services can be denied or degraded through a *DoS* attack wherein, a large volume of network traffic packets can be sent to a target information system, in a short span of time, so that it is crippled and unable to provide its services. *Elevation of Privilege* enables an existing legitimate user of the system to unlawfully elevate its privileges to gain more capabilities required to carry out a cyber-attack. For instance, a user of system may want to elevate his/her privileges for gaining remote access to sensitive data residing on the organization's database server.

The impact of a threat on an information system may be one of the following [16]:

- *Information corruption or loss*: The information system may have become corrupted through the actions of the threat actor leading to loss of some or all the information contained on the affected systems.
- *Information disclosure*: Unlawful, i.e., unauthorized access to information through the exposure, interception, intrusion or any other threat.
- *DoS*: The intentional degradation of services provided by the information systems through the manipulation of system resources, or through blocking of the network traffic flow to the system (traffic flow to/from the system?).
- *Privilege escalation*: The threat actor elevates his or her existing privilege to access a given information system, with the intention to disrupt services or to steal information unlawfully.

## 2.9 Data classification

Data classification is an essential component of information security. Organizations can only provide the most targeted risk containment approach against cyber-threats if information is properly classified and labeled. Proper identification of individuals responsible to protect information must follow proper implementation of data classification schemes. According to the SANS Institute, information classification is comprised of [18]:

- Identification of information sources: the inventory all information sources in the organization and being able to identify the data owners, custodians, security controls in place, and the information format.
- Identification of information classes.
- Mapping of security controls to information classes.

Information or data classification schemes can be generically categorized as commercial or government. Commercial data classification schemes are applied to protect information with monetary value, and also to comply with the law to protect the security and privacy of information. In contrast, government classification schemes are implemented to protect public interests, national security, privacy of entities and individuals, and for compliance with information protection laws.

The Australian Government security classification system classifies information into the following groups [19]:

- Protected—when the compromise of the confidentiality of information in question could lead to damage to national interest, organization, or individuals.
- Confidential—when the compromise of the confidentiality of information in question could lead to significant damage to national interest, organization, or individuals.
- Secret—when the confidentiality of information in question could lead to serious damage to national interest, organization, or individuals.
- Top Secret—when the confidentiality of information in question could lead to exceptionally grave damage to national interest, organization, or individuals.

The Top Secret classification level requires the highest level of protection of the information asset and must be applied through the most pertinent security controls so as to minimize the risk as much as possible.

The North Atlantic Treaty Organization (NATO), which comprises 28 nations, has an obligation on the part of the member nations to comply with NATO rules inclusive of the NATO classification for information. The categories of information as classified by NATO are [20]:

- Cosmic Top Secret—when the confidentiality of information in question could lead to exceptionally grave damage to NATO interests.
- NATO Secret—when the confidentiality of information in question could lead to serious damage to NATO interests.
- NATO Confidential—when the confidentiality of information in question could lead to damage to NATO interests.

- NATO Restricted—when the confidentiality of information in question would be disadvantageous to the interests of the NATO.
- ATOMAL—is defined as information that can either be US-restricted data classified pursuant to the Atomic Energy Act, 1954, or United Kingdom ATOMIC information which has been officially released to NATO. ATOMAL information can be marked as Cosmic Top Secret ATOMAL, NATO Secret ATOMAL, and NATO Confidential ATOMAL.
- NATO unclassified—information which does not fall into the classification groups listed above.

The Graham Leach Bliley Act of 1999 was aimed at the financial services industry in the United States. It requires financial institutions to share their information sharing practices with their customers and to safeguard their sensitive data. Participating financial institutions are mandated to develop solutions for protecting against anticipated threats and hazards including those that may lead to unauthorized access to information systems, thus compromising customer information. Financial institutions are obligated to share their information sharing policies with their customers, including the institutions' policies on disclosing non-public personal information to affiliates and to third parties, disclosing this information after termination of a customer relationship, and protecting the information. The Act allows customers to opt out from limited sharing of non-public data including names, addresses, telephone numbers, social security numbers, and other data as deemed non-public personal information [21].

## 2.10 Information security for the IoT

The IoT is a technological paradigm that has seen an increasing number of electronic devices connect to the Internet to facilitate better services for end-users. The IoT paradigm is comprised of a collection of electronic "objects" or "things" with networking capabilities and is connected to or can interact with other peer electronic-networked devices. The paradigm has pushed information security requirements beyond those that were developed for conventional computers, networks, and mobile devices. Typical examples of "things" include smart phones, smart lighting, smart cameras, printers, building automation systems including security systems/alarms, elevators and air-conditioning, and smart vehicles. Internet-connected IoT devices are readily accessible from remote locations, facilitating control and convenient operation. Since an IoT device is simply any device which is connected to other devices or networks, and as such, IoT device manufacturers do not adhere to a common standard, i.e., common protocols for communication, the process of securing the information that is communicated to and from, is extremely challenging [22]. As such, these devices must rely on higher-order protection mechanisms and concepts such as defense in depth for their security analogous to the challenges seen in control system networks [23].

Several IoT frameworks exist on the market for ready adoption by vendors, including AWS IoT from Amazon, ARM Bed from ARM and other partners, Azure

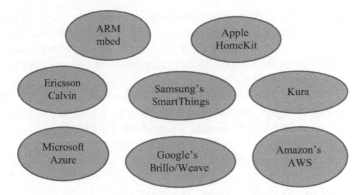

*Figure 2.4    Common IoT frameworks with embedded information security features*

IoT Suite from Microsoft, Brillo/Weave from Google, and Calvin from Ericsson (as shown in Figure 2.4).

A comparative analysis of the various security features that exist on the above-mentioned IoT frameworks is as follows:

1.  The Kura framework [24], while providing security of data and communication messages, does not provide support for security updates and on-the-fly configuration updates for IoT devices. Therefore, a security reconfiguration capability was introduced by open-source tools such as Eurotech [25], to facilitate virtual private network (VPN) over Kura, for secure remote access to IoT devices. Kura also supports the use of public key cryptography through the message queuing telemetry transport (MQTT) protocol [26], support for management of security policies, data integrity checks, and application of runtime security policy enforcement.

2.  SmartThings is an IoT platform that was released by Samsung [27] that facilitates smart services on homes. The SmartThings platform is comprised of IoT devices in the household, all of which are wireless-capable, running ZigBee, Z-Wave, Wi-Fi, or Bluetooth low energy (BLE). Events can be processed locally within the IoT devices of the household, with capability to connect to a backend Cloud facility for data storage, further processing and for communicating with other remote IoT systems. Encryption through SSL/TLS is enabled by default. The SmartThings architecture provides the core components for facilitating information security by ensuring that the IoT devices can access and solicit services only from other authorized IoT devices. For authentication of smart devices running the SmartThings application, the OAuth/OAuth2 protocols are implemented. A service manager module running inside the SmartThings device provides authentication services to external cloud service providers, for device discovery, initiating connections with other smart devices, and for controlling device actions. SmartThings devices also have a capabilities module that ascertains that only users that meet the requisite permissions for accessing a given service are given access. Service access is

comprised of running a set of commands or directives to carry out operations relevant to the application being run on the IoT device. Some examples include access rights for controlling the light switch (On/Off), or a thermostat (On/Off/ Heat/Cool/Fan On, etc.). SmartThings's communications are 128-bit encrypted using the AES standard by default.

3.  HomeKit is an IoT platform developed and released by Apple [28]. Similar to Samsung SmartThings, the HomeKit platform facilitates the management and control of connected IoT devices in a household. Apple's Siri voice recognition service provides access to HomeKit controls through voice and wireless capability is provided through ZigBee and Z-Wave protocols. IoT devices that are not compatible with HomeKit can still connect to the platform through the deployment of a HomeKit Bridge. HomeKit security is comprised of options to facilitate user authentication, authorization and access control, and secure communication. The ed25519 standard [28] is deployed for public key based encryption and digital signature generation and verification. Secret keys are stored in a keychain which is synchronized among various HomeKit IoT devices using the iCloud Keychain [29]. All keys are encrypted using ChaCha20-Poly1305 AEAD and HKDF-SHA-512 derived keys [30]. Authorization is sought from users before the HomeKit platform operates on data on the IoT devices, and the iOS operating system on the HomeKit IoT devices supports layered security. The underlying system files are protected from user access, and users and third-party applications alike are denied access to system level iOS files. Only trusted applications are allowed to be installed and run on the HomeKit devices. AES-256 encryption is applied for data transfer between the temporary memory (flash) and the primary hard drive of the HomeKit system. Devices themselves have unique IDs installed within their core memory by Apple, during manufacturing. Secure inter-device communication is achieved using AES-128-GCM and SHA-256 standards. HomeKit devices also benefit from the Perfect Forward Secrecy property, wherein a fresh session key is generated for each communication session between an Apple user device and any accessories. This session key is generated from the principal key stored in the Apple device.

4.  Calvin is an IoT system developed by Ericsson. The system facilitates the communication between Calvin IoT devices and also with other smart applications hosted on non-Calvin platforms. Authentication of users is performed by one of three processes, namely, local authentication wherein, usernames and passwords are stored in JavaScript object notation (JSON) format within a local directory of the machine for subsequent verification; deployment of a centralized authentication server that performs authentication on behalf of the Calvin IoT device; and thirdly, through the deployment of a RADIUS server, that verifies username and password and replies with attributes of the subject [31]. Authorization of user access to applications on the Calvin system is enabled through the X.509 standard, that helps verify JSON web tokens containing the authorization request/response. Secure communication is optional, but is provisioned by enabling the TLS/datagram transport layer security (DTLS) protocol running elliptic curve cryptographic (ECC) processes. Encryption of data and the generation of digital signatures are both included in the ECC processes.

5. Brillo/Weave is a Google platform that runs the Android operating system. Security is incorporated at design time within the Brillo/Weave architecture. Authentication of devices and users is facilitated through the OAuth 2.0 protocol, which is deployed in addition to digital certificates. Access control to processes on the Brillo/Weave device is enabled by the underlying SELinux kernel of the operating system. Standard UNIX access control rights such as read, write, and execute are implemented by default, and are applicable to both individual users as well as to entire user groups. Sandboxing of processes is another security feature which exists within the Brillo/Weave platform. Through this feature, user processes that are deemed as suspect or malicious can be run in the sandbox that has minimal interaction with other processes, thus protecting against system compromise. Secure communications are facilitated through SSL/TLS, and through the option of full disk encryption of all saved data on the Brillo/Weave IoT device. Brillo also provides a Trusted Execution Environment, and secure boot, so as to protect the system code from compromise, and to provide strong information security to the system [32].

6. Microsoft's Azure IoT suite is a collection of IoT services that enables users of the platform to store, process and exchange information securely, and is the default cloud gateway for IoT devices. The Azure IoT hub enables bidirectional communication between the IoT devices as well as with the backend Azure cloud services, with the underlying communication protocols such as MQTT and HTTP. Other protocols are also supported by the Azure IoT protocol gateway [33]. Mutual authentication between the IoT devices and the Azure IoT hub is facilitated by verifying authentication tokens against shared access policies as well as the security credentials of the IoT device. Security tokens are time restricted, i.e., they expire after a given time. Through this feature, the Azure IoT suite does not rely on the traditional username, password-based authentication procedure. Secure communication is enabled by the SSL/TLS protocol which provides encrypted communications as well as integrity checks through digital signature generation and subsequent validation. The information security of documents is ensured through the storage of data within the DocumentDB or in a secure SQL database [34].

7. The ARM mbed IoT platform was developed for ARM microcontrollers. The ARM platform has a common operating system across all IoT devices, but supports several communication protocols including MQTT, HTTP, and Advanced Message Queuing Protocol (AMQP) [35]. The ARM mbed security functionality is provided through the mbed uVisor device-side security solution that compartmentalizes software processes from each other as well as from the operating system, and the mbed TLS for secure communications between the ARM mbed IoT devices, as well as between the devices and the centralized cloud. Authentication is not explicitly included with the ARM mbed platform, but could be enabled through the proper configuration and operation of the X.509 standard. Some of the ARM microcontrollers are equipped with hardware encryption operations, which complement the security of information that the ARM mbed IoT platform provides through its security features.

8.  AWS (Amazon Web Services) for IoT [36] is a cloud-based IoT platform licensed by Amazon. As with other IoT platforms, AWS for IoT enables secure smart device communication and remote control of devices. In addition, AWS services such as Amazon DynamoDB, S3, Machine learning, are seamlessly extended to the AWS IoT platform. A device gateway must also be deployed in the AWS IoT setup that acts as intermediary between the AWS IoT devices and the AWS cloud server. Authentication is done through the AWS IoT requirement for mutual authentication for all connections. It is provisioned through X.509, AWS group/user roles, and AWS Cognito identities [37,38]. With X.509-based authentication, the AWS cloud serves as the CA and certificates issued by the CA are SSL/TLS based. The platform authenticates AWS IoT devices by requiring and subsequently verifying the X.509 public key-based certificate of the device. AWS Identity and Access Management (IAM) and ASWS Cognito are other standards employed to facilitate mutual authentication in the AWS IoT platform. Authorization of AWS IoT devices is accomplished through policies and derived rules. Such rule definition ensures that only those devices that have been defined as "permitted" within the policy are allowed access to other devices. Secure communications are enabled through SSL/TLS, thus ensuring that all information is encrypted and digitally signed. Storage of private data is also encrypted using standard AES-128 encryption.

## 2.11  Health-care information security standards

The Health Insurance Portability and Accountability Act (HIPAA) act, defined in 1996, was one of the first regulations for health insurance coverage and eHealth, with specific emphasis on security and privacy of health data. The privacy component of HIPAA sets the standards, processes, and procedures for access to personal health information. Unauthorized use and/or disclosure of patient data is considered a breach of the law, with exceptions that exist for law enforcement and legislation [39].

The security component of HIPAA provides an outline on technical safeguards for securing sensitive patient data. Inherently, security considerations such as safeguarding all facilities involved in the handling of patient data are addressed through HIPAA compliance. Examples of misuse cases that ought to be considered and addressed through HIPAA compliance include: who has access to server room facilities, authentication of users of the patient database, policies on network security.

HIPAA security rules cover the following properties of information security [40]:

1.  Confidentiality, integrity, and availability of e-health data at rest and in transit.
2.  Identification and protection against reasonably anticipated threats to security and integrity of information.
3.  Protection against anticipated and/or unlawful information disclosure.
4.  Compliance by the workforce.

The confidentiality rule of HIPAA ascertains that health data is not made available for disclosure to unauthorized personnel. Integrity of health data implies the resilience to alteration and/or destruction without authority. Availability implies the accessibility and usability of health data by authorized personnel.

Risk analysis on health data includes the following components: evaluation of the likelihood and impact of potential risks on health data; adoption and implementation of security controls for mitigating the identified risks; documentation of the security measures implemented and rationale for these choices; and maintenance and continuous update of security controls.

The administrative safeguards of HIPAA include the following: management of security risks; designation of personnel for security policy enforcement and procedure adoption; information access management, preferably role-based access control (RBAC) to information resources of the health infrastructure; training and management of appropriate workforce for enforcing security policies and for making users aware of procedures to be taken for safeguarding health information; evaluation that includes a periodic assessment of security posture of the health-care entity.

Physical safeguards of HIPAA include access control to facilities and device security within the health-care provider premises. Technical safeguards include the deployment and management of access control systems for restricting information access to authorized personnel; audit controls for recording and examining access to information systems containing health data; integrity controls for ensuring that health data is not tampered with or destroyed when a defined policy is violated; and transmission security to restrict the transfer of health data without proper encryption, so as to avoid unwanted disclosure to unauthorized personnel [40].

While HIPAA is the US standard for health-care information security and privacy, the Australian health service providers are required by law to adhere to the Commonwealth's Privacy Act 1988 (Privacy Act) which applies to both the Australian Government and all health service providers in the private sector. The act states that health service providers must take "reasonable steps to protect the information from misuse, interference and loss, as well as unauthorized access, modification or disclosure" [41]. Additionally, and more recently, the *Privacy Amendment (Notifiable Data Breaches) Bill 2016* [41] was passed into law in Australia, which brings additional requirements to health care. In particular, the requirement that any breach of health data must be reported to affected individuals within a very short timeframe. A further modification of the Privacy Act (1988) was made in October 2017 to specifically deal with data breaches related to systems which are considered to pertain to the My Health Records Act (2012).

The Australian Privacy Principles (APP) fact sheet [42] presents 13 principles to be adhered to under the Privacy Act 1988. Information security is ensured with regards to security and privacy of user information including instructions for individual anonymity, data integrity checks, confidentiality of user information, authorized access to information, and the availability of information to both the users as well as the health-care providers. In addition, guidelines are stipulated for proper management of information within the health-care provider systems [42].

Additionally, the "Guide to Mandatory Data Breach Notification in the My Health Record System" is available from the Office of the Australian Information Commissioner. This guide provides a compliance checklist and information on notification, legislative framework, and the regulatory approach.

## 2.12  National Institute of Standards and Technology (NIST)—framework for improving critical infrastructure cybersecurity

The NIST framework for Critical Infrastructure Cybersecurity [43] provides a guideline for business drivers to follow, so as to ensure that cybersecurity activities are sustainable and effective, whilst the risks are considered as part of the overall organization's risk management processes. The framework provides the following five set of guidelines for organizations to follow:

- Description of the current cybersecurity posture
- Description of the target cybersecurity state
- Identification and prioritization of opportunities to improve cybersecurity state
- Assessment of the progress toward the target state
- Communication among the stakeholders (internal and external) on risk posed.

Data security is categorized as follows:

- Data-at-rest is protected.
- Data-in-transit is protected.
- Assets are formally managed during removals, transfers, and disposition.
- Ensuring the availability of information and having controls in place to protect against data leaks.
- Integrity checking mechanisms are in place (software, hardware, and firmware).
- Segregation of development and testing environments from the production environment.

The importance of security controls for information systems and organizations in general, has been emphasized in the NIST 800-53 Security and Privacy Controls for Federal Information Systems and Organizations' document [43]. Three key questions have been posed to organizations that hold security of information as a key management issue, namely:

- Do the security control types and categories required to secure the organization adequately mitigate the risk posed through external and internal threat actors?
- Have the security controls been implemented? Or are to be implemented as per corporate plan?
- Is the desired or required level of assurance provided by the selected security controls?

It is stated that the choice of security controls for a given information system in the organization must be effectively made through a three-tiered approach for addressing the risk to information resources. These three tiers of risk management include: Tier 1: Organization, Tier 2: Mission/Business processes, and Tier 3: Information systems.

Through Tier 1, a connection is established between the organizational mission, its business functions, investment strategies, information technology solutions, and security thereof. Tier 2 is defined to include the various business processes required for supporting the organization's mission, determining the security categories of information systems/assets, incorporating security into the mission, and facilitation of security controls for all information systems and assets. Based on the six steps for risk management, the proposed framework is defined as follows [43]:

- Step 1: Categorization of information systems (SP 800-60, FIPS 199)
- Step 2: Selection of security controls (FIPS 200, SP 800-53)
- Step 3: Implementation of security controls (SP 800-160)
- Step 4: Assessment of security controls (SP 800-53A)
- Step 5: Authorization for information systems (SP 800-37)
- Step 6: Monitoring security controls (SP 800-137).

Through a clear and valid identification of information system assets in step 1, the business mission of inventorying information systems and assets is realized. Without a proper enumeration and subsequent categorization of information assets, the task of provisioning security controls to reduce the risk posed, is encumbered. Subsequent steps including the choice of security controls, its deployment, assessment, authorized access, and maintenance (i.e., monitoring) are therefore implementable.

The choice of security controls is challenging for organizations that are large and comprised of heterogeneous information system hardware and software assets. However, through a fundamental understanding of the business mission and the underlying processes, accompanied with proper inventorying of assets, and categorization based on level of sensitivity of the assets, the entire six-step process of risk management is achievable.

## 2.13 Challenges for information security in the IoT era

Challenges for information security in the era of the IoT are considerable. We categorize some of these challenges as follows.

Vulnerabilities in current heterogeneous devices that are part of the IoT ecosystem, must be identified and categorized based on their respective levels of impact on the underlying information systems. Many current IoT devices do not adhere to a specific standard, as we have described in Section 2.10 earlier. Consequently, the variations in the types of vulnerabilities of each IoT device are impossible to quantify. Vulnerabilities may exist at various levels of operation of IoT devices, and may expose the devices as well as the information system that they are a part of, to cyber threats. Such vulnerabilities may have been acquired by the IoT devices from flawed hardware design, standard operating environments, or third-party applications. Protocol level security vulnerabilities may be exploited by the adversary for carrying out a cyber-attack against the IoT devices. Vulnerabilities in the cloud infrastructure are mostly associated with the operation of virtualized cloud environments. In addition, protocol level vulnerabilities also exist within the cloud. The diversity in the types of vulnerabilities that exist in the above information systems encumbers the process of information system hardening, as required for information security. A solution tailored for the IoT paradigm and devices therein, will not be seamlessly adoptable by the cloud. The other factor to consider while enumerating vulnerabilities for information systems is the type of application that they are supporting. Vulnerability mapping would vary from one application to another, and therefore, a robust evaluation of the information system must be done within the context of the type of application that they run, so as to accurately enumerate all vulnerabilities.

Cybersecurity threats vary from one information system to another, albeit the category of threat can affect one of the followings: confidentiality, integrity, authenticity, availability, and non-repudiation. Information system threat identification and assessment of the resulting impact to information assets is an essential part of information system security. Threats may vary based on the type of hardware platforms of the information system, network and system-level protocols being run, and overlay applications.

Based on Baig, *et al.* [44], the following are foreseeable challenges in securing information systems:

- Data volume
- Data privacy
- Cost of protection
- Heterogeneity of data and systems.

The diverse range of IoT devices that exist in the market pose a challenge for information security. IoT devices that are deployed in the environment for monitoring phenomena, such as temperature and pressure, generally run on batteries with a finite life. Other challenges include the lack of investment in securing these devices before they are released for sale, owing to the high cost in provisioning a security solution. Moreover, IoT devices are not equipped with high-end processing and battery-support capabilities, and the low-power feature of such devices restricts the implementation of any potential security solution. Symmetric key cryptography is known to consume lower power than asymmetric key cryptography, and is therefore more suited for IoT platforms. However, despite the implementation of such solutions, smaller lengths of secret keys for symmetric key cryptography reduce the security of the scheme whilst improving upon battery life, with the trade-off that the secret keys are usually hard coded, and once discovered, cannot be changed, thus rendering the device permanently insecure. Confidentiality of IoT data is compromised when encryption of information is not done. The integrity of data can be checked at the cost of fewer computing and memory resources because the computation of a digital signature does not require significant power use, and therefore, the message integrity can be validated. IoT devices are also prone to DoS attacks [45] that may bring down critical infrastructure resources that are deployed for assessing environmental conditions.

The disparity in data classification standards [18–21] adopted by the varying jurisdictions for information should also be considered when evaluating the security of information. When information is being transferred from one jurisdiction to another, proper measures must be adopted for ascertaining that proper mapping of data classes is performed beforehand, so that the level of security to be provisioned for the transmitted data is not reduced through the transfer. Moreover, a protocol must be agreed on for transferring top secret-level information from one point to another.

## 2.14 Conclusion

The current era of the IoT has witnessed a rapid proliferation of heterogeneous computing devices that follow varying standards and protocols for information storage, transfer, and security. The devices themselves operate with low computing power to preserve battery life, and thus implementation of any security measure must be at the system level rather than at the device level. The issues associated with information security in today's world are highly dynamic and require a robust understanding of the underlying functionality of the information systems. It is also important to adhere to the five fundamental principles of information security, namely, confidentiality, integrity, availability, authenticity, and non-repudiation, and to accordingly design and develop information systems that are resilient to rapidly evolving cyber-threats.

## References

[1]  Longley, D., Shain, M., and Caelli, W. *Information Security Handbook*. Basingstoke: New York, NY; 1991.

[2]  Delfs, H. and Knebl, H. *Introduction to Cryptography: Principles and Applications*. Springer-Verlag: Berlin; 2002.

[3]  Garfinkel, S. 'Public key cryptography.' *Computer*. 1996;**29**(6): 101–104.

[4]  Diffie, W. and Hellman, M. E. 'New directions in cryptography.' *IEEE Trans. on Info. Theory*. 1976;**22**(6): 644–654.

[5]  Schneider, F. *Hashes and Message Digests* [online]. 2005. Available from http://www.cs.cornell.edu/courses/cs513/2005fa/NL20.hashing.html [Accessed 28 Apr 2018].

[6]  Paxson, V. 'An analysis of using reflectors for distributed denial-of-service attacks.' *ACM SIGCOMM Computer Communication Review*. 2001; **31**(3) 38–47.

[7]  CERT Advisories, Software Engineering Institute, Carnegie Mellon University [online], Available from https://resources.sei.cmu.edu/asset_files/WhitePaper/1996_019_001_496172.pdf [Accessed 28 Apr 2018].

[8]  Hang, L., De Luc, A., Smith, M. Richter, M., and Hussmann, H. 'Where have you been? Using location-based security questions for fallback authentication.' *Proceedings of the 11th USENIX Conference on Usable Privacy and Security (SOUPS'15)*, USENIX Association, Berkeley, CA, 2015, pp. 169–183.

[9]  Kung, S., Mak, M., and Lin., S. *Biometric Authentication: A Machine Learning Approach* (First ed.). Prentice Hall Press, Upper Saddle River, NJ; 2004.

[10] Pagnin, E. and Mitrokotsa, A. "Privacy-Preserving Biometric Authentication: Challenges and Directions," *Security and Communication Networks*; 2017, Article ID: 7129505, pp. 1–9; 2017.

[11] McCullagh, A. and Caelli, W. *Non-Repudiation in the Digital Environment* [online]. 2000. Available from http://www.ojphi.org/ojs/index.php/fm/article/ view/778/687 [Accessed 28 Apr 2018].

[12] Menezes, A., Vanstone, S., and Van Oorschot, P. *Handbook of Applied Cryptography* (1st ed.). CRC Press, Inc.: Boca Raton, FL; 1996.

[13] Tilborg, H. and Jajodia, S. *Encyclopedia of Cryptography and Security* (2nd ed.). Springer Publishing Company, Inc.: USA; 2011.

[14] Hardt, D. *The OAuth 2.0 Authorization Framework*, IETF RFC 6749 [online]. Available from https://tools.ietf.org/html/rfc6749 [Accessed 28 Apr 2018].

[15] The Internet Society. *The Kerberos Network Authentication Service (V5)* [online]. Available from https://tools.ietf.org/html/rfc4120 [Accessed 28 Apr 2018].

[16] Jouini, M., Rabai, L., and Aissa, A. 'Classification of security threats in information systems.' *Procedia Computer Science*. 2014;**32**:489–496.

[17] Wagner, D. *Introduction to Microsoft® Security Development Lifecycle (SDL) Threat Modeling* [online] Available from https://people.eecs.berkeley. edu/~daw/teaching/cs261-f12/hws/Introduction_to_Threat_Modeling.pdf [Accessed 28 Apr 2018].

[18] Fowler, S. *Information Classification – Who, Why and How* [online]. Available from https://www.sans.org/reading-room/whitepapers/auditing/ information-classification-who-846 [Accessed 28 Apr 2018].

[19] *Information Security Management Guidelines, Australian Government Attorney-General's Department* [online]. 2018. Available from https://www. protectivesecurity.gov.au/informationsecurity/Documents/INFOSECGuide- linesAustralianGovernmentSecurityClassificationSystem.pdf [Accessed 28 Apr 2018].

[20] *NATO Security Indoctrination* [online]. Available from http://www.act.nato.int/ images/stories/structure/reserve/hqrescomp/nato-security-brief.pdf [Accessed 28 Apr 2018].

[21] *The Gramm-Leach-Bliley Act* (GLBA) [online]. 1999. Available from https://www.epic.org/privacy/glba/ [Accessed 28 Apr 2018].

[22] Ammar, M., Russello, G. and Crispo, B. 'Internet of things: A survey on the security of IoT frameworks.' *Journal of Information Security and Applications*. 2017;**38**: 8–27.

[23] Kuipers, D. and Fabro, M. *Control systems cyber security: Defense in depth strategies*. United States Department of Energy Report, 2006.

[24] Lawton, G. *How to put configurable security in effect for an IoT gateway* [online]. 2017. Available from http://www.theserverside.com/tip/How-to-put-configurable-security-in-effect- for-an-IoT-gateway [Accessed 28 Apr 2018].

[25] The Eurotech Group [online]. Available from https://www.eurotech.com/en/about+eurotech/ [Accessed 28 Apr 2018].

[26] Eclipse Foundation. *MQTT and COAP, IoT protocols* [online]. 2014. Available from https://www.eclipse.org/community/eclipse_newsletter/2014/february/article2.php [Accessed 28 Apr 2018].

[27] SmartThings. *Smart things developer documentation* [online]. Available from https://docs.smartthings.com/en/latest/ [Accessed 28 Apr 2018].

[28] Apple. *The smart home just got smarter* [online]. Available from http://www.apple.com/ios/home/ [Accessed 28 Apr 2018].

[29] Bernstein, D.J., Duif N., Lange, T., Schwabe, P., and Yang, B-Y. 'High-speed high-security signatures.' *J Crypt. Eng.* 2012; **2**(2): 77–89.

[30] Apple. *IOS security* [online]. Available from http://www.apple.com/business/docs/iOS_Security_Guide.pdf [Accessed 28 Apr 2018].

[31] Ericsson. *Security in Calvin* [online]. Available from https://github.com/EricssonResearch/calvin-base/wiki/Security/ [Accessed 28 Apr 2018].

[32] Android. *Hardware-backed keystore* [online]. Available from https://source.android.com/security/keystore [Accessed 28 Apr 2018].

[33] Azure M. *Azure IoT protocol gateway* [online]. Available from https://azure.microsoft.com/en-us/documentation/articles/iot-hub-protocol-gateway/ [Accessed 28 Apr 2018].

[34] Azure M. *Documentdb* [online]. Available from https://azure.microsoft.com/en-us/services/documentdb/ [Accessed 28 Apr 2018].

[35] ARM. *Arm mbed iot device platform* [online]. Available from http://www.arm.com/products/iot-solutions/mbed-iot-device-platform [Accessed 28 Apr 2018].

[36] Amazon. *Aws IoT framework* [online]. Available from https://aws.amazon.com/iot [Accessed 28 Apr 2018].

[37] Amazon. *Iam users, groups, and roles* [online] Available from http://docs.aws.amazon.com/iot/latest/developerguide/iam-users-groups-roles.html [Accessed 28 Apr 2018].

[38] Amazon. *Amazon cognito identities* [online]. Available from http://docs.aws.amazon.com/iot/latest/developerguide/cognito-identities.html [Accessed 28 Apr 2018].

[39] Belbey, J. *Privacy and Security: Learn from Best Practices for HIPAA Compliance*. Forbes [online]. 2015. Available from https://www.forbes.com/sites/joannabelbey/2015/12/19/privacy-and-security-learn-from-best-practices-for-hipaa-compliance/#4c09f2b871b4 [Accessed 28 Apr 2018].

[40] *Summary of the HIPAA Security Rule, Health Information Privacy*. Available from https://www.hhs.gov/hipaa/for-professionals/security/laws-regulations/index.html [Accessed 28 Apr 2018].

[41] Australian Digital Health Agency. *Information Security Guide for Small Healthcare Businesses, Australian Government* [online]. Available from

https://www.digitalhealth.gov.au/about-the-agency/digital-health-cyber-security-centre/information-security-guide-for-small-healthcare-businesses/HD127%20Information%20Security%20Guide%20for%20small%20healthcare%20businesses%20(co-branded%20with%20Stay%20Smart%20Online)%20Online%20Version.pdf [Accessed 28 Apr 2018].

[42]    Australian Government, Office of the Australian Information Commissioner *Australian Privacy Principles* [online]. Available from https://www.oaic.gov.au/individuals/privacy-fact-sheets/general/privacy-fact-sheet-17-australian-privacy-principles#part-4-integrity-of-personal-information [Accessed 28 Apr 2018].

[43]    NIST 800-53. *Security and Privacy Controls for Federal Information Systems and Organizations* [online]. 2013. Available from https://nvlpubs.nist.gov/nistpubs/specialpublications/nist.sp.800-53r4.pdf [Accessed 28 Apr 2018].

[44]    Baig, Z., Szewczyk, P., Valli, C., *et al.* 'Future challenges for smart cities: Cyber-security and digital forensics.' *J. Dig. Inv.* 2017;**22**: 3–13.

[45]    Khan, M., Iqbal, M., Ubaid, F., Amin, R., and Ismail, A. 'Scalable and secure network storage in cloud computing.' *Int. J. Comput. Sci. Inf. Secur.* 2016;**14**(4): 545.

## Chapter 3

# Data authentication algorithms

*Sarah Al-Shareeda[1]*

To successfully secure the emerging cloud technology, Internet of Things (IoT), and big data, the to-be-adopted security framework must meet the specific security prerequisites. One central/critical requirement is **authentication**; in essence, authentication (1) ensures data integrity, i.e., data has not been fabricated, and (2) assures that the data senders are authorized users, i.e., they are certified data originators. The term "data", which we refer to here, might be simply the data originators' usernames and passwords that are sent for validation. It can also be the senders' signatures, or simply their biometric information. The way, the senders' received data is authenticated, is called an **authentication algorithm**. Passwords and hash functions have been used as some simple authentication schemes. However, with the advancement of cryptography, encrypted checksums such as message authentication codes (MAC)s are presented to fulfill the authentication need. A mixture of cryptographic hash functions and MACs is used to create keyed-hashed MACs (HMACs) algorithms for authentication. Besides, when introduced, the cryptographic digital signature algorithms (DSAs) paved the way for more advanced authentication protocols such as the public key infrastructure (PKI). The use of elliptic curves (ECs) has also contributed to have lightweight authentication signatures. On the other hand, aside from these conventional authentication traits, users' biometric features have been widely used for authentication. In addition, stego-based authentication algorithms such as watermarking and steganography are introduced and they represent one of the tracks followed to achieve authentication goals.

In this chapter, our aim is to present a comprehensive classification and overview of the abovementioned authentication algorithms. We will first categorize the available methods, define and identify the strengths and weaknesses of each category, and cover only the most popular algorithms of each category giving their algorithmic details with some examples. We conclude the chapter by connecting the explained algorithms in light of cloud computing, IoT, and big data; finally, some future directions will be identified.

[1]Electrical and Computer Engineering Department, The Ohio State University, USA

## 3.1    Taxonomy of authentication methodologies

Authentication can be identified as a twofold process; on one hand, it is a verification that the obtained data is from an authorized identities or digital entities. On the other hand, it is the process of confirming the integrity of data. Authentication is an essential element of having secure data, communications, systems, clouds, and IoT. Authentication techniques are classified according to the distinguishing characteristics/factors they use; the factors themselves are classified into [1,2]:

- **Knowledge factors such as passwords**. Passwords are weak, however, for two reasons. First, their effectiveness depends on secrecy and it is hard to keep them secret. There are countless ways to sniff or otherwise intercept them, and there is usually no way to detect a successful sniffing attack until damage is done. Second, evolving threats on passwords has made it relatively easy for attackers to figure out the passwords that people are most likely to choose and remember. Even if they choose hard-to-guess passwords, people are more likely to forget them or are obliged to write them down in order to have them available when needed [2].
- **Ownership factors such as a software token, a smart card, and a hardware device.** Token-based authentication is the solidest technique to exploit since it relies on a unique physical object that one must have in order to log into the system [2].
- **Being factors such as a biometric.** A distinguishing characteristic is a physical or behavioral feature that is unique to the user being authenticated. Familiar techniques use a person's voice, fingerprints, written signature, hand shape, iris features, or keystroke typing rhythm for authentication [2].

Traditional authentication uses single-factor authentication rule whereas modern authentication can be a mixture of these factors to offer more security. Nevertheless, the available authentication algorithms can be broadly classified into four main categories as is shown in our focal outline in Figure 3.1. The simplest category is the password authentication and its pure, hashed, and salted passwords sub-types. With the advent of cryptography, cryptographic-based category has emerged as a promising authentication scheme including hashing functions such as secure hash function (SHA), symmetric authentication algorithms such as MAC, and asymmetric authentication such as digital signatures. Since the use of physiological and behavioral traits is more robust in identifying and authenticating users, biometric authentication schemes have been introduced including fingerprint authentication, iris recognition, face recognition, etc. Furthermore, one more class of authentication has used the watermarking and steganography of texts and images to add more robustness to the authentication schemes. We dedicate the following sections to describe the particulars of the first two categories: password and cryptographic authentications where we cover the most popular algorithms alongside with their detailed description. Biometrics and stego-based authentication are briefly discussed as they are explained in detail in other chapters.

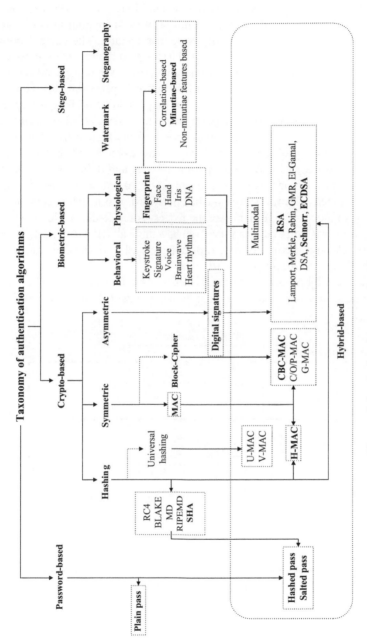

*Figure 3.1  Authentication schemes taxonomy*

## 3.2    Password-based authentication

Being an entity/member in a system/network/cloud/IoT, a user needs to log onto the system to be able to use it. The conventional way of logging in is to enter an account username and a password assigned to that account. The entered information is checked against the stored password of that user at the server's database as in Figure 3.2. If a match occurs, the system accepts the user request otherwise the system rejects it. To preserve the security of the network, password has to be strong: long and contains alphanumeric characters lest they could be easily guessed [3]. In early days, the stored passwords were plain simple text; since attackers could access the system, they can easily download and access all the system users' passwords. As a solution to this problem, hashed passwords were stored at the database. Section 3.3.1 is dedicated for the explanation of types and definition of hash functions. Whenever a user sends its username and password, his/her password is hashed before it is compared with the stored hashed password. If a match occurs, he/she is granted access to the system; otherwise, the request is rejected, see Figure 3.3. With this type of passwords, attackers can try a rainbow table attack where hackers exert a brute force attack on a dictionary of words and the hashes of those words to reveal the correct hash of the correct password.

To defeat the rainbow attack, salted hashes are used for passwords. The idea is to have a dynamic random text (salt) added at the beginning of the user password before

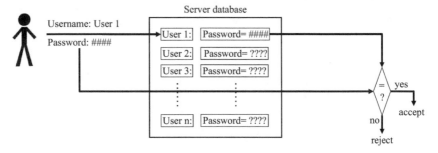

*Figure 3.2    Plain password authentication*

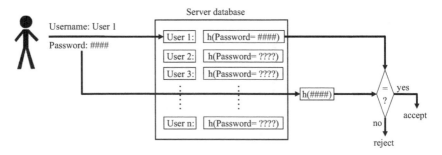

*Figure 3.3    Hashed password authentication*

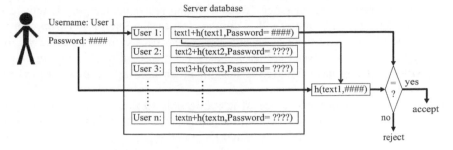

*Figure 3.4 Salted hashed password authentication*

hashing. The database stores that plain salt plus the hashed text plus pass pair. When the user signs in, his/her entered password is combined with the stores plain salt before transferred to the same hashing algorithm; the result will be compared to the stored digest value. If a match occurs, the system authenticates the user; otherwise, his/her request is rejected [3] as in Figure 3.4. In spite of the simplicity of the salted hashed passwords concept, it makes cracking the hashed password much harder, since the rainbow table represents the hashes of individual words of a dictionary. If the hacker tries to compare them to the stored database, he/she will gain no match because he/she is comparing the hashes of individual words to hashes of salts plus words. In this case, to hack on password of **User 1** in Figure 3.4, he/she needs to combine the stored plain salt with every word in his/her dictionary before hashing and see if the result matches the stored salted hashed password. In this sense, with salts cracking passwords is slowed down and takes more processing time and resources [3].

## 3.3 Cryptographic-based authentication

Nowadays, cryptographic building blocks are everywhere. Whether we need authentication, integrity, non-denial, or confidentiality, cryptography is the main instrument to utilize. For authentication, as we see in Figure 3.1, various types of cryptographic systems have been invented over the years. Each has its own strengths and weaknesses. In this section, we will discuss the three main sub-categories of cryptographic authentication schemes; we will delve into the detailed description of only the most popular algorithms in each sub-category.

### 3.3.1 Cryptographic hash functions

A hash function is an essential cryptographic primitive that is used in most of advanced symmetric and asymmetric authentication algorithms of the cloud, the IoT, and wherever big data is used. When a hash function $h$ is applied to a message $m$ of any bit length, the output $h(m)$ is a digest of a fixed length $L$. For the hash function $h$ to be secure, it has to fulfill three important properties:

- One-wayness or preimage resistance. Given a hash digest $h(m)$ over message $m$, the hash function must be computationally infeasible to be reversed, i.e., $m$ cannot be regenerated.

- Second preimage resistance (weak collision resistance). $h(m_1)$ is unique for message input $m_1$ and $h(m_2)$ is unique for message input $m_2$. This property is important in case there is an attacker $A$ who tries to infer message $m_2$ from $h(m_1)$. In theory, weak collision exists, but it is hard to be found in practice since a strong hash function is designed such that no two messages have the same digest $h(m_1) \neq h(m_2)$.
- (Strong) Collision resistance. If it is infeasible to find two different messages $m_1$ and $m_2$ with $h(m_1) = h(m_2)$, the hash function $h$ is called a strong collision resistant hash. This property is harder than the previous weak collision resistance one since the attacker $A$ has the freedom to pick two similar messages or keep altering them until their hashes match. For more details about this property, we refer the reader to [4].

---

**Practical properties of hash function $h:m\in\{0,1\}^* \rightarrow h(m)\in\{0,1\}^L$**

- No fixed bit length for input message $m$
- Fixed bit length for output digest $h(m)$
- $h(m)$ is easy and fast to compute.

**Security properties of hash function $h$**

- One-wayness: $m \rightarrow h(m)$
- Weak collision resistance: $m_1 \neq m_2 = ? \rightarrow h(m_1) \neq h(m_2)$
- Strong collision resistance: $m_1 = ? \neq m_2 = ? \rightarrow h(m_1) \neq h(m_2)$.

---

Hash functions have several applications. In connection to authentication, hash functions are used for storing hashed passwords as we discussed in Section 3.2. They are used for data integrity check, as we will see in Section 3.3.3. Hash functions are typically built based on Merkle–Damgård-iterated design principle. According to this principle, the input is segmented into several blocks to be processed sequentially by an essential component in a hash function design: the compression function. The final output of the function is the fixed bit-length final message digest. Such compression function can be built using block ciphers[1]. Further, block cipher hashes can be categorized into dedicated and not dedicated. The not dedicated block cipher hashes are the ones that use symmetric encryption block ciphers for building their compression functions. This chapter revisits the dedicated hash functions category where the compression function is

---

[1]There are stream ciphers compression functions but they give small bit size of output and need more iteration such as hashes made with Rivest Cipher 4 (RC4) ciphers. BLAKE stream cipher-based hashes are faster than the earlier versions of stream cipher hashes and need less number of rounds.

built from block ciphers dedicated exclusively to work for hashing purposes. This category of hash functions includes message digest (MD) family that contains MD hash functions, RACE integrity primitives evaluation message digest (RIPEMD) hashes, and secure hash algorithms (SHA) hashes. Most of these generally accepted hashes were considered strong at their inauguration, but over time cyber-attackers develop smart math methods to reduce the strength of the bit length of the chosen hash, i.e., shorten the hash's effective bit length. Once this happens, the hash is considered broken and no longer should be used [5]. The first developed MD hash was MD2 by Ronald Rivest in 1989 with 128-bit digest length, but it was not widely used because of its vulnerability to many attacks. In 1990 and 1995, Rivest developed the MD4 and MD5 128-bit hashes; however, they were widely and severely compromised. By 2011, MD4 was regarded obsolete; MD5 was broken in 2016 by a collision resistance attack that shortened its effective bit length from 128 to only 18 bit in less than a second on a regular computer. The successor to MD5 was MD6 developed in 2008 in MIT by Rivest and his team in a response to a call from the National Institute of Standards and Technology (NIST), with up to 512-bit MD6 has been relatively unused due to a plethora of better alternatives. Aside from the MD family, in Leuven, Belgium, RIPEMD hashes were developed in 1996 by a group of researchers led by Hans Dobbertin. The original RIPEMD was structured as a variation on MD4 and therefore it inherited the weaknesses of MD4. Although its successor versions of 160, 256, and 320 bit were strengthened, RIPEMD family has limited success in only some products.

The need for longer digest encouraged the National Security Agency (NSA) in 1993 to design the SHA-0 hash of 160-bit digest rather than the 128-bit output of MD5; SHA-0 version had some flaws. It was revised and introduced as SHA-1 in 1995 by the NIST. Over the course of time, many attacks against SHA-1 shortened its effective bit length; therefore, NSA and NIST introduced its related successor, SHA-2, as the new recommended hashing standard in 2002 [5]. SHA-2 is a set of six hashes: 224, 256, 384, 512, 512/224, and 512/256 bit, all built using Merkle–Damgård structure with a one-way compression function. The most popular one is SHA-256 bits. Although SHA-2 shares some of the same math characteristics as SHA-1 and minor weaknesses have been discovered, in crypto-world it is still considered "strong" for the foreseeable future. Since SHA-512 is the most secure and stable fellow of SHA-2 family, in what follows the SHA-512 hash is explained. The algorithms behind SHA-256, -384, and -512 are quite similar; somehow their lifecycle will be similar to SHA-1's. NIST already approved in 2015 a replacement hash algorithm standard called SHA-3. SHA-3 does not share the same mathematical properties as previous SHA-2 and thus should be resistant to cryptographic attack longer than SHA-2 [5].

### 3.3.1.1  Secure hash algorithm (SHA)-512

The SHA-512 hash algorithm takes an input message $m$ and produces the digest $h(m)$. Message $m$'s length is $L$ bit where $L \leq 2^{128}$. The output digest is of 512-bit length. The algorithm constitutes of the subsequent four phases [6]:

**Phase 1: Preparing input message**

- At first, input $m$ is padded with **padding bits** in the range of 1 bit to 1,024 bits. The padding bits are in the form of 1000000, i.e., 1 followed by the required number of 0s.
- $m$ plus padding is **appended with a block of 128 bits**. This block is the unsigned 128-bit integer representation of $m$'s length $L$.
- The resulted expanded $m$ is divided into 1,024 bit blocks.

The outcome of this phase is an expanded message of sequence of 1,024 bit blocks $m_1, \ldots, m_n$ with the length of 1,024 $n$ bit as can be seen in Figure 3.5.

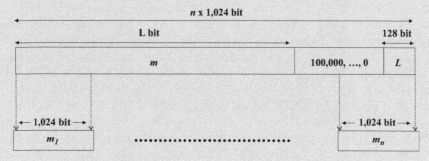

*Figure 3.5   Phase 1: preparing the input of SHA-512*

**Phase 2: Preparing each block $m_i$ for processing (scheduling)**
Each block $m_i$ has to be represented in the form of 80 words $w_0, \ldots w_t \ldots, w_{79}$ each of 64-bit length before being processed by the heart of SHA-512, which is a module $F$ of **80 rounds**:

- For $t = 0 \ldots 15$, $w_t$ are the first 16 words of block $m_i$.
- For $t = 16 \ldots 79$, $w_{16} - w_{79}$ are calculated by $w_t = \alpha_1^{512}(w_{t-2}) + w_{t-7} + \alpha_0^{512}(w_{t-15}) + w_{t-16}$, where:
  - $\alpha_0^{512}(a) = rotr^1(a) \oplus rotr^8(a) \oplus shr^7(a)$,
  - $\sigma_1^{512}(a) = rotr^{19}(a) \oplus rotr^{61}(a) \oplus shr^6(a)$,
  - $rotr^N(a)$ is circular right shift of the 64-bit $a$ by $N$ bits,
  - $shr^N(a)$ is left shift of the 64 bit $a$ by $N$ bits with padding by zeros on the right, and
  - $+$ is addition modulo $2^{64}$.

Phase 2 represents a crucial security advantage of SHA-512 by constructing the new $w_t$ words using $w_t$ preceding values except for $w_0 - w_{15}$ that are the corresponding 16 words of the message block $m_i$, as can be seen in Figure 3.6. This asset will prove its effectiveness in the following phases.

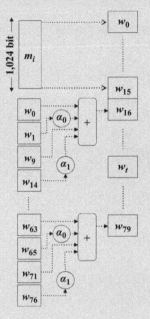

*Figure 3.6   Phase 2: preparing 80 words*

## Phase 3: Preparing 512-bit hash buffer $h_i$

The intermediate and final results of the hash function are stored at $n$ hash buffers $h_1, \ldots h_i, \ldots, h_n$ each of 512-bit length. Each 512-bit chunk is in the form of eight of 64-bit registers $(a, b, c, d, e, f, g, h)$. Their initial value is chosen to be the first 64 bits of the fractional fragments of the square roots of the first eight prime numbers. Here are their hexadecimal values:

- $a = 6A09E667F3BCC908$
- $b = BB67AE8584CAA73B$
- $c = 3C6EF372FE94F82B$
- $d = A54FF53A5F1D36F1$
- $e = 510E527FADE682D1$
- $f = 9B05688C2B3E6C1F$
- $g = 1F83D9ABFB41BD6B$
- $h = 5BE0CD19137E2179$

**Phase 4: Processing *n* blocks of expanded message by module *F***
In SHA-512, module *F* has 80 rounds, each round *t*:

- Inputs the intermediate $h_{i-1}$ hash value to its 512 bit $a, b, c, d, e, f, g, h$ initialized buffer.
- Inputs the 64 bit word $w_t$ value of the current processed block $m_i$.
- Inputs a constant $k_t$ of 64 bit. Each $k_t$ is the first 64 bits of the fractional parts of the cube roots of the first 80 prime numbers. $k_t$s ensure randomizing the input data.
- Outputs its eight updates registers values to the next round.

At the final round, to produce the final value $h_i$, the output of round 79 is added with the input of round 0. The addition is independent for each of the eight registers using addition modulo $2^{64}$, as Figure 3.7 shows. For how the SHA-512 round function works, we refer the reader to [6].

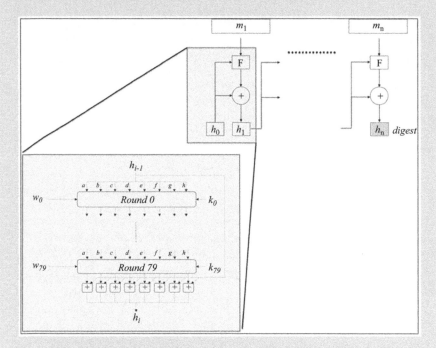

*Figure 3.7    SHA-512 processing of each block and digest generation*

With these three preparation phases in hand, the processing module of SHA-512 algorithm is explained in Phase 4.

After processing all of the *n* blocks, the 512-bit message digest is the output of the *n*th stage as shown in Figure 3.8.

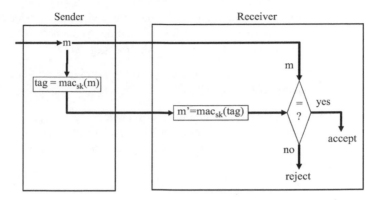

*Figure 3.8    Principles behind MAC*

### 3.3.1.2    SHA-256's strengths and weaknesses

The SHA-512 algorithm's strength comes from the property that every single bit of the input message is an argument to every single bit of the output message. The resulted hash is well mixed because of the redundant repetition of module $F$. Therefore, the preimage resistance feature of hash functions is achieved and no two messages have the same hash. The probability of having two messages $m_1$ and $m_2$ of the same digest is $1/2^{256}$ and the probability of finding a message $m$ with a given digest is $1/2^{512}$ [6]. Since SHA-512 shares some of the math behind SHA-1, as we stated earlier, its lifecycle will follow the SHA-1's lifecycle.

### 3.3.2    Symmetric key authentication

Authentication protocols of the clouds, the IoT, and for the big data use an advanced version of cryptographic authentication schemes; they are symmetric key-based authentication algorithms mainly called MAC algorithms. In essence, an MAC algorithm represents a symmetric-keyed hash function or a symmetric-key encrypted checksum[2]. The main idea behind MAC is to attach an authentication *tag* with an arbitrary bit length message *m*. Applying a function MAC on *m* generates the fixed-length *tag*. The function either uses hash algorithms or block ciphers of a symmetric key $s_k$ at the sending end and the resulted *tag* is verified using the same key $s_k$ at the receiving end, and hence the name "symmetric authentication." $s_k$ is a shared secret symmetric key between the user/sender and the system/receiver. In Figure 3.8, the computed *tag* at the sender is again verified at the receiver. The result $m'$ is compared to the sent *m*. If the message has not been changed or altered, then the result of the re-computation of MAC yields a similar result to the sent message; otherwise, message *m* is rejected. Hence, MAC algorithm achieves

---

[2]Checksums are hash-like verifiers, but without any cryptographic proof behind them to prove they provide reasonably unique outputs for unique inputs [6].

message integrity. Also, user authentication is guaranteed since the sender has the same symmetric key that the receiver used for verification. Since both parties have the same key, it is hard to prove who originates the message $m$.

---

**Security properties of MAC**

- Data integrity: $m \neq m'$ if $m$ was altered or changed.
- Data authentication: both the sender and the receiver have the $s_k$ key.
- No non-repudiation: who originates message $m$ cannot be proven to a third-party entity.

---

To realize and construct MAC algorithms, two different cryptographic primitives are used. MACs can be implemented using cryptographic hash functions or using symmetric **block ciphers**. Below, we briefly explain what block ciphers are although we have already hinted on block ciphers designed from scratch and used for the compression module $F$ inside the SHA-512 hash function description. There are also some fast computable MACs that are created using universal hashing concept[3] [4]. Hash-based MAC (HMAC) algorithm represents the most popular MAC authentication algorithm. In 1996, Bellare *et al.* presented HMAC algorithm [7]. As with any MAC, HMAC verifies message integrity and message originator's authenticity using hash and secret key. The most popular hash functions that are used with HMAC are MD5 and SHA-1; however, with the development of SHA-2 and 3, HMAC becomes more advanced and more secure. For example, if SHA-256 hash is used, HMAC is referred to as HMAC-SHA256. For the inner description and construction of HMAC, Section 3.3.2.1 is dedicated. The other alternative MAC realization is from symmetric encrypting block ciphers. Advanced encryption standard (AES) block cipher is used in a cipher block chaining (CBC) mode; this is known as CBC-MAC algorithm as explained below. Since block cipher-based MACs have been preferred over hashed-based MACs, more types and constructions have been introduced over the years. To have a variable length input CBC-MAC, CMAC is a suggested variant that became a recommendation by the NIST in 2005. The heart of CMAC is a modification of CBC-MAC and was introduced by Black and Rogaway [8]. Its earlier version used three secret keys for security. In an attempt to reduce the number of keys, Iwata and Kurosawa [9] presented one-key MAC (OMAC) as another CBC-MAC-like algorithm; OMAC family has two versions: OMAC 1 and 2 with OMAC1 equivalent to CMAC. Further, Rogaway presented the parallelizable MAC (PMAC) variant of OMAC that has better security. Aside from these CBC-MAC based MACs, Galois MAC (GMAC) algorithm, which is a variant of Galois counter mode (GCM), was introduced. GMAC is used for authentication purposes unlike GCM that can be

---

[3]Universal hashing is to randomly choose a hash function from a family of a certain mathematical property.

used for encryption. GMAC is fast because it is easy to be parallelized and yields more efficient hardware implementations. Another direction of realizing MACs is the use of universal hashing concept [10]. UMAC algorithm proposed in 1999 by Black *et al.* [11]. The idea behind UMAC is to construct it using a hash function chosen from a set of weak functions according to some secret key. The resulting hash value is encrypted to obscure the identity of the used hash. This type of MACs is less computation intensive than other MAC constructions and it is suitable for 32-bit processing units' architectures. To have a 64-bit processing unit architecture universal hash MAC, Krovetz and Dai in 2007 proposed VMAC [12]. Below, we are elaborating on block ciphers, the concept behind CBC-MAC; CBC-MAC is covered. Further, HMAC algorithm is introduced to have a sense of their inner construction and achieved security.

### 3.3.2.1 Block ciphers

Block ciphers are algorithms/transformations/permutations that take fixed-size blocks of plain input of $b$ bits to construct fixed-size encrypted output blocks. Using some fixed secret key $s_k$ of $N$ bit, block ciphers generate their ciphered/encrypted output of $b$ bits. AES is one example of block ciphers. The exact permutations of the block cipher are controlled by the secret key $s_k$. Mostly, block cipher algorithms are from the iterated-style genre, i.e., their inner working is an iteration of an invertible round function; iteration is called a round [13]. At each round, different intermediate form of the fixed size secret key $s_k$ is generated. Besides, at the first and last round, the key is modified/whitened by xoring it with some bits. There are four main types of iterated block ciphers: substitution-permutations networks, Feistel design, Lai–Massey schemes, and Add-Rotate-Xor (ARX) type. Since a block cipher algorithm can be applied only to a single block of a fixed–size length, **modes of operation** have been presented to describe how to repetitively employ the block cipher's single-block operation to larger amounts of input data. Many modes or operations are coined such as: electronic codebook (ECB), CBC, cipher feedback (CFB), output feedback (OFB), counter (CTR), etc. [14]. The difference between these modes is how they cascade the outputs from previous encryption/decryption block or from other deterministic variables into the subsequent encryption/decryption block. All of these modes need two ingredients: **initial value** and **padding**. On one hand, the mode's initial value is a fixed randomly chosen binary format block of bits; it is used to randomize the ciphering of the encryption algorithm to produce dissimilar ciphers even if the same input block is encrypted several times. On the other hand, since we are dealing with variable length input messages and block ciphers need the messages to be divided into fixed-size blocks, the last block of any divided messages might need some padding; padding is the process of appending the last block of input data with some value (zeros or one and zeros) [14].

### 3.3.2.2 CBC mode and CBC-MAC algorithm

CBC mode of operation of block ciphers was presented in 1976 [15]. CBC chains the execution of each block cipher $F$ with the result of the preceding unit. Hence, block $m_i$ of message $m$ is xored with the result of previous encryption before it is

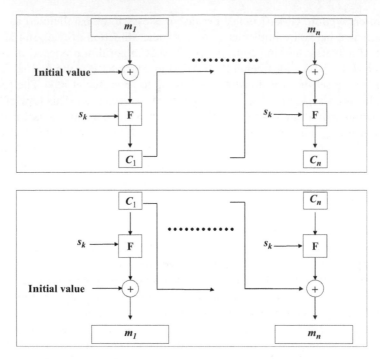

*Figure 3.9    Encryption and decryption in the CBC mode*

input to the current encryption module. This way, each resulted block depends on all input blocks of *m* processed up to that point. CBC uses the initial value ingredient in its first block processing as with any other mode of operation [15], see Figure 3.9 for the description of CBC mode encryption and decryption operations; we notate the encryption/decryption module of the block cipher as *F*. For strengths and weaknesses of CBC mode, we refer the reader to [4].

CBC mode is used in constructing the popular CBC-MAC authentication algorithm. The same structure of Figure 3.9 is followed, but with *F* being the AES encryption/decryption algorithm and decryption is not used for verification[4]. The three phases of the CBC-MAC algorithm are described here.

**Phase 1: CBC-MAC preparation**

- At first, input *m* is divided into *n* bocks: $m_1$ to $m_n$.
- Any needed padding is made in the form of 1000000 . . . .
- Choosing the secret key $s_k$ and *initial value* of the inner AES algorithm. The *initial value* is a random public value while $s_k$ is private.

---

[4]Existing AES standard generates a block of 128-bit length.

**Phase 2: CBC-MAC generation**

On the acquired blocks of message $m$, the CBC-MAC is applied where:

- Iteration 1: using the *initial value*, the first block $m_1$ of $m$, and the secret key $s_k$, the AES encryption is applied to obtain the first output/ciphered block $c_1 = AES_{s_k}(initial\ value \oplus m_1)$.
- Iteration $i$, $1 < i \leq n$: the xor is conducted between the current block $m_i$ and the previous ciphertext $c_{i-1}$ to obtain $c_i = AES_{s_k}(c_{i-1} \oplus m_i)$.

The final output $c_n$ of the last block is the CBC-MAC of message $m$, i.e., $c_n = CBC - MAC(m)$. In the pure CBC mode, the output is the concatenation of all $c$s, i.e., $c_1 | c_2 | \ldots | c_n$.

**Phase 3: CBC-MAC verification**

To verify the correctness of the generated MAC, the CBC-MAC is recomputed for $m$ and compared with the previously received value $c_n$. If a match occurs the message is accepted; otherwise, it is rejected. Just to mention, in the case of the pure CBC mode, the process of phase 2 is reversed to check the correctness:

- Iteration 1: using the *initial value*, the first block $c_1$ of $c$, and the secret key $s_k$, the AES decryption is applied to obtain the first block of message $m$ back $m_1 = initial\ value \oplus AES_{s_k}^{-1}(c_1)$.
- Iteration $i$, $1 < i \leq n$: the xor is conducted between the current block $c_i$ and the previous message block $m_{i-1}$ to obtain $m_i = m_{i-1} \oplus AES_{s_k}^{-1}(c_{i-1})$.

Hence, message $m$ is retrieved back and compared with the received plain message, if a match occurs, the receiver accepts $m$; otherwise, he/she rejects it as being tampered.

### 3.3.2.3 CBC-MAC's strengths and weaknesses

The security of HMAC is related to the security of CBC mode. IF CBC mode is used incorrectly, it yields the CBC-MAC insecure. Common mistakes can be in using the same key $s_k$ for CBC-MAC encryption and authentication. Another mistake is by allowing the initial value to change value. For more detailed description of these two attacks, read the related sections of [6]. As a better choice, HMAC algorithm was introduced.

### 3.3.2.4 HMAC algorithm

There has been increased interest in developing a MAC derived from a cryptographic hash function because they are faster and because the availability of vast underlying hashes' libraries. A hash function such as SHA is not designed for use as an MAC and cannot be used directly for that purpose, because it does not rely on a secret key. There have been a number of proposals for the incorporation of a secret key into an existing hash algorithm. The approach that has received the most support is HMAC

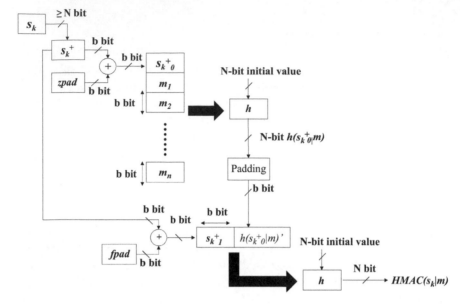

*Figure 3.10    HMAC inner construction*

and it has been chosen as the mandatory-to-implement MAC for the IP security; it is also utilized by other Internet protocols such as SSL. Here, we give a detailed explanation for the HMAC algorithm's four phases with a supporting illustration in Figure 3.10.

**Phase 1: Preparing input message $m$**

- Message $m$ is divided into $n$ blocks $m_0$ to $m_{n-1}$, each of $b$ bit length.

**Phase 2: Choosing the inner hash function $h$**

- The to-be-used hash function is chosen of $N$ bit hash digest.
- Its initial value is set.

**Phase 3: Preparing the intermediate secret keys from input $s_k$**

- Input secret key $s_k$ of length $\geq N$ bits is chosen. If $s_k$ is longer than block size of $b$ bits, then it is passed through the compression function of $h$ to produce an $N$ bit length.
- From $s_k$, another key $s_k^+$ is created. $s_k^+$ is generating by padding $s_k$ with zeros to the left to have a length $b$ key.

- From $s_k^+$ two pseudorandom intermediate keys are generated:

  ○ $s_k^+0$: bit-wise xoring $s_k^+$ with zpad to generate $b$-bit block $s_k^+0$. zpad is 00110110 reiterated $b/8$ times to extend its length to become $b$ bits. *zpad* flips half of bits of $s_k^+$.

  ○ $s_k^+1$: bit-wise xoring $s_k^+$ with fpad to generate $b$-bit block $s_k^+1$. fpad is 01011100 reiterated $b/8$ times. *fpad* flips another half of bits of $s_k^+$.

**Phase 4: Inner operation of HMAC**

- First intermediate key $s_k^+0$ of $b$-bit length is appended to the input $m$.
- The generated stream is entered to the hash function $h$ to produce an output $h(s_k^+0|m)$ of $N$ bits.
- $h(s_k^+0|m)$ is padded with zeros to extend its length to be $h(s_k^+0|m)'$ of $b$ bits.
- $h(s_k^+0|m)'$ is appended with the second intermediate secret key $s_k^+1$ of $b$ length to generate the second stream.
- The second stream is entered to the hash function $h$. The resulted hash is the required HMAC of message $m$ and secret key $s_k$.

After preparing the needed inputs and choosing the inner hash, the HMAC procedure constitutes the following steps:

*HMAC's strengths and weaknesses*
The security of HMAC is proven to be the hardness of the underlying hash function. It has been proved that for the probability of successful forgery against HMAC equals to one of these two attacks on the implanted hash [6]:

- First attack considers HMAC as a mere hash function of an input equals one block of $b$ bits. To countermeasure, the initial value of the hash has be assumed as a random secret $n$ bits value; the attacker probability of success will be $1/2^n$.
- In the second type of attacks, the attacker wants to find collision in the implemented hash, i.e., he/she wants to find two messages that have the same digest. As we stated earlier, the probability of fining a preimage collision is $1/2^{0.5n}$; therefore, if $n$ is large enough, e.g., 128 bit, he/she will need many years to succeed.

The only limitations of HMAC algorithm are the necessity of having $s_k$ shared between the sender and the receiver. Besides, HMAC has no non-denial, i.e., senders can deny their sending of messages. In this sense, the public key authentication schemes such as digital signatures are more effective as discussed below.

### 3.3.3    Asymmetric key authentication

Since symmetric cryptographic primitives such as MACs offer no non-repudiation, the need for more secure authentication means have led the way to the world of public key authentication primitives. The main authentication element is digital signatures. A digital signature $s$ is a technique to bind the identity of the sender with the message $m$ he is sending. Thus, it achieves message/originator authentication; digital signatures are created using a private key $s_k$ over message $m$, i.e., $sign_{s_k}(m)$. They are verified using a public key $p_k$ associated with that private key: $verify_{p_k}(s)$. Normally, DSAs use hash functions $h$ to achieve data integrity; if the message has been modified, the signature is denied. Further, digital signatures achieve the non-repudiation security feature such that a sender cannot deny sending the message if any dispute happens because his/her $s_k$ private key was used to create that signature. Table 3.1 compares the three available cryptographic-based authentication techniques and shows how digital signatures achieve the three required security goals of authentication. Figure 3.11 gives a schematic diagram of digital signature authentication.

Diffie and Hellman coined the notion of digital signatures in 1976, leading the way for presenting the first popular DSA of Rivest–Shamir–Adleman (RSA) in 1977. RSA

*Table 3.1    Cryptographic authentication primitives comparison: in terms of the achieved security requirement*

| | Primitive | | |
|---|---|---|---|
| **Requirement** | **Hash** | **MAC** | **Digital signatures** |
| Integrity | Yes | Yes | Yes |
| Authentication | No | Yes | Yes |
| Non-repudiation | No | No | Yes |
| Keys | None | Secret keys | Asymmetric keys |
| Computation time | Fastest | Fast | Slow |

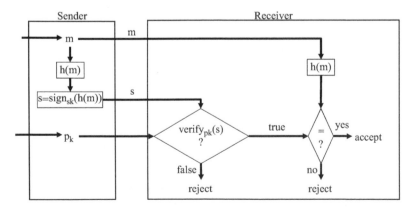

*Figure 3.11    Digital signature authentication*

security is based on the integer factorization of large numbers hardness problem and RSA problem defined below; that is, it is hard to factor large numbers using limited computing resources. To keep the signature secure, the size of the used secret and public keys has to be large enough such as 1,024 bit and 2,046 bit. In Section 3.3.3.1, we sketch main outline of such masterpiece RSA signature. Rabin signature followed the introduction of RSA and also was based on the problem of integer factorization; however, the success of RSA made Rabin signature not widely used. Two other signatures were presented in the late 1970s: Lamport and Merkle signatures; both were built based on the hardness of hash functions with signing keys to be used only one time. In 1984, Goldwasser, Micali, and Rivest rigorously defined the security requirements of digital signatures and presented their GMR signature. At the same time, El-Gamal signature scheme was presented, but its hardness was based on the difficulty of computing discrete logarithm problem (DLP) as defined in [4,16,17].

**Security features achieved with digital signatures**

- Message integrity: The use of a hash function $h$ when constructing a DSA achieves the integrity check for sent message $m$: $h(m) \neq h(m')$.
- Message authentication: Receiver can only verify the signature using $p_k$ public key of the sender who possess the corresponding $s_k$ secret key: $verify_{p_k}(sign_{s_k}(m))$.
- Non-repudiation: Only the real signer knows the $s_k$ secret key used for signing $m$. He/she cannot deny sending the message $m$.

**Definition 1 (Discrete logarithm problem in $Z_p^*$ [4,16,17]):**
*Given modular arithmetic cyclic group $Z_p^*$ and $P$ a generating element of $Z_p^*$. If $p_k \in Z_p^*$, it is computationally infeasible to compute $s_k$ in $p_k = P^{s_k} \bmod p$, where $p$ is a large prime and $Z$ is integer numbers domain.*

Despite its success, El-Gamal signature was not widely used. A variant of it, known as the DSA, was developed by NIST in 1991 and became much more widely used. To shorten the size of keys, Schnorr signature was presented in 1993 and based on the intractability of the DLP. When the public key cryptography started the utilization of ECs, algebraic structures over finite fields, an elliptic curve (EC) version of DSA (ECDSA) was proposed in 1998. ECDSA has shorter keys, shorter signature, and faster processing time because it simply uses ECs. Since ECDSA is an ingredient of most modern authentication protocols that are based on ECs, we dedicate the next section to describe it. Since we are covering EC signatures, we also introduce the EC version of popular Schnorr signature in Section 3.3.3.3. Although ECs mathematical structure and hardness are well covered in [4,16], we will briefly define them when it is needed.

### 3.3.3.1   RSA authentication algorithm

RSA encryption algorithm was introduced in 1977. Since then it was the most widely used scheme of all times. The same algorithm can also be used for authentication purposes. RSA authentication has three phases of keys generation, signature generation, and signature verification.

**Phase 1: Keys generation**

For an $L$-bit security level:

- Two random integer primes $q$ and $p$ are generated.
- Keeping both primes hidden, an $n = q \cdot p$ value is calculated.
- The Euler's phi Function $\Phi(n)$ is calculated for $n$ such that $\Phi(n) = p - 1 \cdot q - 1$.
- From $\Phi(n)$, $e$ is created, where $e$ is a co-prime with $\Phi(n)$ and $1 \leq e \leq \Phi(n)$.

At this point, the two secret and public key of RSA are set such that:

- Secret key $s_k = d = e^{-1}$ using the extended Euclidean algorithm (EEA) algorithm.
- Public key $p_k = (e, n)$.

**Phase 2: Signature generation**

To sign message $m$, the sender needs to compute:

- Hash function of $m$, $h(m)$
- The signature is calculated such that $h(m)$ is raised to the power of the sender secret key $d$ modulus the $n$ value of the public key, i.e. $s = sig_d(m) = h(m)^d \bmod n$.

As a result, the sender sends the message $m$, his signature $s$, and his/her public key $p_k$ to the receiver or server for authentication.

**Phase 3: Signature verification**

To verify the authenticity of received tuple $m$, $s$, $p\_k$, receiver or server:

- Raises $s$ to the power of the sender public key $e$ modulus $n$, i.e., he/she computes $s^e \bmod n \rightarrow h(m)^{d^e} \bmod n \rightarrow h(m)^{d \cdot e} \bmod n$. Because $d = e^{-1}$, the pair $d \cdot e$ dies out and $h(m)$ is retrieved from $s$.
- The received plain message $m$ is hashed and compared with the retrieved digest; if a match occurs, the message is received as an unaltered message; otherwise, it is rejected.

*RSA's strengths and weaknesses*
The RSA algorithm is built upon the hardness of two problems: large integer factorization problem and RSA problem. For the first, it is infeasible to compute the factorization of sufficiently large prime numbers. However, with the advancement of computing resources, fining factors of large primes is not a long shot anymore. The second problem is defined below as:

**Definition 2 (RSA Problem [6]):**
*Given public key $(e, n)$ and ciphertext $c = m^d$ mod $n$, it is hard to compute m, i.e., inverting the RSA function without knowing the secret key d.*

Such problem is hard to solve if the modulus $n$ is large and the message $m$ is random and from large space. If the modulus $n$ can be factored, the task is believed to be solvable with fast computing resources. With the introduction and utilization of ECs, ECDSA signature starts to substitute the use of RSA. Before we delve into the explanation of ECDSA, a formal definition to an EC can be simply stated as:

**Definition 3 (Elliptic curve *E* [4,16]):**
*The elliptic curve E over F_p (Galois field modulus large prime $p > 3$) is the set of all points $(x, y) \in F_p$ which fulfill the short Weierstrass equation $y^2 \equiv (x^3 + ax + b)$ mod p together with an imaginary point at infinity O, where $a, b \in F_p$ and the condition $4a^3 + 27b^2 \neq 0$ mod p must be satisfied to have no self-intersected smooth curves. Number of points on elliptic curve is bounded by Hasse's theorem to $(p + 1 - \bar{t})$ where $\bar{t}$, the Trace of Frobenius, satisfies $|\bar{t}| \leq 2\sqrt{p}$.*

The power of cryptography depends on the ECs' DLP (ECDLP) hardness that is stated as:

**Definition 4 (ECDLP [4,16]):**
*For any two points P and Q on the elliptic curve, it is computationally infeasible to know whether they are multiples of each other, i.e., it is hard to know k in $Q = k \cdot P$.*

### 3.3.3.2 Elliptic curve digital signature algorithm

The ECDSA algorithm has three phases: keys generation, signature generation, and signature verification. The underlying EC parameters are as follows. For $2L$-bit prime number $p$, a Galois field $F_p$ is created and an EC equation $E : y^2 \equiv (x^3 + ax + b)$ mod $p$ is generated, where $a, b, x, y \in F_p$. On such $E$, a subgroup $G$ of $(x, y)$ points is chosen with generating point $P$; $G$ has a prime order $q$. These public parameters are given to all entities in the network. Over these parameters, the following three ECDSA phases are conducted.

**Phase 1: Keys generation**

Generate two keys:

- Private key $s_k = d$ to use for signing messages where $d$ is a random integer and $0 \leq d \leq q$. The secret key is to be held only at sender to generate signatures.
- Public key $p_k = s_k \cdot P$ for verifying signatures, where $P$ is the generator of $G$. The public key is given to receivers to use it for verification.

**Phase 2: Signature generation**

To sign an outgoing message $m$, the signature is created as:

- Message $m$ is hashed first to create $h(m)$.
- Choose random ephemeral private key $k_e$ where $0 \leq k_e \leq q$.
- Calculate another ephemeral public point key $R = k_e \cdot P$, where $R = (X_R, Y_R)$.
- Let $r$ part of the signature equal $X_R$ the $x$-coordinate of point $R$.
- Calculate $s$, the second part of the signature $s = (h(m) + s_k \cdot r)k_e^{-1} \bmod q$ using $s_k$.

The generated signature is $(r, s)$. Now, we have $m$ and $(r, s)$ to be sent to verification end.

**Phase 3: Signature verification**

At the receiving end, to verify the authenticity of the received signature:

- Hash the received message $m$ to obtain $h(m)$.
- From $s$, compute the auxiliary value of $w \neq s^{-1} \bmod q$.
- From $w$ compute two auxiliary values $u_1$ and $u_2$ such that $u_1 \neq w \cdot h(m) \bmod q$ and $u_2 \neq w \cdot r \bmod q$.
- From $u_1$ and $u_2$, compute $\bar{P} = u_1 \cdot p_k + u_2 \cdot P$ using public key $p_k$.
- If the $x$-coordinate $X_P$ of $\bar{P}$ equals $r \bmod q$, accept the received signature as valid; otherwise, reject it as invalid.

*ECDSA's strengths and weaknesses*

The proof of the structured ECDSA signature is easy and can be seen in [4]. The main analytical attack against ECDSA attempts to solve the EC discrete logarithm problem. If an attacker were capable of doing this, he/she could compute the private key $s_k$ and/or the ephemeral key $k_e$. However, the best-known ECC attacks have a complexity proportional to the square root of the size of the group in which the discrete logarithm problem is defined, i.e., proportional to $\sqrt{q}$ where $q$ is large. However, digital signatures are slower than MACs; they are used only when there is not a shared secret or the non-repudiation property is crucially important [4].

**Phase 1: Signature generation**
To sign an outgoing message $m$, the signature is created as:

- The user picks a random private integer key $s_k \in Z_q^*$ and creates a random public point key $p_k = s_k \cdot P \in G$.
- The user calculates two parts $(e, s)$ of Schnorr signature such that $e = h(p_k|m)$ or $e = h(m|p_k)$ and $s = s_k + sk_{PKG} \cdot e \bmod q$, i.e., $s_k = s - sk_{PKG} \cdot e \bmod q$.
- The generated signature $(e, s)$ is sent with message $m$ for verification.

**Phase 2: Signature verification**
At the receiving server, to verify the authenticity of the received signature, the receiver who has $p, q, P, pk_{PKG}, h$ checks whether $h(mp_k) = h(m(s \cdot P - e \cdot pk_{PKG}))$, i.e., whether $(s \cdot P)$ equals $(p_k + e \cdot pk_{PKG})$. If it is valid, the receiver accepts $m \cdot$

### 3.3.3.3 Elliptic curve Schnorr signature algorithm
In 1989, Schnorr presented an efficient short signature whose EC version is known to be ECDLP secure in the random oracle model. In Schnorr signature, the central public key generator (PKG) chooses an elliptic curve $E$ with large parameters $(a, b, q, p, G,$ and $P)$ and a hash function $h$. PKG randomly chooses a master private scalar key $sk_{PKG} \in Z_q^*$ and calculates its master public point key $pk_{\{PKG\}} = sk_{PKG}.P \in G$. PKG publishes these domain parameters to every registered user. Hence, after deployment, two phases of the scheme are conducted [17].

### 3.3.3.4 EC Schnorr signature's strengths and weaknesses
Schnorr signature is short, simple, and secure; that is why it is highly appealing that it will replace ECDSA in the Bitcoin technology. Schnorr signature is not malleable, i.e., active attackers cannot change it. Further, the signature supports multi-signature verification leading to less verification time in comparison to other signatures [18].

Having covered various cryptographic authentication schemes, we switch the gears to sketchily describe a totally different realm of authentication where biometric features of users are the key ingredients of authentication algorithms. In this book, we dedicate chapters to discuss this type of authentication. On the other hand, since authentication can also be implemented using stego-based schemes such as watermarking and steganography, we fully describe the available stego-based authentication schemes and trends in subsequent chapters of this book.

## 3.4 Biometric authentication

Biometric authentication is more secure than mere cryptographic-based authentication. The use of biological traits is more robust in identifying and authenticating users. Fingerprints, palm veins/print, retinal/iris patterns, face, DNA samples, voice/speech, heart cardiogram, brainwave, keystroke rhythm when typing a password, and behavioral patterns are all virtually unique attributes to each individual. Thus, proving user's identity is very difficult to be falsified/spoofed. Since these features represent who we are, another advantage of biometric authentication is that these credentials are with us all the time and we do not need to store or secure them for proper usage [3]. Any biometric recognition system must have the typical stages shown in Figure 3.12. The first time an individual uses a biometric system is called enrollment. During the enrollment, biometric information from an individual is captured and stored. In subsequent uses, biometric information is detected and compared with the information stored at the time of enrollment.

In addition to the unimodal biometric system that authenticates users based only on a single feature, multimodal biometric authentication is utilized. With the multimodal biometric system, sets of features are used from same user at the same time; input sets can be either many features or many versions of a single feature. In multimodal biometric systems, unimodal systems can be fused sequentially, in parallel, or hierarchically. Fusion of the biometrics information can occur at different stages of a recognition system. In case of feature level fusion, the data itself or the features extracted from multiple biometrics are fused.

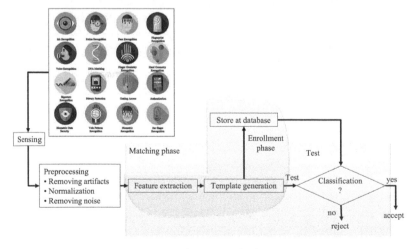

*Figure 3.12    Typical stages of a biometric system*

Matching-score level fusion consolidates the scores generated by multiple classifiers pertaining to different modalities. Finally, in case of decision level fusion the final results of multiple classifiers are combined via techniques such as majority voting. Feature level fusion is believed to be more effective than the other levels of fusion because the feature set contains richer information about the input biometric data than the matching score or the output decision of a classifier. Therefore, fusion at the feature level is expected to provide better recognition results. Despite being vulnerable to user interface attacks, fingerprint authentication is still the most widely used biometric system followed by face recognition systems [19].

Fingerprints were only used to vet criminals and identify victims in the nineteenth century. However, nowadays with the development of IoT and advanced mobile apps, fingerprints are everywhere. Since it is more secure and more convenient than entering passwords to login to systems, fingerprint authentication is widely used to secure smart phones and to approve transactions in online e-shopping. Fingerprint biometric authentication system begins when the user scans his fingerprint image; such image may require minor or major preprocessing depending on its quality [20]. Preprocessing might include enhancement, binarization, extraction of region of interest, hole/island removal, thinning, and noise elimination. The next step is feature extraction where three types of features are recognized [21]: the overall pattern shape of the fingerprint, the specific friction ridge paths, and the intrinsic detail present in a fingerprint. The selection of important/discriminatory features and putting the required algorithms for extracting/measuring these features is the next important step. Finally, the matching algorithm is used to check whether the image matches a stored template; two given fingerprints are compared by a matching algorithm and return either a degree of similarity (matching score) or an acceptance/rejection decision [20]. Over the past decades, many fingerprint authentication algorithms have been proposed. Generally, they are classified into three main categories [22,23]: correlation-based, minutiae-based, and non-minutiae-based algorithms. Furthermore, neural network based approaches have been presented [23]. Due to the extent of this topic, in Figure 3.13, we briefly sketch the possible categories of the fingerprint recognition systems [20–26] and the later chapters will give a comprehensive detailed explanation of these systems.

## 3.5 Learned lessons and future trends

Data authentication algorithms are different from authentication protocols.

- Data authentication algorithms can be mainly classified into four types: password-based, cryptographic-based, biometric-based, and stego-based schemes.
- Password-based authentication is the simplest authentication algorithm; yet it has three forms. The used password can be plain password, hashed password, or an encrypted password with some block cipher encryption to add more security to this type of authentication.

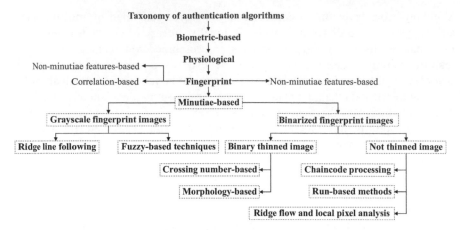

*Figure 3.13    Fingerprint authentication categories*

- Cryptographic-based authentication is well studied over the years. Three sub-categories emerge: cryptographic hash functions, symmetric authentication, and public key authentication, which is the basis of PKI framework of the Internet.
- SHA-256 and SHA-512 are the current standards used by most advanced cryptographic primitives such as MACs and digital signatures.
- The lifecycle of SHA-2 family of hashes will follow that of SHA-1 since they share some structure of the underlying math.
- SHA-3 is the successor for SHA-2 and it may be the best choice for IoT, cloud computing, and big data in the near future with the advancement of computing resources.
- Under symmetric authentication algorithms, MACs are a leading tool.
- Many types of MACs are available, but generally they can be created using block ciphers, hash function, or universal hashing.
- Block ciphers are called so because they handle the input message as a set of fixed-size blocks.
- Block ciphers have various modes of operations and CBC is the most popular one where the result of one stage depends on the inputs of all the preceding stages.
- CBC-MAC authentication algorithm differs from CBC mode of operation. In the CBC mode, the resulted ciphertext is the concatenation of all stages outputs whereas in CBC-MAC, the ciphertext is the output of the last stage only. Another difference is that CBC mode's verification phase is the inverse of its generation phase; in the CBC-MAC algorithm, the verification phase is a second generation of the MAC over the message to compare with the MAC generated at sender.
- HMAC is a hash-based MAC authentication scheme. Its inner working is an iterated usage of hash function over an input message, secret key, and initial value.

- HMAC is preferred over CBC-MAC; therefore, it is a better candidate to use in IoT, clouds, and big data.
- The introduction of the public key cryptography led the way to have the RSA signature scheme.
- In RSA authentication, the user/sender uses his/her secret key to generate the signature and send the signature alongside his/her public key. The verifier has to use the received public key to verify the signature.
- RSA security depends on two hardness problems: large prime factorization and RSA problem are hard to be solved.
- With the advancement of ECs mathematic structures, ECDSA signature becomes the buzzword in the field of authentication. It is used in certificated PKI framework that is used to secure the Internet, the cloud computing, the big data, and the IoT.
- ECDSA security comes from the hardness of soling ECDLP problem on ECs.
- Recent research suggests the use of Schnorr signatures instead of ECDSA for the authentication of the trendy Bitcoin technology.
- Schnorr signature is short, simple, and secure. It is not malleable, i.e., active attackers cannot change it. It allows the verification of multiple signatures at once.
- Biometric authentication uses the features/behavior of the user to authenticate him/her to the system. It is more secure than the previously mentioned types.
- Fingerprint authentication is the most popular form of biometrics and it has four sub-categories: minutiae based, correlation based, non-minutiae features based, and neural networks based. Depending on the quality of the scanned fingerprint image and which type of features to be extracted, each type can be further subcategorized.
- Watermarking and steganography can also be considered as types of authentication algorithms; they are used in secret sharing and authenticating images.

## 3.6    Conclusions

Data authentication algorithms represent the baseline on which advanced authentication protocols can be built. In the realm of cloud computing, IoT, and big data, data authentication algorithms play a vital role to secure the transmitted, stored, and exchanged data and information. These basic and advanced algorithms are categorized into four main types. Passwords and hash functions represent the simplest authentication schemes. Hash functions are used into the more complex constructions of authentication algorithms such as MACs and digital signatures. The choice of the underlined mathematical building blocks, such as ECs, contributed to the improvement of authentication algorithms; nowadays, we have algorithms with efficient computation performance and shorter cryptographic keys. Besides the cryptographic realm of authentication, biometric and steganography schemes have been used as other means of authentication algorithms where the featured of the user are the keys to authenticate him/her into the system. Below, we summarize the overall learned lessons and list some future trends in this area of research.

# References

[1]    John S. *What is data authentication* [Online]. 2018. Available from: https://simplicable.com/new/data-authentication [accessed 20 Feb 2018].

[2]    Smith R. *Authentication: From passwords to public keys.* Addison-Wesley Longman Publishing Co; 2001; Boston, MA, USA.

[3]    Deb S. *Understanding and selecting authentication methods* [Online]. 2018. Tech Republic. Available from: https://www.techrepublic.com/article/understandingandselectingauthenticationmethods [accessed 24 Feb 2018].

[4]    Paar C, and Pelzl J. *Understanding cryptography: A textbook for students and practitioners.* 2nd ed. Springer Science & Business Media; 2009; Springer-Verlag, Berlin, Heidelber.

[5]    Roger G. *All you need to know about the move from SHA-1 to SHA-2 Encryption* [Online]. 2018. CSO. Available from: https://www.csoonline.com/article/2879073/encryption/all-you-need-to-know-about-the-move-from-sha1-to-sha2-encryption.html [accessed 5 Mar 2018].

[6]    Stallings W. *Cryptography and network security: Principles and practice.* 2017; Upper Saddle River, NJ.

[7]    Bellare M, Canetti R, and Krawczyk H. 'Keying hash functions for message authentication'. Proceedings of the Annual International Cryptology Conference; Springer; 1996. pp. 1–15.

[8]    Black J, and Rogaway P. 'A suggestion for handling arbitrary-length messages with the CBC MAC'. Proceedings of the NIST Second Modes of Operation Workshop; 2001.

[9]    Iwata T, and Kurosawa K. 'OMAC: One-key CBC MAC'. Proceedings of the International Workshop on Fast Software Encryption; Berlin, Heidelberg: Springer; 2003. pp. 129–153.

[10]   Stinson DR. 'Universal hashing and authentication codes'. Journal of Designs, Codes and Cryptography. 1994; 4(3): 369–380.

[11]   Black J, Halevi S, Krawczyk H, Krovetz T, and Rogaway P. 'UMAC: Fast and secure message authentication'. Proceedings of the Annual International Cryptology Conference; Springer; 1999; Berlin, Heidelberg. pp. 216–233.

[12]   Krovetz T, and Dai W. *VMAC: Message authentication code using universal hashing.* Technical report, CFRG Working Group, 2007.

[13]   Junod P, and Canteaut A. *Advanced Linear Cryptanalysis of Block and Stream Ciphers (Cryptology and Information Security Series).* IOS Press, 7th ed. 2011; Amsterdam, The Netherlands, The Netherlands.

[14]   NIST Computer Security Division's (CSD) Security Technology Group (STG). *Block cipher modes, Cryptographic Toolkit*, NIST, 2013.

[15]   Ehrsam W, Meyer C, Smith J, and Tuchman W. *Message verification and transmission error detection by block chaining.* US Patent 4074066, 1976.

[16]   Menezes AJ, Van Oorschot PC, and Vanstone SA. *Handbook of applied cryptography.* CRC press; 1996; Boca Raton.

[17]   Al-Shareeda S. *Enhancing security, privacy, and efficiency of vehicular networks.* The Ohio State University; 2017.

[18]  Buntinx JP. *What are Schnorr signatures* [Online]. 2018. Available from: https://nulltx.com/what-are-schnorr-signatures/ [accessed 21 Jul 2018].

[19]  Singla SK, and Kumar S. 'A review of data acquisition and difficulties in sensor module of biometric systems'. Songklanakarin Journal of Science & Technology. 2013; 35(5): 589–597.

[20]  Kothavale M, Markworth R, and Sandhu P. *Computer security ss3: Biometric authentication*. The University of Birmingham. 2004.

[21]  Dyre S, and Sumathi C. *A survey on various approaches to fingerprint matching for personal verification and identification*. Infinite Study; 2016.

[22]  Bahaa-Eldin AM. 'A medium resolution fingerprint matching system'. Ain Shams Engineering Journal. 2013; 4(3): 393–408.

[23]  Maltoni D., Maio D., Jain A.K., and Prabhakar S. *Handbook of fingerprint recognition*. 2009. Springer Science & Business Media, Springer, London.

[24]  Lindoso A, Entrena L, Liu-Jimenez J, and San Millan E. 'Increasing security with correlation-based fingerprint matching'. Proceedings of the 41st Annual IEEE International Carnahan Conference on Security Technology; 2007. pp. 37–43.

[25]  Bazen A.M., Verwaaijen G.T., Gerez S.H., Veelenturf L.P, and Van Der Zwaag B.J. 'A correlation-based fingerprint verification system'. Proceedings of the ProRISC2000 Workshop on Circuits, Systems and Signal Processing, 2000.

[26]  Thakkar D. *Minutiae based extraction in fingerprint recognition* [Online]. 2016. Bayometric. Available from: https://www.bayometric.com/minutiae-based-extraction-fingerprint-recognition [accessed 14 Aug 2018].

*Chapter 4*

# Cryptographic algorithms

*Bahram Rashidi[1]*

## 4.1 Introduction

One part of the science of secure communication is cryptography. It deals with the design and realization of cryptographic algorithms, e.g., data encryption and decryption, secure e-mail, banking transactions, and security for mobile communications. In recent years, cryptographic development has been a high priority and challenging research area in both fields of mathematics and communication. Internet of Things (IoT), Big Data and cloud computing are based on a highly interconnected network of devices, servers, and massive volumes of data where all kinds of communications seem to be possible. Therefore, the security requirement for such technologies becomes critical, which should be provided by cryptographic algorithms. The different types of cryptographic methods are shown in Figure 4.1. Two main categories in cryptography are symmetric key cryptography (block ciphers and stream ciphers) and asymmetric (or public-key) cryptography. The advanced encryption standard (AES) and data encryption standard (DES) are two important block ciphers of the symmetric key cryptography for message encryption and decryption. Also, the practical examples for public-key cryptography (PKC) are Rivest, Shamir, and Adleman (RSA) and elliptic curve cryptosystems (ECCs). Symmetric encryption is a form of cryptography in which encryption and decryption algorithms are performed using the same shared key of a certain size. There are two main hard problems used in modern PKCs, the integer factorization problem (IFP), and discrete logarithm problem (DLP). A particular case of DLP problem is the elliptic curve discrete logarithm problem (ECDLP), which is defined based on point multiplication (or scalar multiplication), is the hard problem for ECCs over finite fields. The applicable methods for PKC are rather slow compared to symmetric key cryptographic algorithms. Therefore, PKC is used as a complement to symmetric key cryptography. The applications of the PKC are including digital signatures, message authentication (a mechanism to verify the integrity of a message), key generation and key exchange. Security services are the objectives of

[1]Department of Electrical Engineering, University of Ayatollah Ozma Borujerdi, Iran

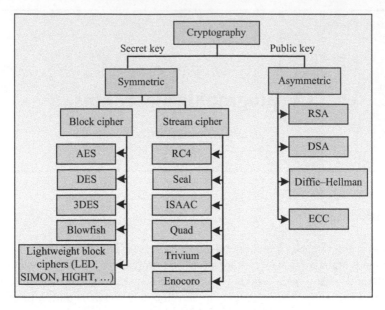

*Figure 4.1    Classification of cryptography*

security systems. The most important security services in many cryptographic applications are as follows:

1.  **Confidentiality**: Information is kept secret from all but authorized parties.
2.  **Integrity:** Messages are not modified in transit.
3.  **Message authentication:** The sender of a message is authentic. An alternative term is data origin authentication.
4.  **Non-repudiation:** The sender of a message cannot deny the creation of the message.

In this chapter, cryptographic algorithms related to symmetric key cryptography and PKC are discussed. Also, authentication methods in regard to new technologies such as IoT and Big Data and cloud computing are presented.

## 4.2    Symmetric cryptography

An encryption scheme is called symmetric-key if it is *computationally easy* to determine decryption key $d$ knowing only encryption key $e$ and vice versa. Based on a symmetric encryption, the plaintext $M$ is converted to the ciphertext $c$ using a secret key and an encryption algorithm. On the other hand, the plaintext $M$ is generated from the ciphertext $c$ by using the same key and decryption algorithm. In the most practical symmetric-key encryption schemes key $e$ is equal to key $d$, the term "symmetric-key" becomes appropriate. In the symmetric-key schemes, a secure communication channel to each pair of users based on a common secret key is provided. In this case, for example, user **A** encrypts her (or his) message $M$ using a symmetric algorithm, and sends the ciphertext $c$. User **B** receives the ciphertext $c$

and decrypts the message. The decryption process is the inverse of the encryption process. The symmetric cryptography is divided into two main groups *block ciphers* and *stream ciphers* [1]. Here, we only explain block cipher. In the block ciphers, $b$ bits of the message at a time is encrypted, where $b$ is the width of the block cipher. However, in the stream cipher, the bits are encrypted individually. Traditional and standard symmetric-key encryption schemes consist of data encryption standard (DES), RC5, RC6, and AES [2]. In addition, in recent years the lightweight block ciphers such as HIGHT, SIMON, SPECK, PRESENT, KATAN for low-cost devices and IoT applications are presented.

One of the most important disadvantages of the symmetric-key encryption is the key distribution between a high number of users. This drawback is solved by using public-key encryption. The important properties of the symmetric-key encryption are as follows:

- The key length can be shorter than public-key schemes for an acceptable level of security.
- Hardware and software implementations of these ciphers have high speed and low cost.

In the following, we describe two important block ciphers AES and DES in more detail.

### 4.2.1 Data encryption standard

One of the most widely used block ciphers is based on the DES. It is proposed in 1977 by the NBS[1], which is now called the NIST, as FIPS[2] PUB 46 [3]. In this algorithm, size of the data blocks and key are 64-bit and 56-bit, respectively. Figure 4.2 shows the structure of the DES as a Feistel cipher. The encryption and decryption schemes are based on the same key. Algorithm 1 shows DES encryption algorithm.

---

**Algorithm 1** DES encryption algorithm

---

**Input:** Plaintext $P$.
**Output:** Ciphertext $C$.

1. $L_0 \| R_0 = \text{IP}(P)$; // $\|$ denotes the concatenation operation
2. **For** $i$ **from** 1 **to** 16 **do**
3. $L_i = R_{i-1}$;
4. $R_i = L_{i-1} \oplus f(R_{i-1}, K_i)$;
5. **End For**;
6. $C = FP(R_{16} \| L_{16})$;
7. **Return** $C$;

---

[1]National Bureau of Standards
[2]Federal Information Processing Standard

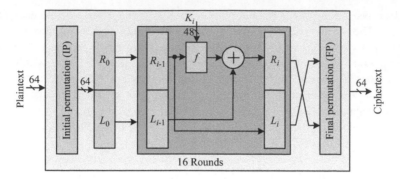

*Figure 4.2    Structure of the DES as a Feistel cipher*

More details about the structure of the $f$-function are presented in [1]. In this structure, first, the 32-bit input is expanded to 48 bits by a special type of permutation (E-box). Next, the 48-bit result is XOR-ed with the round key $K_i$, and the eight 6-bit blocks are applied into 8 different 6-bit input substitution boxes (S-boxes). Therefore, the bit lengths of the input and output of the S-boxes are 6-bit and 4-bit, respectively. The S-boxes are the nonlinear element in the DES algorithm and provide confusion (for obscuring of the relationship between key and ciphertext). Finally, in the $f$-function, to introduces diffusion (to hiding statistical properties of the plaintext), the 32-bit output of the S-boxes is applied to a permutation block. In the DES algorithm, the key length of 56-bit is very short to data encryption nowadays. It can relatively easily be broken with an exhaustive key-search attack [1]. Therefore, the DES algorithm is not suitable for many cryptographic applications.

### 4.2.2  Triple DES (3DES)

As mentioned before, a key length of 56-bit in the DES algorithm is insufficient for most modern cryptographic applications. In this case, three keys and three copies of the main cipher structure often are used. This structure of the DES algorithm is called triple DES or 3DES [3], which consists of three subsequent DES ciphers. The 3DES structure is shown in Figure 4.3. The key length is equal to 168-bit ($3 \times 56$ bits) in the 3DES. The 3DES is considerably more secure than DES, but the speed processing of the 3DES is 1/3 of the DES speed. In particular, 3DES is still secure.

### 4.2.3  Advanced encryption standard

The AES was proposed by Vincent Rijmen and Joan Daemen. It was published by the NIST in 2001 [4]. AES is a symmetric cryptographic algorithm that is used instead of DES algorithm as the confirmed standard for many cryptographic applications. It is the most widely used in several industry standards and many commercial systems [1]. For example, AES is included in the Internet security standard IPsec, TLS, the Wi-Fi encryption standard IEEE 802.11i, the secure shell network protocol SSH, and the Internet phone Skype. In work [5], a survey of different implementations of AES is presented.

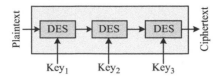

*Figure 4.3    Structure of the 3DES*

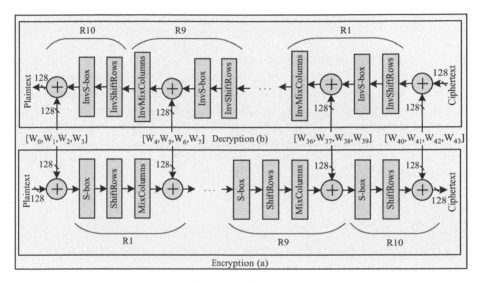

*Figure 4.4    Structure of the AES encryption (a) and decryption (b)*

### 4.2.3.1   Encryption and decryption algorithms

The AES algorithm consists of rounds, where the number of rounds depends on the key length: 10 rounds for a 128-bit key, 12 rounds for a 192-bit key, and 14 rounds for a 256-bit key. Figure 4.4 shows the structure of AES encryption and decryption. The rounds consist of four distinct transformation functions: *SubBytes* (uses an S-box to perform a byte-by-byte substitution of the block), *ShiftRows* (a simple permutation), *MixColumns* (a substitution that makes use of arithmetic over $\mathbb{F}_{2^8}$), and *AddRoundKey* (a simple bit-wise XOR of the current block with a portion of the expanded key). Algorithm 2 shows AES encryption algorithm.

---

**Algorithm 2** AES encryption algorithm

---

**Input:** Plaintext $P$ and the first round key $K_0$.
**Output:** Ciphertext $C$.

1.   $I =$ Key addition $(P, K_0)$;
2.   **For** $i$ **from** 1 **to** 9 **do**

3.  $I = \text{S-box}(I)$;
4.  $I = \text{ShiftRows}(I)$;
5.  $I = \text{MixColumns}(I)$;
6.  $I = \text{Key addition}(I, K_i)$;
7.  **End For**;
8.  $I = \text{S-box}(I)$;
9.  $I = \text{ShiftRows}(I)$;
10. $C = \text{Key addition}(I, K_{10})$;
11. **Return** $C$;

---

### 4.2.3.2   Structure of the AES operations

In this subsection, we describe more details about each of the four transformations used in the AES. For each transformation, we shall first describe the transformation used in the encryption algorithm, and then the inverse of transformation used in decryption algorithm is discussed. In order to understand the data movement in the AES algorithm, the 128-bit data is represented based on state matrix $A$ consisting of 16 bytes $A_0, \ldots, A_{14}, A_{15}$ is arranged in a four-by-four byte matrix which is called the state matrix:

$$\begin{pmatrix} A_0 & A_4 & A_8 & A_{12} \\ A_1 & A_5 & A_9 & A_{13} \\ A_2 & A_6 & A_{10} & A_{14} \\ A_3 & A_7 & A_{11} & A_{15} \end{pmatrix}$$

*Byte Substitution (S-Box) and inverse of Byte Substitution (InvS-Box)*
The substitute byte transformation or S-box is computed in the following steps:

1.  First, we compute inverse of each byte, $A_i = (a_i(7), a_i(6), \ldots, a_i(1), a_i(0))$ in the related state over $\mathbb{F}_{2^8}$, where $0 \le i \le 15$.
2.  If $A_i^{-1} \bmod f(x) = B_i$, where $f(x) = x^8 + x^4 + x^3 + x + 1$ is an irreducible polynomial (all elements have an inverse except for 0 on a finite field), the following transformation is applied to $B_i$:

$$\begin{pmatrix} b_i'(0) \\ b_i'(1) \\ b_i'(2) \\ b_i'(3) \\ b_i'(4) \\ b_i'(5) \\ b_i'(6) \\ b_i'(7) \end{pmatrix} = \begin{pmatrix} 1 & 0 & 0 & 0 & 1 & 1 & 1 & 1 \\ 1 & 1 & 0 & 0 & 0 & 1 & 1 & 1 \\ 1 & 1 & 1 & 0 & 0 & 0 & 1 & 1 \\ 1 & 1 & 1 & 1 & 0 & 0 & 0 & 1 \\ 1 & 1 & 1 & 1 & 1 & 0 & 0 & 0 \\ 0 & 1 & 1 & 1 & 1 & 1 & 0 & 0 \\ 0 & 0 & 1 & 1 & 1 & 1 & 1 & 0 \\ 0 & 0 & 0 & 1 & 1 & 1 & 1 & 1 \end{pmatrix} \times \begin{pmatrix} b_i(0) \\ b_i(1) \\ b_i(2) \\ b_i(3) \\ b_i(4) \\ b_i(5) \\ b_i(6) \\ b_i(7) \end{pmatrix} \oplus \begin{pmatrix} 1 \\ 1 \\ 0 \\ 0 \\ 0 \\ 1 \\ 1 \\ 0 \end{pmatrix} \qquad (4.1)$$

For example, if we have $A_i = (71)_{16}$ as an input of the S-box. The inversion of $(71)_{16} = (01110001)_2$ in $\mathbb{F}_{2^8}$ is equal to $(B7)_{16} = (10110111)_2$. Now, based on (4.1), result of the S-box for input $(71)_{16}$ is equal to $(A3)_{16}$ as follows:

$$
\begin{pmatrix}
1 & 0 & 0 & 0 & 1 & 1 & 1 & 1 \\
1 & 1 & 0 & 0 & 0 & 1 & 1 & 1 \\
1 & 1 & 1 & 0 & 0 & 0 & 1 & 1 \\
1 & 1 & 1 & 1 & 0 & 0 & 0 & 1 \\
1 & 1 & 1 & 1 & 1 & 0 & 0 & 0 \\
0 & 1 & 1 & 1 & 1 & 1 & 0 & 0 \\
0 & 0 & 1 & 1 & 1 & 1 & 1 & 0 \\
0 & 0 & 0 & 1 & 1 & 1 & 1 & 1
\end{pmatrix}
\times
\begin{pmatrix}
1 \\ 1 \\ 1 \\ 0 \\ 1 \\ 1 \\ 0 \\ 1
\end{pmatrix}
\oplus
\begin{pmatrix}
1 \\ 1 \\ 0 \\ 0 \\ 0 \\ 1 \\ 1 \\ 0
\end{pmatrix}
=
\begin{pmatrix}
1 \\ 0 \\ 0 \\ 1 \\ 0 \\ 0 \\ 1 \\ 0
\end{pmatrix}
\oplus
\begin{pmatrix}
1 \\ 1 \\ 0 \\ 0 \\ 0 \\ 1 \\ 1 \\ 0
\end{pmatrix}
=
\begin{pmatrix}
1 \\ 1 \\ 0 \\ 0 \\ 0 \\ 1 \\ 0 \\ 1
\end{pmatrix}
$$

Also, the inverse of the S-box, called InvS-box, is computed based on the following two steps:

1. First input byte $A_i = (a_i(7), a_i(6), \ldots, a_i(1), a_i(0))$ is applied to the following transformation:

$$
\begin{pmatrix}
a_i'(0) \\ a_i'(1) \\ a_i'(2) \\ a_i'(3) \\ a_i'(4) \\ a_i'(5) \\ a_i'(6) \\ a_i'(7)
\end{pmatrix}
=
\begin{pmatrix}
0 & 0 & 1 & 0 & 0 & 1 & 0 & 1 \\
1 & 0 & 0 & 1 & 0 & 0 & 1 & 0 \\
0 & 1 & 0 & 0 & 1 & 0 & 0 & 1 \\
1 & 0 & 1 & 0 & 0 & 1 & 0 & 0 \\
0 & 1 & 0 & 1 & 0 & 0 & 1 & 0 \\
0 & 0 & 1 & 0 & 1 & 0 & 0 & 1 \\
1 & 0 & 0 & 1 & 0 & 1 & 0 & 0 \\
0 & 1 & 0 & 0 & 1 & 0 & 1 & 0
\end{pmatrix}
\times
\begin{pmatrix}
a_i(0) \\ a_i(1) \\ a_i(2) \\ a_i(3) \\ a_i(4) \\ a_i(5) \\ a_i(6) \\ a_i(7)
\end{pmatrix}
\oplus
\begin{pmatrix}
1 \\ 1 \\ 0 \\ 0 \\ 0 \\ 1 \\ 1 \\ 0
\end{pmatrix}
\qquad (4.2)
$$

2. The result of the InvS-box is computed by inversion of the output of the above transformation.

As an example, if input of InvS-box is $A_i = (2A)_{16}$ for the computation of output, we have:

$$
\begin{pmatrix}
0 & 0 & 1 & 0 & 0 & 1 & 0 & 1 \\
1 & 0 & 0 & 1 & 0 & 0 & 1 & 0 \\
0 & 1 & 0 & 0 & 1 & 0 & 0 & 1 \\
1 & 0 & 1 & 0 & 0 & 1 & 0 & 0 \\
0 & 1 & 0 & 1 & 0 & 0 & 1 & 0 \\
0 & 0 & 1 & 0 & 1 & 0 & 0 & 1 \\
1 & 0 & 0 & 1 & 0 & 1 & 0 & 0 \\
0 & 1 & 0 & 0 & 1 & 0 & 1 & 0
\end{pmatrix}
\times
\begin{pmatrix}
0 \\ 1 \\ 0 \\ 1 \\ 0 \\ 1 \\ 0 \\ 0
\end{pmatrix}
\oplus
\begin{pmatrix}
1 \\ 1 \\ 0 \\ 0 \\ 0 \\ 1 \\ 1 \\ 0
\end{pmatrix}
=
\begin{pmatrix}
0 \\ 0 \\ 1 \\ 0 \\ 1 \\ 0 \\ 1 \\ 1
\end{pmatrix}
\oplus
\begin{pmatrix}
1 \\ 1 \\ 0 \\ 0 \\ 0 \\ 1 \\ 1 \\ 0
\end{pmatrix}
=
\begin{pmatrix}
1 \\ 0 \\ 1 \\ 0 \\ 1 \\ 0 \\ 0 \\ 1
\end{pmatrix}
$$

Now, we compute the inverse of $(10001010)_2 = (8A)_{16}$, it is equal to $(10010101)_2 = (95)_{16}$. Therefore, InvS-box of $(2A)_{16}$ is equal to $(95)_{16}$.

*ShiftRows and inverse of ShiftRows operations*

In the ShiftRows transformation, one-byte, two-byte, and three-byte cyclically left shift (rotate) is applied to the second-row, third-row, and fourth-row of the state matrix, respectively. In the first row, the bytes are not shifted. Also, in case of inverse ShiftRows transformation, the bytes in the second, third, and fourth row are cyclically shifted to the right one, two and three bytes, respectively. Here, the 128-bit of the state matrix $A$ is arranged based on 16 bytes $A_{15}, \ldots, A_1, A_0$. In the following, the ShiftRows and inverse of ShiftRows are given by:

$$
\begin{pmatrix} A_0 & A_4 & A_8 & A_{12} \\ A_1 & A_5 & A_9 & A_{13} \\ A_2 & A_6 & A_{10} & A_{14} \\ A_3 & A_7 & A_{11} & A_{15} \end{pmatrix} \xrightarrow{\text{ShiftRows}} \begin{pmatrix} A_0 & A_4 & A_8 & A_{12} \\ A_5 & A_9 & A_{13} & A_1 \\ A_{10} & A_{14} & A_2 & A_6 \\ A_{15} & A_3 & A_7 & A_{11} \end{pmatrix}
$$

$$
\begin{pmatrix} A_0 & A_4 & A_8 & A_{12} \\ A_1 & A_5 & A_9 & A_{13} \\ A_2 & A_6 & A_{10} & A_{14} \\ A_3 & A_7 & A_{11} & A_{15} \end{pmatrix} \xrightarrow{\text{Inverse of ShiftRows}} \begin{pmatrix} A_0 & A_4 & A_8 & A_{12} \\ A_{13} & A_1 & A_5 & A_9 \\ A_{10} & A_{14} & A_2 & A_6 \\ A_7 & A_{11} & A_{15} & A_3 \end{pmatrix}
$$

*MixColumns and inverse of MixColumns operations*

The MixColumns transformation has the main diffusion property in the AES algorithm. In this transformation, each byte of a column in the state matrix is mapped into a value that is a function of all four bytes in that column. The following matrix multiplication on the state matrix is defined for the MixColumns transformation:

$$
\begin{pmatrix} (02)_{16} & (03)_{16} & (01)_{16} & (01)_{16} \\ (01)_{16} & (02)_{16} & (03)_{16} & (01)_{16} \\ (01)_{16} & (01)_{16} & (02)_{16} & (03)_{16} \\ (03)_{16} & (01)_{16} & (01)_{16} & (02)_{16} \end{pmatrix} \times \begin{pmatrix} A_0 & A_4 & A_8 & A_{12} \\ A_1 & A_5 & A_9 & A_{13} \\ A_2 & A_6 & A_{10} & A_{14} \\ A_3 & A_7 & A_{11} & A_{15} \end{pmatrix}
$$

$$
= \begin{pmatrix} A'_0 & A'_4 & A'_8 & A'_{12} \\ A'_1 & A'_5 & A'_9 & A'_{13} \\ A'_2 & A'_6 & A'_{10} & A'_{14} \\ A'_3 & A'_7 & A'_{11} & A'_{15} \end{pmatrix}
$$

In this matrix multiplication, the field addition and field multiplication operations are performed in $\mathbb{F}_{2^8}$ module irreducible polynomial $f(x) = x^8 + x^4 + x^3 + x + 1$. As seen in the MixColumns transformation, we have the computation of multiplication by $(01)_{16}$, $(02)_{16}$ and $(03)_{16}$, which are hex numbers representing finite field elements $1, x$ and $x + 1$, respectively. In case of multiplication by $(02)_{16}$, i.e., $(02)_{16}A_i$, if the MSB-bit $A_i(7)$ of the input $A_i$ is equal to one then the bits of the input are shifted one bit to the left and then XOR-ed with $(00011011)_2$. Otherwise, if the MSB-bit of the input is "0", the only left shift by one bit is performed. Also, the multiplication by $(03)_{16}$ is implemented based on multiplication by $(02)_{16}$ as $(03)_{16}A_i = ((02)_{16}A_i \oplus A_i)$. For the inverse of MixColumns transformation, called InvMixColumns, we have the following matrix multiplication:

$$
\begin{pmatrix}
(0E)_{16} & (0B)_{16} & (0D)_{16} & (09)_{16} \\
(09)_{16} & (0E)_{16} & (0B)_{16} & (0D)_{16} \\
(0D)_{16} & (09)_{16} & (0E)_{16} & (0B)_{16} \\
(0B)_{16} & (0D)_{16} & (09)_{16} & (0E)_{16}
\end{pmatrix}
\times
\begin{pmatrix}
A_0 & A_4 & A_8 & A_{12} \\
A_1 & A_5 & A_9 & A_{13} \\
A_2 & A_6 & A_{10} & A_{14} \\
A_3 & A_7 & A_{11} & A_{15}
\end{pmatrix}
$$

$$
=
\begin{pmatrix}
A_0' & A_4' & A_8' & A_{12}' \\
A_1' & A_5' & A_9' & A_{13}' \\
A_2' & A_6' & A_{10}' & A_{14}' \\
A_3' & A_7' & A_{11}' & A_{15}'
\end{pmatrix}
$$

For example, let $A_0 = (7E)_{16}$, $A_1 = (4A)_{16}$, $A_2 = (99)_{16}$ and $A_3 = (86)_{16}$ be the first column of input state matrix and for computation of the first column of output state matrix, $A_0'$, $A_1'$, $A_2'$ and $A_3'$ are equal to $(3D)_{16}$, $(DC)_{16}$, $(8C)_{16}$ and $(46)_{16}$, respectively.

### Key addition
The key addition is performed based on field addition, byte by byte, the state matrix, and the round key by a bitwise XOR operation (the bitwise XOR operation is for implementation of the addition in the finite field $\mathbb{F}_2$).

### 4.2.3.3 Key schedule
The key schedule takes the main key (of lengths 128, 192, or 256 bits) and generates the round keys $W_0$, $W_1$, $\ldots$, $W_{4r+3}$, where $r$ is the number of the rounds. The number of round keys for AES-(128 bits), AES-(192 bits), and AES-(256 bits) is equal to 11, 13, and 15, respectively. There are three key schedules for the three different AES key sizes of 128, 192, and 256 bits. Figure 4.5(a), (b), and (c) shows key schedule structures for the AES key lengths of 128, 192, and 256 bits, respectively. The key schedule has a recursive structure and the round keys are computed recursively as seen in Figure 4.5. The round keys are stored in a key expansion register W that consists of words, where each word has the length of 32 bits.

The key schedule structures include $g$ and $h$ functions, which are based on field addition and S-box operations. The structures of these functions are shown in Figure 4.6. The $RC[i]$ are round constants can be found in [1], where $i$ is the number of current round.

## 4.3 Asymmetric cryptography or PKC

Diffie and Hellman proposed the PKC in 1976 [6]. In the PKC, we have two keys which are called public and private keys. The public key can be shared with everyone, whereas the private key must be kept secret. Here, we denote the public

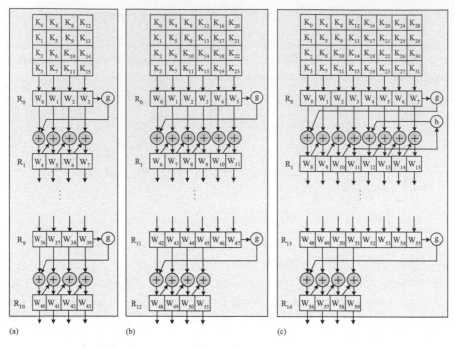

*Figure 4.5    Key schedule structures for AES 128-bit (a), 192-bit (b), and 256-bit (c)*

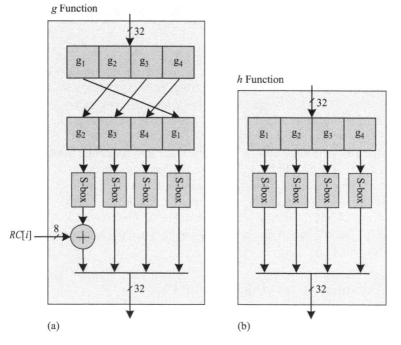

*Figure 4.6    (a) g and (b) h functions in the key schedule structures*

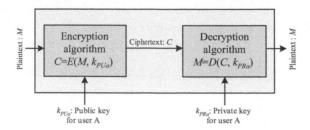

*Figure 4.7 Encryption and decryption in the PKC*

key and private keys for user **A** by $k_{PUa}$ and $k_{PRa}$, respectively. In this case, for the encryption of plaintext $M$, ciphertext $C$ is generated as follows:

$$C = E(M, k_{PUa})$$

where $E$ is the public-key encryption algorithm. Also, for decryption we have $M = D(C, k_{PRa})$, where $D$ is a public-key decryption algorithm. In the following, important aspects of the PKC are presented:

1. Each user generates a pair of the public and private key.
2. Users declare their public key in publicly manner, while the private key is hidden.
3. Everyone is able to send encrypted messages to any user with their public key.
4. Each user can decrypt the encrypted messages with his (or her) private key.

Figure 4.7 shows the encryption and decryption process in the PKC based on these four presented aspects.

### 4.3.1 Rivest, Shamir, and Adleman

In 1978, Rivest, Shamir, and Adleman [7] proposed an algorithm for the implementation of the PKC which is called RSA. The RSA derives its security from the difficulty of factoring large integers that are the product of two large prime numbers. Determining the original prime numbers from the factoring is considered infeasible due to the time it would take. The public and the private key-generation algorithm is the most complex part of the RSA cryptosystem. Two large prime numbers, $p$ and $q$, are generated using the Rabin–Miller primality test algorithm. A modulus $n$ is calculated by multiplying $p$ and $q$. The bit length of modulus $n$ is called the key length. The public key consists of the modulus $n$, and a public exponent $e$, which is normally set at 65537, as its a prime number that is not too large. The private key consists of the modulus $n$ and the private exponent $d$, which is calculated using the extended Euclidean algorithm (EEA) to find the multiplicative inverse with respect to the totient of $n$. RSA key-generation algorithm is shown in Algorithm 3.

---

**Algorithm 3** RSA key-generation algorithm

---

1.  Select two large prime numbers $p, q$
2.  Compute $n = p \times q$; $\varphi(n) = (p - 1)(q - 1)$ // totient $n$
3.  Select small odd integer $e$ relatively prime to $\varphi(n)$ $\gcd(\varphi(n), e) = 1$
4.  Determine $d$: $d \times e = 1 \bmod \varphi(n)$ and $d < \varphi(n)$
5.  **Return** Public key $(n, e)$ and private key $(n, d)$

---

Let us assume a message $M$, the encryption of this message based on the public key $(n, e)$ is as follows:

$$C = M^e \bmod n \tag{4.3}$$

and for decryption of the $C$ we have

$$C^d \bmod n = M \tag{4.4}$$

For example, we select $p = 11$ and $q = 13$, and so, $n = p \times q = 143$. The totient function is equal to $\varphi(n) = (p - 1)(q - 1) = 120$. We chose the public encryption exponent $e = 7$, since we have $\gcd(120, 7) = 1$. Then, by applying the EEA we obtain $d = 103$ since

$$7 \times 103 = 1 \bmod 120$$

suppose the message is $M = 9$, then to encrypt $M$ we have:

$$C = M^e \bmod n = 9^7 \bmod 143 = 48.$$

Now, for decrypting the ciphertext $C = 48$ based on the private key (103,143), we compute:

$$C^d \bmod n = 48^{103} \bmod 143 = 9.$$

For more details about different attacks on RSA, see [8].

### 4.3.2 *ElGamal public-key encryption*

The ElGamal public-key encryption was presented by Taher ElGamal in 1985 [9]. It is the simplest encryption scheme based on the DLP [4]. The ElGamal public-key encryption is part of the free GNU Privacy Guard (GUNPG), OpenSSL, Pretty Good Privacy (PGP), and other encrypto software [1]. There are some public parameters (domain parameters) which can be shared by number of users. The domain parameters are given by

- $p$: a large prime number (around 1,024-bit), such that $p - 1$ is divisible by another medium prime $q$ (around 160-bit).
- $g$: an element of $\mathbb{F}_p^*$ (algebraic closer of finite field $\mathbb{F}_p$) of prime order $q$, i.e., $g = r^{(p-1)/q} \bmod p \neq 1$, for some $r \in \mathbb{F}_p^*$.

All domain parameters $(p, q, g)$ create abelian group $G$ of prime order $q$ with generator $g$. In the ElGamal encryption, the private key is chosen to be an integer $x$, while the public key is given by

$$h = g^x \bmod p.$$

In this case, each user only needs to generate a random number and a modular exponentiation to generate a key pair. To encrypt a message $M \in \mathbb{F}_p^*$, i.e., $(M \in [0, p-1])$, we have:

1. Generate a random ephemeral key $k \in [1, q-1]$
2. Compute $C_1 = g^k \bmod p$
3. Compute $C_2 = M \times h^k \bmod p$

The ciphertext is $C = (C_1, C_2)$. To decrypt a ciphertext $C = (C_1, C_2)$, we have:

$$C_2 \times C_1^{-x} \bmod p = \frac{C_2}{C_1^x} \bmod p = \frac{M \times h^k}{g^{xk}} \bmod p = \frac{M \times g^{xk}}{g^{xk}} \bmod p = M.$$

For example, we choose the domain parameters $q = 101$, $p = 809$, and $g = 3$. The public and private keys are $h = g^x \bmod p = 3^{68} \bmod 809 = 65$, $x = 68$ if $M = 100$, we generate a random ephemeral key $k = 89$ and then $C_1 = g^k = 345$, $C_2 = m \times h^k = 517$. Therefore, the ciphertext is $C = (345, 517)$. Also, for decryption, we have:

$$C_2 \times C_1^{-x} \bmod p = 517 \times 345^{-68} \bmod 809 = 100.$$

### 4.3.3 Elliptic curve cryptosystems

The main advantage of ECC, when compared to other asymmetric cryptosystems such as RSA, is the smaller key length with an equivalent security level. It is based on the ECDLP of the elliptic curve over a finite field [2]. In the two last decades, the elliptic curves have been considered in many cryptographic applications such as banking transactions, mobile security, smart cards, Internet protocols (web transactions and secure document transfers), and network applications. The ECC has been standardized by many standards such as the NIST[3] [10], ANSI[4] [11], IEEE[5] [12], and ISO[6] [13]. The main operation in the ECC is point multiplication. A comprehensive survey of hardware implementations of ECC is presented in [14].

---

[3]National Institute of Standards and Technology
[4]American National Standards Institute
[5]Institute of Electrical and Electronics Engineers
[6]International Organization for Standardization

In this section, we present a brief mathematical background of the ECC and point multiplication operation is described in more detail. An elliptic curve over a field $\mathbb{F}$ can be defined by

$$E : y^2 + a_1xy + a_3y = x^3 + a_2x^2 + a_4x + a_6 \tag{4.5}$$

This equation is called *long Weierstrass* equation, where $a_1, a_2, a_3, a_4$ and $a_6$ are in $\mathbb{F}$. The discriminant of the field is given by

$$\Delta = -d_2^2d_8 - 8d_4^3 - 27d_6^2 + 9d_2d_4d_6 \tag{4.6}$$

where $d_2 = a_1^2 + 4a_2$, $d_4 = 2a_4 + a_1a_3$, $d_6 = a_3^2 + 4a_6$, and $d_8 = a_1^2a_6 + 4a_2a_6 - a_1a_3a_4 + a_2a_3^2 - a_4^2$. $\Delta \neq 0$, since the elliptic curve is nonsingular. The set of affine points $(x, y)$ satisfying the curve equation with the point at infinity denoted by $\mathcal{O}$ construct a group [2]. The set of $\mathbb{F}$-rational points on $E$ is defined as follows:

$$E(\mathbb{F}) = \{(x, y) \in \mathbb{F} \times \mathbb{F} : y^2 + a_1xy + a_3y - x^3 - a_2x^2 - a_4x - a_6 = 0\} \cup \{\mathcal{O}\} \tag{4.7}$$

Based on a group of points defined over an elliptic curve, group law operation for two points $P_1$ and $P_2$, where $P_1 \neq P_2$, defines the point addition (PA) $P_3 = P_1 + P_2$ using the tangent and chord rule as the primary group operation. For $P_1 = P_2$ we have point doubling (PD) $P_3 = 2P_1$. Basically, for an elliptic curve over a finite field $\mathbb{F}$, a point $P$ over the curve can generate all the other points by the point addition operation.

### 4.3.3.1    Elliptic curve over finite field $\mathbb{F}_{2^m}$

The binary elliptic curves defined over a binary finite field $\mathbb{F}_{2^m}$. One of the most important binary elliptic curves is called *Binary Weierstrass curves* (BWCs), it is defined by the following equation:

$$W : y^2 + xy = x^3 + ax^2 + b \tag{4.8}$$

where $a, b \in \mathbb{F}_{2^m}$ and $b \neq 0$. This equation is called *non-super singular* which is suitable for cryptographic applications. The NIST recommended standard elliptic curves {B-163 over $\mathbb{F}_{2^{163}}$, B-233 over $\mathbb{F}_{2^{233}}$, B-283 over $\mathbb{F}_{2^{283}}$, B-409 over $\mathbb{F}_{2^{409}}$, and B-571 over $\mathbb{F}_{2^{571}}$} for this family of curves.

In the following, point addition and point doubling on BWCs in affine coordinate are presented. Let $P_1 = (x_1, y_1)$ and $P_2 = (x_2, y_2)$ be two points on the BWCs with $P_1 \neq \pm P_2$ where $-P_2 = (x_2, x_2 + y_2)$. Then the addition of points $P_1, P_2$ is the point $P_3 = P_1 + P_2 = (x_3, y_3)$, where $x_3 = \lambda^2 + \lambda + x_1 + x_2 + a$, $y_3 = \lambda(x_1 + x_3) + x_3 + y_1$, and $\lambda = \frac{y_1 + y_2}{x_1 + x_2}$. Also for the point doubling we have $P_3 = 2P_1 = (x_3, y_3)$, where $x_3 = \lambda^2 + \lambda + a$, $y_3 = \lambda(x_1 + x_3) + x_3 + y_1$, and $\lambda = x_1 + \frac{y_1}{x_1}$. The computation cost of the point addition and point doubling are equal to $2\mathbf{I} + 4\mathbf{M} + 2\mathbf{S}$, where $\mathbf{I}$, $\mathbf{M}$, and $\mathbf{S}$ are cost of computation field inversion, field multiplication, and field squaring, respectively.

### 4.3.3.2 Elliptic curve over the finite field $\mathbb{F}_p$

Let $p$ be a prime with $p > 3$, an elliptic curve over $\mathbb{F}_p$ is defined the called *short Weierstrass* equation as:

$$E_p : y^2 = x^3 + ax^2 + b \tag{4.9}$$

where $a, b, x, y \in \mathbb{F}_p$ and $4a^3 + 27b^2 \neq 0$. In this curve, the characteristic is not equal 2 and 3 or $p > 3$ . Also group operations on elliptic curves over $\mathbb{F}_p$ are defined.

If the points on an elliptic curve $E_p$ are represented by the points $P = (x_1, y_1)$, $Q = (x_2, y_2)$, and $R = (x_3, y_3) = P + Q$, the point addition and point doubling computation are as follows:

$$R = (x_3, y_3) = P + Q \Rightarrow x_3 = \left(\frac{y_2 - y_1}{x_2 - x_1}\right)^2 - x_1 - x_2,$$

$$y_3 = -y_1 + \left(\frac{y_2 - y_1}{x_2 - x_1}\right)(x_1 - x_3)$$

$$P = Q \Rightarrow R = 2P = (x_3, y_3) \Rightarrow x_3 = \left(\frac{3x_1^2 + a}{2y_1}\right)^2 - 2x_1,$$

$$y_3 = -y_1 + \left(\frac{3x_1^2 + a}{2y_1}\right)(x_1 - x_3).$$

Also, if $P = -Q$, we have $P + Q = \mathcal{O}$. For example, for elliptic curve $y^2 \equiv x^3 + x + 5 \bmod 17$ over $\mathbb{F}_{17}$, the discriminant is equal to $4a^3 + 27b^2 = 4 + 657 = 679 \equiv 16 \bmod 17$. Let $P = (3, 1)$ and $Q = (8, 10)$ be two points on this curve. For point addition, we have:

$$R = P + Q \Rightarrow x_3 = \left(\frac{9}{5}\right)^2 - 3 - 8 \bmod 17 \equiv 14,$$

$$y_3 = -1 + \left(\frac{9}{5}\right)(3 - 14) \bmod 17 \equiv 3$$

and point doubling is computed as follows:

$$P = Q \Rightarrow R = 2P \Rightarrow x_3 = \left(\frac{3 \times 3^2 + 1}{2 \times 1}\right)^2 - 2 \times 3 = 190 \bmod 17 \equiv 3,$$

$$y_3 = -1 + \left(\frac{3 \times 3^2 + 1}{2 \times 1}\right)(3 - 3) = -1 \bmod 17 \equiv 16.$$

The NIST recommended standard elliptic curves over prime fields consist of {$p$-192 over $\mathbb{F}_{192}$, $p$-224 over $\mathbb{F}_{224}$, $p$-256 over $\mathbb{F}_{256}$, $p$-384 over $\mathbb{F}_{384}$, and $p$-521 over $\mathbb{F}_{521}$}.

### 4.3.3.3    Point multiplication

The most important operation in the ECC is called *point multiplication* or *scalar multiplication*. In this operation, we have $Q = kP = P + P + \cdots + P$, where $k$ is a positive integer and $P$ is a point on the curve. The point multiplication can be computed by $k$ times addition of point $P$ by self based on the PA and PD operations. The security of ECCs is based on the computational intractability of the ECDLP. It is defined based on point multiplication, i.e., if we have $Q$ and $P$, on the curve, it is hard to find scaler number $k$ so that $Q = kP$. In this case, $k$ is a $m$-bit number, where $m \geq 160$. Here, we present an example of the point multiplication. This example is based on elliptic curve $y^2 \equiv x^3 + x + 6$ over $\mathbb{F}_{11}$. All points on this curve are as follows:

$$\{(2,4),(2,7),(3,5),(3,6),(3,2),(5,9),(7,2),(7,9),(8,3),(8,8),(10,2),(10,9)\}\cup\{\mathcal{O}\}.$$

If select $P = (8,3)$ as a generator, for the multiples of $P$ by scalar number $n$, we have:

$$2P = (8,3) + (8,3) = (x_2, y_2) \Rightarrow x_2 = \left(\frac{3 \times 8^2 + 1}{2 \times 3}\right)^2 - 16 \bmod 11 \equiv 7,$$

$$y_2 = -3 + 1(8 - 7) \bmod 11 \equiv 9 \Rightarrow 2P = (7,9).$$

For $3P = (8,3) + (7,9)$

$$3P = (x_3, y_3) \Rightarrow x_3 = \left(\frac{9-3}{7-8}\right)^2 - 7 - 8 \bmod 11 \equiv 10,$$

$$y_3 = -9 + \left(\frac{9-3}{7-8}\right)^2 (7 - 10) \bmod 11 \equiv 9 \Rightarrow 3P = (10,9).$$

For $4P = (7,9) + (7,9)$

$$4P = (x_4, y_4) \Rightarrow x_4 = \left(\frac{3 \times 7^2 + 1}{2 \times 9}\right)^2 - 14 \bmod 11 \equiv 2,$$

$$y_4 = -9 + \left(\frac{3 \times 7^2 + 1}{2 \times 9}\right)^2 (7 - 2) \bmod 11 \equiv 4 \Rightarrow 4P = (2,4).$$

Other point multiplications are computed as shown below:

$$5G = (5,2), 6G = (3,6), 7G = (3,5), 8G = (5,9), 9G = (2,7), 10G = (10,2),$$

$$11G = (7,2), 12G = (8,8).$$

The generator $P = (8,3)$ is called a primitive element that generates the multiples. There are several methods in the implementation of point multiplication [2]: right-to-left double and add, Left-to-right double and add, non-adjacent-form (NAF), window NAF method (width-$w$ NAF), sliding window method, $\tau$-adic NAF

($\tau$NAF) method, and Montgomery ladder method. The affine and projective coordinates are used for computations. The projective point $(X, Y, Z), Z \neq 0$ corresponds to the affine point $\left(\frac{X}{Z^c}, \frac{Y}{Z^d}\right)$. In the projective coordinate, the complexity of the PA and PD computations is reduced.

The most popular projective coordinates consist of standard ($c = 1, d = 1$), Jacobeans ($c = 2, d = 3$), and Lopez-Dahab (LD) ($c = 1, d = 2$). For example, in the LD coordinate [15] projective version of the BWCs in (4.6) is computed by replacing $x$ and $y$ with $\frac{X}{Z}$ and $\frac{Y}{Z^2}$ as

$$E : Y^2 + XYZ = X^3 Z + aX^2 Z^2 + bZ^4.$$

Algorithm 4 shows right-to-left point multiplication algorithm. In the algorithm processes, the bits of $k$ are from the right to left. In this algorithm every bit of scalar $k$ is scanned, then based on the value of each bit, "0" or "1", no operation or both PD and PA operations are performed in parallel form. Also, Algorithm 5 shows Montgomery ladder algorithm [16] which is one of the applicable point multiplication algorithms. In the algorithm, for every $k_i$, where $k_i$ is $i$th bit of scalar $k$, both PD and PA operations are performed simultaneously. This is an important property of the Montgomery ladder algorithm for resistance against power and timing attacks.

---

**Algorithm 4** Right-to-left point multiplication algorithm

---

**Input:** $k = (k_{l-1}, k_{l-2}, \ldots, k_2, k_1, k_0), P \in \mathbb{F}_q$
**Output:** $kP$

1. $Q \leftarrow \mathcal{O}$
2. **for** $i$ **from** 0 **downto** $l - 1$ **do**
3.    **if** $k_i = 1$ **then**
4.      $Q \leftarrow P + Q$
5.      $P \leftarrow 2P$
6.    **end if**
7.    **end for**
8. **Return** $Q$

---

---

**Algorithm 5** Montgomery ladder algorithm for point multiplication

---

**Input:** $k = (k_{l-1}, k_{l-2}, \ldots, k_0)$, with $k_{l-1} = 1, P \in \mathbb{F}_q$
**Output:** $kP$

1. $Q_1 \leftarrow P, Q_2 \leftarrow 2P$
2. **for** $i$ **from** $l - 2$ **downto** 0 **do**
3.    **if** $k_i = 1$ **then**
4.      $Q_1 \leftarrow Q_1 + Q_2, Q_2 \leftarrow 2Q_2$

5.  **else**
6.  $Q_2 \leftarrow Q_1 + Q_2, Q_1 \leftarrow 2Q_1$
7.  **end if**
8.  **end for**
9.  **Return** $Q_1$

---

Implementation of the point multiplication is performed in three main steps as follows:

1.  Select the point multiplication method.
2.  Select the coordinates to represent elliptic curve points.
3.  The representation of the field elements (type of basis for the binary fields and structure of the prime number $p$ in the prime fields) is selected.

### 4.3.4 Protocols

In this subsection, we briefly explain the number of cryptographic protocols which provide higher level services based on the application of cryptographic algorithms. A cryptographic protocol is defined as a series of steps and message exchanges between multiple users (users can be persons, organizations, devices, etc.) in order to achieve a specific security purpose. They are widely used for secure application-level data transport. Important properties of a protocol are as follows [17]:

1.  Any user involved in the protocol must know all the steps of the protocol.
2.  Every step must be well defined and there is no chance of misunderstanding. Therefore, the protocol must be unambiguous.
3.  Any user involved in the protocol must agree to follow it.
4.  In the protocol, there is a specified action for every possible situation. In other words, the protocol must be complete.
5.  It should not be possible to do or learn more than what is specified in the protocol.

Some of the applications of cryptographic protocols are presented as follows:

- **Key exchange:** A key exchange protocol allows two parties to agree on a shared secret key such as Diffie–Hellman protocol.
- **Secret sharing (or secret splitting) method:** It is a method of sharing a secret data among a set of participants.
- **Secure multi-party computation (MPC):** Secure multi-party computation can be used to compute answers based on confidential data so that when the protocol is complete the participants know only their own input and the answer.
- **Zero-knowledge proofs:** Proof of knowledge of an information without revealing the information.
- **Blind signatures:** Blind signatures are similar to digital signatures, but are not quite the same. They are generated based on a cryptographic protocol between the sender (signer) and a receiver such that the sender does not see the message being signed. And also, the sender does not learn any suitable information on

the produced signature. Blind signatures can be used for digital credentials and digital cash to prove that a user holds an attribute or right without the obvious identity of the user.

- **Secure elections:** Provide sets of desirable privacy and audit-ability properties for conducting e-voting.
- **Time-stamping:** Secure time-stamping can be used to prove that data existed at a certain time.

In the following, some of the most well-known cryptographic protocols are presented:

- **The Needham–Schroeder Protocol:** This protocol relies on symmetric encryption and makes use of a trusted third party (TTP).
- **Kerberos:** It is an authentication access control service which allows a client to authenticate his(or herself) to multiple services.
- **SSH: Secure Shell (SSH):** It is a network protocol that allows data to be exchanged over a secure channel. It has become a more general tool that is used to provide a secure channel between two networked computers for cryptographic applications such as secure file transfer.
- **Secure sockets layer (SSL)/transport layer security (TLS):** SSL provides security based on allowing applications to encryption of transform data from a client to a server. Also, the TLS protocol is used for securing traffic between an unauthenticated web browser and an authenticated web site.
- **TELNET (telnet):** The telnet lets user connect to a remote computer and work as if user were sitting in front of a computer, no matter how far away you are. By default, telnet does not encrypt data sent over the network, so use with caution.
- **Simple Mail Transfer Protocol (SMTP):** It is the protocol for Internet e-mail and transfers e-mail between computers.
- **Post Office Protocol (POP3):** It provides basic client/server features that help the user download e-mail from an server to a computer. Also, it allow the user to access his (or her) e-mail more freely.
- **Internet Message Access Protocol (IMAP4):** It is a protocol to manage e-mail. IMAP4 protocol provides a richer set of features than that of POP3.
- **Hyper Text Transfer Protocol (HTTP):** It is a protocol for the transmission of data across the Internet. This protocol allows the transfer of Hyper Text Markup Language (HTML) and other related scripting languages to travel from servers to browsers.
- **Hyper Text Transfer Protocol Secure (HTTPS):** It is a safe (secure) version of HTTP. HTTPS protocol simplifies a safe communication over a network.
- **Session Initiation Protocol (SIP):** It is a communications protocol which is commonly used for managing multimedia communications such as voice and video calls over Internet Protocol (IP) networks.
- **Internet Protocol Security (IPsec):** It is a protocol for providing confidentiality, authentication, and integrity for IP data transmitted over untrusted networks such as the Internet. The main use of IPsec has been to create virtual private networks (VPNs).

- **Secure File Transfer Protocol (SFTP):** It is a network protocol for securely transferring files (upload and download) on a network.
- **Simple Network Management Protocol (SNMP):** This protocol used in network management to monitor users connected to the network for conditions that warrant administrative attention.
- **Challenge Handshake Authentication Protocol (CHAP):** It uses shared secrets to authenticate switches.

## 4.4   Digital signatures

In the digital domain, proving a digital message generated by a specific person is a very important issue. The digital signatures similar to handwritten signatures are used to prove that we signed the message by a valid signature. Also, in the digital signatures only signature owner (signer) must be capable of generating a valid signature. The digital signature is an important concept of the PKC, which was proposed by Diffie and Hellman [3]. The digital signatures are widely used today in digital certificates (secure e-commerce) and key establishment over insecure channels. The basics of a digital signature scheme is shown in Figure 4.8. A digital signature algorithm (DSA) provides the basic capability of authentication of digital messages, allowing the holder of a private key to produce signatures on arbitrary messages.

The process of the digital signature scheme is presented based on the following steps:

1.   Generate public and private keys $k_{PU_a}$ and $k_{PR_a}$ by the user **A**
2.   Share public key $k_{PU_a}$
3.   Sign message $S = sign(M)$ by the private key $k_{PR_a}$
4.   Send message and signature by the user **A**
5.   Verify signature $ver(M, S)$ based on $k_{PU_a}$ by the user **B**.

### 4.4.1   RSA digital signature scheme

The RSA PKC can be used for signatures based on RSA encryption [1]. Suppose user **A** wants to send a signed message $M$ to user **B**. In this case, user **A** generates the same RSA keys that were used for RSA encryption as presented in Section 4.3.1. Therefore, we have $k_{PU_a} = (n, e)$ and $k_{PR_a} = (n, d)$ for public and

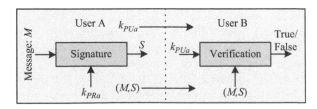

*Figure 4.8   The principle of a digital signature scheme*

private keys, respectively. The signature is the pair $(S, M)$ which is computed based on $S = sign_{k_{PR_a}}(M) \equiv M^d \bmod n$. For verification of the signature, we have:

$$Ver_{k_{PU_a}}(S, M) \equiv S^e \bmod n \begin{cases} \equiv M \bmod n & \text{valid signature} \\ \equiv M \bmod n & \text{invalid signature.} \end{cases}$$

For example, to sign message $M = 4$ based on RSA signature, we choose $P = 3$, $q = 11$. In this case, $n = p \times q = 33$ and $\varphi(n) = (3 - 1) \times (11 - 1) = 20$. Also, we choose $e = 3$ and $d \equiv e^{-1} \bmod \varphi(n) \equiv 3^{-1} \bmod 20 = 7$. Therefore, the public key $k_{PU_a}$ is equal to $(33, 3)$ and $S = M^d \equiv 4^7 \equiv 16 \bmod 33$. The signature is pair $(16, 4)$. On the other hand, for verification of the signature, we have:

$$Ver_{k_{PU_a}}(S, M) \equiv S^e \equiv 16^3 \equiv 4 \bmod 33 \equiv M \bmod n \rightarrow \text{valid signature.}$$

### 4.4.2   ElGamal digital signature scheme

In this subsection, the ElGamal signature scheme is described. As mentioned before, the ElGamal encryption scheme is designed to enable encryption by a user's public-key and decryption by the user's private key. The ElGamal signature scheme involves the use of the private key for encryption and the public key for decryption. To sign a message $M$, $0 \leq m \leq p - 1$, first a random number $k$ such that $\gcd(k, p - 1) = 1$ is selected. The public key is equal to $y \equiv g^x \bmod p$, where, $x < p$ is the private key. Also, we compute $r \equiv g^k \bmod p$. The signature of $M$ is equal to $(r, S), 0 \leq r, S < p - 1$, which is achieved based on the following computations [17]:

$$g^M \equiv y^r r^S \bmod p \equiv (g^x)^r (g^k)^S \bmod p \equiv g^{xr + kS} \bmod p.$$

The $S$ parameter can be computed by the extended Euclidean algorithm. The verification of the signature is achieved if

$$y^r r^S \bmod p \equiv (g^M) \bmod p.$$

For example, to sign a message $M = 6$, we have $(P = 11, g = 7, x = 3)$ and $y \equiv g^x \bmod p \equiv 7^3 \bmod 11 = 2$. Also, we choose a random number $k = 7$ such that $\gcd(k, p - 1) = \gcd(7, 10) = 1$   and   $r \equiv g^k \bmod p \equiv 7^7 \bmod 11 = 6$. Now, we compute the $S$ parameter by

$$M = 6 \equiv xr + kS \bmod p - 1 \equiv 3 \times 6 + 7S \bmod 10$$

where, $7S \equiv 28 \bmod 10$, so, $S \equiv 4 \bmod 10$. In this case, the signature of $M = 6$ equals $(r = 6, S = 4)$. To verify the signature, we have the following computations:

$$y^r r^S \bmod p \equiv (g^M) \bmod p \rightarrow 2^6 6^4 \bmod 11 \equiv (7^6) \bmod 11 \rightarrow$$

$$82944 \bmod 11 \equiv 117649 \bmod 11 \rightarrow 4 \bmod 11 \equiv 4 \bmod 11 \rightarrow \text{valid signature.}$$

### 4.4.3   Schnorr digital signature scheme

The Schnorr signature scheme is based on discrete logarithms [4,17]. The Schnorr scheme minimizes the message-dependent amount of computation required to generate a signature. First, we have the generation of a pair of private and public keys, which consists of the following steps:

1.  Choose primes $p, q$, such that $q$ is prime factor of $p - 1$, i.e., $q|p - 1$.
2.  Choose an integer $a$, where, $a^q = 1 \bmod p$, the values $(a, p, q)$ are global public key which are common for group of the users.
3.  For private key, we choose a random integer $s$, $0 < s < q$.
4.  For user's public key, we have $v = a^{-s} \bmod p$.

For Schnorr digital signature, user **A** with private key $s$ and public key $v$ generates a signature for message $M$ in the following method. First, this user choose a random integer $r$, $0 < r < q$ and calculate $x \equiv a^r \bmod p$. User **A** concatenates the message $M$ and $x$ and computes the hash code $h = H(M \| x)$, where, $H$ is a hash function and $\|$ is used for denoted concatenates operation. Then, $y \equiv (r + se) \bmod q$ is computed. User **A** sends the signature $(h, y)$ to user **B**. User **B**, for verification of the signature, computes $z \equiv a^y \lambda^h \bmod p$ and $h' = H(M \| z)$. If $h = h'$, then user **B** confirms the signature as valid.

For example, for signature of message $M = 12345$, first choose two primes $P = 29$ and $q = 7$ such that $q = 7|28$. Choose an integer $a = 7$, where, $a^q \equiv 1 \bmod p \rightarrow 7^7 \equiv 1 \bmod 29$. We select a private key $s = 4$, $s < q$ and public key is computed as follows:

$$k_{PR_a} = v \equiv a^{-s} \bmod p \equiv 7^{-4} \bmod 29 \equiv 24.$$

User **A** chooses a random integer $r = 5$, $0 < r < q$ and calculate $x \equiv a^r \bmod p \equiv 7^5 \bmod 29 \equiv 16$. Compute the hash code by MD4 hash algorithm; based on the computation, concatenate the message $M = 12345$ and $x = 16$ as follows:

$$h = H(M \| x) = H(12345 \| 16) \bmod q$$
$$= 919671992759145855242593220263016201851705566252 (\bmod 7) \equiv 5.$$

Also, user **A** computes $y \equiv (r + se) \bmod q \equiv (5 + 4 \times 5) \bmod 7 \equiv 4$. The signature is equal to $(h, y) = (5, 4)$, which is sent to user **B**. Now, user **B** verifies the signature, by computations $z \equiv a^y \lambda^h \bmod p \equiv 7^4 \times 24^5 \bmod 29 \equiv 2401 \times 7962624 \bmod 29 \equiv 19118260224 \bmod 29 \equiv 16$ and hash value $H(M \| z)$ as follows:

$$h' = H(M \| z) \bmod q \equiv H(12345 \| 16) \bmod 7 \equiv 5.$$

The user **B** confirms that the signature is a valid signature based on these computations and $h = h'$.

## 4.4.4   Digital signature standard

The digital signature standard (DSS) is a public key technique which is published in 1991 by the NIST. In the DSS, a new and popular digital signature technique that called DSA is presented [4]. In this section, we discuss the original DSS algorithm. In the DSS method, the hash code is provided as input to a signature function along with a random number generated $k$ for this particular signature. The signature function also depends on the sender's private key $k_{PR_a}$ and a set of parameters known to a group of communicating principals. The result of the signature is consisting of two components $(r, s)$. Algorithm 6 shows the DSA signature and verification.

---

**Algorithm 6** DSA signature and verification

---

**Key generation for DSA:**

1. $p$: a prime number, bit length between 512 and 1,024 bits
2. $q$: a prime factor of $p - 1$, bit length of 160-bit
3. $g \equiv h'(p - 1)/q \bmod p > 1$, and $0 < h' < p - 1 \; // (p, q \text{ and } g)$: public parameters
4. $0 < x < q$: random integer (the user's private key), 160-bit
5. $y \equiv g^x \bmod p$: the user's public key, 160-bit

**DSA signature generation for message $M$:**

1. $0 < k < q$: a random number
2. $r \equiv (g^k \bmod p) \bmod q$
3. $S \equiv k^{-1}(H(M) + xr) \bmod q$, where $H(M)$ is a one-way hash function $//(r,S)$: Signature

**DSA signature verification:**

1. $w \equiv S^{-1} \bmod q$
2. $u_1 \equiv H(M) \times w \bmod q$
3. $u_2 \equiv r \times w \bmod q$
4. $v \equiv (g^{u_1} y^{u_2} \bmod p) \bmod q \; //\text{If } v = r$, then the signature is verified.

---

For example, user **A** wants to send a message $M$ to user **B** which is to be signed with the DSA algorithm. Assume the hash value of $M$ to be $H(M) = 10$. Then the key generation, signature, and verification process is as follows:

**Key generation for DSA**

$p = 23$
$q = 11$: a prime factor of $p - 1$
$h' = 16 < p - 1$, $g \equiv 16^2 \bmod 23 \equiv 3 > 1$
$x = 7 < q$: the user's private key
$y \equiv 3^7 \bmod 23 \equiv 2$: the user's public key

**DSA signature generation**

$k = 5 < q$: a random number
$r \equiv (3^5 \bmod 23) \bmod 11 \equiv 13 \bmod 11 \equiv 2$
$S \equiv 5^{-1}(10 + 7 \times 2) \bmod 11 \equiv 216 \bmod 11 \equiv 7 \rightarrow (2,7)$: Signature

**DSA signature verification**

$w \equiv 7^{-1} \bmod 11 \equiv 8$
$u1 \equiv 10 \times 8 \bmod 11 \equiv 3$

$$u2 \equiv 2 \times 8 \bmod 11 \equiv 5$$
$$v \equiv (3^3 2^5 \bmod 23) \bmod 11 \equiv (864 \bmod 23) \bmod 11 \equiv 13 \bmod 11 \equiv 2$$

Since $v = r = 2$, the signature is verified.

## 4.4.5   Elliptic curves digital signature algorithm

The elliptic curve digital signature algorithm (ECDSA) signature and verification computations are presented in this subsection. The ECDSA was proposed in 1992 by Scott Vanstone. It was accepted as an ANSI standard in 1999 and later as IEEE and NIST standards in 2000. The prime field $\mathbb{F}_p$ and binary field $\mathbb{F}_{2^m}$ are used for elliptic curves which are used in the ECDSA [2]. In practice, the $\mathbb{F}_p$ is often preferred. Algorithm 7 shows the ECDSA.

---

**Algorithm 7** Elliptic curve digital signature algorithm (ECDSA)

---

**Key generation for DSA:**

1. Use an elliptic curve $E$ with (modulus $p$, coefficients $a$ and $b$, a point $A$ which generates a cyclic group of prime order $q$)
2. $d$: a random integer with $0 < d < q$, (the user's private key)
3. Compute point multiplication $B = dA$, $(p, a, b, q, A, B)$ are the user's public key

**DSA signature generation for message $M$:**

1. $0 < k_E < q$: a random integer as ephemeral key
2. Compute point multiplication $R = k_E A = (x_R, y_R)$
3. Compute $S \equiv (H(M) + d \times r)k_E^{-1} \bmod q$. // where $H(M)$ is SHA-1 (cryptographic hash function) and $(x_R, S)$: Signature

**DSA signature verification:**

1. $w \equiv S^{-1} \bmod q$
2. $u1 \equiv H(M) \times w \bmod q$
3. $u2 \equiv x_R \times w \bmod q$
4. $P = u_1 A + u_2 B = (x_P, y_P)$ // If $x_P \equiv x_R \bmod q$, then the signature is verified.

---

For example, user **A** uses the elliptic curve $y^2 \equiv x^3 + 2x + 2 \bmod 17$ over $\mathbb{F}_{17}$ and wants to send a message $M$ to user **B** which is to be signed with the ECDSA. Assume the hash value of $M$ to be $H(M) = 26$. Then the key generation, signature, and verification process is as follows:

**Key generation for ECDSA**

1. Use an elliptic curve $E$ with (modulus $p = 17$, coefficients $a = 2$ and $b = 2$, a point $A = (5, 1)$ with order $q = 19$)
2. Choose $0 < d = 7 < q$: the user's private key
3. Compute point multiplication $B = dA = 7(5,1) = (0,6)$, $(p = 17,\ a = 2,\ b = 2,\ q = 19,\ A = (5,1),\ B = (0,6)$ are the user's public key

**ECDSA signature generation**

1. Choose $0 < k_E = 10 < q$: a random integer as ephemeral key
2. Compute point multiplication $R = k_E A = 10(5, 1) = (7, 11) = (x_R, y_R)$
3. Compute $S \equiv (H(M) + d \times r) k_E^{-1} \bmod q \equiv (26 + 7 \times 7)2 \equiv 17 \bmod 19 \equiv 17$.
   // $(x_R, S) = (7, 17)$: Signature and $(M, (7, 17))$ is sent to user **B**.

**ECDSA signature verification**

1. $w \equiv 17^{-1} \bmod 19 \equiv 9$
2. $u1 \equiv 26 \times 9 \bmod 19 \equiv 6$
3. $u2 \equiv 9 \times 7 \bmod 19 \equiv 6$
4. $P = 6(5, 1) + 6(0, 6) = (7, 11) = (x_P, y_P)$, since $x_P \equiv 7 \bmod 19 \equiv 7$, the signature is verified.

## 4.5 Hash functions

Hash functions are an important cryptographic primitive and are widely used in protocols, digital signature, and message authentication. In a hash function $H$, an input data with variable-length $M$ is converted to fixed-length hash value or message digest $h = H(M)$ [4]. Data integrity is the main object of a hash function. To efficiently compute signatures of large messages, first long message is applied to a hash function then hash value is signed. The main properties of hash functions are as follows:

1. **Preimage resistance (one-way)**: For a given hash value $h$, it is computationally hard to find input $M$ such that $H(M) = h$.
2. **Second preimage resistance**: Given $M_1$ is an input, it is computationally hard to find any input $M_2 \neq M_1$ such that $H(M_1) = H(M_2)$.
3. **Collision resistance**: It is computationally difficult to find any input pairs $(M_1, M_2)$ with $M_1 \neq M_2$ such that $H(M_1) = H(M_2)$.

### 4.5.1 Applications of cryptographic hash functions

Hash functions have different use in cryptosystems. One of the essential parts of DSA, protocols, and message authentication codes are hash functions. Also, a cryptographic hash function can be used to construct a pseudo-random number generator (PRNG) for the generation of symmetric keys. In this subsection, the applications are presented in more details.

#### 4.5.1.1 Message authentication

To verify the integrity of a message (the received data are exactly as sent without modification or insertion), the message authentication is used. The hash functions are used to implement the message authentication, in this case, the hash function value is called message digest. Figure 4.9 shows a way in which a hash function can be used to implement message authentication.

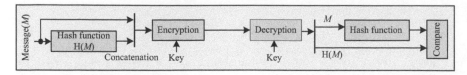

*Figure 4.9   A simple configuration of a hash function in message authentication*

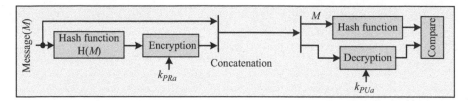

*Figure 4.10   A simple configuration of a hash function in digital signature*

### 4.5.1.2   Digital signatures

Another application of hash functions is in the digital signature. A simple configuration for use of a hash function in digital signature is shown in Figure 4.10. In this
case, the hash value of a message is achieved based on a user's private key. In the
receiver part of the signature scheme (destination), the integrity of the message is
verified based on the user's public key.

## 4.5.2   Secure hash algorithm (SHA)

In recent years, the secure hash algorithm (SHA) are the most widely used hash
functions. The SHA was developed by the NIST and published as FIPS 180 in
1993; this version is referred to as SHA-0. In 1995, a revised version was issued as
FIPS 180-1 (SHA-1), with a hash value of 160-bit. Three new versions of SHA-1
and FIPS 180-2 (SHA-2) were presented in 2002 for higher security. These hash
algorithms are called SHA-256, SHA-384, and SHA-512 with hash value sizes of
256, 384, and 512 bits, respectively [1]. Also, SHA-224 was presented in 2004 in
order to fit the security level of 3DES. These hash functions (SHA-256, SHA-224,
SHA-384, and SHA-512) are referred to as SHA-2. In this subsection, we present a
description of the SHA-512 structure. The other versions of the SHA have a similar
structure.

### 4.5.2.1   SHA-512

The algorithm takes as input a message with a maximum length of less than $2^{128}$
bits and produces as output a 512-bit message digest. The input is processed in
1,024-bit blocks. The input message $M$ (with a length of $L$ bits) is padded in the
range of 1 to 1,024 bits based on a single "1" bit and $k$ "0" bits, where
$k \equiv 1,024 - 128 - 1 - L \equiv 896 - (L + 1) \bmod 1,024$. A block of 128 bits
is appended to the message. This block contains the length of the original message.

The expanded message has length of the $N \times 1,024$ as the 1,024-bit blocks $M_1$, $M_2$, and $M_N$ [4]. Figure 4.11 shows the message digest generation based on SHA-512.

A 512-bit register is used to store intermediate and final results of the hash function. The register can be implemented as eight 64-bit registers $(a, b, c, d, e, f, g, h)$. These registers are loaded by the following eight 64-bit initialize integers: $a = 6A09E667F3BCC908$  $e = 510E527FADE682D1$,  $b = BB67AE8584CAA73B$, $f = 9B05688C2B3E6C1F$,  $c = 3C6EF372FE94F82B$,  $g = 1F83D9ABFB41BD6B$, $d = A54FF53A5F1D36F1$, and $h = 5BE0CD19137E2179$.

The main block of the algorithm is compression function (F function in Figure 4.11) that consists of 80 rounds. In each round, the 512-bit input value is applied to registers $(a, b, c, d, e, f, g, h)$, and contents of the registers are updated. In the $t$th round of algorithm a 64-bit value $W_t$ and $K_t$ (additive constant) are used, where $0 \leq t \leq 79$, for more details see [4]. The $W_t$ are generated using message schedule block based on current 1,024-bit message $M_i$. In the SHA-512 output, 80th round is added to $H_{i-1}$ to generate $H_i$. The additions are computed modulo $2^{64}$. The compression function of SHA-512 is shown in Figure 4.12(a). Computation of each round is as follows:

$$T_1 = h + Ch(e, f, g) + \left(\sum_{1}^{512} e\right) + W_t + K_t$$

$$T_2 = \left(\sum_{0}^{512} a\right) + Maj(a, b, c)$$

$$h = g, \quad g = f, \quad f = e, \quad e = d + T_1, \quad d = c, \quad c = b, \quad b = a, \quad a = T_1 + T_2.$$

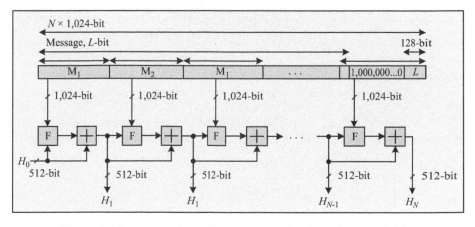

*Figure 4.11   The message digest generation based on SHA-512*

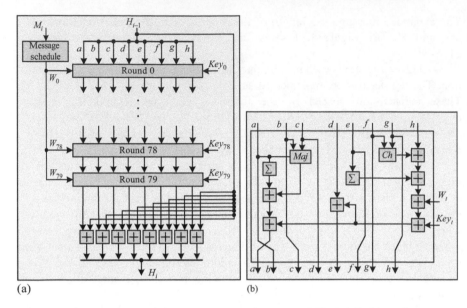

(a)                                                          (b)

*Figure 4.12    Structure of the compression function of SHA-512 (a) and structure of the each round (b)*

*Table 4.1    The building blocks of compression function and message schedule*

| Parameters | Computations |
|---|---|
| $Ch(e, f, g)$ | $(eANDf) \oplus (NOT(e)ANDg)$ |
| $Maj(a, b, c)$ | $(aANDb) \oplus (aANDc) \oplus (bANDc)$ |
| $\left( \sum_0^{512} a \right)$ | $ROTR^{28}(a) \oplus ROTR^{34}(a) \oplus ROTR^{39}(a)$ |
| $\left( \sum_1^{512} e \right)$ | $ROTR^{14}(e) \oplus ROTR^{18}(e) \oplus ROTR^{41}(e)$ |
| $\sigma_0^{512}(x)$ | $ROTR^1(x) \oplus ROTR^8(x) \oplus SHR^7(x)$ |
| $\sigma_1^{512}(x)$ | $ROTR^{19}(x) \oplus ROTR^{61}(x) \oplus SHR^6(x)$ |

$ROTR^n(x)$: Circular right shift of the 64-bit argument $x$ by $n$-bit
$SHR^n(x)$: Left shift of the 64-bit argument $x$ by $n$-bit with padding by zeros on the right.

As mentioned before, the 64-bit word values $W_t$ are generated from the 1,024-bit message. The values of $W_t$ are computed in the message schedule block based on the following equation:

$$W_t = \begin{cases} M_t^i & 0 \leq t \leq 15 \\ \sigma_1^{512}(W_{t-2}) + W_{t-7} + \sigma_0^{512}(W_{t-15}) + W_{t-16} & 16 \leq t \leq 79 \end{cases}$$

The definition of the building blocks of compression function and message schedule is shown in Table 4.1.

### 4.5.3    SHA-3

SHA-3 was proposed as a cryptographic hash standard by the NIST in 2012 [18] through a public competition with five final candidates BLAKE, Grøstl, JH, Keccak, and Skein. The winner candidate was Keccak. It was standardized in 2015 as FIPS-PUB-202 [19]. The SHA-3 inputs and outputs can be represented in two forms. The first form is to represent the data as a string $S[l]$ of $b$-bits, where, $b$ is equal to $\{25, 50, 100, 200, 40, 800, 1,600\}$ and $0 \leq l \leq b - 1$. The second form is to represent the data as a three-dimensional state array $A[x,y,z]$ with three indices $0 \leq x, y < 5$, and $0 \leq z < w$. The mapping form the first form ($S[l]$) to the second form ($A[x,y,z]$) is given by $A[x,y,z] = S[w(5y + x) + z]$. In the SHA-3 input state array, for $b = 1,600$, consists of 1,600-bit that is arranged in the form of $5 \times 5$ matrix of 64-bit words, it is shown in Figure 4.13. The computation steps in the first round of SHA-3 (Keccak) are presented as follows:

$\theta-$***step:***$(0 \leq x, y \leq 4, 0 \leq z \leq 63)$,

$$C[x,y,z] = A[x,0,z] \oplus A[x,1,z] \oplus A[x,2,z] \oplus A[x,3,z] \oplus A[x,4,z]$$

$$D[x,z] = C[(x - 1),z] \oplus ROT(C[(x + 1),1])$$

$$A'[x,y,z] = A[x,y,z] \oplus D[x,z].$$

$\rho-$***step:***$(0 \leq x, y \leq 4)$,

$$A[x,y,z] = ROT(A'[x,y,z], r[x,y]).$$

$\pi-$***step:***$(0 \leq x, y \leq 4, 0 \leq z \leq 63)$,

$$B[y, (2x + 3y), z] = A[x,y,z].$$

$\chi-$***step:***$(0 \leq x, y \leq 4, 0 \leq z \leq 63)$,

$$A'[x,y,z] = B[x,y,z] \oplus (NOT(B[(x + 1),y,z])AND(B[(x + 2),y,z])).$$

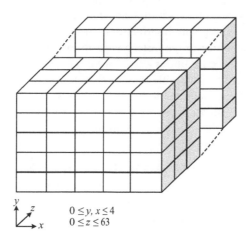

$0 \leq y, x \leq 4$
$0 \leq z \leq 63$

*Figure 4.13    SHA-3 1,600-bit state matrix*

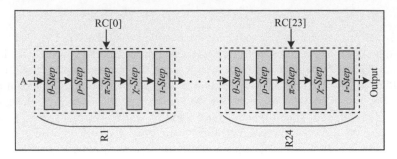

*Figure 4.14    The structure of SHA-3*

$\iota-step:(0 \leq z < 63)$,

$$A'[0,0,z] = A[0,0,z] \oplus RC[z].$$

In the above steps, the value of $r[x,y]$ (cyclic shift offset) and $RC[z]$ (round constant) can be found in [19]. $A[x,y]$ denotes a particular 64-bit word in that state and $B[x,y]$, $C[x]$, and $D[x]$ are intermediate variables. The $ROT$ denotes the bit-wise cyclic shift operation. Figure 4.14 shows the structure of 24 rounds of the SHA-3. As seen in this figure, each round includes five steps. For the SHA-3 algorithm, no attacks are known to date, and it is one of the safest choices when selecting a hash function nowadays technologies.

## 4.6  Authenticated encryption

Message authenticity, message confidentiality, and integrity are desirable goals over a network. Authenticated encryption is a scheme which simultaneously achieves these properties. This type of encryption can be constructed based on a message authentication scheme (a message authentication code (MAC) is more commonly used to message authentication) combined with a symmetric block cipher (encryption scheme) as generic composition. In this case, the encryption scheme is semantically secure under a chosen plaintext attack and also the message authentication scheme is unforgeable under a chosen message attack. Authenticated encryption schemes have been standardized in the ISO/IEC and NIST. Authenticated encryption has applications in SSH, SSL/TLS, and IPsec protocols. There are three ways for constructing an authenticated encryption in practical cryptosystems and these are listed as follows [20]:

- **Authenticate-then-Encrypt (AtE):** The sender computes a tag on the plaintext by a hash function, the tag is appended to the plaintext, then the result is encrypted by encryption scheme. To recovery of the tag and the plaintext, the receiver decrypts the ciphertext. In this case, if the tag verifies correctly, it returns the plaintext; otherwise, it returns.
- **Encrypt-then-Authenticate (EtA):** The sender encrypts the plaintext by encryption scheme, also computes a tag on the ciphertext by a hash function,

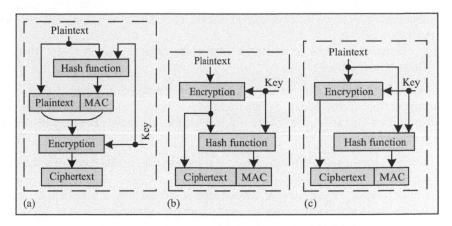

*Figure 4.15 Authenticated encryption schemes (a) AtE, (b) EtA, and (c) E&A*

then appends the tag to the ciphertext and sent together. The tag and the ciphertext are recovered by the receiver. If the tag verifies correctly, the receiver decrypts the ciphertext and returns the plaintext; otherwise, it returns.

• **Encrypt-and-Authenticate (E&A):** The sender computes a tag on the plaintext by a hash function. It then encrypts the plaintext by encryption scheme, then appends the tag to the ciphertext and sent together. The tag and the ciphertext are recovered by the receiver, and then ciphertext is decrypted. If the tag verifies correctly the plaintext is returned, otherwise, it returns.

Figure 4.15(a), (b), and (c) shows authenticated encryption schemes AtE, EtA, and E&A, respectively. In these structures, when the length of the message is relatively large compared to the size of data block in the block cipher, the performance of the authentication step can be improved by using alternative constructions. Most widely used is MACs based on hash functions (HMAC), which produces a tag by hashing a message (e.g., SHA-256) and a key together.

## 4.7 Authentication techniques and security of the IoT, big data, and cloud computing

As mentioned before, authentication is verifying the identity of the user. An authentication method can be selected based on security effectiveness, ease of implementation, ease of use and user attitude and acceptance. RSA authentication is explained based on the work [21] as follows:

1. The server encrypting a message using the client's public key and sends this message to the client.
2. The client decrypts this message using its own private key.
3. The client encrypts this message using the server's public key and sends it back to the server.

4.  The server receives the message and it can decrypt the message using its own private key.
5.  If the message is the same as the original message the server knows that the client is authorized to login.

Also, in [22], a secure ECC-based mutual authentication protocol for secure communication of embedded devices and cloud servers using HTTP cookies has been proposed (Figure 4.16). There are three main approaches to user authentication as follows [23]:

*   **Knowledge-based authentication:** An authentication based on what the user knows, such as a password. This approach is the most widely used type of authentication. Examples of knowledge-based authentication include passwords, pass phrases (or pass sentences), graphical passwords, pass faces, and personal identification numbers (PINs).
*   **Possession-based (or token-based) authentication:** It is an authentication based on what the user has, such as physical objects like memory cards and smart card tokens. It should be noted that presentation of a valid token does not prove ownership, as it may have been stolen or duplicated.
*   **Biometric-based authentication:** An authentication based on what the user is unique, such as *physiological characteristics* or *behavioral features* reliably distinguish one user from another. The main physiological characteristics consist of face recognition, fingerprint, and iris recognition. Also, the main behavioral features consist of Gait recognition (Gait is a behavioral biometric that uses a sequence of video images of a walking person to measure several movements to identify a mobile's user), voice recognition, keystroke, and signature recognition. The collection and the comparison of these characteristics are the main operations

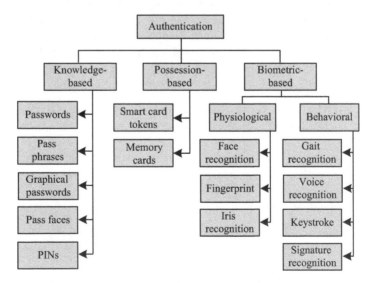

*Figure 4.16    Authentication techniques*

in the biometric-based authentication. Therefore, a biometric system can be constructed based on three main parts: the sensor part, the feature extraction part, and the feature matching part.

### 4.7.1   Security of IoT

The IoT is a network used to interconnect embedded devices, such as sensors, which are able to generate, communicate, and share data with one another. In large-scale networks of interconnected smart devices, the identification of a specific device raises a fundamental challenge that influences all other functions of the system, such as its governance, privacy features, and access control [23–27]. The IoT extends the Internet to the physical world and thus poses many new security and privacy challenges. Some of the problems are due to the intrinsic characteristics of the IoT. To ensure that no untrusted users can get access to the devices, some form of authentication method has to be implemented. Authentication technique is used for identifying devices in a network to restrict access. It provides the ability for users to authenticate an IoT device. Many IoT authentication scenarios are machine-to-machine based without any human intervention, such as Baimos Technologies, Covisint, Device Authority, Entrust Datacard, and Gemalto. Normally, this is achieved using PKC such as RSA or ECC and symmetric key cryptography such as block ciphers. In [23], a comprehensive survey of authentication protocols for IoT is presented.

### 4.7.2   Security of Big Data

Big Data is the term used to describe massive volumes of data that are very difficult to process [28–31]. In this case, many companies are using the technology to store and analyze petabytes of data related to their companies. Therefore, information classification becomes even more critical. If a security breach occurs to Big Data, it can be irreparable. For making Big Data secure, techniques such as encryption, logging, honey-pot detection must be necessary. The main topics related to security in Big Data consist of Infrastructure Security of data, data privacy (unlike security, privacy should be considered as an asset), data management and integrity and reactive security [30,31]. Figure 4.17 shows graphical representation of Big Data security challenges. With the increase in the use of Big Data in business, many companies are encountered with privacy issues [32]. The challenge of detecting and preventing advanced threats and malicious intruders must be solved using Big Data-style analysis.

### 4.7.3   Security of cloud computing

Cloud computing is a technology which depends on the sharing of computing resources to handle the applications. The word *Cloud* means *The Internet*, so the cloud computing means a type of computing in which services are delivered through the Internet [33,34]. In this case, the aim is to increase the computing power to execute millions of instructions per second. Cloud computing uses networks of a large group of servers to distribute data processing. The challenges of security in cloud computing can be categorized into network level (network

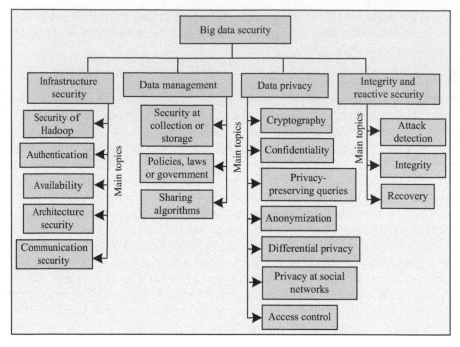

*Figure 4.17   Big Data security challenges*

*Figure 4.18   A general framework for data protection in cloud computing*

protocols and network security such as distributed nodes, distributed data, Inter-node communication), user authentication level (encryption/decryption techniques, authentication methods), data level (data integrity and availability such as data protection and distributed data) and generic issues (traditional security tools, and use of different technologies) [33]. As mentioned earlier, in [22], a secure ECC-based mutual authentication protocol for secure communication of embedded devices and cloud servers using HTTP cookies has been proposed.

A general framework for data protection in cloud computing is shown in Figure 4.18. The encryption function can be a homomorphic encryption. Homomorphic encryption allows the server to do the operation on ciphertext without knowing the original plaintext. In other words, in this encryption scheme complex mathematical operations to be performed on encrypted data without using the original data. An encryption method is called homomorphic over an operation ☆ if it supports the following equation [35]:

$$E(m_1) \star E(m_2) = E(m_1 \star m_2), \forall m_1, m_2 \in M \tag{4.10}$$

where $E$ is the encryption function and $M$ is the set of all possible messages. In order to create an encryption scheme allowing the homomorphic evaluation of arbitrary function, it is sufficient to allow only addition and multiplication operations because addition and multiplication are functionally complete sets over finite fields. Therefore, operation $*$ can be multiplication $\times$ or addition $+$. For example, RSA and ElGamal schemes are homomorphic encryption over the multiplication operation also, Benalh, Paillier, and Okamoto uchiyama schemes are homomorphic encryption over the addition operation.

## 4.8   Advantages and disadvantages of the cryptographic algorithms

Advantages and disadvantages of the cryptographic algorithms are presented in this section. The symmetric cryptographic algorithms have high-speed and low-cost implementation compared to PKC algorithms. In the symmetric cryptography, keys should be distributed before transmission between users. The key distribution among so many users is the main problem of symmetric cryptography. The PKC algorithms are used to solve the problem of key distribution.

The elliptic curves have several advantages over RSA and discrete logarithm schemes like ElGamal encryption. In particular, for ECCs, bit lengths in the range of 160–256-bit provide security level equivalent to 1,024–3,072-bit compared to RSA scheme. The shorter bit length of ECC leads to shorter computation time in digital signatures and authentication protocols.

The authentication methods have benefits and drawbacks, trade-offs need to be made among security effectiveness, usability, ease of implementation, and ease of administration. Authentication types can be implemented alone or in combination. To strengthen the authentication process, the use of at least two types authentication is recommended. Multiple layers of different types of authentication provide substantially better protection.

## 4.9   Research challenges and future perspectives

In recent years, providing security in IoT, Big Data, and Cloud computing is a very important issue. This security can be realized based on the cryptographic algorithms such as symmetric key algorithms, authentication methods, secure network protocols, etc. Also, the new PKC approaches such as post-quantum cryptography [36] and fully homomorphic encryption (FHE) (which allows computations of data in encrypted form) [37] have attracted widespread attention. FHE is used for numerous cryptographic applications including private information retrieval, private search, data aggregation, homomorphic secret sharing, homomorphic signatures for network coding, outsourced computation, e-voting, and biometrics.

Post-quantum cryptography aims to provide new public-key encryption algorithms that are resistant to attacks possible by high-speed quantum technologies. Code-based algorithms, hash-based algorithms, supersingular elliptic curve isogeny cryptography, multivariate-based cryptography, and lattice-based algorithms are some of the proposed post-quantum algorithms. Lattice-based cryptography is one of the most interesting post-quantum approaches. It can be used in the implementation of encryption, digital signatures, key exchange, attribute-based encryption, and FHE. The lattice-based encryption primitives are based on finding solution to linear equations when an error is introduced as a hard problem. Also, lattice-based cryptography has shorter key sizes compared to other schemes of post-quantum algorithms.

Therefore, summary, research challenges, and future perspectives are presented as follows:

- It is important to implement cryptographic algorithms in the constrained environments (with acceptable performance). Therefore, the number of researches which implement the cryptographic algorithms in the low-cost microcontroller-based devices is increasing.
- The design and implementation of the hardware structures for the point multiplication on binary Edwards curves (BECs) can be a popular research topic [38], because BECs are complete, without exception points and intrinsically resistant to simple power analysis.
- The hardware implementation of the ECC for lightweight, flexible, scalable and multi-point multiplication applications based on FPGA and ASIC design has been a popular research topic.
- New lightweight block ciphers such as HIGHT, SIMON, SPECK, PRESENT, KATAN, etc., are attractive subjects for providing security in IoT [39], Big Data, and cloud computing.
- Security and privacy in the new technologies can be resolved using data encryption. However, data must be accessed quickly and encryption process does not affect processing times.
- Implementation of the new cryptographic hash functions such as SHA-3 is a research challenge in recent years.
- Software and hardware attacks on cryptographic algorithms are important subjects in cryptography, which are as research challenges, for example, simple power analysis (SPA), differential power analysis (DPA), refined power analysis (RPA), zero-value point attack (ZPA), zero power analysis (ZPA), template attack, timing attack, classical correlation power analysis, address-bit DPA, doubling attack, carry leakage attack, same values power analysis (SVA), big Mac attack, classical horizontal power analysis, differential fault attack, and hardware Trojan.
- Encrypting data at rest and in transit between IoT devices and back-end systems using standard cryptographic algorithms is an importation topic.

• Cloud computing has numerous security issues because it includes many technologies such as networks, databases, operating systems, virtualization, resource scheduling, transaction management, load balancing, concurrency control, and memory management. Hence, security issues of these systems and technologies are applicable to cloud computing. For example, it is very important for the network which interconnects the systems in a cloud to be secure. Also, mapping of the virtual machines to the physical machines has to be performed very securely. Therefore, providing security in cloud computing has been a popular research topic.

## 4.10 Conclusion

In this chapter, different types of cryptographic algorithms applicable for security in IoT, cloud computing, and Big Data are presented. IoT, cloud computing, and Big Data are based on a highly interconnected network of devices, servers, and massive volumes of data where all kinds of communications seem to be possible. Therefore, the security requirement for such technologies becomes critical, which should be provided by cryptographic algorithms. Two main categories in cryptography are symmetric key cryptography and asymmetric or PKC. The applicable methods for PKC are rather slow compared to symmetric key cryptographic algorithms. Therefore, PKC is used as a complement to symmetric key cryptography for providing security in IoT, cloud computing, and Big Data.

## References

[1]  Paar, C. and Pelzl, J., *Understanding Cryptography*, First Edition, Springer, New York, 2010.
[2]  Hankerson, D., Menezes, A., and Vanstone, S., *Guide to Elliptic Curve Cryptography*, First Edition, Springer-Verlag, New York, 2003.
[3]  Smart, N., *Cryptography: An Introduction*, Second Edition, McGraw-Hill, New York, 2003.
[4]  Stallings, W., *Cryptography and Network Security Principles and Practice*, Fifth Edition, Prentice Hall, New York, 2011.
[5]  Rezaeian Farashahi, R., Rashidi, B., and Sayedi, S.M., 'FPGA Based Fast and High-Throughput 2-Slow Retiming 128-bit AES Encryption Algorithm', *Microelectronics Journal*, 2014, Vol. 45, pp. 1014–1025.
[6]  Diffie, W. and Hellman, M., 'New Directions in Cryptography', *IEEE Trans. on Information Theory*, 1976, Vol. 22, pp. 644–654.
[7]  Rivest, R.L., Shamir, A., and Adleman, L., 'A Method for Obtaining Digital Signatures and Public-Key Cryptosystems', 1978, *Communications of the ACM*, Vol. 21, pp. 120–126.
[8]  Boneh, D., 'Twenty Years of Attacks on the RSA Cryptosystem', *Notices of the AMS*, 1999, Vol. 46, pp. 203–213.
[9]  ElGamal, T., 'A Public Key Cryptosystem and a Signature Scheme Based on Discrete Logarithms', *IEEE Trans. on Information Theory*, 1985, Vol. 31, pp. 469–472.

[10] FIPS 186-2, *NIST: Digital Signature Standard (DSS)*, U.S. Department of Commerce 2000.

[11] ANSI X9.62-1999, *The Elliptic Curve Digital Signature Algorithm, ANSI*, Washington, D.C., USA, 1999.

[12] IEEE P1363, *Editorial Contribution to standard for Public Key Cryptography*, 2000.

[13] ISO/IEC 14888-3, *Information Technology Security Techniques Digital Signatures with Appendix Part 3*, 2006.

[14] Rashidi, B., 'A Survey on Hardware Implementations of Elliptic Curve Cryptosystems', *arXiv preprint arXiv:1710.08336*, 2017.

[15] Lopez, J. and Dahab, R., 'Improved Algorithms for Elliptic Curve Arithmetic in $GF(2^n)$', *Proceedings of the Sel. Areas Cryptography*, 1999, pp. 201–212.

[16] Montgomery, P.L., 'Speeding the Pollard and Elliptic Curve Methods of Factorization', *Mathematics of Computation*, 1987, Vol. 48, pp. 243–264.

[17] Young Rhee, M., *Internet Security Cryptographic Principles, Algorithms and Protocols*, First Edition, John Wiley & Sons, West Sussex, 2003.

[18] NIST, *NIST Selects Winner of Secure Hash Algorithm (SHA-3) Competition*, 2012.

[19] FIPS PUB 202, *SHA-3 Standard: Permutation-Based Hash and Extendable-Output Functions. Tech. Rep. NIST*, 2015.

[20] Degabriele, J.P., *Authenticated Encryption in Theory and in Practice*, PhD dissertation, University of London, 2014.

[21] Xiaolin, Y., Nanzhong, C., Zhigang, J., and Xiaobo, C., 'Trusted Communication System Based on RSA Authentication', *Second International Workshop on Education Technology and Computer Science*, 2010, Vol. 1, pp. 329–332.

[22] Kalra, S. and Sood, S., 'Secure Authentication Scheme for IoT and Cloud Servers', *Pervasive and Mobile Computing*, 2015, Vol. 24, pp. 210–223.

[23] Ferrag, M.A., Maglaras, L.A., Janicke, H., Jiang, J., and Shu, L., 'Authentication Protocols for Internet of Things: A Comprehensive Survey', *Security and Communication Networks*, 2017, Vol. 2017, pp. 1–41.

[24] Atzori, L., Iera, A. and Morabito, G., 'The Internet of Things: A survey', *Computer Networks*, 2010, Vol. 54, pp. 2787–2805.

[25] Liu, X., Zhao, M., Li, S., Zhang, F., and Trappe, W., 'A Security Framework for the Internet of Things in the Future Internet Architecture', *Future Internet*, 2017, Vol. 9, pp. 1–28.

[26] Li, C.T., Wu, T.Y., Chen, C.L., Lee, C.C., and Chen, C.M., 'An Efficient User Authentication and User Anonymity Scheme with Provably Security for IoT-Based Medical Care System' *Sensors*, 2017, Vol. 17(1482), pp. 1–18.

[27] Sicari, S., Rizzardi, A., Grieco, L.A., and Coen-Porisini, A., 'Security, Privacy & Trust in Internet of Things: The Road Ahead', *Computer Networks*, 2015, Vol. 76, pp. 146–164.

[28] Bertino, B., 'Big Data-Security and Privacy', *IEEE International Congress on Big Data*, 2015, pp. 756–760.

[29] Li, R., Asaeda, H., Li, J., and Fu, X., 'A Distributed Authentication and Authorization Scheme for In-Network Big Data Sharing', *Digital Communications and Networks*, 2017, Vol. 3, pp. 226–235.

[30] Moreno, J., A. Serrano, M., and Fernández-Medina, E., 'Main Issues in Big Data Security', *Future Internet*, 2017, Vol. 8, pp. 1–16.

[31] Acharjya, D.P., and Ahmed, K., 'A Survey on Big Data Analytics: Challenges, Open Research Issues and Tools', *International Journal of Advanced Computer Science and Applications*, 2016, Vol.7, pp. 511–518.

[32] Ahmed, E., Yaqoob, I., Targio Hashem, I.A., *et al.*, 'The Role of Big Data Analytics in Internet of Things', *Computer Networks*, 2017, Vol. 129, pp. 459–471.

[33] Inukollu, V.N., Arsi, S., and Ravuri, S.R., 'Security Issues Associated with Big Data in Cloud Computing', *International Journal of Network Security & Its Applications'*, 2014, Vol. 6, pp. 45–56.

[34] Singh, S., Jeong, Y.S., and Park, J.H., 'A Survey on Cloud Computing Security: Issues, Threats, and Solutions', *Journal of Network and Computer Applications*, 2016, Vol. 75, pp. 200–222.

[35] Acar, A., Aksu, H., Uluagac, A.S., and Conti, M., 'A Survey on Homomorphic Encryption Schemes: Theory and Implementation', *arXiv preprint arXiv:1704.03578v2*, 2017.

[36] Bernstein D.J., Johannes, B., and Erik, D., *Post-quantum Cryptography*, First edition., Springer-Verlag, Berlin, Heidelberg, 2009.

[37] C. Gentry, *A fully Homomorphic Encryption Scheme,* PhD dissertation, Stanford University, 2009.

[38] Rashidi, B., 'Efficient Hardware Implementations of Point Multiplication for Binary Edwards Curves', *International Journal of Circuit Theory and Applications*, 2018, Vol. 46, pp. 1–18.

[39] Beaulieu, R., Shors, D., Smith, J., Treatman-Clark, S., Weeks, B., and Wingers, L., 'Simon and Speck: Block Ciphers for the Internet of Things', *NIST Lightweight Cryptography Workshop*, 20–21 July 2015, pp. 1–15.

*Chapter 5*

# Digital watermarking algorithms for multimedia data

*SK Hafizul Islam[1], Arup Kumar Pal[2], Shiv Prasad[2], Soumitra Roy[3], Raunak Rungta[1] and Shikha Verma[1]*

Nowadays, the remarkable growth of Internet technology makes multimedia applications popular. However, the security issue of multimedia data is a big concern due to the openness of the Internet. The threats may occur in terms of illegal copying and/or unauthorized manipulation of multimedia data. From the last few decades, digital watermarking has been considered as one of the promising solutions for controlling the content from unlawful manipulation and redistribution. In watermarking, a watermark or logo is embedded in the original image. The watermark can be extracted later for applications such as copyright protection, ownership verification, content authentication, and so on. In this context, the watermarking is addressing broadly into two application areas such as copyright protection using robust watermarking and to detect illegal content manipulation through fragile watermarking approach. One more type of watermarking, called semi-fragile watermarking, is also quite popular. It is sustainable against certain attacks for the purpose of copyright protection and is applicable for reinforcing the authentication property of multimedia documents. So, the aim of this chapter is to discuss watermarking approaches such as robust, fragile, and semi-fragile in the context of basic requirements or principles, and developing procedures. We also discuss the state-of-the-art as well as some possible research scope in this particular area.

## 5.1 Introduction

In recent years, the multimedia-based information-sharing over the Internet has grown tremendously due to the availability of high-speed Internet and portable computing devices. Trustworthy multimedia data like images play a vital role in applications

[1]Department of Computer Science and Engineering, Indian Institute of Information Technology Kalyani, West Bengal, India
[2]Department of Computer Science and Engineering, Indian Institute of Technology [IIT(ISM)] Dhanbad, Jharkhand, India
[3]Department of Computer Science and Engineering, Dr. B.C. Roy Engineering College, Durgapur, West Bengal, India

including health care, defense communication, security surveillance, education, etc. Since the Internet is an open channel, and thus some cryptographic approaches [1] are adopted to ensure the security of digital data during transmission. In cryptography, several data encryption algorithms such as Data Encryption Standard (DES), Advanced Encryption Standard (AES), CAST (named after Carlisle Adams and Stafford Tavares), International Data Encryption Algorithm (IDEA), RSA (named after Ron Rivest, Adi Shamir, and Leonard Adleman), and so on are widely used for protecting the confidentiality of the digital data. In general, the user transmits the secret data in encrypted form to the authorized recipients for preserving the confidentiality of data. However, in such type of applications, once the secret data is decrypted, then there is no control to monitor the illegal redistribution of the decrypted content due to the easy availability of multimedia manipulation software. Here, the security threats come in terms of authentication/copyright and integrity [2]. So, protecting the integrity and the authenticity independently of a data is another major issue.

Authentication and integrity of multimedia data are protected using robust and fragile watermarking approaches. Basically, digital watermarking [3] is a method for embedding some information to the cover image, which can later be extracted or detected for protecting the authentication and/or integrity of the cover image. In robust watermarking schemes [4,5], it is not possible to remove the copyright information absolutely even after any kind of modification on the watermarked image, which ensures the authenticity of the watermarked image. But in the fragile watermarking scheme, the watermark or copyright information is destroyed when some kind of modification or alteration is done on the watermarked image. This property ensures the integrity of the watermarked image. Fragile watermarking [6] is mostly used in some critical applications, such as medical imaging and forensic image archiving, where the integrity is the major concern since any modification to the dataset leads to wrong diagnosis or judgment in the medical domain or criminal offense, respectively. In general, the fragile watermarking should meet some basic requirements, such as the watermark information should be invisible after embedding onto the cover image; the tampering can be localized even after any kind of modification or alteration of the watermarked image. The purpose of both the robust and fragile watermarking is focused on two different directions, i.e., to protect the copyright of the digital content and to preserve the integrity of digital content, respectively. However, semi-fragile watermarking supports the properties of robust and fragile watermarking to some extent. This kind of watermarking is capable of tolerating certain number of image manipulation attacks as well as it is suitable to locate the manipulated image region.

## 5.1.1 Chapter organization

We organized this chapter as follows. Section 5.2 discusses various properties of the digital watermarking scheme. The basic requirements and the applications of digital image watermarking are discussed in Section 5.3. The classification of digital watermarking is presented in Section 5.4. The working procedure and related works of robust, fragile, and semi-fragile are presented in Section 5.5. Section 5.6 concludes this chapter. Section 5.7 provides some future scopes of the different techniques discussed in this chapter.

*Table 5.1    Properties of digital watermarking*

| Properties | Purposes |
| --- | --- |
| Transparency | The data, which is watermarked, should be consumable at the planned user device without giving distress to the user. Watermark only appears to a watermark-detector device. |
| Security | The data, which is watermarked, should be available to the legitimate person only. The legitimate person has the authority to change that content. For the prevention of watermarked information from the unauthorized person, we can use encryption. |
| Robustness | Robustness of digital watermarking is suitable to prevent various types of attacks and threats for signal-processing operations. If someone tries to attempt any manipulation whether intentionally or unintentionally, then it has a power to change the information and treats it like an attack. In digital watermarking, it plays an essential role against the attack in robustness and this technology helps in the protection of copyright, which depends on its stability and opposition to attacks. |
| Scalability | Another important property of a watermarking system is its scalability with each generation of computers. As the technology is growing tremendously, the present-generation detector might be computationally reasonable and transportable but might not be as strong as next generation detectors that are capable of handling more rigid forms of attacks. |
| Fidelity | In the system of watermarking, it is effective when it has a level of high fidelity and it is also one of the key requirements of watermarking. The fidelity property must ensure that the watermark should not be perceptible to the viewer and should not degrade the quality of the watermarked image. |

## 5.2    Properties of digital watermarking

We listed some important properties of the watermarking techniques in Table 5.1. These properties serve various security objectives in different applications. During designing of an effective watermarking scheme, these security properties are incorporated in most of the cases. The main strength of any digital watermarking relies on these properties.

## 5.3    Applications of digital watermarking

Digital watermarking is applied in several fields to protect the multimedia data. Here, we briefly described some applications of watermarking in various aspects to protect the multimedia data.

### 5.3.1    Copyright protection

Copyright protection [7] of digital data is one of the foremost useful application of digital watermarking where the user inserts his/her copyright protection information such as company's/sender's logo/signature into the original cover media to prove the actual originator of the digital content. Digital data manipulations, duplicity, and spreading of the content are some of the major illegal processes, which can be restricted by copyright protection. The unauthorized copies of the data can even be controlled and traced by encoding the identification of buyer along with the copyright holder ownership.

### 5.3.2    Transaction tracing fingerprinting

Fingerprint watermark [8] behaves like a transitional watermark. This helps to trace the supply of prohibited repeating of the data. The holder will infix totally various distinctive watermarks for various owners. Fingerprinting technique will be used to detect the source from where the data are being copied. During the fingerprinting embedding chain technique, the holder or various middle layer recipients/clients embed their identity information into cover data using the corresponding watermarking method. In the receiver side, holder can restore the original cover medium and can rebuild the information about the middle layer embedding chain. It gives permission to the holder to spot client who has violated license agreement by providing the information to the third party. It is straightforward or can say very easy to trace out the accountable client if someone is misusing the digital information.

### 5.3.3    Broadcast monitoring

This application employs broadcasting the watermarked data at a particular time and place by some advertisers. Application of watermarking finds that is to observe or tracking data be broadcasted, with noting down the time as well as the location of broadcasting. Some highly specialized equipment is being used to monitor the broadcasted channels. It's additionally helpful in finding the criminal of broadcasting copyright data [9]. For inserting a watermark in industrial advertisements, an automatic observance system will check whether the advertisements that are broadcasted are as per contract or not. Owners of proprietary videos need to induce their royalties on every occasion their broadcasting the property.

### 5.3.4    Tamper proofing

Tamper proofing [10,11] is applied to discover counterfeit when data is being counterfeit evil-mindedly and deliberately by inserting the watermark simply broken by micro-operation. As an example, security instrument like CCTV has a born-again from an A/D (analog to digital) system, however, all information are saved in a digital format. Operation on digital data can be done by a normal user who has the system is a major drawback of it. There are various types of instrument, which help in the process such as Digital Video Recorder, digital camera, etc.

## 5.4    Classification of digital watermarking

The digital watermarking can be categorized into various aspects, such as human perception, watermark detection process, application specific, depending on cover media, and watermark embedding domain. Based on human perception, two types of watermarking applications are found. First one is known as visible [28] and the second one is known as invisible. For visible watermarking scheme, the watermark is noticeable by human visual perception. However, for invisible watermarking, it is hard to identify or locate the watermark in the cover image. The second category is comparatively secure since the watermark removal is reasonably hard here. To validate the copyright protection or integrity, the watermark can be detected by the authorized user using blind and non-blind watermarking process, respectively. In the blind watermarking approach [12], the original watermark or original cover media is not required to locate the watermark but in case of the non-blind watermarking category, that additional information is essential to detect the watermark from the watermarked image. The blind watermarking schemes are more effective than non-blind watermarking schemes since the watermark can be directly identified without considering the original watermark or original cover media. Further, the watermarking based applications are found for image, audio, and video data [13]. So, according to the cover media, the watermarking areas are divided into image watermarking, audio watermarking, and video watermarking. According to the applications or properties of security aspects, the watermarking schemes are found in different types such as robust [14], fragile [33], and semi-fragile [15]. The robust watermarking is used to protect the copyright of the digital content. The main purpose of robust watermarking is to resist meaningful digital data manipulation from any eavesdroppers. In this watermarking, after performing attacks, the extracted actual/approximate watermark remains intact. As a result, the copyright property of digital data is retained. On the other hand, the fragile watermarking is exclusively used to protect the integrity property of the digital data. In this category of watermarking approach, any alteration causes drastic changes in the extracted watermark. However, the semi-fragile watermarking schemes satisfy the partial property of robust watermarking as well as the fragile watermarking. The watermark embedding process may be done either by directly modifying the pixels of the cover image or by modifying the coefficients of the transformed cover media. So, based on the watermark embedding process, the watermarking schemes are found as spatial domain, transform domain, and hybrid domain. In the hybrid domain, multiple transformation tools are collectively used to achieve more robustness. In general, some widely used transformation tools such as Discrete Cosine Transform (DCT) [16], Discrete Wavelet Transform (DWT) [17], and Singular Value Decomposition (SVD) [18] are used during the development of any robust watermarking scheme. Figure 5.1 summarizes the classification of watermarking in different aspects.

## 5.5 Watermarking procedure

In this section, we are giving a general outline of the watermarking procedure in the context of robust, fragile, and semi-fragile watermarking schemes, respectively. We also incorporate some current state-of-the-art approaches in this particular area.

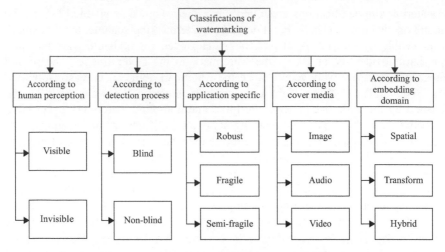

*Figure 5.1    Classification of digital watermarking*

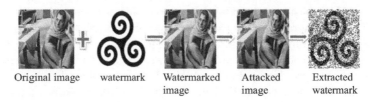

| Original image | watermark | Watermarked image | Attacked image | Extracted watermark |

*Figure 5.2    Robust watermarking scheme*

## 5.5.1    Robust watermarking

### 5.5.1.1    Principle

As discussed earlier, robust watermarking is used to protect the copyright infor-mation of digital data. The robust watermarking scheme is shown in Figure 5.2. In this procedure, a watermark/logo is initially embedded into the cover image. The watermark with the cover image is known as the watermarked image. Later, the attacker intentionally modifies the watermarked image with the intention to remove the watermark from the watermarked image. In Figure 5.2, the approximate watermark is obtained when the watermarked image is manipulated; otherwise, the original watermark will be found.

Further, Figure 5.3 shows the watermark embedding process where a water-mark or logo is hidden into a cover image. Sometimes, a secret key may be used to enhance the security level. In general, transform domain-based watermarking schemes [18] are more effective than spatial domain watermarking schemes. In the transform domain watermarking scheme, initially, the cover media is trans-formed by suitable transformation tool(s). The multiple transformation tools are considered during devising the hybrid robust watermarking scheme. Later, the original

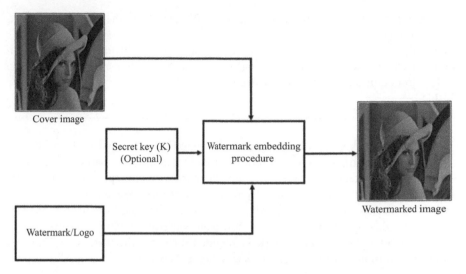

*Figure 5.3    Watermark embedding procedure in robust watermarking scheme*

watermark or transformed watermark is embedded after modifying the coefficients of the transformed cover image. In this particular procedure, the coefficients of the transformed cover image are first divided into three parts, i.e., the low-frequency band coefficients, middle-frequency band, and high-frequency band coefficients. The low-frequency band coefficients convey most of the information and this particular region is not suitable to hide the watermark since after the watermark embedding causes severe distortion in the watermarked image. On the other hand, the high-frequency band components/coefficients are discarded in the time of lossy compression process. So, the middle-frequency band coefficients are more preferable to hide the watermark. After selection of suitable embedding zone, the watermark is concealed directly into the transformed cover image. Later, the inverse transformation is performed on the modified transformed cover image to obtain the final watermarked image. The watermarked image is generally found robust since the watermark is embedded asymmetrically throughout the cover media. The main algorithmic steps of the robust watermarking scheme are mentioned in Algorithm 1. After watermark embedding processes, it is not feasible to locate the watermark directly in cover media in the spatial domain.

---

**Algorithm 1:** Watermark embedding procedure of robust watermarking scheme

---

**Input:** A cover image and a logo/watermark
**Output:** The watermarked image
**Begin**
Step 1: Read a cover image and subsequently, transform the cover image using suitable transformation tool(s).

Step 2: Select the middle-frequency band coefficients from the transformed cover image.

Step 3: Embed the watermark/logo into the selected middle band coefficient region.

Step 4: Perform the inverse transformation on the modified transformed cover image to obtain the watermarked image.

**End**

---

The watermark extraction process is shown in Figure 5.4, where the original or approximate watermark is identified from the original watermarked or attacked watermarked image, respectively. In the watermark extraction process, initially, the watermarked image is transformed by forward transformation and subsequently, in the blind watermarking procedure, the watermark is extracted from the middle band coefficients directly. But in cases of non-blind watermark extraction process, the original cover image or watermark is required to locate the watermark from the watermarked image. The watermark extraction procedure is given in Algorithm 2.

---

**Algorithm 2:** Watermark extraction procedure of robust watermarking scheme

---

**Input:** The watermarked image
**Output:** The extracted watermark/logo
**Begin**
Step 1: Read the watermarked image and subsequently, transform the watermarked image using corresponding transformation tool(s).

Step 2: Select the middle-frequency band coefficients from the transformed watermarked image.

Step 3: Extract the watermark/logo from the selected middle-frequency band coefficient region.

**End**

---

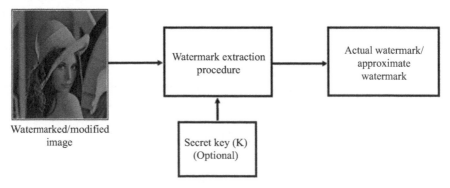

*Figure 5.4    Watermark extraction procedure in robust watermarking scheme*

## 5.5.1.2 Related works

Several effective robust watermarking schemes are suggested by the researcher using different transformation tools. Generally DCT-based robust watermarking scheme, the middle-band coefficients are mostly preferred for embedding the watermark information. Barni *et al.* [19] have proposed a DCT-based robust watermarking scheme where a pseudo-random sequence is embedded as a watermark into some selective DCT coefficients of the cover image. Another DCT-based watermark scheme is suggested by Chu [20]. In their scheme, before embedding the watermark, DCT is applied on sub-images, which are obtained by sub-sampling of the image. A DCT domain-based blind image watermarking [21] is found in the literature. Their scheme was block based where DC coefficients of each block are used to predict suitable AC component in that particular block. Later, the selected AC component is modified based on the watermark bit. Their effectiveness depends on the selection of the proper AC component. Another DCT-based blind watermarking scheme is found in [22], where the authors have proposed repetition code based watermark embedding procedure. Their scheme is suitable to hide multiple watermarks even in a color image. A DWT-based robust watermarking scheme is suggested by Tay *et al.* [23] where the watermark insertion is realized into the mid-frequency wavelet channel. Liu *et al.* [24] have suggested a DWT-based blind scheme. An SVD transformation-based watermarking scheme is given by Chang *et al.* [25]. However, the false positive problem is the main demerit of the SVD-based image watermarking scheme. In the false positive problem, a correct watermark from an unauthorized image can be identified. To overcome this problem, in [26], the authors have proposed an improved SVD-based watermarking scheme. A secret key-based watermarking [27] is devised to enhance the security. In their scheme, prior to embedding, the watermark was scrambled by a secret key sequence. Several hybrid watermarking schemes are also popular due to its high robustness. In [28], the authors have incorporated RDWT-DCT for devising a robust and blind watermarking scheme. In [29], three transformation tools such as DWT, SVD, and DCT are used to survive from JPEG and JPEG2000 compression attacks. A robust watermarking scheme is effective when the embedded watermark survives against various image manipulation attacks. Figure 5.5 shows all possible attacks on the robust watermarking scheme. After performing these attacks, if the watermark still survives then it satisfies the robustness property. So, different transformation domain-based watermarking schemes are popular and acceptable to resist different image manipulation attacks.

## 5.5.2 Fragile watermarking

### 5.5.2.1 Principle

The basic idea behind the fragile watermarking scheme is to insert a watermark or authentication code into the cover image to form a watermarked image. Later, if the watermarked image is manipulated then the watermark bits or authentication code is not identified in the modified region. It means that the watermark bits will be removed where the alteration of the watermarked image occurs. Figure 5.6(a)

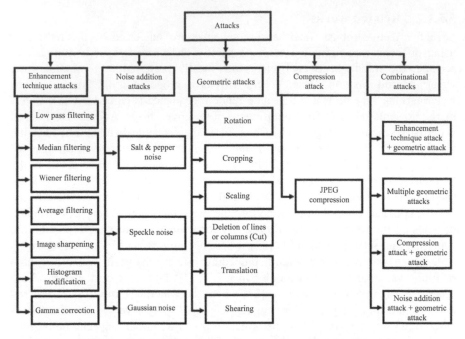

*Figure 5.5    Different attacks on robust watermarking*

(a)                          (b)                          (c)

*Figure 5.6    (a) The watermarked image; (b) tampered image; and (c) actual
tampered regions*

shows the watermarked image. The image has been tampered and it is shown in
Figure 5.7(b). The purpose of an effective fragile watermarking scheme is to locate
the tampered region as shown in Figure 5.7(c). So, in the fragile watermarking
scheme, two major phases are watermark/authentication code embedding and
tamper detection. Figure 5.7 depicts the watermark embedding procedure. In general, the watermark embedding procedure is carried out either in the pixel or block
level. In the pixel level, a watermark may be directly embedded into the least

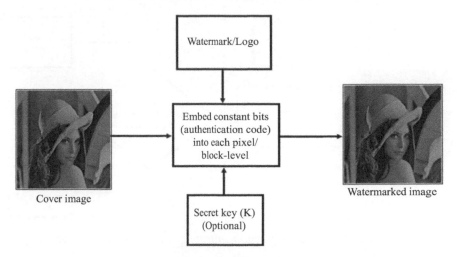

*Figure 5.7   Watermark embedding procedure in fragile watermarking scheme*

significant bit positions or an authentication code may be generated from the most significant bits of a pixel and the same will inserted into the least significant bit positions. Similarly, in the block level, the earlier procedure is carried out on a set of pixels from a particular block. In the tamper detection process, the extracted watermark bits are compared with the corresponding original watermark bits. A pixel is found unaltered when the extracted watermark bits and the original watermark bits are same. For the case of the authentication code, in a similar way, the code is generated from the watermarked content and is compared with extracted code. The pixel is found unchanged when both the codes are same. In the block-level watermarking scheme, the same process is considered whatever is done at the pixel level. Figure 5.8 is the outline of the tamper detection process in the fragile watermarking scheme. Algorithms 3 and 4 describe the watermark embedding procedure and the tamper detection procedure, respectively, in the fragile watermarking scheme.

---

**Algorithm 3:** Watermark embedding procedure of the fragile watermarking scheme

---

**Input:** A cover image and a watermark/logo
**Output:** The watermarked image
**Begin**
Step 1: Read a cover image.
Step 2: Compute a hash value/signature from the most significant bits of a particular pixel (in case of pixel-based fragile watermarking scheme) or a set of pixels of a particular block (in case of the block-based fragile watermarking scheme).

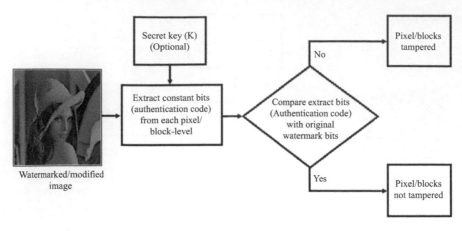

*Figure 5.8    Tamper detection in fragile watermarking scheme*

Step 3: Find the authentication code using the watermark/logo and embed the derived authentication code into the least significant bits position of the particular pixel/a set of pixels of a block.

Step 4: Process rest of pixels/block of pixels using Step 2 to Step 3 to obtain the watermarked image.

**End**

---

**Algorithm 4:** Tamper detection procedure of fragile watermarking scheme

---

**Input:** The watermarked image and the watermark/logo
**Output:** The tampered detected image
**Begin**
Step 1: Read the watermarked image.
Step 2: Compute a hash value/signature from the most significant bits of a particular pixel (in case of pixel-based fragile watermarking scheme) or a set of pixels of a particular block (in case of the block-based fragile watermarking scheme).
Step 3: Extract the embedded watermark bit(s) from the least significant bits position of the particular pixel/a set of pixels of a block with the help of bit streams obtained from Step 2.
Step 4: Compare the extracted watermark bit(s) with the original watermark bit(s).
Step 5: If the comparison is true, then there is no tampering in pixel/block else the pixel/block is marked as tampered
Step 6: Process rest of pixels/block of pixels using Step 2 to Step 5 to mark the tampered region into the watermarked image.
**End**

---

### 5.5.2.2 Related works

In [30], the suggested fragile watermarking scheme works for both pixel level and block level. The authors have shown that their scheme locate the tampered region effectively. In [31], the authors have generated an authentication code using Hamming code from MSBs of a set of pixels from a block. The generated code is embedded into LSBs of pixels. Their scheme finds the tampered region in block level. In [32], the authors have performed preprocessing using fuzzy transform prior to embed the watermark. The tamper detection accuracy for their scheme is well acceptable. Trivedy and Pal [11] have considered a logistic map-based secret sequence to embed the authentication code and later the same secret sequence is used to identify the tampered region. They have achieved the high accuracy during tamper detection process. Another block level fragile watermarking scheme is proposed by Chuan *et al.* [33] and they have introduced adaptive LSB layers concept to hide authentication code. Their scheme is also found suitable in terms of tamper detection. In [34], the authors have used vector quantization (VQ) based compressed image during watermark insertion time. Their scheme is well suited to locate the tampered region. In [35], the proposed fragile watermarking scheme is designed for security purpose of medical images. An SVD-based fragile watermarking is given by Ahmad *et al.* [36] where they have considered encrypted watermark for improving the security. Azeroual and Afdel [37] have developed another fragile watermarking scheme in DWT domain. Recently, researchers are trying to incorporate some suitable error-correcting codes in the fragile watermarking scheme to locate and correct the tampered region simultaneously. The effectiveness and efficiency of the fragile watermarking is estimated by a number of quantitative measures like the false negative rate (FNR) and the false positive rate (FPR). An efficient scheme has very less values of FNR and FPR. Based on FNR and FPR, the accuracy is computed for evaluating the performance of tamper detection in the digital image content. In this particular filed, the researcher's main concern is to improve the accuracy. The fragile watermarking schemes are mostly used in medical images to protect the integrity property.

## 5.5.3 Semi-fragile watermarking

### 5.5.3.1 Principle

A semi-fragile watermarking satisfies partially robustness property of robust watermarking scheme. It survives some of the common image processing attacks such as additive noise, contrast adjustment, Gaussian low-pass filtering, and median filtering. This scheme is also known as soft authentication as the integrity-checking criteria is relatively flexible as compared to that of fragile watermarking. So, the semi-fragile watermark defends the certain degree of robustness property of digital contents.

### 5.5.3.2 Related works

Several semi-fragile digital image watermarking schemes have been discussed in the literature. In [38], the authentication is done by extracting the watermark from the original image and inserting it back again into the image which avoids additional signature files. The user's private key is used for encryption and decryption of watermark. In [39], the suggested semi-fragile watermarking scheme has considered random bias and non-uniform quantization to protect robustness against lossy compression. In [40], the proposed scheme can perform the automatic authentication and restoration of the content of digital images. Peng *et al.* [15] have given a novel semi-fragile watermarking based on the log-polar coordinate mapping. Their scheme is robust against rotation, translation and scaling operations. In this particular area, the researcher's main concern is to satisfy the integrity property as well as to ensure the robustness property against the maximum number of image manipulation attacks.

## 5.6    Chapter summary

This chapter covers the principles of watermarking, and discusses several characteristics of watermarks that might be desirable for various applications. Numerous related methods for digital image watermarking are analyzed and attempted to identify their strengths and weaknesses. The aim of any watermarking scheme is to resist both the intentional and unintentional attacks. So, in this area, a researcher has a lot of scope to explore some new attacks as well as to develop more efficient watermarking schemes. In future, the watermarking can be further studied on different datasets as well as in different environments to ensure the high level of security in various application aspects.

## 5.7    Future research directions

To solve the inherent security problem of the digital data, in digital watermarking, certain information such as signature, logo, secret key uniquely related to the owner or distributor is permanently embedded into digital data. With the imperceptibility, to make this related watermark information secure and robust, confidentiality integrity and authenticity/copyright protection property of digital data should be preserved. So, the main objective of any proposed watermarking algorithm is to design a framework to carry out the recent development of watermarking schemes for digital images, video, and audio data. To accomplish this goal, modern researchers begin their work by developing some robust, fragile, and semi-fragile watermarking techniques for the digital data. While designing these blind and non-blind watermarking schemes, to improve the effectiveness, balance should be achieved between the imperceptibility, robustness, and the embedding capacity of watermarking schemes.

All the available single watermarking schemes are not suitable to prove the authenticity of multiple owners/creators of digital object. For these types of digital object, multiple watermarking schemes should be designed. In general, the watermark is an inseparable part of the host object and after the insertion of watermark data, the host/cover object is permanently distorted in an imperceptible manner. These types of watermarking methods are termed as irreversible watermarking scheme where the cover image is permanently modified after the embedding of watermark data. In today's world, watermarking can be used in sensitive applications such as medical diagnosis, military identification where this slight and permanent modification of the cover object cannot be acceptable. Reversible watermarking technique, where cover object is restored almost bit by bit after watermark data extraction, is the most suitable solution for these applications. In these types of applications, important valuable information actually remains in the host object. So, designing of suitable reversible watermarking schemes is one of the main future directions of this field. Still, there is no proper benchmarking tool available for the evaluation of watermarking algorithms. Researchers can design suitable benchmarking tool for different watermarking algorithms.

# References

[1] William Stallings. *Cryptography and Network Security: Principles and Practices*. India: Pearson Education, 5th ed., 2007.

[2] Shiguo Lian. *Multimedia Content Encryption: Techniques and Applications*. New York: CRC Press, 2009.

[3] Chun-Shien Lu. *Multimedia Security: Steganography and Digital Watermarking Techniques for Protection of Intellectual Property*. Idea Group Publishing, 1st ed., 2005.

[4] Yang Liu, Shanyu Tang, Ran Liu, Liping Zhang, and Zhao Ma, 'Secure and robust digital image watermarking scheme using logistic and RSA encryption', *Expert Systems with Applications*, 2018; **97**:95–105.

[5] Satendra Pal Singh, and Gaurav Bhatnagar, 'A new robust watermarking system in integer DCT domain', *Journal of Visual Communication and Image Representation*, 2018; **53**:86–101.

[6] Chuan Qin, Ping Ji, Xinpeng Zhang, Jing Dong, and Jinwei Wang, 'Fragile image watermarking with pixel-wise recovery based on overlapping embedding strategy', *Signal Processing*, 2017; **138**:280–293.

[7] Fawad Ahmad, and Lee-Ming Cheng, 'Authenticity and copyright verification of printed images', *Signal Processing*, 2018; **148**:322–335.

[8] Dipanjan Roy, and Anirban Sengupta, 'Low overhead symmetrical protection of reusable IP core using robust fingerprinting and watermarking during high level synthesis', *Future Generation Computer Systems*, 2017; **71**:89–101.

[9] Ming Li, Jinhua Zhang, and Wenying Wen, 'Cryptanalysis and improvement of a binary watermark-based copyright protection scheme for remote sensing images', *Optik*, 2014; **125**:7231–7234.

[10] Raphael C.-W. Phan, 'Tampering with a watermarking-based image authentication scheme', *Pattern Recognition*, 2008; **41**: 3493–3496.

[11] Saswati Trivedy, and Arup Kumar Pal, 'A logistic map-based fragile watermarking scheme of digital images with tamper detection', *Iranian Journal of Science and Technology, Transactions of Electrical Engineering*, 2017; **41(2)**:1–11.

[12]    Soumitra Roy, and Arup Kumar Pal, 'An indirect watermark hiding in discrete cosine transform–singular value decomposition domain for copyright protection'. *Royal Society Open Science*, 2017; **4(6)**. DOI: http://dx.doi.org/10.1098/rsos.170326.

[13]    Ingemar Cox, Matthew Miller, Jeffrey Bloom, Jessica Fridrich, and Ton Kalker. *Digital Watermarking and Steganography*. Morgan Kaufmann, Burlington, MA, 2007.

[14]    Soumitra Roy, and Arup Kumar Pal. 'A hybrid domain color image watermarking based on DWT–SVD'. *Iranian Journal of Science and Technology, Transactions of Electrical Engineering*, 2018; 1–17. DOI: https://doi.org/10.1007/s40998-018-0109-x.

[15]    Fei Peng, Re-Si Guo, Chang-Tsun Li, and Min Long, 'A semi-fragile watermarking algorithm for authenticating 2D CAD engineering graphics based on log-polar transformation', *Computer-Aided Design*, 2010;**42(12)**: 1207–1216.

[16]    Mehdi Khalili, 'DCT-Arnold chaotic based watermarking using JPEG-YCbCr', *Optik- International Journal for Light and Electron Optics*, 2015; **126(23)**:4367–4371.

[17]    Mehul S Raval, and Priti P Rege, 'Discrete wavelet transform based multiple watermarking scheme', In TENCON 2003. Conference on Convergent Technologies for the Asia-Pacific Region, **vol. 3**, pp. 935–938. IEEE, 2003.

[18]    Ruizhen Liu, and Tieniu Tan, 'An SVD-based watermarking scheme for protecting rightful ownership', *IEEE Transactions on Multimedia*, 2002; **4 (1)**:121–128.

[19]    Mauro Barni, Franco Bartolini, Vito Cappellini, and Alessandro Piva, 'A DCT domain system for robust image watermarking', *Signal Processing*, 1998; **66(3)**:357–372.

[20]    Wai C Chu, 'DCT-based image watermarking using subsampling', *IEEE Transactions on Multimedia*, 2003; **5(1)**:34–38.

[21]    Yulin Wang, and Alan Pearmain, 'Blind image data hiding based on self-reference', *Pattern Recognition Letters*, 2004; **25(15)**:1681–1689.

[22]    Soumitra Roy, and Arup Kumar Pal, 'A blind DCT based color watermarking algorithm for embedding multiple watermarks', *International Journal of Electronics and Communications*, 2016; **72**:149–161.

[23]    R Tay, and JP Havlicek, 'Image watermarking using wavelets. In Circuits and Systems', 2002. MWSCAS-2002. The 2002 45th Midwest Symposium on, **vol. 3**, pp. III–III. IEEE, 2002.

[24]    Jiang-Lung Liu, Der-Chyuan Lou, Ming-Chang Chang, and Hao-Kuan Tso, 'A robust watermarking scheme using self-reference image', *Computer Standards & Interfaces*, 2006; **28(3)**:356–367.

[25]    Chin-Chen Chang, Piyu Tsai, and Chia-Chen Lin, 'SVD-based digital image watermarking scheme', *Pattern Recognition Letters*, 2005; **26(10)**:1577–1586.

[26]    Jing-Ming Guo, and HeriPrasetyo, 'False-positive-free SVD-based image watermarking', *Journal of Visual Communication and Image Representation*, 2014;**25(5)**:1149–1163.

[27] Zhao Yantao, Ma Yunfei, and Li Zhiquan. 'A robust chaos-based DCT-domain watermarking algorithm'. *In 2008 International Conference on Computer Science and Software Engineering*, **vol. 3**, pp. 935–938. IEEE, 2008.

[28] Soumitra Roy, and Arup Kumar Pal, 'A robust blind hybrid image watermarking scheme in RDWT-DCT domain using Arnold scrambling', *Multimedia Tools and Applications*, 2017; **76(30)**:3577–3616.

[29] Hwai-Tsu Hu, and Ling-Yuan Hsu, 'Exploring DWT-SVD-DCT feature parameters for robust multiple watermarking against JPEG and JPEG2000 compression', *Computers & Electrical Engineering*, 2015; **41**:52–63.

[30] Xinpeng Zhang, and Shuozhong Wang, 'Fragile watermarking scheme using a hierarchical mechanism', *Signal Processing*, 2009; **89(4)**:675–679.

[31] Chin-Chen Chang, Kuo-Nan Chen, Chin-Feng Lee, and Li-Jen Liub, 'A secure fragile watermarking scheme based on chaos-and-hamming code', *Journal of Systems and Software*; 2011; **84(9)**:1462–1470.

[32] Ferdinando Di Martino, and Salvatore Sessa, 'Fragile watermarking tamper detection with images compressed by fuzzy transform', *Information Sciences*, 2012; **195**:62–90.

[33] Chuan Qin, Ping Ji, Xinpeng Zhang, Jing Dong, and Jinwei Wang, 'Fragile image watermarking with pixel-wise recovery based on overlapping embedding strategy', *Signal Processing*, 2017; **138**:280–293.

[34] Archana Tiwari, Manisha Sharma, and Raunak Kumar Tamrakar, 'Watermarking based image authentication and tamper detection algorithm using vector quantization approach', *International Journal of Electronics and Communications (AEÜ)*; 2017; **78**:114–123.

[35] Abdulaziz Shehab, Mohamed Elhoseny, Khan Muhammad, *et al.*, 'Secure and robust fragile watermarking scheme for medical images', *IEEE Access*, 2018; **6**:10269–10278.

[36] Irshad Ahmad Ansari, Millie Pant, and Chang WookAhn, 'SVD based fragile watermarking scheme for tamper localization and self-recovery', *International Journal of Machine Learning and Cybernetics*, 2015; **7(6)**:1225–1239.

[37] AssmaAzeroual, and Karim Afdel, 'Real-time image tamper localization based on fragile watermarking and Faber-Schauder wavelet', *International Journal of Electronics and Communications (AEÜ)*, 2017; **79**:207–218.

[38] Xiang Zhou, Xiaohui Duan, and Daoxian Wang, 'Semi fragile watermark scheme for image authentication', *10th International Multimedia Modelling Conference Proceedings*, 2004, 374–377.

[39] Kurato Maeno, Qibin Sun, Shih-Fu Chang, and Masayuki Suto, 'New semi-fragile image authentication watermarking techniques using random bias and nonuniform quantization', *IEEE Transactions on Multimedia*, 2006; **8(1)**: 32–45.

[40] Xunzhan Zhu, Anthony T.S. Ho, and Pina Marziliano, 'A new semi-fragile image watermarking with robust tampering restoration using irregular sampling', *Signal Processing: Image Communication*, 2007; **22(5)**:515–528.

*Chapter 6*

# Biometric authentication

*Alawi A. Al-Saggaf[1] and Mohammed Abdul Majid[1]*

User authentication is an essential tool for granting access control in various digital environment applications such as e-commerce, e-banking, e-government, e-passport, e-health and a number of forensic applications. In addition, the tremendous development and implementation of cloud technology has made a great impact on businesses around the world. However, privacy is one of several concerns in the current cloud technology, such as the privacy of user data and transaction during the outsourcing data. In generic information security systems, user authentication based on traditional methods such as password, token, or both, which fall apart if the password is not kept secret. Additionally, the passwords and token can be stolen, lost or forgotten and cannot establish the true user's identity.

It is obvious for every organization that securing information is of special significance. The limitations of the traditional authentication methods can be mitigated by the incorporation of highly secure mechanisms for user authentication. Biometrics refers to 'automated recognition of individuals based on their behavioural and biological characteristics such as fingerprints, iris, face, hand, voice, and gait.' Compared to traditional authentication methods, biometrics are easy to use, convenient, not possible to share, reliable, and cannot be forgotten or lost. Compensating for this need, this chapter will focus on the biometric authentication systems which help to prevent unauthorized access to the local server and cloud resources. First, we give a historical overview of biometrics. This chapter also provides some details of physiological and behavioural biometrics modalities along with the performance of each biometric modality. Biometric authentication system procedures along with the performance measures are discussed, and then different known attacks that can be encountered by a biometric authentication system are then illustrated. Next, to prevent the biometric data from different attacks, a survey of the biometric template protection systems is presented. Additionally, this chapter gives details of how we can deploy the biometric into remote user authentication. The last section of the chapter discussed some case studies and research challenges of integrating the biometric authentication systems on the cloud computing and IoT technologies.

[1]Mathematical Sciences Department, Dammam Community College, King Fahd University of Petroleum & Minerals, Dhahran, Saudi Arabia

## 6.1    Introduction

The protection of confidential information has never been as challenging as it is now in today's highly technologically connected world with all types of smart gadgets around us. A total reliance on security codes and password keys possesses serious security loopholes, and moreover maintaining a reliable track has never been easy for people of all ages and professions. More sophisticated digital thefts and threats are carried out these days by hackers and imposters such as duplicating or using a counterfeited ID cards. Hence, the science of biometrics seems to offer and revolutionize the identification, verification and authentication of digital data using some of the unique human features which have stood the tests of times.

In this section, we will provide a brief overview and historical perspective of biometrics and we will set the scene of how critical is the need to establish the true identity in this highly technological world. An astounding fact among the human beings is that there are certain genetic characteristics features that make us unique from each other. This is true in the absolute sense of the word 'uniqueness' to confirm our identity. From the cradle to grave this would remain the case irrespective of how exponentially the human population increases. This difference also can be visibly seen how people around the world vary in terms of their socio-economic strata, availability of opportunities naturally and so on.

The term 'biometrics' is a combination of the word 'bio' derived from the Greek meaning 'life' and 'metrics' means 'to measure'. In [1], the author defined biometrics as 'the use of computer science technology to extract the unique features of an individual, whether it be physical or behavioural traits, in order to positively verify and/or identify the identity of an individual, so that they may have access to certain resources.' It can also be defined more briefly as the unique (personal) physical/logical characteristics or traits of a human body. It is used to measure the physiological or the behavioural features of an individual for the purpose of verifying or recognizing the identity. The unique features of a human being are used to establish his/her identity. The characteristic feature of the biometric data is the fact that it uses the uniqueness of the human body and as are several areas and or points which do not have a close match even in identical twins. Unique identifiers help us in identification and authentication processes. In the words of Francis Galton in 'Nature' 1888 on fingerprints, 'Perhaps the most beautiful and characteristic of all superficial marks are the small furrows with the intervening ridges and their pores that are disposed of in a singularity complex yet even order on the under surfaces of the hands and feet'. The universality and repetitive relentless persistence of the fingerprints have been established since time immemorial.

The uniqueness of some of the characteristics features of the human being changes over time due to the ageing process. These dynamic changes occur mainly due to the biological, physiological, environmental, psychological, behavioural and social changes. Consequently, they present challenges in the identification of individual and hence weakening their credible value as being unique features.

## 6.2 Fundamentals and types of errors

### 6.2.1 Identification, authentication and verification

Identification: One of the most important preliminary steps in biometrics is the identification of an individual to avoid fakes. The identification is based on the measurements of certain features of the human body. Traditional methods are still largely in place for establishing identities based on the ID cards such as passports, National ID, as well as on ones' memory. However, these methods need to change due to their vulnerability to dangers. Historic records reveal that the biometrics particularly fingerprints have been in practice dating back to the eighteenth century.

Authentication: The authentication is the process of authenticating an identity of an individual to a system. To authenticate or to validate means, to check if the attributes of a person match with that of the existing database. It is used for the purpose of verification of the identity based on characteristics that are unique to an individual. The data available in databases is matched based on a certain threshold. The authentication follows an algorithm and if the person's attributes match nearly as identical then it passes the test.

Verification: In this process, the identity of an individual is verified to provide access to a secured system. It is checked whether or not the person is the same as he or she claims to be. The system uses certain unique characteristic features which are only unique to one person for authenticating and verifying in a large database of information.

### 6.2.2 Types of errors

There are also downsides of the biometric systems which are examined as errors and they are broadly classified as types I and II. Not suitably addressing these errors in a biometric system might have serious negative implications in terms of the financial cost as well as raises several questions about its reliability. Type I errors occur due to the improper calibration of the biometric system set to an incorrect accuracy level. When an unauthorized or unsolicited user attempts to get access to a system, Type II errors occur. This leads to a very important consideration that the accuracy and precision levels must be appropriately set in order to avoid serious security breach or consequences.

## 6.3 Biometric authentication modalities

Biometrics can be broadly classified as physiological and behavioural. Some of the physiological modalities are fingerprint recognition, iris recognition and facial recognition, etc. The behavioural classification includes voice recognition and signature recognition, etc. Both these types offer unique characteristic features which make them essential in the entire biometric process. One is considered more reliable and feasible over the other. Measuring the manner an individual carries out certain tasks is behavioural. Physiological biometrics, if not all, are more common and accurate. A brief introduction of these biometric modalities is provided in the section below.

## 6.3.1    Fingerprint recognition

A remarkable fact of the fingertips is that it contains unique and invariant ridges and valleys which do not match with any other human beings in the world. This technology is in practice dating back to hundreds of years and considered as a yardstick for centuries as an identification method. The Galton Points, the method developed by Francis Galton around the nineteenth century, is one of the most popular classical methods of identification. It is used to prove the identity of individuals using their fingerprints. The use of computers and their applications has automated this method and hence the name 'biometrics'. A typical impression of a fingerprint is usually a dark band of lines, ridges and valleys. It is a multi-step approach in which fingerprint image is acquired, analysed and identified through the scanning machines. The acquisition of the image gets interrupted by the system if the extraneous data collected exceeds a set threshold. Because the more extraneous data of an image is produced, the more it would be difficult in the identification process. Therefore, a new image needs to be acquired. With the advent of smartphones and technological advances, the image-processing devices have improved their performance significantly and the quality of images collection has drastically improved. The technology nowadays is working in the form of biometric templates which is, according to [1], a digital representation of the unique features (either physical or behavioural) of the raw image that is captured from the individual in question.

There are degrees of acceptability of various technologies. Although the fingerprinting technology has been truly an old and universal method, however, the other technology which is picking up a fast pace now is the iris recognition. The fingerprints are prone to faking, forgery and identity theft by the use of a synthetic material. For more information, readers can refer to article [2].

## 6.3.2    Iris recognition

In the nineteenth century, the iris technology was first introduced to confirm the identity of an individual. Compared with the face recognition, the iris is an overwhelmingly more reliable and accurate visual recognition partly because of the uniqueness of its features and variations in patterns. Iris of a person does not change over time and even genetically identical twins also have different irises. Thus more sophisticated computer software and hardware are required to capture and analyse the iris-based imaging technology. Complex mathematical algorithms have been developed to map the iris and later a unique barcode id is assigned to each individual. Iris recognition is nowadays considered as one of the most accurate biometric recognition techniques.

An image of an eye can be recorded with ease from some distance as the region that is under study is relatively small that makes it is user-friendly. However, the segmentation presents challenges as the focused area has some constraints.

Thomas *et al.* [3] presented a system which is claimed to be less constrained in terms of imaging conditions and their proposed scheme outperforms Hough transformed result in iris localization. It is gaining momentum now as a popular identification method due to its robustness.

### 6.3.3    Facial recognition

It is a sensor-based technology in which sensors of various types and digital video cameras are used to capture multiple images. Pictures are recorded in mono and multi-colours and then features which are unique in nature are analysed. The distances between vital parts of the face are measured. However, there are some serious issues and challenges attached to this technology which make it less reliable and accurate. Human face change over time due to ageing, weather, surgical operations and many other factors that make it a less desirable technology in biometrics.

A number of issues are reported in the literature on the challenges of using this technology. There is an accuracy of image collection; people use eyeglasses/contact lenses, forgery of faces represented as disguised, ageing and so on. The computing technology works basically on numbers such as binary data, etc. and deciphering and encrypting the image to a number for finding its exact one to one match is a cumbersome and complicated process. The error calculation estimate is not very accurate in this system.

### 6.3.4    Voice recognition

Voice or speech recognition is a way of voice communication using devices/ machines. The sounds of language, a minimal unit of sound, termed as 'voice phoneme' is used to distinguish between voices of two persons. Phonemes use vowels and consonants and then further branching of this classification. In the early nineteenth century, spectrographs were used to record the speech of a person for identification purpose. It is a biometric technology in which speech/voice recognition is performed and the telephone was used for this purpose earlier but these days the smartphones are also being used predominantly. Text-dependent and text-independent methods are used for voice recognition in a soundproof environment for maintaining a high quality of speech. Some standard voice recognition models are developed and used.

### 6.3.5    Ear recognition

Although human body experience changes due to ageing or some other disease-related issues, the ear is an exception to a much greater extent. It is amazingly virtually invariant and its characteristic features make it a suitable choice over fingerprint and other biometrics. Its images can be captured without the knowledge of the individual and moreover from some distance. Whether the uniqueness of the ear appearance is universal needs deeper understanding through empirical studies. The methods to recognize human using ear biometrics are still in the developmental stages now.

## 6.3.6    Hand geometry

The hand geometry consists of the measurement of hand features which include shape, size, palm, length and thickness of fingers, etc. It is one of the oldest methods of identification and verification and its application is found in historical records at least one hundred years old. Unlike other biometric methods, a person's willingness for recording his/her information is mandatory. The uniqueness of this method is acceptable to a certain degree of accuracy as variations of geometric features are observed over time or due to some accidents. Therefore, mainly it is used for the verification purposes only and it is used as a supplemental method to other more reliable methods.

## 6.3.7    Vein pattern recognition

Vein or vascular pattern recognition is a more sophisticated computerized contact-less biometric method compared to fingerprinting, hand geometry and others, etc. Images of blood vessels are transmitted using infrared light for either the dorsum of the hand or palm or fingers. These parts of the hand form a unique pattern among all human beings. Recently, software and hardware technologies have been developed a lot to improve the performance, accuracy and precision of the images. Its ease of use and fast and quick verification method make it a favourable choice.

## 6.3.8    Signature verification

This method has been in practice for a long time not only for the purpose of confirming the identity of individuals but also for more formal and legal business transactions in which signatures bind two parties. Digital signatures are also prevalent in business transactions in which the encrypted data in bit strings are transferred, authenticated and approved.

Nowadays, for signature recognition, a writing stylus pen is used for signature on a tablet and the transaction is completed through software and an attached camera. The signature is recognized by the system with the existing database. There is always a threat of duplication of signatures in visual appearance; however, the behavioural aspects of individuals such as pressure and speed at which a signature is carried out vary. In comparison with the other superior technologies such as iris, this recognition system has a number of inherent drawbacks. The demerits include the signature of a person can greatly change over time due to several physiological reasons. The use of neural network technology which can detect minute variations in the signature has greatly improved this recognition method. In spite of attempts to resolve and improve the system, its credibility relies heavily on the high quality of hardware and software needed for this technology which makes it less favourite compared with the other technologies.

## 6.3.9    Keystroke dynamics

This behavioural technology is considered among the simplest and quite reasonable in terms of the cost of implementing it. Moreover, no sophisticated training is needed for the users of this technology. All of us are unique in the way we type on a keyboard. Specialized software is used for recording our typing patterns.

## 6.3.10 Gesture biometrics

Gesture recognition works on identifying the human gestures which are captured using basically the infrared cameras which are mounted at a suitable angle. The cameras use electromagnetic radiations which are of invisible wavelengths to humans. The hand gestures are used for contactless interaction with devices and they are analysed. The hand gesture technology has made the life much easier as one can control the volume of an electronic device remotely without bothering to use a remote controller and they can choose what content to watch at their own ease.

Gesture recognition has witnessed a revolution with the conception of sixth sense technology proposed by Pranav Mistry, an Engineer-Scientist at Samsung Research America. The technology can be used for processing images by simply using some sensors attached to fingertips for establishing a connection between the digital and the physical worlds. The digital data, beyond the perception of human senses, can be made available in varied formats with the use of this technology.

## 6.4 Biometric authentication systems

It is largely believed that the advancement in computer technology, in general, has made life easier. The information is so accessible to each one of us that it is a mouse click away from us and the digitization of data is ubiquitous. However, these innovations and inventions pose several technologically inherent threats to its developers and consumers. The illegitimate and unauthorized access to one's personal and financial data is one of the major threats causing great losses to both individuals and organizations. Several methods of securing data are used such as highly encrypted codes, complex alpha-numeric passwords and ID cards. These measures have been partially successful; however, the cyber-attacks are also evidently on the rise. These attacks are mainly due to the vulnerability of these systems to attacks and their inherent security flaws.

A typical biometric system (Figure 6.1) consists of four basic components. The first component is the data/sample acquisition sensors through which the individuals' biometrics are scanned and produced its digital representation which is stored in the form of a template with user's identity in order to facilitate identification. The second component functionality is utilized with the use of the component called feature extraction. This module extracts the biometric features and stores these unique features of images into the form of a template with the user's identity in the database system. The third component is called the matching unit of the system which determines the relationship between the new biometric images collected with that of the template stored in the database. The fourth component is the decision module which makes the decision whether to accept the identity or not based on the matching criteria. This is performed under threshold-based authentication.

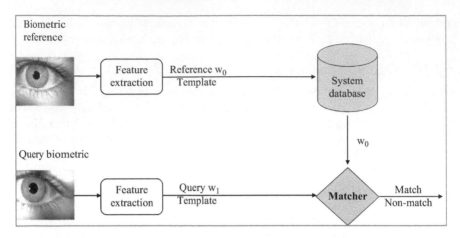

*Figure 6.1    Basic operation of biometric authentication system*

## 6.4.1    Biometric authentication system design

The design of a biometrics-based personal authentication system is a blueprint of a detailed and well-planned action plan. The functionality of a good design of a biometric device is determined by assessing whether or not the subject that is being verified is a true person itself or not. Schuckers and Michael [4] have outlined universality, uniqueness, permanence, collectability, performance, acceptability and circumvention as the seven characteristic features that a biometric ideally must have. Universality pertains to the majority of users who have that particular bio-metric. The uniqueness of fingerprints is mainly due to papillary ridges in skin patterns which make humans unique and it is true even in identical twins. Perma-nence is related with a trait which would remain intact over time. The collection of data quantitatively is termed as collectability. The ease of use of a biometric, minimizing error and processing terms are related to performance. A biometric which is relatively universal in acceptance by its users is called acceptability. Some biometrics are highly acceptable than others such as fingerprints. How foolproof/ theft-proof is the system is studied under circumvention. Generating copies of fingerprints, hand geometry and ear prints, etc. are highly unlikely for duplication.

## 6.4.2    Performance of biometric systems

The performance evaluation of biometric systems plays an important role in mak-ing correct decisions about the suitability and feasibility of a security system. False acceptance rate and false rejection rate provide the basic criteria in the assessment and evaluation of the performance of a system. The system is evaluated by passing several samples of genuine and fake identifications and a similarity score under a certain threshold is calculated and plotted. A comparison is performed to examine the accuracy of the system as shown in Table 6.1. A number of techniques derived from statistics and mathematics are used such as detection error trade-off and receiver operating characteristic depending upon the level of accuracy required.

Table 6.1  *Comparison between biometrics traits: high, medium and low are denoted by H, M and L, respectively* [5]

| Biometrics | University | Uniqueness | Permanence | Collectability | Performance | Acceptability | Circumvention |
|---|---|---|---|---|---|---|---|
| Face | H | L | M | H | L | H | L |
| Fingerprint | M | H | H | M | H | M | H |
| Hand geometry | M | M | M | H | M | M | M |
| Keystrokes | L | L | L | M | L | M | M |
| Hand veins | M | M | M | M | M | M | H |
| Iris | H | H | H | M | H | L | H |
| Retinal scan | H | H | M | L | H | L | H |
| Signature | L | L | L | H | L | H | L |
| Voice | M | L | L | M | L | H | L |
| Facial thermogram | H | H | L | H | M | H | H |
| Odour | H | H | H | L | L | M | L |
| DNA | H | H | H | L | H | L | L |
| Gait | M | L | L | H | L | H | M |
| Ear recognition | M | M | H | M | M | H | M |

## 6.4.3   Attacks on biometric authentication systems

The security of biometric systems is crucial in ensuring that the input sample to the biometric system was indeed that of its legitimate owner, and subsequently, the system indeed matched the input pattern with genuinely enrolled pattern samples [6]. The need and the development of biometric systems have grown significantly as the classical methods of patterns recognition do not simply offer the flexibility, convenience and capability. With the growing demand for security systems, the natural questions that come to mind are the data privacy issues and their security. Do we have full privacy for our personal and financial data? In spite of the robustness and viability of biometrics security, the systems are still considered vulnerable to all sorts of cyber-attacks and they are susceptible to all kinds of digital threats. A discussion on vulnerable points of biometric systems, threats and their countermeasures can be found in [7].

In the domain of biometrics, the biometric attacks have been broadly classified as direct and indirect due to several weak points in the system and at least eight such types have been identified so far [8,9]. Some of these attacks happen remotely without the imposter being physically available at the site.

Type 1 attack is basically presenting the fake identification using a synthetic material such as an artificial face or a finger. It happens at the point of capturing a sample using biometric sensors. A biometric sensor recognition system is used to capture the biometric image. The research studies such as [10,11] have tested a number of fingerprint sensors by creating dummy fingers.

The second attack type occurs between the process of capturing the sample and sending it through to the feature extractor unit. While the extractor module attempts to receive the captured image for matching with the existing database template, the image is intercepted and the process is hindered and the previously stored image from the original database is displayed. The sensor is by-passed in the entire process, and the more-sophisticated and intelligent is the sensor the lesser is the likelihood of being attacked.

The third type of attack occurs at the feature extractor. A feature extraction unit of a biometric recognition system is used to extract the qualitative area of the image which is vital for the identification purpose. The ability of feature extractor is obstructed and the intruder forces it to generate fake values, not the features based on the primary genuine database.

The communication between feature extractor and the matcher module is disabled by the imposter causing the attack type 4. The feature values of the user are stolen. A biometric matcher unit is used to primarily perform matching and comparing the biometric features of an image and providing the output using some match score criteria. The output score represents the similarity or dissimilarity of the two captured biometric images.

The decision-making unit, based on the values generated by the matcher module, decides how closely the two images are related. Irrespective of the values generated, the matcher module is tampered to produce fake values which result in an attack type 5. This attack occurs at match module unit.

The attack 6 happens when an unreal template is added to the system or the existing one is unlawfully modified by imposters. In this type of attack, the biometric template is either altered or stolen which happens between the match module and the storage in the main database. The security of the database is breached intelligently with the deep knowledge of the intricacies of the system.

The attack type 7 is due to the tampering of the template being transmitted. An imposter attacks the template and attempts to alter the original message at the time of transmission between the matcher module and the source database.

The acceptance or rejection decision has tampered and this is called type 8 attack. The matching criterion is invaded and the false match score is transmitted.

Currently, the research in this area is intense and several techniques have been investigated. The authors in [66] outlined some countermeasures and models such as the Naïve model and complex model for thwarting biometric attacks. The point 1 attack type can be handled by introducing finger conductivity/pulse sensing behaviour. By placing the biometric components in a secure place can also be effective in overcoming the attacks mentioned above. A countermeasure method to tackle the problems of faking in fingerprinting [12] is presented. The method based on back propagation neural network (BPNN) is used to detect the perspiration pattern of a finger to overcome fake biometric attacks. The sweating pattern is quantified to measure the vitality of the fingerprint.

The modern biometric methods by far demonstrate the most effective authentication and verification in the identification process, still, the challenges of ensuring the robust and 100% secured systems are yet to be seen. The hardware, software and human resources need to work in cohesion in order to effectively operate these security systems. In spite of its vulnerabilities to attacks, they are still preferred over passwords, pins and other traditional identifications procedures.

## 6.5    Biometric template protection techniques

Recently, biometric systems are embedded in smart devices such as smartphones and tablets. Despite the proliferation of biometric systems in various applications, the utilization of biometric raises several security, privacy and integrity concerns:

- *Security:* The biometric template may be replaced by a Trojan horse program that produces pre-determined feature sets and the legitimate biometric template may be replaced with synthetic template.
- *Secrecy:* The biometric is not secret, can be easily recorded and misused without the user's explicit knowledge. Face and iris can be easily captured using infrared cameras, user left information about their fingerprint in the surfaces, and voice can be recorded.
- *Renewability:* The biometrics is permanently associated with the user and cannot be renewed if it is compromised. Unlike the password and the key, user has limited number of bio-passwords [13].

- *Cross-matching*: If a biometric template is hacked once, it is compromised forever and hence cannot be used for all applications where the biometric is used.

Biometric template protection techniques are designed to bridge the gap between the exactitude of cryptographic techniques and the fuzziness of biometrics and ensure the desired security, privacy and integrity [14]. There are two main approaches to protect biometric template and commonly categorized as biometric cryptosystems and cancellable biometrics [15].

### 6.5.1  Biometric cryptosystems

Biometric cryptosystems are designed to securely binding a digital key to a biometric data or generate a digital key from biometric data [15,16]. Biometric cryptosystems offer solutions to the stored template attack and achieve substantial security [17] and the biometric template matching is performed indirectly. Biometric cryptosystem is often referred to as helper data [6], which is typically constructed by combining techniques from cryptography and error correcting code areas. In the biometric cryptosystem framework (Figure 6.2), the system consists of two phases' registration and authentication. In the registration phase, the biometric reference template $w_0$ is concealed along with the encoded key $C_0$ using the function $F(w_0, c_0) = (HD, f(c_0))$, where the public information, the Helper Data $HD$ and $f(c_0)$, ($f$ is a cryptographic algorithm) are stored in the system database. At the authentication phase, the biometric query template $w_1$ which is sufficiently close to the reference template $w_0$ according to a suitable metric distance $M_d(w_0, w_1)$ and not necessarily identical should generate the code word $c_1$ and then the key $k$ using

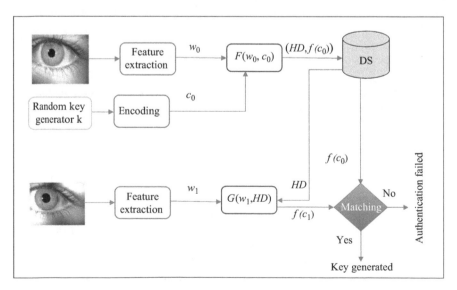

*Figure 6.2    Basic operation of biometric cryptosystems*

the generation function $G(w_1, HD)$. The key will be generated if the biometric matches successfully by testing the $f(c_1)$ against the stored $f(c_0)$. However, it has theoretically been proved that it is computationally infeasible to extract the key $k$ or the biometric reference template $w_0$ from the public information $F(w_0, c_0)$ and the attacker is able to authenticate himself/herself using different biometric template $w_2$ such that $M_d(w_0, w_2)$ is greater than the threshold of the system in probability time only if he/she is able to break the cryptographic algorithm [18].

There are two biometric key binding cryptosystem approaches: firstly when the randomly key generated is securely bounded to the biometric template, and the other approach is when a key is generated from the biometric template. Examples of key binding are fuzzy commitment scheme [19], fuzzy vault scheme [20], and key generation examples secure sketch [21] and fuzzy extractor [22].

### 6.5.1.1   Fuzzy commitment scheme: application implementation

In 1999, Jules and Wattenberg [19] combined well-known techniques from the areas of cryptography and error-correcting codes to achieve a new cryptographic primitive referred to fuzzy commitment scheme. In the fuzzy commitment scheme, the function $F$ is defined as $F(w_0, c_0) = (w_0 - c_0, h(c_0))$, where $h$ is a cryptographic hash function. Each $w_1$, which is sufficiently close to $w_0$ according to appropriate metric distance $M_d(w_0, w_1)$, should be able to construct the code word $c_1 = w_1 - (w_0 - c_0)$ with $M_d(c_0, c_1) = M_d(w_0, w_1)$. A hash of the result $h(c_1)$ is tested against the stored $h(c_0)$.

The fuzzy commitment scheme was applied to different biometric traits (Table 6.2). The scheme was applied to iris-based biometric authentication system by Hao *et al.* [23]. During the enrolment, a 140-bit cryptographic key $k_0$ is bounded and retrieved using a 2,048-bit iris reference template $w_0$, the key is prepared with Hadamard and Reed–Solomon error correction codes to produce $c_0$. The iris template $w_0$ and the code word $c_0$ are input for the function $F(w_0, k_0) = (w_0 \oplus c_0, h(k_0))$ and the result is stored in the system database, where $\oplus$ is the

*Table 6.2   Application and implementation of the fuzzy commitment scheme*

|  | [23] | [24] | [25] | [26] | [27] | [28] |
|---|---|---|---|---|---|---|
| Biometric characteristics | Iris | Iris | Face | Finger vein | Gait | Iris |
| Error correction code | Hadamard and Reed–Solomon | Hadamard and Reed–Solomon | BCH | Product codes | BCH | Reed–Solomon |
| Complexity of the algorithm | MD5 | SAH-1 | SHA-256 | – | SHA | – |
| Cryptography key length (bit) | 140 | 128 | 36 | – | 139 | 400 |
| Sample size | 70 | About 100 | 68 | 60 | 38 | – |
| FA/FR rates (%) | 0/0.47 | 0/4.64 | 0/30 | 0.01/4.3 | 0/16.2 | 0/3.75 |

bitwise xorring. At the authentication, a 2048-bit iris query template $w_1$ extracted and xorred with $c_1 = w_1 \oplus (w_0 \oplus c_0)$. According to Reed–Solomon and Hadamard decoding a 140-bit cryptographic key generated $k_1$, hashed if $h(k_1) = h(k_0)$ the authentication is successful and the cryptographic is generated $k_1 = k_0$. The system was evaluated using iris samples from 70 different eyes, with 10 samples from each eye. Rathgeb and Uhl [24] provide a systematic approach to the construction of iris-based biometric, Reed–Solomon and Hadamard codes are applied. In different work [29], the authors extracted iris template using context-based reliable component selection and then bounded to Hadamard code words in order to apply fuzzy commitment scheme. Adamovic *et al.* [30] extracted homogeneous regions of high entropy from iris biometrics and applied to fuzzy commitment scheme. Further iris-based biometric cryptosystems are proposed [31–33] to improve the performance of the system.

Fuzzy commitment scheme was applied to fingerprint-based biometric. Teoh and Kim [34] applied a randomized dynamic quantization transformation to binaries fingerprint features extracted from a multichannel Gabor filter. Feature vectors of 375 bits are extracted and Reed–Solomon codes are applied to construct the fuzzy commitment scheme. Nandakumar [35] obtained a binary fixed-length of fingerprint minutiae points by quantizing the Fourier-phase spectrum of a minutia set and used it in a fuzzy commitment scheme. A vein extraction technique adapted to template protection and used it to apply a fuzzy commitment scheme [36]. A fuzzy commitment scheme is also applied to face [25,37,38], online signature [39] and gait [27].

### 6.5.1.2 Fuzzy vault scheme and implementation

In 2002, Juels and Sudan [20] derived a new cryptographic primitive known as fuzzy vault based on polynomial reconstruction problem. The basic operation of fuzzy vault from fuzzy commitment scheme [19] is designed to enhance the security and privacy of biometric template. In the fuzzy vault, the cryptographic key $k$ encoded using a polynomial $P$ ($k$ formed the coefficients of $P$). The function $F$ computes as follows: the biometric template $w_0$ projected onto the polynomial $P$, i.e. $P(w_0)$. Additionally, chaff points $R$ are added in order to obscure genuine points of the polynomial $(w_0, P(w_0))$, the helper data $HD = R \cup \{(w_0, P(w_0))\}$ as output of $F$, where $R$ is a set of chaff points. Each set $(w_1, P(w_1))$ overlaps the set with $(w_0, P(w_0))$ to a certain extent in order to locate a sufficient amount of points in $HD$ that lie on $P$. Applying error correction codes, $P$ can be reconstructed and, thus $k$.

The fuzzy vault was applied to different biometric traits. The first implementation of fuzzy vault was done by Clancy *et al.* [40], by encoding a 128-bit random key using Reed–Solomon codes. Several other approaches to address this problem are suggested [41–46] such as the original concept of fingerprint fuzzy vault in terms of using the polynomial [47–50]. Chaff points generation algorithms for fuzzy vault have been proposed [51–56] to improve the security of the biometric template and the key. In other work, fuzzy vault applied and implemented to iris biometrics [57–60], to face [61], to palm [62,63] and to online signature [64].

## 6.5.2   Cancellable Biometrics

Cancellable biometrics are referred to as a feature transformation which are designed in a way that it should be computationally hard to recover the original biometric [15] (Figure 6.3). Cancellable biometric applies a one way function to biometric image or template and matches the transformed template forms. In the cancellable biometrics, a one-way function $T(w_0, p_0)$ is applied to the biometric template or biometric image using a parameter $p_0$ (key or password), whereas the transformed template or image is stored in the database system as $CB_0$, the transformation parameter is stored secret as $p_0$. During authentication, the same transformation applies to the query $w_1$ with the same parameter $p_0$, $T(w_1, p_0)$. The result is transformed biometric $CB_1$ which is compared with the stored $CB_0$. Thus, the biometric matching takes place indirectly in terms of transformed forms. In addition, correlation of several transformed templates must not reveal any information about the original biometrics [15]. Cancellable biometrics are classified into two main categories, namely, non-invertible transformations and biometric salting [6,15].

*Non-invertible transforms*: Non-invertible transforms are usually one way transformation functions that are easy to compute but computationally hard to invert. In these transforms, biometric image or template is modified into a new form using parameters such as password or random key in order to update the biometric data. The merit of applying these transformations is that it is hard for an

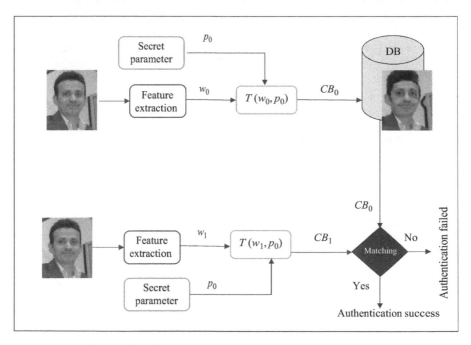

*Figure 6.3   Basic operation of cancellable biometrics*

attacker to recover the original biometric if the transformation is compromised. The disadvantage of non-invertible transforms tends to compromise discriminability of the transformed templates, thereby a decrease in the performance [65].

The first work of a non-invertible transform was presented by Ratha *et al.* [66]. In further work, multiple cancellable biometrics were constructed from fingerprint data [67,68] and from iris biometric [69] using different non-invertible transformations. Hämmerle *et al.* [70] applied the transformation to iris biometric suggested in [69]. In [71], non-invertible transformation applied to iris biometric using row permutations to obtain iris cancellable biometric. Cancellable templates from online signature obtained using linear convolution of sequences [72–74]. Boult *et al.* [75,76] proposed cryptographically secure technique biotokens, which is called Biotope$^{TM}$, uses a feature space transformation applied to fingerprint and face. Further work in cancellable biometric is applied to iris biometric [77] and fingerprint [78].

*Biometric salting*: Biometric salting usually denotes transforms of biometric templates which are selected to be invertible [15] in which the transformation parameters have to be kept secret and have to present at each authentication. BioHashing technique [79] is a kind of biometric salting in which a pseudo random number is binding with biometric template to generate Biocodes. In this technique, biometric templates are projected on an orthonormal random matrix generated by pseudo random number followed by a two level quantization using thresholding function which results in binary codes called BioCodes. Teoh *et al.* [80] proposed a new BioHashing technique referred to MRP to obtain cancellable fingerprint. In further subsequent research studies, some methods have been proposed to generate cancellable features from face [81], speech [82], and online signature. Kuan *et al.* [83] proposed a method to generate cancellable keys out of dynamic hand signatures based on the random mixing step. Wang and Hu [84] developed a blind system identification approach to the design of alignment free cancellable fingerprint templates. Recently, Zhe *et al.* [85] proposed a ranking-based locality sensitive hashing inspired two-factor cancellable biometrics, dubbed 'Index-of-Max' (IoM) hashing for fingerprint biometric template.

## 6.6    Biometric-based remote user authentication

Remote user authentication is an essential tool for granting access control in various digital environment applications such as e-commerce, e-banking, e-government, e-passport, e-health and a number of forensic applications. Many researchers proposed different types of remote user authentication schemes based on requirements. A password-based user authentication using smart card is the most popular system which is known as t-factor authentication system. However, people use simple passwords, which are pretty easy to crack or complex passwords, which are difficult to remember. Furthermore, a common user with more than one account in different applications will have to remember multiple passwords. Finally, some people use the same password for multiple accounts, if that password is compromised, it may provide access to their entire online world.

It is obvious for every organization that securing information is of special significance. The limitations of the traditional authentication mechanisms can be mitigated by incorporation of highly secure methods, biometrics. There are sundry biometric based remote user authentication schemes using smart cards presented in the literature. Accordingly, such schemes should satisfy the following desirable security and functionality requirements [86]:

- *Resist tampering with stored biometric templates attacks*: A tampering with a stored biometric template attack is when the user's biometric template can be modified by the attacker's template in the system database to gain server authentication.
- *Resist stolen biometrics template attacks*: If the user's biometric template stored in the system is stolen by an attacker, she/he can use it for other purposes.
- *Resist privileged insider attacks*: A privileged insider attack is when the registration centre receives the user's password and biometric data in the registration phase.
- *Resist smart card attack*: Assume that the smart card of the user is lost or stolen. The attacker having the smart card has no way to retrieve the sensitive information saved in the card.
- *User anonymity property*: An important security arising as a result of remote user authentication is the confidentiality of the user's identity. For obvious reasons, it is desirable to keep this information secret from attackers.
- *Resist masquerade attacks*: An attacker may try to masquerade as a legitimate user to communicate with a valid system or masquerade as a valid system in order to communicate with users.
- *Resist replay attacks*: An attacker tries to hold up the messages between the user and the server and then impersonate other legal party to replay the fake messages for further deceptions.
- *Resist man-in-the-middle attacks*: An attacker may intercept the messages during transmissions and then can change or delete or modify the contents of the messages delivered to the recipients.
- *Resist denial-of-service attacks*: If an attacker blocks the messages from reaching the server and the users, the server as well as the users should know about malicious dropping of such control messages.
- *Provide proper verification*: The system should provide proper user verification at login phase.
- *Provide mutual authentication*: The scheme provide mutual authentication between the user and the server and after successful authentication, a secret session key should be established between them for further communication.
- *Efficiency*: The schemes should be efficient in terms of communication and computational overheads.
- *Freely change credentials*: The schemes should support that the user freely change the password, if it is compromised.

### 6.6.1 Biometric-based remote user authentication systems using smart cards

Biometrics-based remote user authentication schemes are protocols in which a remote server verifies the legitimacy of a user over an unsecured communication channel using his biometric data. The schemes rely on passwords or biometric or both. The schemes employ the conventional biometric authentication systems. Typically schemes consists of four phases, namely, the registration phase, the login phase, the authentication and key agreement phase and the change password phase.

In the registration phase, the user registers his/her ID, password and biometric with the server. The server performs the necessary steps to secure the user's credentials and loads it to the user's smart card.

In the login phase, the user presents his/her smart card, password and biometrics in order to login to the system. If the system verifies the user, the smart card performs some operation and passed the login message to the server for authentication.

In the authentication phase, when the server receives the login message, the server system performs several steps. After the user authenticated, the server and user communicate several messages which will lead to establish session secret key.

In the password change phase, this phase invoked whenever the user wants to change his/her old password to a new one. First, the user has to verify his biometrics, if it is a success then the user can change the old password by following some steps.

Numerous developments to remote user authentication schemes using smart cards based on biometric technology have been introduced. In 2002, Lee *et al.* [87] introduced fingerprint to the remote user authentication using smart card based on ElGamal's public key cryptosystem to improve the security of the password methods schemes. In 2004, Lin and Lai [87] identified that the scheme proposed by Lee *et al.* is vulnerable to masquerade attack and proposed a new scheme. Khan and Zhang [88] improved the security of Lin and Lai's scheme which performs only unilateral authentication (not mutual authentication) and they proposed an improved scheme.

### 6.6.2 Biometric template protection-based remote user authentication systems using smart cards

Utilization of conventional biometric technology in the remote user authentication systems leads to a privacy and security concerns against the misuse and storage of biometric data. Biometric template protection techniques discussed in Section 6.5, biometric cryptosystems and cancellable addressing these concerns and improving the public confidence of acceptance biometrics [15]. Therefore, it is important to protect the biometric data using cryptography (biometric template protection) in remote user authentication schemes.

Several biometrics-based remote user authentication schemes using smart cards have been proposed in the literature [86,89–97]. A number of biometric-based remote user authentication schemes have been put forward for different applications such as secure multi-server environments [98–102] and telecare medicine information system [103–105]. A robust three-factor remote user authentication schemes are proposed in [106] and [107] using discrete logarithm problem and elliptic curve cryptosystem, respectively. Li and Hwang [86] proposed an efficient biometric-based remote user authentication scheme using smart cards, but Li *et al.* [89] and Das [90] found that Li and Hwang's scheme had some security and design flaws and proposed two different and improved schemes based on the traditional biometrics technology. In these cases, the user biometric template is matched against the template stored in the system database with other security improvements to overcome the detected flaws. Later, An [91] pointed out that Das's scheme was still insecure against password guessing, user impersonation and insider attacks and presented an improved scheme. In 2013, Khan and Kumari [92] showed that there existed loopholes in An's scheme which would be detrimental for security and proposed an improved biometric based remote user authentication scheme with the user anonymity property eradicating the flaws of An's scheme. Recently, Sarvabhatla *et al.* [93] and Wen *et al.* [97] demonstrated that Khan and Kumari's scheme is insecure against password guessing attacks and user impersonation attacks and subsequently two new schemes are proposed, respectively, to overcome the security weakness.

The above-mentioned schemes make use of user's biometrics to protect the user's password and enhance the user's secrecy and privacy. Unfortunately, the usage of biometrics verification in [86,91–93,97] schemes fail to provide proper biometrics authentication because of the direct implementation of the cryptographic hash function on the biometric templates as two biometrics readings of the same feature are rarely identical. Li *et al.* [89] and Das [90] schemes do not protect the stored biometric templates because of the usage of traditional biometrics verification. To overcome these issues, biometric cryptosystems are designed to provide proper authentication and protect the stored biometric templates. In 2015, Das and Goswami [94] presented a robust biometric-based remote user authentication scheme using smart cards. The biometric template is protected using fuzzy extractor techniques and BiohHashing. However, their scheme is costly in terms of communication and computation overheads and it requires the user to remember a complex password. Zhao *et al.* [96] presented a new technology called a fuzzy negotiation structure based on well-known fuzzy extractor technology for securing a body sensor network (BSN). In the initiation of the structure, each biosensor node is preloaded with secret keys in order to secure and verify the commitment. While implementing the fuzzy negotiation structure in the scenario of remote user authentication is a solution, it tends to be complicated because the user and server should agree about secret key before starting the protocol. Qi and Tang [95] developed a new biometrics authentication scheme for session initiation protocol using a fuzzy extractor technique. However, the Roy *et al.* and Qi and Tang schemes have high computational and communication costs.

## 6.7 Challenges and research in biometrics cloud

In the last decade, the proliferation of online services in the fields of Internet of Things (IoT) and cloud computing have tremendously changed the way we live and work. In the cloud computing, users are unlikely to be aware of the location of their data and, consequently, this raises several (known and unresolved) challenges

[108]. Several security issues, requirements and challenges that associated with holding data in cloud service providers are discussed [108,109]: (1) Is the cloud service provider compliant with national laws and standards?; (2) Does the cloud service provider ensure that destroyed biometric data are no longer available in the cloud in any form and no any other copy exists after deletion?; (3) Does the cloud service provider inform the user about where the data is stored?; and (4) Does the cloud service provider notify the user when privacy breaches occur?

This highlights the increasing need to design a secure authentication system in a cloud-computing environment to ensure the security and privacy. Biometric authentication methods can replace the traditional password and personal identification number authentication methods because of their advantages over remembering hundreds or tens of passwords every day. However, the biometric data/template is highly susceptible to a number of security and privacy attacks as discussed in the previous section. The biometric template protection schemes have been identified as potential solutions for securing biometric data/template. For instance, biometric cryptosystems can provide protection to the template as well as generate securely a cryptographic key which can be used in the cloud instead of the password. On the other hand, the cancellable biometrics can provide a solution to revoking the biometric data of the person when the cancellable biometric is compromised. Furthermore, it was pointed out that there are a number of challenges in offering Biometric-as-a Service (BaaS).

In recent years, several research papers for biometric technologies deployment in the cloud have been written. In 2013, Yuan and Yu [110] proposed an efficient privacy-preserving biometric identification scheme which achieves efficiency by exploiting the power of cloud computing. In their scheme, the biometric database is encrypted and outsourced to the cloud servers. To perform a biometric identification, the database owner generates a credential for the candidate biometric trait and submits it to the cloud. The cloud servers perform identification over the encrypted database using the credential and return the result to the owner. However, Zhu *et al.* [111] observed that the encrypted data set in Yuan's scheme can be broken by the collusion attack without deducing the key. In 2015, Wang *et al.* [112] investigated the privacy-preserving biometric identification outsourcing problem and proposed the scheme CloudBI-II which used random diagonal matrices to realize biometric identification. Later, the authors in [113] identified several serious attacks in Wang *et al.*' scheme. Recently, in [114], the authors examined the biometric identification scheme [110] and showed its insufficiencies and security weakness under the proposed level-3 attack. To improve the security, in their scheme, an efficient privacy-preserving biometric identification outsourcing scheme has been proposed.

## 6.8   Conclusion

In this chapter, the need and significance of biometric authentication have been highlighted as it is becoming an essential tool for granting access control in various digital environment applications. The challenges of traditional methods of user authentication which are based on password and token, etc. have also been discussed as well as the privacy of data. This chapter primarily focused on the biometric authentication systems which help to prevent unauthorized access to the local server and cloud resources. A historical overview of biometrics was given followed by some details of physiological and behavioural biometrics modalities along with the performance of each biometric modality. Furthermore, biometric authentication system procedures along with the performance measures are discussed, and then different known attacks that can be encountered by a biometric authentication system are also highlighted with illustrations. A survey of the techniques of biometric template protection systems is presented for the protection of biometric data from different attacks. How biometric technology can be deployed into remote user authentication has also been investigated. The chapter was concluded with the presentation of some case studies and research challenges of integrating the biometric authentication systems on the cloud computing and IoT technologies.

# References

[1]   Das, R.: 'Biometric Technology: Authentication, Biocryptography, and Cloud-Based Architecture' (Boca Raton, FL:CRC Press, 2014, 1st edn.).

[2]   Uludag, U., and Jain, A.K.: 'Attacks on biometric systems: A case study in fingerprints', in 'Proc. SPIE 5306, Security, Steganography, and Watermarking of Multimedia Contents' (2004), p. 622.

[3]   Thomas, T., George, A., and Devi, K.P.I.: 'Effective iris recognition system' *Procedia Technol.*, 2016, **25**, pp. 464–472.

[4]   Schuckers, M.E.: 'Some statistical aspects of biometric identification device performance' *Stats*, 2002, **33**, (3), pp. 3–7.

[5]   Jain, A.K., Ross, A., and Pankanti, S.: 'Biometrics: A tool for information security' *IEEE Trans. Inf. Forensics Secur.*, 2006, **1**, (2), pp. 125–143.

[6]   Nandakumar, K., Jain, A.K., and Nagar, A.: 'Biometric template security' *EURASIP J. Adv. Signal Process.*, 2008, **2008**, Article ID 579416, pp. 1–17.

[7]   Omar Alaswad, A., Montaser, A.H., and Elhashmi Mohamad, F.: 'Vulnerabilities of biometric authentication "threats and countermeasures"' *Int. J. Inf. Comput. Technol.*, 2014, **4**, (10), pp. 947–958.

[8]   Ratha, N.K., Connell, J.H., and Bolle, R.M.: 'An analysis of minutiae matching strength' *Audio-Video-Based Biometric Pers. Authentication*, 2001, **2091**, pp. 223–228.

[9]   Dugelay, J.L., Junqua, J.C., Kotropoulos, C., Kuhn, R., Perronnin, F., and Pitas, I.: 'Recent advances in biometric person authentication' *ICASSP, IEEE Int. Conf. Acoust. Speech Signal Process. - Proc.*, 2002, **4**, pp. 4060–4063.

[10]  Putte, T., and Keuning, J.: 'Biometrical fingerprint recognition: Don't get your fingers burned', in 'Smart Card Research and Advanced Applications' (2000), pp. 289–303.

[11]  Matsumoto, T., Matsumoto, H., Yamada, K., and Hoshino, S.: 'Impact of artificial "Gummy" fingers on fingerprint systems', in 'SPIE' (2002), p. 148.

[12]    Derakhshani, R., Schuckers, S.A.C., Hornak, L.A., and O'Gorman, L.: 'Determination of vitality from a non-invasive biomedical measurement for use in fingerprint scanners' *Pattern Recognit.*, 2003, **36**, (2), pp. 383–396.

[13]    Al-Saggaf, A.A.: 'Crisp commitment scheme based on noisy channels', in 'Saudi International Electronics, Communications and Photonics Conference 2011, SIECPC 2011' (2011).

[14]    Nandakumar, K., and Jain, A.K.: 'Biometric template protection: Bridging the performance gap between theory and practice' *IEEE Signal Process. Mag.*, 2015, **32**, (5), pp. 88–100.

[15]    Rathgeb, C., and Uhl, A.: 'A survey on biometric cryptosystems and cancelable biometrics' *EURASIP J. on Info. Security*, 2011, **2011**, (3), https://doi.org/10.1186/1687-417X-2011-3.

[16]    Cavoukian, A., and Stoianov, A.: 'Biometric encryption' *Biometric Technol. Today*, 2007, **15**, (3), p. 11.

[17]    Jain, A.K., Ross, A., and Uludag, U.: 'Biometric template security: Challenges and solutions' *Secur. Watermarking Multimed.*, 2002, **4675**, (IV), pp. 629–640.

[18]    Al-Saggaf, A.A., and Haridas, A.: 'Statistical hiding fuzzy commitment scheme for securing biometric templates' *Int. J. Comput. Netw. Inf. Secur.*, 2013, **5**, (4), pp. 8–16.

[19]    Juels, A., and Wattenberg, M.: 'A fuzzy commitment scheme', in 'Proceedings of the 6th ACM Conference on Computer and Communications Security – CCS '99' (1999), pp. 28–36.

[20]    Juels, A., and Sudan, M.: 'A fuzzy vault scheme' *Des. Codes, Cryptogr.*, 2006, **38**, (2), pp. 237–257.

[21]    Chang, Y., Zhang, W., and Chen, T.: 'Biometrics-based cryptographic key generation' Int. Conf. Multimed. Expo, 2004, pp. 2203–2206.

[22]    Dodis, Y., Reyzin, L., and Smith, A.: 'Fuzzy extractors', in 'Security with Noisy Data: On Private Biometrics, Secure Key Storage and Anti-Counterfeiting' (2007), pp. 79–99.

[23]    Hao, F., Anderson, R., and Daugman, J.: 'Combining cryptography with biometrics effectively' *IEEE Trans. Comput.*, 2006, **55**, (9), pp. 1081–1088.

[24]    Rathgeb, C., and Uhl, A.: 'Systematic construction of iris-based fuzzy commitment schemes', in 'Lecture Notes in Computer Science (including subseries Lecture Notes in Artificial Intelligence and Lecture Notes in Bioinformatics)' (2009), pp. 940–949.

[25]    Lu, H., Martin, K., Bui, F., Plataniotis, K.N., and Hatzinakos, D.: 'Face recognition with biometric encryption for privacy-enhancing self-exclusion', in 'DSP 2009: 16th International Conference on Digital Signal Processing, Proceedings' (2009).

[26]    Favre, M.S.P.B.: 'Balancing is the key: Performing finger vein template protection using fuzzy commitment', in '2015 International Conference on Information Systems Security and Privacy (ICISSP)' (2015).

[27]    Hoang, T., Choi, D., and Nguyen, T.: 'Gait authentication on mobile phone using biometric cryptosystem and fuzzy commitment scheme' *Int. J. Inf. Secur.*, 2015, **14**, (6), pp. 549–560.

[28]    Adamovic, and S.M.M.M.V.: 'Fuzzy commitment scheme for generation of cryptographic keys based on iris biometrics' *IET Biometrics*, 2017, **6**, (2), pp. 89–96.

[29]    Rathgeb, C., and Uhl, A.: 'Context-based biometric key generation for Iris' *IET Comput. Vis.*, 2011, **5**, (6), p. 389.

[30]    Adamovic, S., Milosavljevic, M., Veinovic, M., Sarac, M., and Jevremovic, A.: 'Fuzzy commitment scheme for generation of cryptographic keys based on iris biometrics' *IET Biometrics*, 2017, **6**, (2), pp. 89–96.

[31]    Zhang, L., Sun, Z., Tan, T., and Hu, S.: 'Robust biometric key extraction based on iris cryptosystem', in 'Lecture Notes in Computer Science (including subseries Lecture Notes in Artificial Intelligence and Lecture Notes in Bioinformatics)' (2009), pp. 1060–1069.

[32]    Ignatenko, T., and Willems, F.: 'Achieving secure fuzzy commitment scheme for optical PUFs', in 'IIH-MSP 2009 – 2009 5th International Conference on Intelligent Information Hiding and Multimedia Signal Processing' (2009), pp. 1185–1188.

[33]    Cimato, S., Gamassi, M., Piuri, V., Sassi, R., and Scotti, F.: 'A multi-biometric verification system for the privacy protection of iris templates', in 'Advances in Soft Computing' (2009), pp. 227–234.

[34]    Teoh, A.B.J., and Jaihie, K.: 'Secure biometric template protection in fuzzy Commitment scheme' *IEICE Electron. Express*, 2007, **4**, (23), pp. 724–730.

[35]    Nandakumar, K.: 'Fingerprint matching based on minutiae phase spectrum', in 'Proceedings – 2012 5th IAPR International Conference on Biometrics, ICB 2012' (2012), pp. 216–221.

[36]    Favre, M., Picard, S., Bringer, J., and Hervé, C.: 'Balancing is the key: Performing finger vein template protection using fuzzy commitment', in '2015 International Conference on Information Systems Security and Privacy (ICISSP)' (2015).

[37]    van der Veen, M., Kevenaar, T., Schrijen, G.-J., Akkermans, T.H., and Zuo, F.: 'Face biometrics with renewable templates', in 'Security, Steganography, and Watermarking of Multimedia Contents' (2006), p. 60720J.

[38]    Ao, M., and Li, S.Z.: 'Near infrared face based biometric key binding', in 'Lecture Notes in Computer Science (including subseries Lecture Notes in Artificial Intelligence and Lecture Notes in Bioinformatics)' (2009), pp. 376–385.

[39]    Maiorana, E., Campisi, P., and Neri, A.: 'User adaptive fuzzy commitment for signature template protection and renewability' *J. Electron. Imaging*, 2008, **17**, (1), pp. 1–12.

[40]    Clancy, T.C., Kiyavash, N., and Lin, D.J.: 'Secure smartcardbased fingerprint authentication', in 'Proceedings of the 2003 ACM SIGMM Workshop on Biometrics Methods and Applications – WBMA '03' (2003), p. 45.

[41]    Li, P., Yang, X., Cao, K., Tao, X., Wang, R., and Tian, J.: 'An alignment-free fingerprint cryptosystem based on fuzzy vault scheme' *J. Netw. Comput. Appl.*, 2010, **33**, (3), pp. 207–220.

[42]  Chung, Y., Moon, D., Lee, S., Jung, S., Kim, T., and Ahn, D.: 'Automatic alignment of fingerprint features for fuzzy fingerprint vault', in 'International Conference on Information Security and Cryptology' (2005), pp. 358–369.

[43]  Yang, S., and Verbauwhede, I.: 'Automatic secure fingerprint verification system based on fuzzy vault scheme', in 'ICASSP, IEEE International Conference on Acoustics, Speech and Signal Processing – Proceedings' (2005).

[44]  Uludag, U., and Jain, A.: 'Securing fingerprint template: Fuzzy vault with helper data', in 'Proceedings of the IEEE Computer Society Conference on Computer Vision and Pattern Recognition' (2006).

[45]  Uludag, U., and Jain, A.K.: 'Fuzzy fingerprint vault', in: Kanade T., Jain A., Ratha N.K. (eds) Audio- and Video-Based Biometric Person Authentication. AVBPA 2005. Lecture Notes in Computer Science, vol 3546. Springer, Berlin, Heidelberg, 20054.

[46]  Nandakumar, K., Jain, A.K., and Pankanti, S.: 'Fingerprint-based fuzzy vault: Implementation and performance' *IEEE Trans. Inf. Forensics Secur.*, 2007, **2**, (4), pp. 744–757.

[47]  Arakala, A.: 'Secure and private fingerprint-based authentication' *Bull. Aust. Math. Soc.*, 2009, **80**, (2), pp. 347–349.

[48]  Nagar, A., Nandakumar, K., and Jain, A.K.: 'Securing fingerprint template: Fuzzy vault with minutiae descriptors', in '2008 19th International Conference on Pattern Recognition' 2008, pp. 1–4.

[49]  Nagar, A., and Chaudhury, S.: 'Biometrics based asymmetric cryptosystem design using modified fuzzy vault scheme', in 'Proceedings – International Conference on Pattern Recognition' (2006), pp. 537–540.

[50]  Daesung, M., Choi, W.Y., Kiyoung, M., and Yongwha, C.: 'Fuzzy fingerprint vault using multiple polynomials', in 'Digest of Technical Papers – IEEE International Conference on Consumer Electronics' (2009), pp. 290–293.

[51]  Dellys, H.N., Benadjimi, N., Boubakeur, M.R., Sliman, L., and Ali, F.: 'Fingerprint fuzzy vault chaff point generation by squares method', in 'Proceedings of the 2015 7th International Conference of Soft Computing and Pattern Recognition, SoCPaR 2015' (2016), pp. 357–362.

[52]  Nguyen, M.T., Truong, Q.H., and Dang, T.K.: 'Enhance fuzzy vault security using nonrandom chaff point generator' *Inf. Process. Lett.*, 2016, **116**, (1), pp. 53–64.

[53]  Ha, Y., Nguyen, T.H., Li, R., and Wang, Y.: 'Performance and security-enhanced fuzzy vault scheme based on ridge features for distorted fingerprints' *IET Biometrics*, 2015, **4**, (1), pp. 29–39.

[54]  Dang, T.K., Nguyen, M.T., and Truong, Q.H.: 'Chaff point generation mechanism for improving fuzzy vault security' *IET Biometrics*, 2016, **5**, (2), pp. 147–153.

[55]  Arrahmah, A.I., Gondokaryono, Y.S., and Rhee, K.H.: 'Fast non-random chaff point generator for fuzzy vault biometric cryptosystems', in 'Proceedings of the 2016 6th International Conference on System Engineering and Technology, ICSET 2016' (2017), pp. 199–204.

[56] Hartato, B.P., Adji, T.B., and Bejo, A.: 'A review of chaff point generation methods for fuzzy vault scheme' 2016, pp. 180–185.

[57] Wu, X., Qi, N., Wang, and K., Zhang, D.: 'A novel cryptosystem based on iris key generation', in 'Proceedings – 4th International Conference on Natural Computation, ICNC 2008' (2008), pp. 53–56.

[58] Wu, X., Qi, N., Wang, K., and Zhang, D.: 'An iris cryptosystem for information security', in 'Proceedings – 2008 4th International Conference on Intelligent Information Hiding and Multimedia Signal Processing, IIH-MSP 2008' (2008), pp. 1533–1536.

[59] Lee, Y.J., Bae, K., Lee, S.J., Park, K.R., and Kim, J.: 'LNCS 4642 – Biometric key binding: Fuzzy vault based on iris images' in: Lee S.W., Li S.Z. (eds) Advances in Biometrics. ICB 2007. Lecture Notes in Computer Science, Springer, Berlin, Heidelberg, 2007, **4642**, pp. 800–808.

[60] Reddy, E.S., and Babu, I.R.: 'Performance of iris based hard fuzzy vault', in 'Proceedings – 8th IEEE International Conference on Computer and Information Technology Workshops, CIT Workshops 2008' (2008), pp. 248–253.

[61] Wu, Y., and Qiu, B.: 'Transforming a pattern identifier into biometric key generators', in '2010 IEEE International Conference on Multimedia and Expo, ICME 2010' (2010), pp. 78–82.

[62] Wu, X., and Wang, K.: 'A cryptosystem based on palmprint feature' *Sci. Technol.*, 2008, (c), pp. 1–4.

[63] Kumar, A., and Kumar, A.: 'Development of a new cryptographic construct using palmprint-based fuzzy vault' *EURASIP J. Adv. Signal Process.*, 2009, **2009**, (13).

[64] Alisher KholmatovBerrin Yanikoglu: 'Biometric Cryptosystem Using Online Signatures', in 'International Symposium on Computer and Information Sciences' (2006), pp. 981–990.

[65] Kaur, H., and Khanna, P.: 'Gaussian Random Projection Based Non-invertible Cancelable Biometric Templates', in 'Procedia Computer Science' (2015), pp. 661–670.

[66] Ratha, N.K., Connell, J.H., and Bolle, R.M.: 'Enhancing security and privacy in biometrics-based authentication systems' *IBM Syst. J.*, 2001, **40**, (3), pp. 614–634.

[67] Ratha, N.K., Chikkerur, S., Connell, J.H., and Bolle, R.M.: 'Generating cancelable fingerprint templates' *IEEE Trans. Pattern Anal. Mach. Intell.*, 2007, **29**, (4), pp. 561–572.

[68] Ratha, N.K., Connell, J.H., Bolle, R.M., and Chikkerur, S.: 'Cancelable biometrics: A case study in fingerprints', in 'Proceedings – International Conference on Pattern Recognition' (2006), pp. 370–373.

[69] Zuo, J., Ratha, N.K., and Connell, J.H.: 'Cancelable iris biometric', in '2008 19th International Conference on Pattern Recognition' (2008), pp. 1–4.

[70] Hämmerle-Uhl, J., Pschernig, E., and Uhl, A.: 'Cancelable iris biometrics using block re-mapping and image warping', in 'Lecture Notes in Computer Science (including subseries Lecture Notes in Artificial Intelligence and Lecture Notes in Bioinformatics)' (2009), pp. 135–142.

[71]    Rathgeb, C., and Uhl, A.: 'Secure iris recognition based on local intensity variations', in 'Lecture Notes in Computer Science (including subseries Lecture Notes in Artificial Intelligence and Lecture Notes in Bioinformatics)' (2010), pp. 266–275.

[72]    Maiorana, E., Martinez-Diaz, M., Campisi, P., Ortega-Garcia, J., and Neri, A.: 'Template protection for HMM-based on-line signature authentication', in '2008 IEEE Computer Society Conference on Computer Vision and Pattern Recognition Workshops, CVPR Workshops' (2008).

[73]    Maiorana, E., Campisi, P., Ortega-Garcia, J., and Neri, A.: 'Cancelable biometrics for HMM-based signature recognition', in 'BTAS 2008 – IEEE 2nd International Conference on Biometrics: Theory, Applications and Systems' (2008).

[74]    Maiorana, E., Campisi, P., Fierrez, J., Ortega-Garcia, J., and Neri, A.: 'Cancelable templates for sequence-based biometrics with application to on-line signature recognition' *IEEE Trans. Syst. Man, Cybern. Part A Systems Humans*, 2010, **40**, (3), pp. 525–538.

[75]    Boxilt, T.: 'Robust distance measures for face-recognition supporting revocable biometric tokens', in 'FGR 2006: Proceedings of the 7th International Conference on Automatic Face and Gesture Recognition' (2006), pp. 560–566.

[76]    Boult, T.E., Scheirer, W.J., and Woodwork, R.: 'Revocable fingerprint biotokens: Accuracy and security analysis', in 'Proceedings of the IEEE Computer Society Conference on Computer Vision and Pattern Recognition' (2007).

[77]    Farooq, F., Bolle, R.M., Jea, T.Y., and Ratha, N.: 'Anonymous and revocable fingerprint recognition', in 'Proceedings of the IEEE Computer Society Conference on Computer Vision and Pattern Recognition' (2007).

[78]    Lee, C., and Kim, J.: 'Cancelable fingerprint templates using minutiae-based bit-strings' *J. Netw. Comput. Appl.*, 2010, **33**, (3), pp. 236–246.

[79]    Teoh, A.B.J., and Ngo, D.C.L.: 'Biophasor: Token supplemented cancellable biometrics', in '9th International Conference on Control, Automation, Robotics and Vision, 2006, ICARCV '06' (2006).

[80]    Teoh, A.B.J., and Yuang, C.T.: 'Cancelable biometrics realization with multispace random projections' *IEEE Trans. Syst. Man, Cybern. Part B Cybern.*, 2007, **37**, (5), pp. 1096–1106.

[81]    Teoh, A.B.J., and Chong, L.Y.: 'Secure speech template protection in speaker verification system' *Speech Commun.*, 2010, **52**, (2), pp. 150–163.

[82]    Yip, W.K., Teoh, A.B.J., and Ngo, D.C.L.: 'Replaceable and securely hashed keys from online signatures' *IEICE Electron. Express*, 2006, **3**, (18), pp. 410–416.

[83]    Kuan, Y.W., Teoh, A.B.J., and Ngo, D.C.L.: 'Secure hashing of dynamic hand signatures using wavelet-fourier compression with BioPhasor mixing and 2N discretization' *EURASIP J. Adv. Signal Process.*, 2007, **2007**, (1), p. 32.

[84]    Wang, S., and Hu, J.: 'A blind system identification approach to cancelable fingerprint templates' *Pattern Recognit.*, 2016, **64**, pp. 14–22.

[85]  Jin, Z., Hwang, J.Y., Lai, Y.L., Kim, S., and Teoh, A.B.J.: 'Ranking-based locality sensitive hashing-enabled cancelable biometrics: Index-of-max hashing' *IEEE Trans. Inf. Forensics Secur.*, 2018, **13**, (2), pp. 393–407.

[86]  Li, C.-T., and Hwang, M.-S.: 'An efficient biometrics-based remote user authentication scheme using smart cards' *J. Netw. Comput. Appl.*, 2010, **33**, (1), pp. 1–5.

[87]  Lee, J.K., Ryu, S.R., and Yoo, K.Y.: 'Fingerprint-based remote user authentication scheme using smart cards' *Electron. Lett.*, 2002, **38**, (12), pp. 554–555.

[88]  Khan, M.K., and Zhang, J.: 'Improving the security of "a flexible biometrics remote user authentication scheme"' *Comput. Stand. Interfaces*, 2007, **29**, (1), pp. 82–85.

[89]  Li, X., Niu, J.-W., Ma, J., Wang, W.-D., and Liu, C.-L.: 'Cryptanalysis and improvement of a biometrics-based remote user authentication scheme using smart cards' *J. Netw. Comput. Appl.*, 2011, **34**, (1), pp. 73–79.

[90]  Das, A.: 'Analysis and improvement on an efficient biometric-based remote user authentication scheme using smart cards' *Inf. Secur. IET*, 2011, (June 2010), pp. 145–151.

[91]  An, Y.: 'Security analysis and enhancements of an effective biometric-based remote user authentication scheme using smart cards'. *J. Biomed. Biotechnol.*, 2012, **2012**, pp. 1–6.

[92]  Khan, M.K., and Kumari, S.: 'An improved biometrics-based remote user authentication scheme with user anonymity' *Biomed Res. Int.*, 2013, **2013**.

[93]  Sarvabhatla, M., Giri, M., and Vorugunti, C.S.: 'A secure biometrics-based remote user authentication scheme for secure data exchange', in 'International Conference on Embedded Systems, ICES 2014' (2014), pp. 110–115.

[94]  Das, A.K., and Goswami, A.: 'A robust anonymous biometric-based remote user authentication scheme using smart cards' *J. King Saud Univ. – Comput. Inf. Sci.*, 2015, **27**, (2), pp. 193–210.

[95]  Xie, Q., and Tang, Z.: 'Biometrics based authentication scheme for session initiation protocol' *Springerplus*, 2016, **5**, (1).

[96]  Zhao, H., Chen, C., Hu, J., and Qin, J.: 'Securing body sensor networks with biometric methods: A new key negotiation method and a key sampling method for linear interpolation encryption' *Int. J. Distrib. Sens. Networks*, 2015.

[97]  Wen, F., Susilo, W., and Yang, G.: 'Analysis and improvement on a biometric-based remote user authentication scheme using smart cards' *Wirel. Pers. Commun.*, 2015, **80**, (4), pp. 1747–1760.

[98]  Kumari, S., Li, X., Wu, F., Das, A.K., Choo, K.K.R., and Shen, J.: 'Design of a provably secure biometrics-based multi-cloud-server authentication scheme' *Futur. Gener. Comput. Syst.*, 2017, **68**, pp. 1–508.

[99]  Lu, Y., Li, L., Yang, X., and Yang, Y.: 'Robust biometrics based authentication and key agreement scheme for multi-server environments using smart cards' *PLoS One*, 2015, **2015**, Article ID 764919, pp. 1–11.

[100]  Chaturvedi, A., Das, A.K., Mishra, D., and Mukhopadhyay, S.: 'Design of a secure smart card-based multi-server authentication scheme' *J. Inf. Secur. Appl.*, 2016, **30**, pp. 1–118.

[101] Chaudhry, S.A.: 'A secure biometric based multi-server authentication scheme for social multimedia networks' *Multimed. Tools Appl.*, 2016, **75**, (20), pp. 12705–12725.

[102] Odelu, V., Das, A.K., and Goswami, A.: 'A secure biometrics-based multi-server authentication protocol using smart cards' *IEEE Trans. Inf. Forensics Secur.*, 2015, **10**, (9), pp. 1953–1966.

[103] Moon, J., Choi, Y., Kim, J., and Won, D.: 'An improvement of robust and efficient biometrics based password authentication scheme for telecare medicine information systems using extended chaotic maps' *J. Med. Syst.*, 2016, **40**, (3), pp. 1–11.

[104] Jiang, Q., Wei, F., Fu, S., Ma, J., Li, G., and Alelaiwi, A.: 'Robust extended chaotic maps-based three-factor authentication scheme preserving biometric template privacy' *Nonlinear Dyn.*, 2016, **83**, (4), pp. 2085–2101.

[105] Das, A.K.: 'A secure user anonymity-preserving three-factor remote user authentication scheme for the telecare medicine information systems' *J. Med. Syst.*, 2015, **39**, (3).

[106] Li, X., Niu, J., Wang, Z., and Chen, C.: 'Applying biometrics to design three-factor remote user authentication scheme with key agreement' *Secur. Commun. Networks*, 2014, **7**, (10), pp. 1488–1497.

[107] Li, X., Niu, J., Khan, M.K., Liao, J., and Zhao, X.: 'Robust three-factor remote user authentication scheme with key agreement for multimedia systems' *Secur. Commun. Networks*, 2016, **9**, (13), pp. 1916–1927.

[108] Castiglione, A., Choo, K.K.R., Nappi, M., and Narducci, F.: 'Biometrics in the cloud: Challenges and research opportunities' *IEEE Cloud Comput.*, 2017, **4**, (4), pp. 12–17.

[109] Popovic, K., and Hocenski, Z.: 'Cloud computing security issues and challenges' *MIPRO, 2010 Proc. 33rd Int. Conv.*, 2010, pp. 344–349.

[110] Yuan, J., and Yu, S.: 'Efficient privacy-preserving biometric identification in cloud computing', in 'Proceedings – IEEE INFOCOM' (2013), pp. 2652–2660.

[111] Zhu, Y., Takagi, T., and Hu, R.: 'Security analysis of collusion-resistant nearest neighbor query scheme on encrypted cloud data' *IEICE Trans. Inf. Syst.*, 2014, **E97–D**, (2), pp. 326–330.

[112] Wang, Q., Hu, S., Ren, K., He, M., Du, M., and Wang, Z.: 'CloudBI: Practical privacy-preserving outsourcing of biometric identification in the cloud', in 'Lecture Notes in Computer Science (including subseries Lecture Notes in Artificial Intelligence and Lecture Notes in Bioinformatics)' (2015), pp. 186–205.

[113] Pan, S., Yan, S., and Zhu, W.T.: 'Security analysis on privacy-preserving cloud aided biometric identification schemes', in 'Lecture Notes in Computer Science (including subseries Lecture Notes in Artificial Intelligence and Lecture Notes in Bioinformatics)' (2016), pp. 446–453.

[114] Zhu, L., Zhang, C., Xu, C., Liu, X., and Huang, C.: 'An efficient and privacy-preserving biometric identification scheme in cloud computing' *IEEE Access*, 2018, **4**, (c), pp. 19025–19033.

*Chapter 7*

# Lightweight block ciphers with applications in IoT

*Meltem Kurt Pehlivanoğlu[1], Muharrem Tolga Sakallı[2], Sedat Akleylek[3] and Nevcihan Duru[1]*

Internet of Things (IoT) devices bring not only benefits but also security risks because the use of these devices has increased dramatically. Security risks can be avoided by using lightweight cryptographic algorithms that need to be well designed and implemented efficiently on these resource-constrained devices. The selection of a cryptographic algorithm is important because it affects system requirements in terms of cost, area, speed, latency, and bandwidth. In the literature, there are several studies and projects that have focused on performance benchmarking of the different lightweight block ciphers for IoT-based applications, comparing implementations of these ciphers on three single embedded platforms (8-bit, 16-bit, and 32-bit micro-controllers). In this chapter, the design techniques of lightweight block ciphers are presented. We particularly focus on diffusion layers, which aid in providing the required diffusion in a block cipher. Moreover, we present some important requirements for the construction of perfect diffusion layers and the design rationale for lightweight block ciphers. The hardware efficiency of diffusion matrices was analyzed by using the XOR metric. Some problems were revealed expressed as the following questions.

- First, what are the requirements for real-world applications to ensure the practical security and privacy considerations for IoT devices?
- Second, is there any standardization for lightweight implementations focusing on cipher components such as diffusion and confusion layers?

This chapter aims to provide a comprehensive survey of lightweight block ciphers that have been designed for resource-constrained IoT platforms. The implementations of 10 lightweight block ciphers are compared on 8-bit, 16-bit, and 32-bit microcontrollers by using evaluation metrics such as power and energy consumption, latency, security level, throughput, and efficiency metrics. Furthermore, advantages

[1]Department of Computer Engineering, Kocaeli University, Turkey
[2]Department of Computer Engineering, Trakya University, Turkey
[3]Department of Computer Engineering, Ondokuz Mayıs University, Turkey

and disadvantages of these ciphers are discussed. The software performance bench-marking of PRESENT [1], HIGHT [2], and SIMON and SPECK [3] lightweight block ciphers is given for the WeMos D1 ESP8266 IoT Wi-Fi board. Finally, authentication problems and solutions for IoT devices are discussed in detail. Some open problems in this challenging area are provided for future research directions.

## 7.1 Block ciphers design primitives

The simplest definition of a block cipher is that which converts plaintext blocks into ciphertext blocks by using an encryption algorithm and a secret key. The inverse of this process is called decryption which converts ciphertext blocks into original plaintext blocks by using the same encryption key. A block cipher is formed by the same round functions which consist of substitution, diffusion, and key addition layers. Round keys or sub-keys which are generated by using a key scheduling algorithm are used in every round. A block cipher is constructed by using simpler operations to form a much stronger function; such a cipher is called a product or iterated block cipher, a process formalized by Claude Shannon [4]. In Figure 7.1, the encryption algorithm of the product cipher is given, which is a sequence of round functions $f_i$ where the input to the first round is the plaintext $P$, the output of each round is sent to the following round as its input, and the output of the last round $f_r$ is the ciphertext $C$. Each round gets, as one of its inputs, the round key $K_i$ which is derived from the key scheduling algorithm by using the master key $K$.

Even though many improvements have been made in the design of crypto-graphically strong block ciphers, the basic desirable properties have remained the same. These properties in a block cipher are:

- Non-linearity: It hides the distribution or the pattern of the plaintext characters inside the ciphertext;
- Avalanche effect: It ensures a substantial change (half of the output bits) in the ciphertext when a slight change (flipping a single bit) in the plaintext or key is made;
- Strict avalanche criterion (SAC): It is formulated as when a single bit is changed in the input data (plaintext or key), the output data bits (ciphertext) should change with a probability of 1/2;
- Bit independence criterion (BIC): It is formulated as when any single input bit is inverted, two output bits should change independently of each other. This is also considered for all bits.

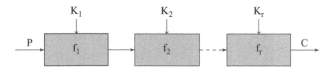

*Figure 7.1 A product block cipher*

Diffusion and confusion properties protect the system from the statistical analysis. Good confusion hides the relationship between the ciphertext and the key while good diffusion hides the statistical distribution property of the plaintext through the ciphertext, i.e., if a slight change is made in the key bits, the ciphertext bits are dramatically influenced by this change. Moreover, SAC and BIC criteria ensure the effectiveness of the confusion property.

Shannon also proposed two important design principles, reduction and making the system secure against all the known attacks. Reduction means that the system security can be reducible to some difficult problems. That principle is more appropriate for public-key cryptosystems [5]. Moreover, Shannon proposed the idea which uses logically separated substitution and diffusion functions to get good confusion and diffusion in a block cipher [4].

Substitution-permutation networks (SPNs) and Feistel networks are the two important block cipher design structures. An SPN structure has two separated functions (layers), namely, substitution and diffusion. A cipher without a substitution layer (also known as confusion layer or confusion function, e.g., S-box) only consists of some linear operations that makes the system vulnerable to cryptographic attacks. Non-linear function (e.g., S-box) maps $n$ input bits to $m$ output bits to achieve confusion in a block cipher. Diffusion layer (permutation layer or P-Box) can be built by permuting positions of the input bits or using some linear transformations. The round has a substitution layer, a diffusion layer, and a key mixing operation (usually performed by XOR operation) in the SPN structure. SPN-based block ciphers need two different circuits for both encryption and decryption.

In the Feistel structure, the input block is split into two branches. (The first half is called the source, and the second half is called the target branch.) The F-function is computed by using the source branch and the round key, and then the result is composed with the target branch. The composition of the source and the target branch is usually done by an XOR operation. Thus, the source branch remains unchanged. In the last step, the branches are swapped to compose the next round input. It is clear that, in the Feistel structure, only half of the state is changed at each round; therefore, the source branch plays an important role in providing confusion and diffusion in a block cipher. Moreover, the F-function should have good avalanche characteristics and should be non-linear in order to resist cryptographic attacks. When compared to the SPN structure, the Feistel structure needs higher number of rounds in a block cipher to ensure the same security level for the same block size and the key sizes. However, these rounds are lighter than SPN rounds, and the decryption process is almost the same with the encryption process. On the other hand, the SPN structure ensures faster confusion and diffusion and higher parallelism with efficient hardware and software optimized implementations [4]. Ideally, block cipher design strategies aim to maximize the randomness and mix the output bits of encryption process as much as possible.

Details about confusion and diffusion layers which are important on the design of block ciphers are given in Section 7.1.1.

## 7.1.1 Confusion and diffusion layers

SPN-based block ciphers include two basic layers: confusion and diffusion. The confusion layer is a non-linear operation, and the diffusion layer is a linear operation which mixes the output of the confusion layer.

The confusion function called the S-box maps the state values to the other values. This function can be represented as a vectorial Boolean function that maps $n$ input bits to $m$ output bits from $\mathbb{F}_2^n$ into $\mathbb{F}_2^m$ given in the following [4]:

$$S : \mathbb{F}_2^n \rightarrow \mathbb{F}_2^m$$

$$(x_0, \ldots, x_{n-1}) \mapsto (y_0, \ldots, y_{m-1})$$

Such a function, called a $(n, m)$-function, can be defined as a vector of $m$ Boolean functions with the same $n$ inputs which are independent from each other [4]. The use of vectorial Boolean functions for S-boxes and cryptography is studied [6]. The aim is to achieve the desired resistance with S-boxes.

One of the most critical and expensive operations of the block cipher is the S-box layer; therefore, designing an S-box with optimal and desired requirement is a challenging area. A lightweight in terms of the required hardware area, a secure and optimal 4-bit to 4-bit S-box is especially suited for the IoT applications [7]. The S-boxes used in some SPN-based lightweight block ciphers, 4-bit to 4-bit S-box $S : \mathbb{F}_2^4 \mapsto \mathbb{F}_2^4$, are given in Table 7.1 in hexadecimal notation. Details for all of these ciphers can be found in [8]. The S-box of the KLEIN cipher, which is involutory, satisfies $S(S(x)) = x, x \in \mathbb{F}_2^4$, so it can be used both in encryption and decryption processes. PRESENT and LED ciphers use the same S-box, which is non-involutory. The Midori cipher uses two S-boxes, two of them given in the table. The S-boxes of the Midori cipher ensure a faster signal delay than the S-boxes of the PRINCE and PRESENT ciphers.

In a block cipher, the internal state is first transformed by a non-linear function S-box; then bits of the state are permuted with a diffusion layer by using fixed bit permutations or a linear transformation. The bit permutation is a simple bit-shifting operation in which bit $i$ of the state is moved to bit position $P(i)$ [1]. The linear

Table 7.1  *Four-bit to 4-bit S-boxes used in some SPN-based lightweight block ciphers*

| Cipher | 0 | 1 | 2 | 3 | 4 | 5 | 6 | 7 | 8 | 9 | A | B | C | D | E | F |
|---|---|---|---|---|---|---|---|---|---|---|---|---|---|---|---|---|
| PRESENT | C | 5 | 6 | B | 9 | 0 | A | D | 3 | E | F | 8 | 4 | 7 | 1 | 2 |
| KLEIN | 7 | 4 | A | 9 | 1 | F | B | 0 | C | 3 | 2 | 6 | 8 | E | D | 5 |
| LED | C | 5 | 6 | B | 9 | 0 | A | D | 3 | E | F | 8 | 4 | 7 | 1 | 2 |
| Midori | C | A | D | 3 | E | B | F | 7 | 8 | 9 | 1 | 5 | 0 | 2 | 4 | 6 |
| Midori | 1 | 0 | 5 | 3 | E | 2 | F | 7 | D | A | 9 | B | C | 8 | 4 | 6 |
| PRINCE | B | F | 3 | 2 | A | C | 9 | 1 | 6 | 7 | 8 | 0 | E | 5 | D | 4 |
| PRIDE | 0 | 4 | 8 | F | 1 | 5 | E | 9 | 2 | 7 | A | C | B | D | 6 | 3 |
| RECTANGLE | 6 | 5 | C | A | 1 | E | 7 | 9 | B | 0 | 3 | D | 8 | F | 4 | 2 |

transformation can be a matrix multiplication in $\mathbb{F}_{2^4}$ or $\mathbb{F}_{2^8}$. The balance between good diffusion and software performance lets us make a choice. Because using bit permutation in a block cipher actually causes the loss of the software efficiency, e.g., the PRESENT lightweight block cipher, which use bit-shifting as a diffusion layer, is a hardware-oriented cipher [1]. The KLEIN and LED ciphers use matrix multiplication in $\mathbb{F}_{2^4}$ with a fixed polynomial. Midori cipher's diffusion layer is composed of cell-permutation and matrix multiplication in $\mathbb{F}_{2^4}$ and $\mathbb{F}_{2^8}$ with a fixed polynomial for the 64-bit and 128-bit variants. The state is multiplied with a matrix in the PRINCE and PRIDE cipher. The RECTANGLE cipher's diffusion layer is composed of three bit-rotations.

A combination of the confusion and diffusion layers with a key addition operation is called a round function of an SPN structure. A round function of an SPN is given in Figure 7.2, where $m^i$ is the plaintext in the $i$th round, $S$ is the confusion layer, $P$ is the diffusion layer, and $k_i$ is the $i$th round key produced from a key scheduling algorithm by using the master key $K$. $m^{i+1}$ is the output of the $i$th round function, and that is used as the next round's input. In the key addition process, the XOR operation or modular addition operations are used. They have almost the same cost for software implementation. However, hardware implementation of a modular addition is more expensive than the XOR operation because of the cost of latency. These layers can be used with different combinations in SPN-based block cipher such as key addition-substitution-key addition-permutation (KSKP) and SPSPS-PKP round structures [4]. Using the key addition process at the beginning of the round or at the end of the round are efficient design structures for round functions [4].

Design requirements of an efficient key scheduling algorithm are an open problem [4]. Even if a cipher has a perfect design, if it has weak key schedule

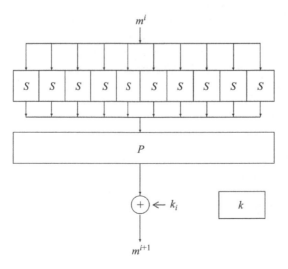

*Figure 7.2   A round function in an SPN*

algorithm, it is vulnerable to key-related attacks. Round keys must be independent of each other. Ideally, it is required that key length be very large; in general, for a $n$-bit ideal block, the cipher key length should be $n \times 2^n$ bits [9] to cope with statistical attacks. However, it is impossible to implement this length of bits.

In the literature, there are several ways to construct key scheduling algorithms. They can be grouped as follows [4]:

- use a linear key scheduling structure with bit permutations, extractions and other linear operation;
- use a round constant in addition to the first structure;
- add non-linear components to the two previous methods;
- or use a different block or stream cipher to generate round keys.

The role of the key schedule is important in terms of preventing vulnerability in a block cipher. In the literature, there are lots of studies [10–13] specifically related to the cryptanalysis of the key schedule algorithm in a block cipher.

The confusion layer affects both the diffusion layer and the round state in a block cipher. Therefore, it is important to get the maximum number of active S-boxes (input difference bits are non-zero) with a small number of rounds.

Surprisingly, the design of good diffusion layers is still an open problem. There are only few known constructions. Simply, two general approaches, an ad-hoc strategy and a wide-trail strategy, can be defined. The ad-hoc strategy requires computer-aided tools to find optimal trails (such as heuristic search techniques) and does not utilize general design techniques. Serpent [14] and Keccak [15] ciphers use this approach. A wide-trail strategy proposed in [16] specifically copes with linear and differential attacks. The main theme of the wide-trail strategy is to spend as much possible on a few more resources for large S-boxes. Then, design of round transformations should be without low bundle weight trails to construct a full dif-fusion [17]. Briefly, good linear codes should be chosen that correspond to good diffusion layers for increasing the active S-boxes number. PRINCE [18], mCrypton [19], LED [20], Anubis [21], Grøstl [22], Khazad [23], and more ciphers use the wide-trail strategy. Even if the wide-trail strategy ensures a good idea for the design structure of the diffusion layer, the authors in [24] assert that this strategy does not help to find the answer to the question, "How can an efficient diffusion layer or linear code with a suitable number of S-box be designed?"

In general, the following three diffusion layer structures are used to achieve good diffusion:

- Bit permutation-based diffusion layers: In this structure, S-box output bits are mixed by using bit permutation. It is efficient for low-cost hardware imple-mentations which are quite compact. In this structure, an output bit influences only a single input bit of the next layer. Therefore, diffusion is quite slow, and the cipher needs a larger number of rounds [4].
- XOR and rotations-based diffusion layers: In this structure, rotations and XOR operations are used. It aims to find trade-offs between diffusion, hardware, and software costs. ASCON [25], ITUbee [26], Hummingbird-2 [27], and Noekeon

[28] ciphers use XOR and rotation-based diffusion layers. The major aim of XOR and rotations-based diffusion is to find trade-offs between diffusion and low cost in hardware and software by using rotations with XORs.

• Linear algebra-based diffusion layers: Matrices defined over a finite field are used as linear algebra-based diffusion layers. Constructing optimal diffusion matrices for efficient implementation is a challenging problem. There are two basic approaches to design these types of diffusion layers, and these are the maximum distance binary linear (MDBL) matrices and the maximum distance separable (MDS) matrices. MDS matrices can be derived from MDS codes over a finite field. In 1994, Vaudenay suggested using MDS matrices to ensure perfect diffusion with multi-permutation [29,30]. Daemen, inspired by this notation, proposed the branch number metric for the first time in [16]. MDS matrices have a maximum branch number and ensure a balance between diffusion and cost. Cost means that the elements of an MDS matrix should not be too expensive for the multiplication operation. An MDS matrix should have the maximum number of 1's and a minimum number of distinct elements, i.e., these elements should have as low a hamming weight [4] as possible. The lightweight block ciphers of Piccolo [31], LED [20] use MDS matrices as diffusion layers. Camellia [32], ARIA [33], and PRIDE [24] ciphers use binary matrices as diffusion layers.

There are several methods for constructing MDS matrices such as the Cauchy matrices, the Vandermonde matrices, the Hadamard matrices, circulant and companion matrices, and BCH codes [4]. The diffusion layer is important for the implementation of the encryption and decryption modules. When the diffusion matrix is involutory, the inverse of this matrix is the same as itself. There is no general construction method for finding involutory MDS matrices except the Hadamard matrices and random generation techniques given in [34].

The efficiency of MDBL or MDS matrices can be defined with the multiplication cost in a finite field. The XOR metric was introduced as the required number of XOR gates to multiply an element with another arbitrary element [35]. Finding MDS matrices with minimum XOR count for minimization of the hardware area is an open problem because it is not easy to find (involutory) MDS matrices with low multiplication complexity due to the huge search space. New matrix forms and different searching methods have been proposed to generate (involutory) MDS matrices in the literature [36–40].

Comparisons to the previous existing best-known XOR count results for involutory MDS and non-involutory MDS matrices are given in Tables 7.2–7.5. The first column of the tables shows that the matrix is involutory or non-involutory. The second column shows the reference of the given matrix, and the third column gives the finite field and irreducible polynomial of the given matrix in hexadecimal notation. The fourth column shows the type of the MDS matrix, and the last column gives the required XOR count to implement the $n \times n$ MDS matrix.

Table 7.2 includes the best-known XOR count results, $4 \times 4$ (involutory) MDS matrices over $\mathbb{F}_{2^4}$ and $\mathbb{F}_{2^8}$. Table 7.3 shows $8 \times 8$ (involutory) MDS matrices over

*Table 7.2    Comparison of the best-known XOR count results: 4×4 involutory MDS and non-involutory MDS matrices over $\mathbb{F}_{2^4}$ and $\mathbb{F}_{2^8}$*

| | Reference | Finite field | Matrix type | XOR counts |
|---|---|---|---|---|
| Involutory | [40] | $\mathbb{F}_{2^4}/0 \times 13$ | GHadamard | $64\ (=16+4\cdot 3\cdot 4)$ |
| Involutory | [38] | $\mathbb{F}_{2^4}/0 \times 13$ | Form (14) | $64\ (=16+4\cdot 3\cdot 4)$ |
| Involutory | [41] | $\mathbb{F}_{2^4}/0 \times 13$ | Hadamard | $72\ (=24+4\cdot 3\cdot 4)$ |
| Non-involutory | [38] | $\mathbb{F}_{2^4}/0 \times 19$ | Toeplitz | $58\ (=10+4\cdot 3\cdot 4)$ |
| Non-involutory | [35] | $\mathbb{F}_{2^4}/0 \times 13$ | Serial/circulant | $60\ (=12+4\cdot 3\cdot 4)$ |
| Non-involutory | [20] | $\mathbb{F}_{2^4}/0 \times 13$ | Serial | $64\ (=16+4\cdot 3\cdot 4)$ |
| Non-involutory | [41] | $\mathbb{F}_{2^4}/0 \times 13$ | Hadamard | $68\ (=20+4\cdot 3\cdot 4)$ |
| Involutory | [40] | $\mathbb{F}_{2^8}/0 \times 1c3$ | GHadamard | $158\ (=62+4\cdot 3\cdot 8)$ |
| Involutory | [41] | $\mathbb{F}_{2^8}/0 \times 165$ | Hadamard | $160\ (=64+4\cdot 3\cdot 8)$ |
| Involutory | [38] | $\mathbb{F}_{2^8}/0 \times 165$ | Form (14) | $160\ (=64+4\cdot 3\cdot 8)$ |
| Non-involutory | [38] | $\mathbb{F}_{2^8}/0 \times 1c3$ | Toeplitz | $123\ (=27+4\cdot 3\cdot 8)$ |
| Non-involutory | [37] | $\mathbb{F}_{2^8}/0 \times 1c3$ | Left-circulant | $128\ (=32+4\cdot 3\cdot 8)$ |
| Non-involutory | [35] | $\mathbb{F}_{2^8}/0 \times 11d$ | Serial/circulant | $132\ (=36+4\cdot 3\cdot 8)$ |
| Non-involutory | [41] | $\mathbb{F}_{2^8}/0 \times 11d$ | Hadamard | $148\ (=52+4\cdot 3\cdot 8)$ |

*Table 7.3    Comparison of the best-known XOR count results: 8 × 8 involutory MDS and non-involutory MDS matrices over $\mathbb{F}_{2^4}$ and $\mathbb{F}_{2^8}$*

| | Reference | Finite field | Matrix type | XOR counts |
|---|---|---|---|---|
| Involutory | [40] | $\mathbb{F}_{2^4}/0 \times 13$ | GHadamard | $407\ (=183+8\cdot 7\cdot 4)$ |
| Involutory | [41] | $\mathbb{F}_{2^4}/0 \times 13$ | Hadamard | $512\ (=288+8\cdot 7\cdot 4)$ |
| Non-involutory | [40] | $\mathbb{F}_{2^4}/0 \times 13$ | GHadamard | $380\ (=156+8\cdot 7\cdot 4)$ |
| Non-involutory | [39] | $\mathbb{F}_{2^4}/0 \times 13$ | Toeplitz | $394\ (=170+8\cdot 7\cdot 4)$ |
| Non-involutory | [41] | $\mathbb{F}_{2^4}/0 \times 13$ | Hadamard | $432\ (=208+8\cdot 7\cdot 4)$ |
| Involutory | [41] | $\mathbb{F}_{2^8}/0 \times 1c3$ | Hadamard | $494\ (=46+8\cdot 7\cdot 8)$ |
| Involutory | [23] | $\mathbb{F}_{2^8}/0 \times 11d$ | Hadamard | $546\ (=98+8\cdot 7\cdot 8)$ |
| Involutory | [42] | $\mathbb{F}_{2^8}/0 \times 11b$ | Hadamard–Cauchy | $570\ (=122+8\cdot 7\cdot 8)$ |
| Non-involutory | [39] | $\mathbb{F}_{2^8}/0 \times 1c3$ | Toeplitz | $680\ (=232+8\cdot 7\cdot 8)$ |
| Non-involutory | [37] | $\mathbb{F}_{2^8}/0 \times 1c3$ | Circulant | $688\ (=240+8\cdot 7\cdot 8)$ |
| Non-involutory | [41] | $\mathbb{F}_{2^8}/0 \times 1c3$ | Hadamard | $768\ (=320+8\cdot 7\cdot 8)$ |

$\mathbb{F}_{2^4}$ and $\mathbb{F}_{2^8}$. Tables 7.4 and 7.5, respectively, include the best-known XOR count results $16 \times 16$ and $32 \times 32$ (involutory) MDS matrices over $\mathbb{F}_{2^8}$ [41]. MDS matrices should guarantee a partially optimal number of S-boxes but, when compared to other structures, they need a higher implementation cost. Therefore, finding MDS matrices which have the best minimum XOR count is still an open problem. For general design, authors in [24] suggested using a near-MDS matrix or a matrix which has a sub-optimal branch number.

*Table 7.4   Comparison of the best-known XOR count results: 16×16 involutory MDS and non-involutory MDS matrices over* $\mathbb{F}_{2^8}$

|  | Reference | Finite field | Matrix type | XOR counts |
|---|---|---|---|---|
| Involutory | [41] | $\mathbb{F}_{2^8}/0 \times 1c3$ | Hadamard–Cauchy | $2{,}178\ (= 258 + 16 \cdot 15 \cdot 8)$ |
| Involutory | [42] | $\mathbb{F}_{2^8}/0 \times 11b$ | Hadamard–Cauchy | $2{,}258\ (= 338 + 16 \cdot 15 \cdot 8)$ |
| Non-involutory | [41] | $\mathbb{F}_{2^8}/0 \times 1c3$ | Hadamard–Cauchy | $2{,}152\ (= 232 + 16 \cdot 15 \cdot 8)$ |

*Table 7.5   Comparison of the best-known XOR count results: 32×32 involutory MDS and non-involutory MDS matrices over* $\mathbb{F}_{2^8}$

|  | Reference | Finite field | Matrix type | XOR counts |
|---|---|---|---|---|
| Involutory | [41] | $\mathbb{F}_{2^8}/0 \times 165$ | Hadamard–Cauchy | $8{,}546\ (= 610 + 32 \cdot 31 \cdot 8)$ |
| Involutory | [42] | $\mathbb{F}_{2^8}/0 \times 11b$ | Hadamard–Cauchy | $8{,}611\ (= 675 + 32 \cdot 31 \cdot 8)$ |
| Non-involutory | [41] | $\mathbb{F}_{2^8}/0 \times 1c3$ | Hadamard–Cauchy | $8{,}532\ (= 596 + 32 \cdot 31 \cdot 8)$ |

The diffusion layer is an important component for a block cipher, but, without a confusion layer, a cipher has only simple linear operations. The confusion layer brings non-linearity to the cipher. As mentioned above, S-boxes should have a good design to achieve resistance against attacks. Mutually incompatible algebraic structures and S-boxes are sometimes used together to increase the non-linearity of the cipher, e.g., GOST [43] and Blowfish [44] block ciphers.

According to [4], S-boxes should have some desirable cryptographic properties:

- statistical dependency between plaintext and ciphertext
- resistance to differential attacks
- a high degree of algebraic functions
- high algebraic immunity
- highly nonlinear functions to avoid linear attacks
- a distribution uniform as possible to resist differential cryptanalysis
- satisfaction of the SAC test
- and no non-zero linear structure.

In recent years, lightweight cryptosystems have been designed due to the increased usage of resource-constrained devices. In the following section, lightweight cryptography and lightweight cryptographic algorithms are given in detail.

## 7.2    Lightweight cryptography

Ensuring an effective balance between security and efficiency is important, especially for resource-constrained environments, so lightweight cryptography has become more popular as a field of study, e.g., IoT, sensor networks, healthcare, automotive systems, cyber physical systems.

If we imagine all of the devices are in a spectrum server, desktops, tablets, and smartphones are located in the high end of the spectrum. Embedded systems, radio frequency identification (RFID), and sensor networks are located at the lower end of the spectrum [45]. In embedded systems, 8-bit, 16-bit, and 32-bit microcontrollers which have instruction sets with small number of simple instructions are widely used. In the recent years, 4-bit microcontrollers are preferred because they support ultra-low applications. Some of the constrained parameters are time, power, and gate equivalent (GE). So, these limitations must be considered for the cryptographic algorithms performed over these devices. Conventional cryptographic algorithms are used to ensure security for devices which are on the high end of the spectrum. As distinct from conventional cryptographic algorithms, lightweight cryptography are used on devices which function in the low end of the device spectrum. Lightweight cryptography focuses on providing functionality and security in the environments which has significantly low or limited cost requirements in software/hardware.

There are some open questions regarding lightweight cryptography such as, "How should we design a lightweight cryptographic algorithm?" and "Is there any standardization for lightweight cryptographic algorithms?" We will discuss the answer to these questions in the rest of this chapter.

### 7.2.1    Standardization for lightweight cryptography

In 2013, the National Institute of Standards and Technology's (NIST) Information Technology Laboratory investigated studies that include efficient implementation of lightweight algorithms and protocols and organized two lightweight cryptography workshops in 2015 and 2016. The goals were to create standardization for lightweight cryptographic algorithms and to show the real-world implementations of these algorithms through these studies.

In 2017, the NIST also published a report that summarized the findings about lightweight cryptography that resulted from the projects and workshops. This report can be summarized under the following three headings [46]:

- devices targeted lightweight cryptography
- design of lightweight algorithms
- and standardization of lightweight cryptography.

The NIST published the Draft Submission Requirements and Evaluation Criteria for the Lightweight Cryptography Standardization Process in April 2018. This will be a competitive challenge for researchers.

Environment and application are important criteria for device-targeted lightweight cryptography. As mentioned before, lightweight cryptography targets devices are located at the lower end of the spectrum; however, it is necessary to implement lightweight cryptographic algorithms for devices located at the high end of the spectrum. For example, a sensor may need to send information to the server which is located at the high end of device spectrum, but the sensor is not a resource-constrained device which means that while sensors are using lightweight algorithms, servers should also support these algorithms. Briefly, all devices in the application should be taken into consideration while using lightweight algorithms because all of them interact with each other, and some of these devices can support conventional standards.

There should be a trade-off between performance and cost when designing a lightweight cryptography. Performance can be expressed by using latency, power consumption, energy consumption, and throughput metrics. Cost is expressed by different metrics for hardware and software implementations. While using a gate equivalent (GE) metric for hardware implementation, random-access memory (RAM) and read-only memory (ROM) size (consumption) metrics are used for software implementation. Important metrics used to design a lightweight block cipher have been summarized as follows [47,48]:

- GE: It is the area occupied by a two-input NAND (NAND2) gate. GE is calculated by dividing the layout area of the cipher circuit in $\mu m^2$ by the area of the NAND2 gate. GE is dependent on fabrication technology and cell libraries. Ideally, a desired GE count is between 2,000 and 4,000 for lightweight block ciphers [47].
- Cycles: It is the required number of clock cycles needed to execute a certain operation and get a result.
- Time: It is the ratio of the number of cycles to the operating frequency.
- Throughput: The Kb/s, the cipher's encryption operation achieved at a specific frequency, is expressed as Kbps. In the literature, 100 kHz and 4 MHz frequencies are used for hardware and software implementations, respectively, in most of the papers related to lightweight cryptography [47].
- Latency: It is the required number of clock cycles to encrypt a single block of the cipher.
- Energy: It is the energy consumption at a certain time, expressed as $\mu J$. It is also calculated by dividing the multiplication result of latency (cycles/block) and power consumption ($\mu W$) metrics by the block size (bits).
- Efficiency: It is the trade-off between performance and the implementation area. While hardware efficiency is calculated by dividing the throughput (Kbps) by the complexity (KGE) [47], software efficiency is calculated by dividing the throughput (Kbps) by the code size (KB) [47].

Lightweight cryptographic algorithms ensure more performance than conventional cryptographic algorithms even though they are specifically purposed for limited range of applications [45].

In this chapter, lightweight block ciphers are analyzed. The choice of parameters such as block size, key size, round structure, and key scheduling algorithm is important for designing of a lightweight block cipher. Using a small block size is good for memory consumption, e.g., 64-bit, 80-bit block size. Key size should also be small for efficiency. According to [49], the minimum key size should be 112-bit. Rounds should also be simple, for example, using a 4-bit S-box instead of an 8-bit S-box reduces GE. The key scheduling algorithm should be simple to reduce latency, power, and memory consumption. However, a simple key scheduling algorithm causes susceptibility to attacks [49].

Lightweight cryptography is handled in various projects and standards [45].

- The International Organization for Standardization/International Electrotechnical Commission (ISO/IEC) 29192 specifies ciphers that are suitable for lightweight cryptograph which consists of six parts: general, block ciphers, stream ciphers, mechanisms using asymmetric techniques and amendment 1, hash functions, and message authentication codes (MACs).

The general part [50] includes security requirements for the lightweight cryptography implementation and classification. According to this part, the minimum security strength of the lightweight cryptography is 80 bit. Chip area and energy consumption metrics are used for hardware implementation, and code and RAM size metrics are used for the software implementation. Input performance and latency are other performance classification metrics. This part also includes mechanisms which use symmetric (especially lightweight block ciphers and stream ciphers) and asymmetric techniques.

First, PRESENT and CLEFIA [51] lightweight block ciphers were introduced in the block ciphers part. Its amendment version was updated in 2014, and then SIMON and SPECK lightweight block ciphers were given in this updated version. The third part is related to Enocoro [52] and Trivium [53] stream ciphers. The fourth part is related to mechanisms that use asymmetric techniques. These mechanisms are divided into three parts [50]: (1) unilateral authentication mechanisms based on discrete logarithms on elliptic curves, (2) unilateral authentication and lightweight key exchange mechanism (including the establishment of a session key), and (3) mechanisms based on the identity-based signature. In 2014, this part was updated and an elliptic curve-based authentication scheme was added to this version.

The fifth part includes PHOTON [54], SPONGENT [55], and Lesamnta–LW [56] hash functions.

The sixth part includes MAC algorithms such as Chaskey [57] and this part is still under development.

- ISO/IEC 29167 [58]: This part is called automatic identification and data capture techniques. It describes security services, especially for air interface communications-based resource-constrained devices. It consists of 13 different parts that purpose to design a common secure cryptosystem for RFID devices. Part 1 includes architecture, security mechanisms, NS file management for RFID devices. The other nine parts, respectively, define cryptographic mechanisms using AES-128, PRESENT-80, ECC-DH, Grain-128A, AES OFB, XOR, ECDSA-ECDH, cryptoGPS, and RAMON ciphers to ensure security on RFID devices. Moreover, three of these parts, RAMON, SIMON, and SPECK ciphers, are still under development.

- Cryptography Research and Evaluation Committees (CRYPTREC) Project [59]: It aims to assure the security of e-Government. In 2003, an e-Government Recommended Ciphers List was published within this project, and in 2009 and in 2013, the list was revised. In 2009, ciphers given in the previous list were called CRYPTREC Ciphers. In 2013, lightweight cryptographic algorithms were specifically investigated for the security of the e-Government system. All of these investigations and technical reports were published within this project.

- The Lightweight Cryptography Project: It aims not only to develop standards and guidelines for all cryptographic primitives and modes for resource-constrained devices but also to adapt these standards to the others. Lightweight cryptography should cope with quickly changing goals or study areas because a standard is insufficient until it is a global standard. Competitions were held to take recommendations for algorithm standardization during this project [45]. According to this project, desired properties for lightweight cryptography are summarized as follows [45]; security strength should be at least 112 bits, and an algorithm should support various implementations on a single platform. (It should be flexible.) Some properties that arose during the execution of the crypto-graphic algorithms (e.g., timing, power consumption) could be used as a vulnerability; therefore, algorithms should be resistant to side channel and fault attacks. Moreover, the same keys should not be chosen for the encryption process, and the round keys should be independent of each other and generated randomly.

In Section 7.2.2, lightweight block ciphers which are suitable for IoT device security are given in detail.

## 7.2.2   Lightweight block ciphers for IoT

IoT, briefly, is everything that is connected to the Internet, e.g., sensors, actuators, virtual objects, networks, platforms, services, and people. According to the estimation of the experts, by 2020, IoT will include almost 50 billion objects. However, IoT brings some security risks, and poor security technology is the top of these risks including vulnerabilities like insecure web interfaces, incorrect authentication/authorization, insecure web services, and unencrypted communication. IoT ensures simultaneous connections, but it also increases data traffic and sometimes causes packet losses.

It is clear that lightweight cryptography should be used to handle insecure applications of these limited resources. According to [60], over 1,600 papers about lightweight cryptography have been published in the last 10 years. New design techniques are proposed for efficient IoT implementations. These techniques have a smaller block size and key size, simple linear and non-linear transformations, simple rounds, and simple key scheduling algorithms. On the other hand, all of these simple structures make the cipher vulnerable to various attacks especially side-channel attacks.

Finding an optimal trade-off between security, cost, and performance depends on the target technology. In the literature, there are lots of studies [61–64] and projects about performance benchmarking of lightweight block ciphers on different hardware and software platforms.

In the BLOC [65] project, authors implemented 21 lightweight block ciphers on the WSN430 sensor which was based on 16-bit MSP430 microcontroller, and they also compared all of these ciphers in terms of execution time, RAM requirements, and code size metrics.

In the ECRYPT Benchmarking of Cryptographic Systems (eBACs) project [66], there are four different competition sections which are aBATS (for public-key systems), eBASC (for stream ciphers), eBASH (for hash functions), and eBAEAD (for authenticated-encryption schemes). Under the same project, the SUPERCOP toolkit was developed to measure the performance of cryptographic primitives for software implementations. An expanded version of SUPERCOP is the eXternal Benchmarking eXtension (XBX) project that is the first project to benchmark cryptographic primitives on embedded devices. They compared algorithms on different microcontrollers in terms of code size, cycle count, and RAM consumption metrics, and new metrics, RAM footprint and ROM consumption, were proposed in the same project.

Automated Tools for Hardware EvaluatioN (ATHENa) project [67] was designed, inspired from the eBACs project. In this project, some comparisons of cryptographic algorithms, architectures, implementations, hardware platforms, languages, and tools were given.

In [68], the authors developed an open framework which compares lightweight block ciphers by using execution time, RAM footprint, and code size metrics; they also proposed a new metric named Figure Of Merit (FOM). They compared software implementations of 13 lightweight block ciphers on 8-bit ATmega, 16-bit MSP430, and 32-bit ARM microcontrollers. The performance comparison results can be accessed from the website [69].

In [70], the authors analyzed software implementations of some lightweight block ciphers and stream ciphers by using code size, RAM consumption, and execution time metrics. Eight-bit AVR (ATmega128), 16-bit MSP (MSP430F1611), and 32-bit ARM (Atmel SAM3X8 Cortex M3) microcontrollers are used for software comparison. They also shared the open-source codes and results in [71].

Marchand *et al.* [72] gave the hardware implementations of KLEIN, LED, Lilliput, and Ktantan lightweight block ciphers on FPGA (Xilinx Spartan 6 and Xilinx Spartan 3).

Hatzivasilis *et al.* [47] compared 52 block cipher implementations by using security, cost, and performance evaluations. Eight-bit, 16-bit, and 32-bit microcontrollers were used for software implementations, and 0.09, 0.13, 0.18, 0.25, and 0.35 μm complementary metal oxide semiconductor (CMOS) technologies were used for hardware implementations. The aim of using different technologies is that the same cipher takes up a different number of GEs on different technologies. According to this paper, implementations based on device capability can be categorized as ultra-lightweight, low cost, and lightweight.

In [73], authors compared PRESENT, SIMON, SPECK, and KHUDRA lightweight block ciphers on ASIC and FPGA platforms in terms of area, power consumption, and resistance of side-channel attack.

In Table 7.6, mCrypton, HIGHT, PRESENT, PRINTcipher, KLEIN, TWINE, Piccolo, PRINCE, SIMON, and SPECK lightweight block ciphers's key size, block size, design structure (SPN, Feistel, generalized Feistel structure (GFS), generalized Feistel networks (GFN), addition, rotation and XOR (ARX), and number of rounds are given.

Table 7.7 shows hardware implementation comparisons of the ciphers given in Table 7.6 for 0.09, 0.13, 0.18, 0.25 μm. In the table latency, throughput, area, efficiency, power, and energy consumption evaluation metrics have been given for the ciphers. In the table, latency, throughput, area, efficiency, power, and energy consumption evaluation metrics have been given for the ciphers. In the literature, the most commonly used CMOS technologies for hardware-based lightweight block cipher implementations are 0.13 and 0.18 μm. The creation of the table benefited from some comparing results given in [47]. According to this table, the Piccolo cipher has the best results with higher throughput and the least energy consumption. SIMON and SPECK ciphers have the least power consumption. PRINCE, SPECK, and mCrypton have low latency, so they are suitable for efficient implementations. PRINT cipher takes up a smaller area compared to other ciphers given in the table. PRESENT and TWINE ciphers provide good performance.

Software implementation comparisons of these lightweight block ciphers are provided in Table 7.8 for 8-bit, 16-bit, and 32-bit microcontrollers. The code size, RAM consumption, and execution time results taken from scenario 1 are given in [68] except mCrypton, PRINTcipher, and KLEIN ciphers. According to the results, SIMON and SPECK ciphers achieve good performance for all microcontrollers. In [47], authors analyzed mCrypton, PRINTcipher, and KLEIN ciphers on these microcontrollers. As a result, software implementations of PRINTcipher, mCrypton

*Table 7.6   General cryptographic properties of some lightweight block ciphers*

| Cipher | Key size (bits) | Block size (bits) | Design structure | Rounds |
|---|---|---|---|---|
| mCrypton | 64, 96, 128 | 64 | SPN | 13 |
| HIGHT | 128 | 64 | GFS | 32 |
| PRESENT | 80, 128 | 64 | SPN | 31 |
| PRINT cipher | 80, 160 | 48, 96 | SPN | 48, 96 |
| KLEIN | 64, 80, 96 | 64 | SPN | 12, 16, 20 |
| TWINE | 80, 128 | 64 | GFN | 36 |
| Piccolo | 80, 128 | 64 | GFN | 25, 31 |
| PRINCE | 128 | 64 | SPN | 12 |
| SIMON | 64, 72, 96, 128, 144, 192, 256 | 32, 48, 64, 96, 128 | Feistel | 32, 36, 42, 44, 52, 54, 68, 69, 72 |
| SPECK | 64, 72, 96, 128, 144, 192, 256 | 32, 48, 64, 96, 128 | ARX | 22, 23, 26, 27, 28, 29, 32, 33, 34 |

*Table 7.7    Hardware implementation comparisons of some lightweight block ciphers in different technologies [47]*

| Cipher | Latency (cycles/ block) | Throughput @ 100 kHz (Kbps) | Area (GE) | Efficiency (Kbps/KGE) | Power (µW) | Energy (µJ/bit) |
|---|---|---|---|---|---|---|
| *0.25* | | | | | | |
| HIGHT | 34 | 188 | 3,048 | 61.67 | 5.48 | 29.14 |
| *0.18* | | | | | | |
| mCrypton-128 | 190 | 33.51 | 2,760 | 12.14 | 4.14 | 122.90 |
| PRESENT-80 | 32 | 200 | 1,570 | 127.38 | 2.35 | 11.17 |
| PRESENT-128 | 32 | 200 | 1,886 | 106.04 | 2.82 | 14.14 |
| PRINTcipher-80 | 48 | 100 | 503 | 198.80 | 0.75 | 7.54 |
| PRINTcipher-160 | 96 | 100 | 967 | 103.41 | 1.45 | 14.50 |
| KLEIN-64 | 207 | 30.9 | 1,220 | 25.32 | 1.83 | 59.18 |
| KLEIN-80 | 271 | 23.62 | 1478 | 15.98 | 2.21 | 93.878 |
| *0.13* | | | | | | |
| mCrypton-96 | 13 | 492.3 | 2,681 | 183.62 | 2.68 | 5.45 |
| Piccolo-80 | 27 | 237.04 | 1,136 | 208.66 | 1.13 | 4.80 |
| Piccolo-128 | 33 | 193.94 | 1,197 | 162.02 | 1.20 | 6.18 |
| PRINCE | 12 | 533.3 | 2,953 | 180.59 | 2.95 | 5.53 |
| SIMON-96 with 48-bit block | 304 | 15.8 | 763 | 20.70 | 0.76 | 48.32 |
| SIMON-96 with 64-bit block | 45 | 142.2 | 1,216 | 116.94 | 1.21 | 8.55 |
| SPECK-96 with 48-bit block | 400 | 12 | 884 | 13.57 | 0.88 | 73.67 |
| PECK-96 with 64-bit block | 29 | 220.7 | 1,522 | 145.00 | 1.52 | 6.89 |
| *0.09* | | | | | | |
| TWINE-80 | 36 | 178 | 1,503 | 118.42 | 1.05 | 5.91 |
| TWINE-128 | 36 | 178 | 1,866 | 95.39 | 1.30 | 7.34 |
| PRESENT-80 | 31 | 206.4 | 1,704 | 121.12 | 1.19 | 5.77 |

*Table 7.8    Software implementation comparisons of some lightweight block ciphers on 8-bit, 16-bit, 32-bit microcontrollers [68]*

| Cipher | 8-bit, 16-bit, 32-bit Code size (bytes) | RAM (bytes) | Execution time (cycles) |
|---|---|---|---|
| PRESENT | 2,840, 2,230, 2,528 | 458, 454, 526 | 245,853, 201,885, 270,603 |
| TWINE | 4,236, 3,796, 2,464 | 646, 564, 442 | 297,265, 393,320, 257,039 |
| Piccolo | 2,672, 1,824, 1,604 | 324, 318, 430 | 407,890, 349,423, 291,401 |
| PRINCE | 5,358, 4,174, 4,304 | 374, 240, 548 | 243,396, 405,552, 202,445 |
| SIMON | 2,304, 9,104, 898 | 380, 380, 428 | 82,085, 176,700, 24,019 |
| SPECK | 1,644, 1,342, 792 | 305, 300, 356 | 59,612, 93,239, 19,529 |
| HIGHT | 2,624, 2,370, 2,196 | 347, 340, 416 | 166,480, 363,829, 173,762 |

are not efficient because of high latency. In contrast, the KLEIN cipher is very compact for software implementations.

In this chapter, we compared PRESENT, HIGHT, SIMON, and SPECK lightweight block ciphers which have good performance in hardware and software implementations. In the next section, these block ciphers' software comparison results for IoT Wi-Fi module are discussed in detail.

### 7.2.3 Software performance analysis of some of the lightweight block ciphers on ESP8266 Wi-Fi module for IoT implementations

According to studies in the literature, 8-bit, 16-bit, and 32-bit microcontrollers are usually used for software benchmarking of the lightweight block ciphers. Unlike previous studies, in this study, we used a WeMos D1 ESP8266 Wi-Fi board which ensures IoT applications. To our knowledge, this is the first study to compare software implementations of the lightweight block ciphers on this IoT board.

In this section, we aim to provide a guideline for designers to choose lightweight block ciphers for applications which targeting low-cost Wi-Fi module IoT platforms. This study compares software implementations of PRESENT, HIGHT, SIMON, and SPECK lightweight block ciphers.

Lightweight block ciphers have been encrypted with the CBC mode. We used two IoT devices (two WeMos D1 ESP8266 Wi-Fi boards) to ensure secure communication between the two devices and proposed a scenario for this communication. According to this scenario, sensitive data is encrypted by using a lightweight block cipher on the first Wi-Fi board, and then encrypted data is sent to the other Wi-Fi board. The data is decrypted by using the same lightweight block cipher on the second board. Also, the master key and round keys are stored in RAM.

In Table 7.9, performance comparison (in cycles/byte) of these ciphers for different message lengths is given. In our benchmarking, we use message (single messages) sizes from 128 bytes to 1,024 bytes. Performance measurement results of the various message lengths have been listed for encryption, decryption, and key scheduling execution times. Different message lengths have been encrypted and decrypted for all ciphers using the CBC mode. As a result, SIMON and SPECK, particularly SPECK ciphers, achieved the best performance on the IoT board. This is a usual result because, according to previous studies, the same ciphers also achieved the best performance on 8-bit, 16-bit, and 32-bit microcontroller platforms. PRESENT is a hardware targeted cipher, so, as expected, it achieved a slower performance than others.

In the next section, authentication problems and solutions for IoT devices have been given in detail.

## 7.3 Authentication problems and solutions for IoT devices

Confidentiality, integrity, and availability terms define the policies for secure communication. Authenticity can be defined as an additional concept to these security objectives. It means that the user knows each arriving information comes

*Table 7.9    Software performance comparisons of PRESENT, HIGHT, SIMON, and SPECK ciphers on WeMos D1 ESP8266 Wi-Fi board*

| Cipher | Size of data (bytes) | Encryption time (cycles/byte) | Decryption time (cycles/byte) | Key sch. time (cycles/byte) |
|--------|------|------|------|------|
| PRESENT | 128 | 15,423.62 | 15,347.22 | 289.71 |
|         | 256 | 15,471.52 | 15,510.20 | 292.17 |
|         | 512 | 15,486.89 | 15,486.15 | 293.39 |
|         | 1024 | 15,482.26 | 15,512.73 | 301.99 |
| HIGHT | 128 | 593.25 | 555.53 | 163.57 |
|       | 256 | 592.14 | 552.22 | 162.23 |
|       | 512 | 580.04 | 565.14 | 175.77 |
|       | 1024 | 816.34 | 890.01 | 254.43 |
| SIMON | 128 | 89.84 | 92.41 | 2.48 |
|       | 256 | 89.84 | 92.41 | 4.96 |
|       | 512 | 91.07 | 96.09 | 9.93 |
|       | 1024 | 174.72 | 246.71 | 22.32 |
| SPECK | 128 | 61.63 | 58.13 | 0.46 |
|       | 256 | 61.63 | 58.13 | 0.91 |
|       | 512 | 63.73 | 58.13 | 1.83 |
|       | 1024 | 61.63 | 141.56 | 11.02 |

from a trusted part. In a block cipher, if we have longer or shorter messages than the block size, operation modes are used, e.g., electronic codebook (ECB), CBC, cipher feedback (CFB), output feedback (OFB), and counter (CTR) modes. These modes ensure data confidentiality.

Two-party communication techniques have been developed to handle confidentiality and authenticity problems. Fully homomorphic encryption (FHE), secure multi-party computation (MPC), and zero-knowledge proofs (ZK) are two-part communication techniques. Symmetrically encrypted MPC values are stored in MPC applications. First, messages are encrypted with encryption algorithms, and then the cloud homomorphically decrypts the messages. All processes are done on the encrypted messages in FHE schemes. Thus, a huge ciphertext expansion is avoided. In the FHE scheme, if it is possible to evaluate Boolean circuit or arithmetic function efficiently on ciphertexts. Designing a computational model with almost free linear operations in FHE scheme influences positively on latency and throughput metrics. Almost free linear operations optimize or minimize AND-depth, the number of ANDs per bit, and the number of ANDs. In the literature, there are recently published papers which aim to minimize the number of ANDs such as LowMC, Kreyvium, FLIP, and MiMC [74].

The increased complexity of the communication technology has brought along lots of different attacks; therefore, new mechanisms should be designed to deal with these attacks. For example, masquerade, content modification, sequence modification, timing modification attacks can be prevented by using a message authentication mechanism. Message authentication is a mechanism that verifies that these messages come from the expected source and have not been altered. Basically, message authentication has low and high levels of functionality. At the low level, the function produces an authenticator to authenticate the messages. Then, this function is used as a primitive at the high level to verify the authenticity of the messages. Message encryption, hash function, and message authentication code (MAC) can be used to produce an authenticator. The ciphertext can be used as the authenticator in the message encryption. In the hash function, a function is defined, and this function maps the message to a fixed-length hash value. This hash value can be used as an authenticator (e.g., secure hash algorithm (SHA). SHA-0, SHA-1, SHA-2, and SHA-3 are hash functions; more details are given in [4]). MAC is known as a cryptographic checksum. By using a function of the message and a shared secret key, a fixed length value is produced. This value can be used as an authenticator. When the MAC function is compared with an encryption function (algorithm), MAC function does not need to be reversible.

Symmetric encryption provides authentication too, but why do we need to use MAC? Three scenarios which use MAC, given in the following, ensure more efficiency than encryption algorithms [9]:

- In this system, there are lots of applications in which the same message is broadcast to several destinations. The system needs to monitor all of them. Thus, it is cheaper to have only one supervisor destination to monitor the authentication.
- This is a system in which one side has a heavy load and does not have enough time to decrypt all incoming messages. Authentication is performed by choosing messages randomly to control the system.
- In this system, authentication of a program is needed. It can be efficient to attach MAC to the program to ensure the integrity of the program, instead of decrypting it every time.

More scenarios can be found in [9]. The success of the MAC function is evaluated in terms of time (time spent for forgery) and message-tag pairs (pairs which are created with the same key) metrics. Importantly, MAC does not ensure a digital signature because two parties (sender–receiver) share the same key.

There are MAC-based structures that use symmetric block ciphers, hash-based message authentication code (HMAC), data authentication algorithm (DAA), and cipher-based message authentication code (CMAC). HMAC uses hash functions, and its security depends on the cryptographic strength of this function. DAA and CMAC use block ciphers. The DES cipher is used with a CBC mode to encrypt messages, and the final block of the message is used as MAC in DAA. However, DAA is not secure for variable-length messages. Two keys and a padding process are used to overcome the message size limitation of the DAA in CMAC.

Encryption and MAC are used together to ensure confidentiality and authenticity in the authenticated encryption. While encryption guarantees that the attacker cannot learn anything about the sensitive message, MAC guarantees that attacker cannot manipulate data. There are different approaches to combine encryption and MAC. These are hashing followed by encryption, authentication followed by encryption (mildly insecure), encryption followed by authentication (secure), and independent encryption and authentication (generically insecure) [9]. Decryption and verification are quite simple in the authenticated encryption. In the encryption followed by authentication approach, the verification process is done first, and then decryption is done. In the other three approaches, decryption is done first, and then verification is done.

The requirements for a good authenticated encryption design can be summarized as follows [9]:

- MACs should be resistant to cryptanalytic attacks, e.g., brute force.
- MACs should have some resistances, e.g., collision resistance and preimage resistance.
- MACs should be uniformly distributed.
- MACs should be unique, meaning it should not be possible to obtain more than one message with the same MAC.
- MAC value should be dependent on all the message bits.

In authenticated encryption, the message is encrypted with an encryption algorithm where a tag value authenticates the associated data and message. Adding nonce value randomizes the structure. In the decryption process, if the tag value is true, the message is shown.

According to [9], counter with cipher block chaining-message authentication code (CCM) and Galois counter mode (GCM) are two examples of the authenticated encryption modes. Additionally, CCM and GCM are standardized by the NIST. The CCM mode has two algorithms, namely, the CTR mode encryption algorithm and the CBC-MAC authentication algorithm. In this mode, it should be a trade-off between lengths of the nonce and the tag. Moreover, an encryption key is used both to generate tag and to encrypt plaintext pairs. The GCM mode provides low cost and low latency because of the parallelizable structure. It is designed as encryption followed by authentication approach. Additionally, the GCM-SIV mode is based on the SIV paradigm. It was designed in 2015 and revised in 2017. It uses authentication followed by encryption (using AES algorithm) design and guarantees security against nonce reuse [75].

In the literature, many lightweight authenticated encryption schemes have been proposed for secure applications of low-cost embedded systems. C-QUARK, ASC-1, ALE, FIDES, ACORN (v1, v2, v3), ASCON, Joltik, Ketje, SCREAM&iSCREAM, LAC, Sablier, and Hummingbird-2 are lightweight authenticated encryption schemes [76]. This question is important "Are the standard authenticated encryption modes suitable for the lightweight cryptography?" Unfortunately, lightweight cryptography ciphers have practical limitations. Generally, block and key sizes should be chosen as an acceptable value in lightweight cryptography, but this makes the standard modes theoretically vulnerable to the attacks. Memory consumption and circuit size are insignificant for some standard modes; however, these metrics are crucial for lightweight hardware implementations. Nevertheless, the lightweight authenticated schemes given above are dedicated design, so they do not use a mode of operation that converts a scheme into an authenticated cipher.

SILC and JAMBU are two lightweight authenticated modes which are used to convert lightweight block ciphers into a lightweight authenticated encryption scheme.

Both modes have nonce-reuse resistance. The JAMBU mode, which is hardware efficient (SIMON-JAMBU, AES-JAMBU), can be a good choice especially for resource-constrained devices such as IoT because it has the minimum state size compared to other authenticated encryption modes. According to hardware comparison results given in [77], the SILC mode of operation has the same performance as the CCM mode.

## 7.4   Conclusion

In recent years, many algorithms have been developed for highly constrained applications. Lightweight block ciphers, in particular, can cope with the limitations of these applications. The selection of a lightweight block cipher is important because it affects the requirements of the system in terms of cost, area, speed, latency, and bandwidth.

In this chapter, lightweight block ciphers and components and metrics that are important while designing a lightweight block cipher were handled in detail, and the requirements for constructing perfect diffusion layers and their design rationale for lightweight block ciphers were given. The hardware efficiency of the linear algebra-based diffusion matrices was analyzed by using the XOR count metric. The existing best-known XOR count results for efficient MDS matrices were compared.

Additionally, efficient implementations of the lightweight algorithms and protocols were examined for lightweight cryptography standards. mCrypton, HIGHT, PRESENT, PRINTcipher, KLEIN, TWINE, Piccolo, PRINCE, SIMON, and SPECK lightweight block ciphers were compared on 8-bit, 16-bit, and 32-bit microcontrollers. Different from previous studies, a software performance comparison of PRESENT, HIGHT, SIMON, and SPECK ciphers was given for the WeMos D1 ESP8266 Wi-Fi board. We aimed to provide a guideline for designers in choosing lightweight block ciphers for applications that target low-cost Wi-Fi module IoT platforms. According to results, SIMON and SPECK ciphers achieved the best performance for this platform.

Also in this chapter, some open problems were described, such as whether there is any standardization of lightweight applications in which components are required for a cipher, and what are the requirements of real-world applications to ensure practical security and privacy for IoT devices?

## Acknowledgment

Sedat Akleylek is partially supported by OMU under Grant No. PYO.MUH. 1906.17.003.

## References

[1]   Bogdanov A, Knudsen LR, Leander G, *et al.* PRESENT: An Ultra-Lightweight Block Cipher. In: Paillier P and Verbauwhede I, editors. Cryptographic Hardware and Embedded Systems – CHES 2007: Proceedings of the

International Workshop on Cryptographic Hardware and Embedded Systems. Lecture Notes in Computer Science: Springer, Berlin, Heidelberg; 2007. p. 450–466.

[2] Hong D, Sung J, Hong S, *et al.* HIGHT: A New Block Cipher Suitable for Low-Resource Device. In: Goubin L and Matsui M, editors. Cryptographic Hardware and Embedded Systems – CHES 2006: Proceedings of the International Workshop on Cryptographic Hardware and Embedded Systems. Lecture Notes in Computer Science: Springer, Berlin, Heidelberg; 2006. p. 46–59.

[3] Beaulieu R, Shors D, Smith J, Treatman-Clark S, Weeks B, and Wingers L. The SIMON and SPECK Families of Lightweight Block Ciphers. Cryptology ePrint Archive: Report 2013/404; 2013 [cited 2018 Feb 28]. Available from: https://eprint.iacr.org/2013/404.pdf.

[4] Avanzi R. A Salad of Block Ciphers. IACR Cryptology ePrint Archive; 2016.

[5] Schneier B. Self-study course in block cipher cryptanalysis. *Cryptologia*. 2000;24(1):18–34.

[6] Crama Y and Hammer PL, editors. *Boolean Models and Methods in Mathematics, Computer Science, and Engineering*. 1st ed. New York: Cambridge University; 2010.

[7] Prathiba A and Kanchana Bhaaskaran VS. Lightweight S-Box Architecture for Secure Internet of Things. *Information*. 2018;9(1):1–13.

[8] CryptoLUX Wiki. Lightweight Block Ciphers; 2018 [cited 2018 Mar 30]. Available from: https://www.cryptolux.org/index.php/Lightweight_Block_Ciphers.

[9] Stallings W, editor. *Cryptography and Network Security: Principles and Practice*. 6th ed. England: Pearson Education Limited; 2014.

[10] Ahmadian Z, Salmasizadeh M, and Aref MZ. Biclique cryptanalysis of the full-round KLEIN block cipher. *IET Information Security*. 2015;9(5):294–301.

[11] Huang J, Vaudenay S, and Lai X. On the Key Schedule of Lightweight Block Ciphers. In: Meier W and Mukhopadhyay D, editors. Progress in Cryptology – INDOCRYPT 2014: Proceedings of the International Conference in Cryptology in India. Lecture Notes in Computer Science: Springer, Cham; 2014. p. 124–142.

[12] Chen J, Wang M, and Preneel B. Impossible Differential Cryptanalysis of the Lightweight Block Ciphers TEA, XTEA and HIGHT. In: Mitrokotsa A and Vaudenay S, editors. Progress in Cryptology – AFRICACRYPT 2012: Proceedings of the International Conference on Cryptology in Africa. Lecture Notes in Computer Science: Springer, Berlin, Heidelberg; 2012. p. 117–137.

[13] Ozen O, Varıcı K, Tezcan C, *et al.* Lightweight Block Ciphers Revisited: Cryptanalysis of Reduced Round PRESENT and HIGHT. In: Boyd C, Nieto JG, editors. Information Security and Privacy – ACISP 2009: Proceedings of the Australasian Conference on Information Security and Privacy. Lecture Notes in Computer Science: Springer, Berlin, Heidelberg; 2009. p. 90–107.

[14] Anderson, R, Biham, E, and Knudsen, L. Serpent: A Proposal for the Advanced Encryption Standard; 1998 [cited 2018 Mar 07]. Available from: http://www.cl.cam.ac.uk/~rja14/Papers/serpent.pdf.

[15]   Bertoni G, Daemen J, Peeters M, *et al.* The Making of KECCAK. *Cryptologia.* 2014;38(1):26–60.

[16]   Daemen J. Cipher and Hash Function Design, Strategies Based On Linear and Differential Cryptanalysis [PhD Thesis]. Katholieke Universiteit Leuven. Belgium; 1995.

[17]   Daemen J and Rijmen V. The Wide Trail Design Strategy. In: Honary B, editor. Cryptography and Coding: Proceedings of the IMA International Conference on Cryptography and Coding. Lecture Notes in Computer Science: Springer, Berlin, Heidelberg; 2001. p. 222–238.

[18]   Borghoff J, Canteaut A, Güneysu T, *et al.* PRINCE – A Low-Latency Block Cipher for Pervasive Computing Applications. In: Wang X, Sako K, editors. Advances in Cryptology – ASIACRYPT 2012: Proceedings of the International Conference on the Theory and Application of Cryptology and Information Security. Lecture Notes in Computer Science: Springer, Berlin, Heidelberg; 2012. p. 208–225.

[19]   Lim CH and Korkishko T. mCrypton – A Lightweight Block Cipher for Security of Low-Cost RFID Tags and Sensors. In: Song JS, Kwon T, and Yung M, editors. Information Security Applications – WISA 2005: Proceedings of the International Workshop on Cryptographic Hardware and Embedded Systems. Lecture Notes in Computer Science: Springer, Berlin, Heidelberg; 2006. p. 243–258.

[20]   Jian Guo J, Peyrin T, Poschmann A, *et al.* The LED Block Cipher. In: Preneel B and Takagi T, editors. Cryptographic Hardware and Embedded Systems – CHES 2011: Proceedings of the International Workshop on Cryptographic Hardware and Embedded Systems. Lecture Notes in Computer Science: Springer, Berlin, Heidelberg; 2011. p. 326–341.

[21]   Barreto PSLM and Rijmen V. The Anubis block cipher; 2001 [cited 2018 Mar 15]. Available from: http://www.larc.usp.br/~pbarreto/anubis-tweak.zip.

[22]   Gauravaram P, Knudsen LR, Matusiewicz K, *et al.* Grøstl – a SHA-3 candidate. Submission to NIST (2008) [cited 2018 Mar 15]. Available from: http://www.groestl.info/.

[23]   Barreto P and Rijmen V. The Khazad Legacy-Level Block Cipher. First Open NESSIE Workshop, KU-Leuven; 2000 [cited 2018 Mar 15].

[24]   Albrecht MR, Driessen B, Kavun EB, *et al.* Block Ciphers – Focus on the Linear Layer (feat. PRIDE). In: Garay JA and Gennaro R, editors. Advances in Cryptology – CRYPTO 2014: Proceedings of the International Cryptology Conference. Lecture Notes in Computer Science: Springer, Berlin, Heidelberg; 2014. p. 57–76.

[25]   Dobraunig C, Eichlseder M, Mendel F, and Schläffer M. Ascon – A Family of Authenticated Encryption Algorithms; 2014 [cited 2018 Mar 15]. Available from: http://ascon.iaik.tugraz.at.

[26]   Karakoç F, Demirci H, and Harmancı AE. ITUbee: A Software Oriented Lightweight Block Cipher. In: Avoine G, Kara O, editors. Lightweight Cryptography for Security and Privacy – LightSec 2013: Proceedings of the International Workshop on Lightweight Cryptography for Security and

Privacy. Lecture Notes in Computer Science: Springer, Berlin, Heidelberg; 2013. p. 16–27.

[27] Engels D, Saarinen MO, Schweitzer P, *et al.* The Hummingbird-2 Lightweight Authenticated Encryption Algorithm. In: Juel A and Paar C, editors. RFID. Security and Privacy – RFIDSec 2011: Proceedings of the International Workshop on Radio Frequency Identification: Security and Privacy Issues. Lecture Notes in Computer Science: Springer, Berlin, Heidelberg; 2012. p. 19–31.

[28] Daemen J, Peeters M, Van Assche G, and Rijmen V. The NOEKEON Block Cipher. First Open NESSIE Workshop, KU-Leuven; 2000 [cited 2018 Mar 15]. Available from: http://gro.noekeon.org/Noekeon-spec.pdf.

[29] Vaudenay S. On the need for multipermutations: Cryptanalysis of MD4 and SAFER. In: Preneel B, editor. Fast Software Encryption – FSE 1994: Proceedings of the International Workshop on Fast Software Encryption. Lecture Notes in Computer Science: Springer, Berlin, Heidelberg; 1994. p. 286–297.

[30] Schnorr CP and Vaudenay S. Black box cryptanalysis of hash networks based on multipermutations. In: De Santis A, editor. Advances in Cryptology – EUROCRYPT'94: Proceedings of the Workshop on the Theory and Application of Cryptographic Techniques. Lecture Notes in Computer Science: Springer, Berlin, Heidelberg; 1995. p. 47–57.

[31] Shibutani K, Isobe T, Hiwatari H, *et al.* Piccolo: An Ultra-Lightweight Blockcipher. In: Preneel B and Takagi T, editors. Cryptographic Hardware and Embedded Systems – CHES 2011: Proceedings of the International Workshop on Cryptographic Hardware and Embedded Systems. Lecture Notes in Computer Science: Springer, Berlin, Heidelberg; 2011. p. 342–357.

[32] Aokı K, Ichıkawa T, Kanda M, *et al.* Camellia: A 128-Bit Block Cipher Suitable for Multiple Platforms – Design and Analysis. In: Stinson DR and Tavares S, editors. Selected Areas in Cryptography – SAC 2000: Proceedings of the International Workshop on Selected Areas in Cryptography. Lecture Notes in Computer Science: Springer, Berlin, Heidelberg; 2001. p. 39–56.

[33] Daesung Kwon D, Kim J, Park S, *et al.* New Block Cipher: ARIA. In: Lim JI and Lee DH, editors. Information Security and Cryptology – ICISC 2003: Proceedings of the International Conference on Information Security and Cryptology. Lecture Notes in Computer Science: Springer, Berlin, Heidelberg; 2004. p. 432–445.

[34] Youssef AM, Mister S, and Tavares S. On the Design of Linear Transformations for Substitution Permutation Encryption Networks. Proceedings of Selected Areas in Cryptography (SAC'97); 1997. p. 40–48.

[35] Khoo K, Peyrin T, Poschmann AY, *et al.* FOAM: Searching for Hardware-Optimal SPN Structures and Components with a Fair Comparison. In: Batina L and Robshaw M, editors. A Cryptographic Hardware and Embedded Systems – CHES 2014: Proceedings of the International Workshop on Cryptographic Hardware and Embedded Systems. Lecture Notes in Computer Science: Springer, Berlin, Heidelberg; 2014. p. 433–450.

[36] Li Y and Wang M. On the Construction of Lightweight Circulant Involutory MDS Matrices. In: Peyrin T, editor. Fast Software Encryption – FSE 2016:

Proceedings of the International Conference on Fast Software Encryption. Lecture Notes in Computer Science: Springer, Berlin, Heidelberg; 2016. p. 121–139.

[37] Liu M and Sim SM. Lightweight MDS Generalized Circulant Matrices. In: Peyrin T, editor. Fast Software Encryption – FSE 2016: Proceedings of the International Conference on Fast Software Encryption. Berlin, Heidelberg: Springer; 2016. p. 101–120.

[38] Sarkar S and Syed H. Lightweight Diffusion Layer: Importance of Toeplitz Matrices. *IACR Transactions on Symmetric Cryptology*. 2016;2016(1):95–113.

[39] Sarkar S and Syed H. Analysis of Toeplitz MDS Matrices. In: Pieprzyk J and Suriadi S, editors. Information Security and Privacy – ACISP 2017: Proceedings of the Australasian Conference on Information Security and Privacy. Lecture Notes in Computer Science: Springer, Cham; 2017. p. 3–18.

[40] Kurt Pehlivanoğlu M, Sakallı MT, Akleylek S, *et al.* Generalization of Hadamard Matrix to Generate Involutory MDS Matrices for Lightweight Cryptography. *IET Information Security*. 2018;12(4):348–355.

[41] Sim SM, Khoo K, Oggier F, *et al.* Lightweight MDS Involution Matrices. In: Leander G, editor. Fast Software Encryption – FSE 2015: Proceedings of the International Workshop on Fast Software Encryption. Lecture Notes in Computer Science: Springer, Berlin, Heidelberg; 2015. p. 471–493.

[42] Chand Gupta K and Ghosh Ray I. On Constructions of Involutory MDS Matrices. In: Amr Youssef A, Nitaj A, and Hassanien AE, editors. Progress in Cryptology – AFRICACRYPT 2013: Proceedings of the International Conference on Cryptology in Africa. Lecture Notes in Computer Science: Springer, Berlin, Heidelberg; 2013. p. 43–60.

[43] Poschmann A, Ling S, and Wang H. 256 Bit Standardized Crypto for 650 GE – GOST Revisited. In: Mangard S and Standaert FX, editors. Cryptographic Hardware and Embedded Systems, CHES 2010: Proceedings of the International Workshop on Cryptographic Hardware and Embedded Systems. Lecture Notes in Computer Science: Springer, Berlin, Heidelberg; 2010. p. 219–233.

[44] Schneier B. The Blowfish Encryption Algorithm. *Dr Dobb's Journal*. 1994;19(4):38–40.

[45] NISTIR 8114. Report on Lightweight Cryptography. National Institute of Standards and Technology U.S. Department of Commerce; 2017 [cited 2018 Feb 13]. Available from: https://doi.org/10.6028/NIST.IR.8114.

[46] ITL Bulletin. Toward Standardizing Lightweight Cryptography [NIST Pubs]. National Institute of Standards and Technology U.S. Department of Commerce; 2017.

[47] Hatzivasilis G, Fysarakis K, Papaefstathiou I, *et al.* A review of lightweight block ciphers. *Journal of Cryptographic Engineering*. 2017;8(2):141–184.

[48] Poschmann AY. Lightweight Cryptography – Cryptographic Engineering for a Pervasive [PhD Thesis]. Ruhr University. Bochum, Germany; 2009.

[49] Transitions: Recommendation for Transitioning the Use of Cryptographic Algorithms and Key Lengths [NIST Pubs]. NIST Special Publication (SP) 800-131A Revision 1, National Institute of Standards and Technology; 2015.

[50] Chen L. Lightweight Cryptography Standards Developed in ISO/IEC SC27; 2016 [cited 2018 Feb 27]. Available from: https://www.nist.gov/sites/default/files/documents/2016/10/17/chen-presentation-lwc2016.pdf.

[51] Shirai T, Shibutani K, Akishita T, *et al*. The 128-Bit Blockcipher CLEFIA (Extended Abstract). In: Biryukov A, editor. Fast Software Encryption – FSE 2007: Proceedings of the International Workshop on Fast Software Encryption. Lecture Notes in Computer Science: Springer, Berlin, Heidelberg; 2007. p. 181–195.

[52] Watanabe D, Ideguchi K, Kitahara J, Muto K, and Furuichi H. Enocoro-80: A Hardware Oriented Stream Cipher [The Third International Conference on Availability, Reliability and Security]; 2008 [cited 2018 Feb 28]. Available from: http://ieeexplore.ieee.org/stamp/stamp.jsp?arnumber=4529493.

[53] De Cannière C and Preneel B. The SIMON and SPECK Families of Lightweight Block Ciphers [ECRYPT Stream Cipher Project]; 2006 [cited 2018 Feb 28]. Available from: http://www.ecrypt.eu.org/stream/p3ciphers/trivium/trivium_p3.pdf.

[54] Guo J, Peyrin T, and Poschmann A. The PHOTON family of lightweight hash functions. In: Rogaway P, editor. Advances in Cryptology – CRYPTO 2011: Proceedings of the Annual Cryptology Conference. Lecture Notes in Computer Science: Springer, Berlin, Heidelberg; 2011. p. 222–239.

[55] Bogdanov A, Knežević M, Leander G, *et al*. Spongent: A Lightweight Hash Function. In: Preneel B and Takagi T, editor. Cryptographic Hardware and Embedded Systems – CHES 2011: Proceedings of the International Workshop on Cryptographic Hardware and Embedded Systems. Lecture Notes in Computer Science: Springer, Berlin, Heidelberg; 2011. p. 312–325.

[56] Hirose S, Ideguchi K, Kuwakado H, *et al*. A Lightweight 256-Bit Hash Function for Hardware and Low-End Devices: Lesamnta-LW. In: Rhee K and Nyang D, editors. Information Security and Cryptology – ICISC 2010: Proceedings of the International Conference on Information Security and Cryptology. Lecture Notes in Computer Science: Springer, Berlin, Heidelberg; 2010. p. 151–168.

[57] Mouha N, Mennink B, Van Herrewege A, Watanabe D, Preneel B, and Verbauwhede I. Chaskey: An Efficient MAC Algorithm for 32-bit Microcontrollers [Cryptology ePrint Archive: Report 2014/386]; 2014 [cited 2018 Mar 01]. Available from: https://eprint.iacr.org/2014/386.pdf.

[58] Automatic Identification and Data Capture Techniques. International Organization for Standardization [cited 2018 Mar 01]. Available from: https://www.iso.org/ics/35.040.50/x/.

[59] CRYPTREC. Cryptography Research and Evaluation Committees [cited 2018 Mar 02]. Available from: http://www.cryptrec.go.jp/english/index.html.

[60] Grance T. The Internet of Things; Epic Change to Follow. National Institute of Standards and Technology; 2016 [cited 2018 Mar 15]. Available from: https://csacongress.org/wp-content/uploads/2015/12/Tim-Grance-The-Internet-of-Things-Epic-Change-to-Follow.pdf.

[61] Law YW, Doumen J, and Hartel P. Survey and benchmark of block ciphers for wireless sensor networks. *ACM Transactions on Sensor Networks (TOSN)*. 2006;2(1):65–93.

[62] Kerckhof S, Durvaux F, Hocquet C, *et al.* Towards green cryptography: a comparison of lightweight ciphers from the energy viewpoint. In: Prouff E and Schaumont P, editors. Cryptographic Hardware and Embedded Systems – CHES 2012: Proceedings of the International Workshop on Cryptographic Hardware and Embedded Systems. Lecture Notes in Computer Science: Springer, Berlin, Heidelberg; 2012. p. 390–407.

[63] Knežević M, Nikov V, and Rombouts P. Low-Latency Encryption – Is "Lightweight = Light + Wait"? In: Prouff E and Schaumont P, editors. Cryptographic Hardware and Embedded Systems – CHES 2012: Proceedings of the International Workshop on Cryptographic Hardware and Embedded Systems. Lecture Notes in Computer Science: Springer, Berlin, Heidelberg; 2012. p. 426–446.

[64] Matsui M and Murakami Y. Minimalism of Software Implementation. In: Moriai S, editor. Fast Software Encryption – FSE 2013: Proceedings of the International Workshop on Fast Software Encryption. Lecture Notes in Computer Science: Springer, Berlin, Heidelberg; 2014. p. 393–409.

[65] Cazorla M, Gourgeon S, Marquet K, and Minier M. Implementations of lightweight block ciphers on a WSN430 sensor; 2013 [cited 2018 Mar 15]. Available from: http://bloc.project.citi-lab.fr/library.html.

[66] Bernstein DJ and Lange T. eBACS: ECRYPT Benchmarking of Cryptographic Systems. ECRYPT II [cited 2018 Mar 16]. Available from: https://bench.cr.yp.to/.

[67] ATHENa: Automated Tools for Hardware EvaluatioN Project Website. George Mason University [cited 2018 Mar 16]. Available from: http://cryptography.gmu.edu/athena/.

[68] Dinu D, Le Corre Y, Khovratovich D, Perrin L, Großschädl J, and Biryukov A. Triathlon of lightweight block ciphers for the internet of things [Cryptology ePrint Archive: Report 2015/209]; 2015 [cited 2018 Mar 16]. Available from: https://eprint.iacr.org/2015/209.pdf.

[69] FELICS Triathlon; 2015 [cited 2018 Mar 16]. Available from: https://www.cryptolux.org/index.php/FELICS_Triathlon.

[70] Dinu D, Biryukov A, Großschädl J, Khovratovich D, Le Corre Y, and Perrin LA. FELICS – Fair Evaluation of Lightweight Cryptographic Systems. NIST Lightweight Cryptography Workshop 2015; 2015 [cited 2018 Mar 15]. Available from: https://csrc.nist.gov/csrc/media/events/lightweight-crypto-graphy-workshop-2015/documents/papers/session7-dinu-paper.pdf.

[71] CryptoLUX. FELICS – Fair Evaluation of Lightweight Cryptographic Systems. National Institute of Standards and Technology; 2015 [cited 2018 Mar 15]. Available from: https://www.cryptolux.org/index.php/FELICS.

[72] Marchand C, Bossuet L, and Gaj K. Ultra-Lightweight Implementation in Area of Block Ciphers. In: Bossuet L and Torres L, editors. Foundations of

Hardware IP Protection. Lecture Notes in Computer Science: Springer, Cham; 2017. p. 177–203.

[73]  Sadhukhan R, Patranabis S, Ghoshal A, *et al.* An Evaluation of Lightweight Block Ciphers for Resource-Constrained Applications: Area, Performance, and Security. Journal of Hardware and Systems Security. 2017;1(3):203–218.

[74]  Dobraunig C, Eichlseder M, Grassi L, *et al.* Rasta: A cipher with low ANDdepth and few ANDs per bit; 2018 [cited 2018 Mar 27]. Available from: https://eprint.iacr.org/2018/181.pdf.

[75]  Gueron S and Lindell Y. GCM-SIV: Full Nonce Misuse-Resistant Authenticated Encryption at Under One Cycle per Byte [Cryptology ePrint Archive: Report 2015/102]; 2017 [cited 2018 Mar 30]. Available from: https://eprint.iacr.org/2015/102.pdf.

[76]  CryptoLUX Wiki. Lightweight Authenticated Encryption; 2018 [cited 2018 Mar 30]. Available from: https://www.cryptolux.org/index.php/Lightweight_Authenticated_Encryption#C-QUARK.

[77]  The JAMBU Lightweight Authentication Encryption Mode (v2.1). CAESAR Competition; 2016 [cited 2018 Mar 30]. Available from: https://competitions.cr.yp.to/round3/jambuv21.pdf.

*Chapter 8*

# Identification schemes in the post-quantum area based on multivariate polynomials with applications in cloud and IoT

*Sedat Akleylek[1] and Meryem Soysaldı[1]*

In this chapter, we survey the identification schemes based on multivariate polynomials over a finite field. We provide some basic definitions needed to construct the structure of identification schemes based on multivariate polynomials over a finite field. Then, we provide a brief survey of identification schemes based on multivariate polynomials by considering applications in different platforms. We analyze them in view of the zero knowledge property and the number of passes such as 3-pass and 5-pass. By considering open problems in the literature, we propose a novel identification scheme based on multivariate quadratic polynomials. Then, we compare them in terms of efficiency. We also provide a discussion for cloud, IoT, and big data applications of quantum secure identification schemes.

## 8.1 Introduction

Cryptosystems have been used to achieve information security concepts such as confidentiality, integrity, authentication, and non-repudiation. Many of them have been broken and revealed to be insecure. Some of them have been further enhanced in terms of security. Nowadays, there are many cryptosystems that known to be secure such as RSA, DSA, and ECDSA in classical computers. However, we have a new-generation computation device: quantum computer.

The idea of quantum computer was suggested by Richard Feymann in 1982 [1]. In 1997, the first 2-qubit quantum computer was built [2]. In 2001, the factorization was achieved with 5-qubit quantum computers [2]. With these developments, the same companies like IBM, Google, and Intel have started to compete to build the quantum computers. In November 2017, the IBM announced to build 50-qubit quantum computer. In early 2018, the company is also working a 20-qubit system through its cloud-computing platform. Google announced in March 2018 in the report of the

[1]Department of Computer Engineering, Ondokuz Mayıs University, Turkey

American Physical Society that they were testing a 72-qubit quantum computer that would surpass IBM's 50-qubit quantum computer announcement [3].

Advances in quantum computers threaten public-key cryptosystems. They are based on the hardness of discrete logarithm problem or factorization problems to solve daily-life problems such as digital signature, key exchange, authentication, and identification. There is no polynomial-time algorithm that can solve these problems in classical computers. However, Shor proposed a polynomial-time algorithm that can solve these problems in quantum computers in 1994 [4]. With this algorithm, all public-key cryptosystems that we currently use will become insecure after quantum computers [5,6]. Therefore, quantum-secure cryptosystems are needed. There are a variety of proposals for signature, public-key encryption schemes, key exchange, and identification schemes based on the quantum secure cryptosystems [5]. The National Institute of Standards and Technology (NIST) has emphasized the importance of post-quantum cryptography and started a project to find and standardize quantum-resistant algorithms [7]. Because of this, researchers have begun to investigate quantum-resistant systems. There are many computationally hard problem families to construct quantum-secure cryptosystems. These are hash-based, code-based, lattice-based, isogeny-based, and multivariate cryptosystems [6]. In [8], recent developments in post-quantum cryptography were surveyed. They focused on the construction and security of lattice and multivariate polynomial-based cryptosystems. A state-of-the-art for multivariate polynomial cryptosystems is given in [9,10]. They mainly provide the construction ideas and the security properties of multivariate polynomial cryptosystems.

There are many identification schemes based on multivariate polynomials [11–13], [14]. The identification schemes have a great importance for signature schemes since they are the basis of signature schemes. In [15], a 5-pass identification scheme is transformed to signature scheme.

Traditional public key cryptosystems such as RSA, DSA, and ECDSA will be broken with quantum computer and this threatens the security of the IoT and cloud security in terms of authentication [16]. It is necessary to work on how cryptosystems known to be quantum secure can be efficiently adapted to IoT devices [17]. It is known that multivariate polynomials and lattice-based cryptosystems are efficient for IoT devices in post-quantum world [16]. In this chapter, we survey identification schemes based on multivariate polynomials.

## 8.1.1    Motivation

Identification schemes are very important for authentication and digital signature in cloud and IoT applications. The security of these authentication and digital signature systems depends computationally hard problems such as integer factorization and discrete logarithm problem which are solved in quantum computers in polynomial time by using Shor's algorithm. So, there is a huge need quantum-secure identification schemes. There are many identification schemes based on multivariate polynomials over a finite field since they have good performance than others in terms of efficiency and can be used in systems with fewer resources such as smart cards and sensors.

## 8.1.2    Organization

The rest of this chapter is organized as follows. In Section 8.2, we present some basic definitions. In Section 8.3, we recall some proposed identification schemes based on multivariate polynomials. We provide a discussion in terms of memory requirements, commitment length, and computation time. Then, we compare the identification schemes. In Section 8.4, we explain the importance of identification schemes for IoT and cloud applications. In Section 8.5, we present the challenges and future directions. In Section 8.6, the conclusion is stated.

## 8.2    Preliminaries

In this section, we give some definitions to understand the topics in this chapter. In Table 8.1, all notations used in this chapter are listed.

### 8.2.1    Basics of identification schemes

Identification is required to be sure of the identity of the other party. Identification is a method that one party can verify his/her identity to the other party without giving the important knowledge [18]. An identification scheme has two parties, namely, prover and verifier. The prover has public and private keys whereas the verifier has only the prover's public key. An identification scheme takes place in three phases. Firstly, the prover makes a commitment to the verifier. The verifier challenges the given commitment. Then the prover responds to the verifier's commitment. The prover tries to convince the verifier with his/her responses. The verifier takes the corresponding responses and at the end of the scheme, the verifier accepts or rejects the prover's commitment. An identification scheme is also called an interactive scheme since this scheme is performed as challenge-response between the prover and the verifier. An identification scheme is shown in Figure 8.1.

*Table 8.1    Notations*

| Notation | Definition |
|----------|------------|
| $\mathbb{F}_q$ | Finite field with $q$ elements |
| $\mathbb{F}_q^n$ | $n$-dimensional vector space of $q$ elements |
| *Com* | The commitment function |
| $v = F(s)$ | Public key |
| *Ch* | The challenge value |
| *Rsp* | The response value |
| *hc* | The hash value of commitment values |
| *s* | Secret key |
| *F* | A system of multivariate polynomials |
| *m* | The number of equations in $F$ polynomial system |
| *n* | The number of variables in $F$ polynomial system |
| *G* | A polar form of $F$ polynomial system |

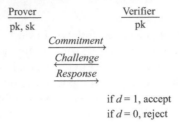

*Figure 8.1    An identification scheme*

**Definition 1:** *[12] An identification scheme consists of Setup, Keygen, P, and V algorithms, respectively.*

- *An identification scheme begins with Setup algorithm that inputs security parameter $1^\lambda$ and outputs a system parameter param.*
- *KeyGen is randomized key generation algorithm that inputs param and outputs a public key pk and a secret key sk.*
- *P and V are interactive algorithms. P algorithm that takes sk as input is performed by the prover. The verifier runs V algorithm that inputs the prover's public key pk. V algorithm returns a decision bit d as output if $d = 1$, the verifier accepts or if $d = 0$ then, the verifier rejects.*

A zero knowledge identification scheme restricts the information transferred between the prover and the verifier [19]. Underlying idea of the zero knowledge is to create a system to prove that you know the knowledge without telling what you know [20]. In a zero knowledge identification scheme, when the prover proves his/her identity to the verifier, the verifier cannot learn any useful information from the prover's public key or commitment values. A cheating prover does not deceive the verifier by claiming that he/she knows the secret key. The cheating prover may be successful several times, but as the challenge-response count increases, the success probability decreases significantly. On the contrary, the verifier cannot deceive the prover. In addition, the verifier cannot cheat another party by showing himself as a prover (pretending to be a prover), even if he/she has copied all of his communications with the prover. The verifier has only a copy of the prover's responses corresponding to his/her own challenges.

An interactive system $(P, V)$ must satisfy the following properties in order to be able to create such a zero knowledge identification scheme.

**Definition 2 (Completeness):** *[20] If the prover convinces the verifier that the prover is really the person he claims to be and the verifier accepts the prover's claim at the end of the $(P, V)$ interactive system, the completeness is satisfied.*

**Definition 3 (Soundness):** *[20] If the verifier is not deceived by a cheating prover who impersonate someone (except negligible probability $\varepsilon > 0$), the soundness is succeeded.*

Commitment schemes are used in many cryptosystems because they allow a party to make a commitment to the other party by keeping the values that construct the commitment secret. We use commitment schemes in the identification schemes to construct a zero-knowledge scheme. There are two phases in a commitment scheme denoted as *Com*: the commit phase and the reveal phase. A sender generates a commitment value $c \leftarrow Com(m, s, g)$, where $m$, $s$, $g$ are the sender's secret parameters before the commit phase starts. In commit phase, the sender commits a specific value $c$ without giving parameters that allow to compute commitment values. Then the reveal phase starts when the sender reveals the parameters $m$, $s$ and $g$. The receiver computes $c' = Com(m, s, g)$. If $c = c'$, the receiver verifies the commitment value and accepts otherwise rejects.

The main properties to be satisfied are given in Definitions 4 and 5.

**Definition 4 (Statistically hiding):** *[21] It should not be able to predict which parameters the sender use to obtain the commitment values even if the receiver has very high computational power. In other words, the receiver cannot distinguish between $c = Com(m, s)$ and $c' = Com(m, g)$.* The values produced by *Com* must be statistically close to each other. The hiding property is identified with a locked box. Because of this feature, the receiver cannot know what is in the commitment values when the sender makes a commitment.

**Definition 5 (Computationally binding):** *[21] After the commit phase, the sender should not change the parameters that used for generating the commitment value. In other words, it is hard to find the values $s'$ and $m'$ as $c = Com(m, s)$ and $c = Com(m', s')$.*

### 8.2.2 Multivariate polynomials system

Let $\mathbb{F}_q$ be finite field with $q$ elements, where $q$ is a prime power and $\mathbb{F}_q^n$ be $n$-dimensional vector space of $q$ elements.

**Definition 6:** *[6] A system of multivariate polynomials is constructed with large number of polynomials. Let $n \in \mathbb{N}$ be the number of variables, $m \in \mathbb{N}$ be the number of equations and $\alpha_{i \cdots j}^{(k)}$, $\beta_i^{(k)}$, $\gamma^{(k)} \in \mathbb{F}_q$ for $1 \le i \le j \le n$, $1 \le k \le m$ be the coefficients. A system of the multivariate $d - degree$ polynomials $F = (f_1, \cdots, f_m)$ can be given as follows:*

$$f_1(x_1, \ldots, x_n) = \sum_i^n \cdots \sum_j^n \alpha_{i \cdots j}^{(1)} \cdot \overbrace{x_i \cdot \ldots \cdot x_j}^{d} + \ldots + \sum_{i=1}^n \beta_i^{(1)} \cdot x_i + \gamma_1$$

$$f_2(x_1, \ldots, x_n) = \sum_i^n \cdots \sum_j^n \alpha_{i \cdots j}^{(2)} \cdot \overbrace{x_i \cdot \ldots \cdot x_j}^{d} + \ldots + \sum_{i=1}^n \beta_i^{(2)} \cdot x_i + \gamma_2$$

$$\vdots$$

$$f_m(x_1, \ldots, x_n) = \sum_i^n \cdots \sum_j^n \alpha_{i \cdots j}^{(m)} \cdot \overbrace{x_i \cdot \ldots \cdot x_j}^{d} + \ldots + \sum_{i=1}^n \beta_i^{(m)} \cdot x_i + \gamma_m. \tag{8.1}$$

The system of multivariate polynomials is called multivariate quadratic (MQ) or cubic (MC) polynomial system for $d = 2$ or $d = 3$, respectively. In Definition 7, the multivariate problem is given.

**Definition 7:** *[6] The multivariate problem is to solve the system $F(x) = 0$ over a finite field and find any $x = (x_1, \cdots, x_n)$ solution vector. In general, the multivariate problem is NP– complete over a finite field. The hardness of solving this problem depends on some parameters. A challenge has been initiated to solve this problem [22].*

To construct an identification scheme, one needs linearization of the elements. This can be achieved by bilinearity and polar form given in Definitions 8 and 9, respectively. The used polar form is changeable according to the degree of multivariate polynomials.

**Definition 8:** *[23] Let $x_1, x_2 \in A$, $y \in B$ and $\alpha$ be a constant. A bilinear form $G : A \times A \rightarrow B$ is a function that satisfies the following conditions:*

- $G(x_1 + x_2, y) = G(x_1, y) + G(x_2, y)$
- $G(\alpha x_1 + x_2, y) = \alpha G(x_1, y) + G(x_2, y)$

**Definition 9:** *[11][13] Let $x, y \in \mathbb{F}_q^n$ and $G$ be a bilinear function. $G$ is defined as polar form of $F$ that is a system of multivariate quadratic polynomials in Definition 6. It is shown that*

$$G(x, y) = F(x + y) - F(x) - F(y) \tag{8.2}$$

*If the multivariate cubic polynomials are used, the polar form $G$ satisfies:*

$$F(x + y) = F(x) + G(x, y) + G(y, x) + F(y) \tag{8.3}$$

**Definition 10:** *[14] Let $x_1, x_2, x_3 \in A$, $y \in B$ and $z \in C$ and $\alpha$ be a constant. A trilinear form $G : A \times B \times C \rightarrow D$ is a function that satisfies the following conditions:*

$$G(x_1 + x_2 + x_3, y, z) = G(x_1, y, z) + G(x_2, y, z) + G(x_3, y, z)$$

**Definition 11:** *[14] Let $x, y, z \in \mathbb{F}_q^n$ and $G$ be a trilinear function. $G$ is defined as polar form of $F$ which is a system of multivariate cubic polynomials. It is shown that*

$$G(x, y, z) = F(x + y + z) - F(x + y) - F(x + z) - F(y + z) + F(x) + F(y) + F(z) \tag{8.4}$$

## 8.3    Identification schemes in the post-quantum era

In this section, we introduce identification schemes based on multivariate polynomials over a finite field. Firstly, we recall the proposed 3-pass and 5-pass identification schemes in the literature. Then, we present a novel 3-pass identification

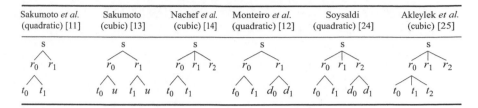

*Figure 8.2   Dividing techniques of all identification schemes based on multivariate polynomials*

scheme based on multivariate polynomials over finite field. Finally, we compare all identification schemes based on multivariate polynomials in view of memory requirements, communication length, and computation time.

In literature, there are some identification schemes based on multivariate polynomials over a finite field. The main idea behind the identification schemes is cut-and-choose approach. According to this approach, a prover sends some values to verifier without giving the secret key after separating the secret key into parts. Then, the verifier can perform the verification process of the values sent by the prover according to his/her choice. Therefore, in studies related to these schemes, the secret key is divided into parts using different techniques. The techniques used in the studies are summarized in Figure 8.2.

### 8.3.1   Sakumoto et al.'s identification schemes based on MQ polynomials

In [11], Sakumoto *et al.* proposed public key identification schemes based on multivariate quadratic polynomials over a finite field. Thus, they found a new dividing method to divide the secret key. They presented a new polar form $G$ of the multivariate quadratic polynomial system $F$ given in Definition 6 by using the property of the bilinear functions given in Definition 8. By means of the polar form, the parts of the secret key are removed from each other as much as possible. The secret key $s$, is initially represented by two parts. The one part of the secret key is the sum of the other two parts $r_0 = t_0 + t_1$ given in Figure 8.2. Finally, the secret key is obtained from the sum of the three parts.

The used construction is briefly described as follows. Let $s$ be a secret key, $F$ be a system of the multivariate quadratic polynomials as given in Definition 6 and $v = F(s)$ be a public key. Let $G$ be polar form of $F$. The public key is represented as $v = F(r_0 + r_1)$ since the secret key is divided into two parts. By using the polar form $G$ of $F$, the public key is presented as $v = F(r_0) + G(r_0, r_1) + F(r_1)$. They consider that $r_0 = t_0 + t_1$ and $F(r_0) = e_0 + e_1$. Since $r_0$ is regarded as the sum of two parts, we can write $v = e_0 + e_1 + G(t_0, r_1) + G(t_1, r_1) + F(r_1)$. Finally, it is obtained that $v = F(r_0 + r_1) = F(s)$ by using the bilinearity property of the polar form $G$ and the parts of the $F(r_0)$. The 3-pass identification scheme is given in Figure 8.3.

In the proposed 3-pass identification scheme as given in Definition 1, the prover selects randomly the parts of the secret key. Then, the prover computes the

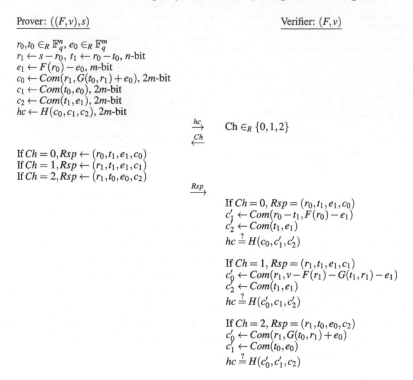

*Figure 8.3   A 3-pass identification scheme by Sakumoto et al.*

commitment values by using the string commitment function *Com* and commits the verifier. Recall that the identification schemes have zero knowledge property as long as the commitment scheme has statistically hiding and computationally binding as given in Definitions 4 and 5. In the second pass, the verifier makes a challenge. The prover sends responses the corresponding challenge. After the last pass, the verifier can verify the commitment since (8.5) is satisfied.

$$G(t_0, r_1) + e_0 = v - F(r_1) - G(t_1, r_1) - e_1$$
$$(t_0, e_0) = (r_0 - t_1, F(r_0) - e_1)$$
(8.5)

By using the above equations and the polar form, we can obtain $v = F(r_0 + r_1)$. The verifier does not find a solution $s$ for $v = F(s)$ although he/she has the parts of the secret key and public key. To be able to show that the identification schemes are secure, identification schemes must have some properties that expressed with two theorems. It is difficult to prove these two theorems for all the identification schemes. For simplicity, we provide detailed proofs for the new scheme in Section 8.3.6.

In [11], the 5-pass identification scheme based on multivariate polynomial system was also proposed. The structures used in the 5-pass identification scheme are very similar to the 3-pass scheme. The main differences are the number of the passes and random element usage in the challenge part. The parts of the secret key depend on $\alpha$ as $\alpha r_0 = t_0 + t_1$ and $\alpha F(r_0) = e_0 + e_1$. The second difference of 5-pass identification scheme from 3-pass ones is two passes that comes after commitment pass. The verifier randomly chooses $\alpha \in \mathbb{F}_q$ and sends the prover after the prover commits the commitment values. The prover uses $\alpha$ to compute the parts of the secret key as $t_1 = \alpha r_0 - t_0$ and $e_1 = \alpha F(r_0) - e_0$. Then, the prover sends $(t_1, e_1)$ to the verifier as continuation of the commitment values. The last two passes are same with 3-pass scheme that are challenge and response passes.

In the 5-pass identification scheme, either $r_0$ or $r_1$ is the response of the corresponding challenge. The parts of the secret key are determined by $\alpha$ sent by the verifier. In addition, the prover sends separately the response of the corresponding challenges and the parts of the secret key. For this reason, the 5-pass identification scheme reduces the probability of the impersonation. In Figure 8.4, the 5-pass identification scheme is given.

The verifier can verify the commitment values $(c_0, c_1)$ with (8.6).

$$G(t_0, r_1) + e_0 = \alpha(v - F(r_1)) - G(t_1, r_1) - e_1 \tag{8.6}$$

By using the properties of bilinear function and polar form given in Definitions 8 and 9, we have

$$\begin{aligned} G(t_0, r_1) + e_0 &= \alpha v - \alpha F(r_1) - G(t_1, r_1) - e_1 \\ G(t_0 + t_1, r_1) + e_0 + e_1 &= \alpha v - \alpha F(r_1) \end{aligned} \tag{8.7}$$

With considering the parts of the secret key, it is obtained as $v = F(r_0 + r_1) = F(s)$.

Prover: $((F,v),s)$                                                        Verifier: $(F,v)$

$r_0, t_0 \in_R \mathbb{F}_q^n, e_0 \in_R \mathbb{F}_q^m$
$r_1 \leftarrow s - r_0, n\text{-bit}$
$c_0 \leftarrow Com(r_0, t_0, e_0), 2m\text{-bit}$
$c_1 \leftarrow Com(r_1, G(t_0, r_1) + e_0), 2m\text{-bit}$

$\xrightarrow{(c_0, c_1)}$
$\xleftarrow{\alpha}$    $\alpha \in_R \mathbb{F}_q$

$t_1 \leftarrow \alpha r_0 - t_0$
$e_1 \leftarrow \alpha F(r_0) - e_0$

$\xrightarrow{(t_1, e_1)}$
$\xleftarrow{Ch}$    $Ch \in_R \{0, 1\}$

If $Ch = 0, Rsp \leftarrow r_0$
If $Ch = 1, Rsp \leftarrow r_1$

$\xrightarrow{Rsp}$

If $Ch = 0, Rsp = r_0$
$c_0 \stackrel{?}{=} Com(r_0, \alpha r_0 - t_1, \alpha F(r_0) - e_1)$

If $Ch = 1, Rsp = r_1$
$c_1 \stackrel{?}{=} Com(r_1, \alpha(v - F(r_1)) - G(t_1, r_1) - e_1)$

*Figure 8.4 A 5-pass identification scheme by Sakumoto et al.*

## 8.3.2    Sakumoto's identification schemes based on MC polynomials

When Sakumoto *et al.* constructed 3-pass and 5-pass identification schemes based on multivariate quadratic polynomials in [11], the first question that comes to mind was whether or not identification schemes could be constructed with multivariate polynomials of degree greater than two. They presented new 3- and 5-pass identification schemes based on multivariate cubic polynomials. In [13], a new polar form $G$ of $F$ was described for the multivariate cubic polynomials and called the associated linear-in-one-argument form.

Let $x$, $y \in \mathbb{F}_q^n$ be the parts of the secret key and $F$ be a system of the multivariate cubic polynomials as given in Definition 6. This associated linear-in-one-argument $G$ satisfies:

$$G(x,y) + G(y,x) = F(x+y) - F(x) - F(y) \tag{8.8}$$

Sakumoto succeeded in dividing the secret key according to his new linear-in-one-argument. They divided the secret key $s = r_0 + r_1$ and then the parts of the secret key yield as $r_0 = u + t_0$, $r_1 = u + t_1$ and $F(r_0) = e_0 + e_1$.

A new 3-pass identification scheme based on multivariate cubic polynomials was presented by using this dividing technique. In Figure 8.5, the 3-pass identification scheme based on multivariate cubic polynomials is given.

The prover can prove the verifier the commitment values in the scheme that satisfies:

$$G(u,r_1) + e_1 = v - F(r_1) - G(t_0,r_1) - e_0$$
$$G(u,r_0) - e_0 = e_1 - F(r_0) - G(t_1,r_0) \tag{8.9}$$

By using (8.8), (8.9), and the parts of the secret key, $v = F(r_0 + r_1)$ is obtained.

Sakumoto proposed a 5-pass identification scheme in addition to 3-pass identification scheme in [13]. The proposed 5-pass identification scheme is given in Figure 8.6. The main idea was not changed. The difference from 3-pass is that the same subpart is not used in the secret key dividing and $\alpha \in \mathbb{F}_q$ sent by the verifier. The secret key is divided into two parts $r_0$ and $r_1$ that are again divided as $\alpha r_0 = t_0 + u_0$ and $\alpha r_1 = t_1 + u_1$. In the 5-pass identification scheme, the prover randomly selects the secret key $s$, $r_0$, $u_0$, $u_1 \in \mathbb{F}_q$. Then the prover computes the other part $r_1 = s - r_0$.

The subsequent parts are tied to a random value $\alpha \in \mathbb{F}_q$ coming from the verifier. The prover computes $t_0 = \alpha r_0 - u_0$, $t_1 = \alpha r_1 - u_1$, and $e_1 = \alpha F(r_0) + \alpha G(r_1, r_0) - e_0$ and sends the verifier. After sending the values, the challenge-response starts between the prover and the verifier. At the end of the scheme, the verifier outputs 0 or 1. If this bit equals 0, it means that the verifier rejects otherwise accepts. The prover can prove commitment as long as (8.10) is satisfied:

$$\alpha(v - F(r_1)) - G(t_0,r_1) - e_1 = G(u_0,r_1) + e_0$$
$$e_1 - \alpha F(r_0) - G(t_1,r_0) = G(u_1,r_0) - e_0 \tag{8.10}$$

Prover: $((F,v),s)$                                                 Verifier: $(F,v)$

$r_0, u \in_R \mathbb{F}_q^n, e_0 \in_R \mathbb{F}_q^m$
$r_1 \leftarrow s - r_0, t_0 \leftarrow r_0 - u, t_1 \leftarrow r_1 - u, n\text{-bit}$
$e_1 \leftarrow F(r_0) + G(r_1, r_0) - e_0, m\text{-bit}$
$c_0 \leftarrow Com(r_1, G(u, r_1) + e_1, 2m\text{-bit}$
$c_1 \leftarrow Com(r_0, G(u, r_0) - e_0), 2m\text{-bit}$
$c_2 \leftarrow Com(t_0, e_0), 2m\text{-bit}$
$c_3 \leftarrow Com(t_1, e_1), 2m\text{-bit}$
$c_4 \leftarrow Com(u), 2m\text{-bit}$

$$\xrightarrow{\ (c_0, c_1, c_2, c_3, c_4)\ }$$
$$\xleftarrow{\ Ch\ }$$
$Ch \in_R \{0, 1, 2, 3\}$

If $Ch = 0, Rsp \leftarrow (r_0, u, e_0)$
If $Ch = 1, Rsp \leftarrow (r_0, t_1, e_1)$
If $Ch = 2, Rsp \leftarrow (r_1, u, e_1)$
If $Ch = 3, Rsp \leftarrow (r_1, t_0, e_0)$

$$\xrightarrow{\ Rsp\ }$$

If $Ch = 0, Rsp = (r_0, u, e_0)$
$c_1 \stackrel{?}{=} Com(r_0, G(u, r_0) - e_0)$
$c_2 \stackrel{?}{=} Com(r_0 - u, e_0)$
$c_4 \stackrel{?}{=} Com(u)$

If $Ch = 1, Rsp = (r_0, t_1, e_1)$
$c_1 \stackrel{?}{=} Com(r_0, e_1 - F(r_0) - G(t_1, r_0))$
$c_3 \stackrel{?}{=} Com(t_1, e_1)$

If $Ch = 2, Rsp = (r_1, u, e_1)$
$c_0 \stackrel{?}{=} Com(r_1, G(u, r_1) + e_1)$
$c_3 \stackrel{?}{=} Com(r_1 - u, e_1)$
$c_4 \stackrel{?}{=} Com(u)$

If $Ch = 3, Rsp = (r_1, t_0, e_0)$
$c_0 \stackrel{?}{=} Com(r_1, v - F(r_1) - G(t_0, r_1) - e_0)$
$c_2 \stackrel{?}{=} Com(t_0, e_0)$

*Figure 8.5   A 3-pass identification scheme based on MC polynomials by Sakumoto*

When the polar form given in (8.8) and the properties of the bilinear function given in Definition 8 are used, $v = F(r_0 + r_1) = F(s)$ is obtained by considering the dividing technique.

In [13], identification schemes based on multivariate cubic polynomials were presented. However, it has not yet known how to construct structures when multivariate polynomials of degree $d \geq 4$ are used. This remains as an open problem because the proposed structure for identification scheme based on multivariate cubic polynomials cannot be generalized for multivariate polynomials of degree $d \geq 4$. Open problem given in [13] is as follows:

**Open Problem** [13] "Efficient constructions based on multivariate polynomials of degree $d \geq 4$ remain as an open problem. However, it might be difficult to construct them by using techniques similar to those of [11] or of ours."

Prover: $((F,v),s)$                                                          Verifier: $(F,v)$

---

$r_0, u_0, u_1 \in_R \mathbb{F}_q^n, e_0 \in_R \mathbb{F}_q^m$
$r_1 \leftarrow s - r_0,$ $n$-bit
$c_0 \leftarrow Com(r_0, u_0, G(u_1, r_0) - e_0,$ $2m$-bit
$c_1 \leftarrow Com(r_1, u_1, G(u_0, r_1) + e_0,$ $2m$-bit

$\xrightarrow{(c_0, c_1)}$      $\alpha \in_R \mathbb{F}_q$
$\xleftarrow{\alpha}$

$t_0 \leftarrow \alpha r_0 - u_0, t_1 \leftarrow \alpha r_1 - u_1$
$e_1 \leftarrow \alpha F(r_0) + \alpha G(r_1, r_0) - e_0$

$\xrightarrow{(t_0, t_1, e_1)}$      $Ch \in_R \{0, 1\}$
$\xleftarrow{Ch}$

If $Ch = 0, Rsp \leftarrow r_0$
If $Ch = 1, Rsp \leftarrow r_1$

$\xrightarrow{Rsp}$

If $Ch = 0, Rsp = r_0$
$c_0 \overset{?}{=} Com(r_0, \alpha r_0 - t_0, e_1 - \alpha F(r_0) - G(t_1, r_0))$

If $Ch = 1, Rsp = r_1$
$c_1 \overset{?}{=} Com(r_1, \alpha r_1 - t_1, \alpha(v - F(r_1)) - G(t_0, r_1) - e_1)$

*Figure 8.6    A 5-pass identification scheme based on MC polynomials by Sakumoto*

## 8.3.3    *Nachef et al.'s identification schemes*

In [14], a solution for open problem defined in [13] was proposed. A generalization was made to construct identification schemes based on multivariate polynomials of any degree $d$ over a finite field. In addition, a new polarization identity was defined in order to be able to construct identification scheme using the multivariate polynomials of any degree $d$. The polarization identity is given in Definition 12.

**Definition 12:** *[14] Let $F$ be a function of multivariate $d$-degree of polynomials as given Definition 6. $G$ defined from $(\mathbb{F}_q^n)^d \rightarrow \mathbb{F}_q^m$ is a $d$-linear form of $F$ and it satisfies*

$$G(r_0, r_1, \ldots, r_{d-1}) = \sum_{i=1}^{d} (-1)^{d-i} \sum_{\substack{S \subset \{0, \cdots, d-1\} \\ |S|=i}} F\left(\sum_{j \in S} r_j\right). \tag{8.11}$$

Firstly, the 3-pass identification scheme based on multivariate cubic polynomials over a finite field was proposed. The secret key is divided into parts as given with Nachef *et al.* in Figure 8.2. We note that the used polarization identity for $d = 3$ is as follows:

$$G(r_0, r_1, r_2) = F(s) - F(r_0 + r_1) - F(r_0 + r_2) - F(r_1 + r_2) + F(r_0)$$
$$+ F(r_1) + F(r_2) \tag{8.12}$$

where $F$ is the system of the multivariate cubic polynomial over a finite field and $G$ is polarization function like polar form in [11].

Prover: $((F,v),s)$                                                                                          Verifier: $(F,v)$

$r_0, r_1, t_0 \in_R \mathbb{F}_q^n, e_0, f_0, h_0 \in_R \mathbb{F}_q^m$
$r_2 \leftarrow s - r_0 - r_1, t_1 \leftarrow r_0 - t_0,$ $n$-bit
$e_1 \leftarrow F(r_0) - e_0, f_1 \leftarrow F(r_0 + r_1) - f_0,$ $m$-bit
$h_1 = F(r_0 + r_2) - h_0,$ $m$-bit
$c_0 \leftarrow Com(r_1, r_2, G(t_0, r_1, r_2) - e_0 + f_0 + h_0),$ $2m$-bit
$c_1 \leftarrow Com(r_1, t_0, e_0, f_0),$ $2m$-bit
$c_2 \leftarrow Com(r_1, t_1, e_1, f_1),$ $2m$-bit
$c_3 \leftarrow Com(r_2, t_0, e_0, h_0),$ $2m$-bit
$c_4 \leftarrow Com(r_2, t_1, e_1, h_1),$ $2m$-bit

$$\xrightarrow{(c_0, c_1, c_2, c_3, c_4)}$$   $Ch \in_R \{0,1,2,3\}$
$$\xleftarrow{Ch}$$

If $Ch = 0, Rsp \leftarrow (r_0, r_1, t_1, e_1, f_1)$
If $Ch = 1, Rsp \leftarrow (r_0, r_2, t_1, e_1, h_1)$
If $Ch = 2, Rsp \leftarrow (r_1, r_2, t_1, e_1, f_1, h_1)$
If $Ch = 3, Rsp \leftarrow (r_1, r_2, t_0, e_0, f_0, h_0)$

$$\xrightarrow{Rsp}$$

If $Ch = 0, Rsp = (r_0, r_1, t_1, e_1, f_1)$
$c_1 \overset{?}{=} Com(r_1, r_0 - t_1, F(r_0) - e_1,$
$F(r_0 + r_1) - f_1)$
$c_2 \overset{?}{=} Com(r_1, t_1, e_1, f_1)$

If $Ch = 1, Rsp = (r_0, r_2, t_1, e_1, h_1)$
$c_3 \overset{?}{=} Com(r_2, r_0 - t_1, F(r_0) - e_1,$
$F(r_0 + r_2) - h_1)$
$c_4 \overset{?}{=} Com(r_2, t_1, e_1, h_1)$

If $Ch = 2, Rsp = (r_1, r_2, t_1, e_1, f_1, h_1)$
$c_0 \overset{?}{=} Com(r_1, r_2, v - G(t_1, r_1, r_2) + e_1 -$
$f_1 - h_1 - F(r_1 + r_2) + F(r_1) + F(r_2))$
$c_2 \overset{?}{=} Com(r_1, t_1, e_1, f_1)$
$c_4 \overset{?}{=} Com(r_2, t_1, e_1, h_1)$

If $Ch = 3, Rsp = (r_1, r_2, t_0, e_0, f_0, h_0)$
$c_0 \overset{?}{=} Com(r_1, r_2, G(t_0, r_1, r_2) - e_0 +$
$f_0 + h_0)$
$c_1 \overset{?}{=} Com(r_1, t_0, e_0, f_0)$
$c_3 \overset{?}{=} Com(r_2, t_0, e_0, h_0)$

*Figure 8.7   A 3-pass identification scheme based on MC polynomials by using trilinear form*

$G$ is in trilinear form since it is used in the multivariate cubic polynomials and satisfies:

$$G(r_0, r_1, r_2) = G(t_0, r_1, r_2) + G(t_1, r_1, r_2)$$

When $r_0$ is divided into two subparts, the terms containing $r_0$ in (8.12) are expressed as $F(r_0 + r_1) = f_0 + f_1$ and $F(r_0 + r_2) = h_0 + h_1$. Thus, the parts of the secret key are successfully distributed. In Figure 8.7, their identification scheme based on multivariate cubic polynomials is given.

We prove the correctness of the proposed scheme when it satisfies:

$$G(t_0, r_1, r_2) - e_0 + f_0 + h_0 = v - G(t_1, r_1, r_2) + e_1 - f_1 - h_1 - F(r_1 + r_2)$$
$$+ F(r_1) + F(r_2) \tag{8.13}$$

By using the parts of the secret key and (8.12), the correctness of this scheme is proved as follows:

$$v = G(t_0 + t_1, r_1, r_2) + f_0 + f_1 + h_0 + h_1 + F(r_1 + r_2) - e_0 - e_1 - F(r_1) - F(r_2)$$

$$v = G(r_0, r_1, r_2) + F(r_0 + r_1) + F(r_0 + r_2) + F(r_1 + r_2) - F(r_0) - F(r_1) - F(r_2)$$

$$v = F(s)$$

$$(8.14)$$

In [14], a general identification scheme was also proposed to show how to construct an identification scheme based on multivariate polynomials of any degree $d$. A solution was proposed by this scheme for open problem in Section 8.3.2. The polarization identity given in Definition 12 was used in this general identification scheme. The secret key is firstly divided into $d$ parts when the multivariate $d$th degree polynomials is used in the proposed scheme. Then the first part of the secret key is divided into two subparts. In this general scheme, the commitment values are more complex since the secret key is denoted large number of parts. In addition, the challenge values are higher than the previous schemes (for more details, see [14]).

### 8.3.4    Monteiro et al.'s identification scheme

In [12], Monteiro *et al.* presented a new 3-pass identification scheme based on multivariate quadratic polynomials over a finite field. They improved Sakumoto's secret key dividing technique in [11] to construct more efficient scheme than the previous ones.

We recall that Sakumoto divided the secret key $s$ into two parts as $s = r_0 + r_1$. Then, they considered $r_0$ as two subparts $t_0$ and $t_1$. Monteiro *et al.* also divided $r_1$ into two subparts as $d_0$ and $d_1$ as shown in Figure 8.2. They used the polar form given in Definition 9.

Their scheme is given in Figure 8.8. In the scheme, $P$ and $G$ denote a system of multivariate quadratic polynomials and the polar form of $P$, respectively. In addition, $P(r_0)$ and $P(r_1)$ are represented as $P(r_0) = e_0 + e_1$ and $P(r_1) = u_0 + u_1$.

The correctness of the their identification scheme is represented by the following equations:

$$G(t_0, r_1) + e_0 = v - P(r_1) - G(t_1, r_1) - e_1$$
$$G(r_0, d_1) + u_1 = v - P(r_0) - G(r_0, d_0) - u_0$$

$$(8.15)$$

From (8.15), it is obtained the public key by using the polar form given in Definition 9. Finally, the verifier has the public key $v = P(r_0 + r_1)$ and verifies the prover's identity when the equations given in (8.15) are satisfied.

### 8.3.5    Soysaldi's identification scheme

In [24], Soysaldi presented a 3-pass identification scheme based on multivariate quadratic polynomials over a finite field. In the proposed scheme, different partition technique is used. When multivariate quadratic polynomials are used, the

Prover: $((P,v),s)$                                     Verifier: $(P,v)$

$c_0 \leftarrow Com(r_0, G(r_0,d_1) + u_1)$, $2m$-bit
$c_1 \leftarrow Com(r_1, G(t_0,r_1) + e_0)$, $2m$-bit
$c_2 \leftarrow Com(t_0, e_0)$, $2m$-bit
$c_3 \leftarrow Com(t_1, e_1)$, $2m$-bit
$c_4 \leftarrow Com(d_0, u_0)$, $2m$-bit
$c_5 \leftarrow Com(d_1, u_1)$, $2m$-bit
$hc \leftarrow H(c_0,c_1,c_2,c_3,c_4,c_5)$, $2m$-bit

$$\overset{hc}{\longrightarrow}$$
$$\overset{Ch}{\longleftarrow}$$
$\mathrm{Ch} \in_R \{0,1,2,3\}$

If $Ch = 0, Rsp \leftarrow (r_1,t_1,e_1,d_0,u_0,c_0,c_2)$
If $Ch = 1, Rsp \leftarrow (r_1,t_0,e_0,d_1,u_1,c_0,c_3)$
If $Ch = 2, Rsp \leftarrow (r_0,t_0,e_0,d_1,u_1,c_1,c_4)$
If $Ch = 3, Rsp \leftarrow (r_0,t_1,e_1,d_0,u_0,c_1,c_5)$

$$\overset{Rsp}{\longrightarrow}$$

If $Ch = 0$, $Rsp = (r_1,t_1,e_1,d_0,u_0,c_0,c_2)$
$c'_1 \leftarrow Com(r_1, v - P(r_1) - G(t_1,r_1) - e_1)$
$c'_3 \leftarrow Com(t_1, e_1)$
$c'_4 \leftarrow Com(d_0, u_0)$
$c'_5 \leftarrow Com(r_1 - d_0, P(r_1) - u_0)$
$hc \overset{?}{=} H(c_0,c'_1,c_2,c'_3,c'_4,c'_5)$

If $Ch = 1$, $Rsp = (r_1,t_0,e_0,d_1,u_1,c_0,c_3)$
$c'_1 \leftarrow Com(r_1, G(t_0,r_1) + e_0)$
$c'_2 \leftarrow Com(t_0, e_0)$
$c'_4 \leftarrow Com(r_1 - d_1, P(r_1) - u_1)$
$c'_5 \leftarrow Com(d_1, u_1)$
$hc \overset{?}{=} H(c_0,c'_1,c'_2,c_3,c'_4,c'_5)$

If $Ch = 2$, $Rsp = (r_0,t_0,e_0,d_1,u_1,c_1,c_4)$
$c'_0 \leftarrow Com(r_0, G(r_0,d_1 + u_1))$
$c'_2 \leftarrow Com(t_0, e_0)$
$c'_3 \leftarrow Com(r_0 - t_0, P(r_0) - e_0)$
$c'_5 \leftarrow Com(d_1, u_1)$
$hc \overset{?}{=} H(c'_0,c_1,c'_2,c'_3,c_4,c'_5)$

If $Ch = 3$, $Rsp = (r_0,t_1,e_1,d_0,u_0,c_1,c_5)$
$c'_0 \leftarrow Com(r_0, v - P(r_0) - G(r_0,d_0) - u_0)$
$c'_2 \leftarrow Com(r_0 - t_1, P(r_0) - e_1)$
$c'_3 \leftarrow Com(t_1, e_1)$
$c'_4 \leftarrow Com(d_0, u_0)$
$hc \overset{?}{=} H(c'_0,c_1,c'_2,c'_3,c'_4,c_5)$

*Figure 8.8   A 3-pass identification scheme by Monteiro et al.*

secret key is divided into three parts. The partition technique of the secret key is given in Figure 8.2. In addition, $F(r_0)$ is represented to sum of $e_0$, $e_1$, and $F(r_2)$ with the sum of $u_0$, $u_1$. The polar form given in Definition 9 for quadratic polynomials is used. The proposed scheme is given in Figure 8.9.

The prover proves his/her identity as long as the scheme satisfies:

$$G(t_0,r_1 + r_2) + e_0 = v - G(t_1,r_1 + r_2) - e_1 - F(r_1 + r_2) \tag{8.16}$$

$$G(r_0 + r_1,d_1) + u_1 = v - G(r_0 + r_1,d_0) - u_0 - F(r_0 + r_1) \tag{8.17}$$

Prover: $((F,v),s)$                                                                      Verifier: $(F,v)$

$r_0, r_2, t_0, d_0 \in_R \mathbb{F}_q^n,$
$e_0, u_0 \in_R \mathbb{F}_q^m,$
$r_1 \leftarrow s - r_0 - r_2, t_1 \leftarrow r_0 - t_0, d_1 \leftarrow r_2 - d_0,$ n-bit
$e_1 \leftarrow F(r_0) - e_0, u_1 \leftarrow F(r_1) - u_0,$ m-bit
$c_0 \leftarrow Com(r_1, r_2, G(t_0, r_1 + r_2) + e_0),$ 2m-bit
$c_1 \leftarrow Com(r_0, r_1, G(r_0 + r_1, d_1) + u_1),$ 2m-bit
$c_2 \leftarrow Com(r_2, t_0, e_0),$ 2m-bit
$c_3 \leftarrow Com(r_2, t_1, e_1),$ 2m-bit
$c_4 \leftarrow Com(r_0, d_0, u_0),$ 2m-bit
$c_5 \leftarrow Com(r_0, d_1, u_1),$ 2m-bit

$$\xrightarrow{(c_0, c_1, c_2, c_3, c_4, c_5)}$$   $Ch \in_R \{0,1,2,3,4,5\}$
$$\xleftarrow{Ch}$$

$Ch = 0, Rsp \leftarrow (r_0, r_1, d_1, u_1)$
$Ch = 1, Rsp \leftarrow (r_0, r_1, d_0, u_0)$
$Ch = 2, Rsp \leftarrow (r_0, r_2, t_1, e_1)$
$Ch = 3, Rsp \leftarrow (r_1, r_2, t_0, e_0)$
$Ch = 4, Rsp \leftarrow (r_1, r_2, t_1, e_1)$
$Ch = 5, Rsp \leftarrow (r_0, r_2, d_1, u_1)$

$$\xrightarrow{Rsp}$$

If $Ch = 0$, $Rsp \leftarrow (r_0, r_1, d_1, u_1)$
$c_1 \overset{?}{=} Com(r_0, r_1, G(r_0 + r_1, d_1) + u_1)$
$c_5 \overset{?}{=} Com(r_0, d_1, u_1)$

If $Ch = 1$, $Rsp \leftarrow (r_0, r_1, d_0, u_0)$
$c_1 \overset{?}{=} Com(r_0, r_1, v - G(r_0 + r_1, d_0) - u_0 - F(r_0 + r_1))$
$c_4 \overset{?}{=} Com(r_0, d_0, u_0)$

If $Ch = 2$, $Rsp \leftarrow (r_0, r_2, t_1, e_1)$
$c_2 \overset{?}{=} Com(r_2, r_0 - t_1, F(r_0) - e_1)$
$c_3 \overset{?}{=} Com(r_2, t_1, e_1)$

If $Ch = 3$, $Rsp \leftarrow (r_1, r_2, t_0, e_0)$
$c_0 \overset{?}{=} Com(r_1, r_2, G(t_0, r_1 + r_2) + e_0)$
$c_2 \overset{?}{=} Com(r_2, t_0, e_0)$

If $Ch = 4$, $Rsp \leftarrow (r_1, r_2, t_1, e_1)$
$c_0 \overset{?}{=} Com(r_1, r_2, v - G(t_1, r_1 + r_2) - e_1 - F(r_1 + r_2))$
$c_3 \overset{?}{=} Com(r_2, t_1, e_1)$

If $Ch = 5$, $Rsp \leftarrow (r_0, r_2, d_1, u_1)$
$c_4 \overset{?}{=} Com(r_0, r_2 - d_1, F(r_2) - u_1)$
$c_5 \overset{?}{=} Com(r_0, d_1, u_1)$

*Figure 8.9    A 3–pass identification scheme by Soysaldi*

By using the parts of the secret key, the polar form and the bilinearity, the correctness of the scheme is shown with the following equations:

$$v = G(r_0 + r_1, d_0 + d_1) + F(r_0 + r_1) + u_0 + u_1$$
$$= G(r_0 + r_1, r_2) + F(r_0 + r_1) + F(r_2)$$
$$= F(r_0 + r_1 + r_2) = F(s)$$
$$v = G(t_0 + t_1, r_1 + r_2) + e_0 + e_1 + F(r_1 + r_2)$$
$$= G(r_0, r_1 + r_2) + F(r_0) + F(r_1 + r_2)$$
$$= F(r_0 + r_1 + r_2) = F(s)$$

### 8.3.6 Akleylek et al.'s identification scheme

In [25], Akleylek *et al.* proposed a new identification scheme based on multivariate cubic polynomials. They used a different technique for dividing the secret key. They improved the technique given in [14]. Note that Nachef *et al.* divided the secret key into three parts and then divided the first part into two subparts in [14]. Firstly, Akleylek *et al.* divided the secret key into three parts as $r_0 + r_1 + r_2$. Then, they divided $r_0$ into three subparts as $r_0 = t_0 + t_1 + t_2$. The dividing technique is demonstrated in Figure 8.2. According to the dividing technique, the other parts of the secret key is shown as $F(r_0) = e_0 + e_1 + e_2$. The terms, including $r_0$ in polar form, are expressed in terms of other variables such as $F(r_0 + r_1) = f_1 + f_2 + f_3$ and $F(r_0 + r_2) = h_1 + h_2 + h_3$ since $r_0$ is divided into three parts. Their proposed identification scheme is given in Figure 8.10.

Prover: $((F,v),s)$

Verifier: $(F,v)$

$r_0, r_1, t_0, t_1, \in \mathbb{F}_q^n$,
$e_0, e_1, f_0, f_1, h_0, h_1 \in \mathbb{F}_q^m$,
$r_2 \leftarrow s - r_0 - r_1, t_2 \leftarrow r_0 - t_0 - t_1$, $n$-bit
$e_2 \leftarrow F(r_0) - e_0 - e_1$, $m$-bit
$f_2 = F(r_0 + r_1) - f_0 - f_1$, $m$-bit
$h_2 = F(r_0 + r_2) - h_0 - h_1$, $m$-bit
$c_0 \leftarrow Com(r_1, r_2, G(t_0 + t_1, r_1, r_2) + f_0 + f_1 +$
$h_0 + h_1 + F(r_1 + r_2) - e_0 - e_1)$, $2m$-bit
$c_1 \leftarrow Com(r_1, t_0, e_0, f_0)$, $2m$-bit
$c_2 \leftarrow Com(r_2, t_0, e_0, h_0)$, $2m$-bit
$c_3 \leftarrow Com(r_1, t_1, e_1, f_1)$, $2m$-bit
$c_4 \leftarrow Com(r_2, t_1, e_1, h_1)$, $2m$-bit
$c_5 \leftarrow Com(r_1, t_2, e_2, f_2)$, $2m$-bit
$c_6 \leftarrow Com(r_2, t_2, e_2, h_2)$, $2m$-bit

$\xrightarrow{(c_0, c_1, c_2, c_3, c_4, c_5, c_6)}$

$Ch \in_R \{0, 1, 2, 3\}$

$\xleftarrow{Ch}$

$Ch = 0, Rsp \leftarrow (r_0, r_2, t_0, t_2, e_0, e_2, h_0, h_2)$
$Ch = 1, Rsp \leftarrow (r_1, r_2, t_0, t_2, e_0, e_1, f_0, f_1, h_0, h_1)$
$Ch = 2, Rsp \leftarrow (r_1, r_2, t_2, e_2, f_2, h_2)$
$Ch = 3, Rsp \leftarrow (r_0, r_1, t_0, t_2, e_0, e_2, f_0, f_2)$

$\xrightarrow{Rsp}$

$Ch = 0, Rsp = (r_0, r_2, t_0, t_2, e_0, e_2, h_0, h_2)$
$c_2 \leftarrow Com(r_2, t_0, e_0, h_0)$
$c_4 \leftarrow Com(r_2, r_0 - t_0 - t_2, F(r_0) - e_0 - e_2,$
$F(r_0 + r_2) - h_0 - h_2)$
$c_6 \leftarrow Com(r_2, t_2, e_2, h_2)$

$Ch = 1, Rsp = (r_1, r_2, t_0, t_2, e_0, e_1, f_0, f_1, h_0, h_1)$
$c_0 \leftarrow Com(r_1, r_2, G(t_0 + t_1, r_1, r_2) + f_0 + f_1 +$
$h_0 + h_1 + F(r_1 + r_2) - e_0 - e_1)$
$c_1 \leftarrow Com(r_1, t_0, e_0, f_0)$
$c_2 \leftarrow Com(r_2, t_0, e_0, h_0)$
$c_3 \leftarrow Com(r_1, t_1, e_1, f_1)$
$c_4 \leftarrow Com(r_2, t_1, e_1, h_1)$

$Ch = 2, Rsp = (r_1, r_2, t_2, e_2, f_2, h_2)$
$c_0 \leftarrow Com(r_1, r_2, v - G(t_2, r_1, r_2) + e_2 - f_2 -$
$h_2 + F(r_1) + F(r_2))$
$c_5 \leftarrow Com(r_1, t_2, e_2, f_2)$
$c_6 \leftarrow Com(r_2, t_2, e_2, h_2)$

$Ch = 3, Rsp = (r_0, r_1, t_0, t_2, e_0, e_2, f_0, f_2)$
$c_1 \leftarrow Com(r_0, t_0, e_0, f_0)$
$c_3 \leftarrow Com(r_1, r_0 - t_0 - t_2, F(r_0) - e_0 - e_2,$
$F(r_0 + r_1) - f_0 - f_2)$
$c_5 \leftarrow Com(r_1, t_2, e_2, f_2)$

*Figure 8.10  A 3-pass identification scheme based on multivariate cubic polynomials by Akleylek et al.*

In the proposed identification scheme, a trilinear polar form given in Definition 11 is used since each part is represented by three subparts. The correctness of the identification scheme is based on this polar form and trilinearity as follows:

$$v - G(t_2, r_1, r_2) + e_2 - f_2 - h_2 + F(r_1) + F(r_2) = G(t_0 + t_1, r_1, r_2) + f_0 + f_1$$

$$+ h_0 + h_1 + F(r_1 + r_2) - e_0 - e_1$$

$$v = \overbrace{G(t_0 + t_1, r_1, r_2) + G(t_2, r_1, r_2)}^{G(r_0, r_1, r_2)} + \overbrace{f_0 + f_1 + f_2}^{F(r_0 + r_1)} + \overbrace{h_0 + h_1 + h_2}^{F(r_0 + r_2)} + F(r_1 + r_2)$$

$$- e_0 - e_1 - e_2 - F(r_1) - F(r_2)$$

$$v = G(t_0 + t_1 + t_2, r_1, r_2) + F(r_0 + r_1) + F(r_0 + r_2) + F(r_1 + r_2) - F(r_0) - F(r_1) - F(r_2)$$

$$v = G(r_0, r_1, r_2) + F(r_0 + r_1) + F(r_0 + r_2) + F(r_1 + r_2) - F(r_0) - F(r_1) - F(r_2)$$

$$v = F(r_0 + r_1 + r_2)$$

$$v = F(s)$$

Now, we explain how the proposed identification scheme works. Note that an identification has two parts: the prover and the verifier. Before the interactive identification scheme begins, the prover runs some algorithm given in Definition 1. The prover has $(v, s)$ the public and private key and $F \in_R MC(n, m, \mathbb{F}_q)$ multivariate cubic polynomial system after *Setup* and *KeyGen* algorithm. After the prover generates randomly $r_0, r_1, t_0, t_1 \in \mathbb{F}_q^n$ and $e_0, e_1, f_0, f_1, h_0, h_1 \in \mathbb{F}_q^m$, the prover computes $r_2 = s - r_0 - r_1$, $t_2 = r_0 - t_0 - t_1$, $e_2 = F(r_0) - e_0 - e_1$, $f_2 = F(r_0 + r_1)$ $- f_0 - f_1$, $h_2 = F(r_0 + r_2) - h_0 - h_1$. The prover, holding all parts of the secret key, computes the commitment values and sends these values to the verifier as commitment. The commitment takes place in the first pass for 3-pass identification scheme. In the second pass, the verifier challenges the prover. In the last pass, the prover sends responses to the verifier and the verifier can compute the commitment values. If the verifier computes the same commitment values, the verifier accepts the prover's commitment. Otherwise, the verifier rejects.

The verifier can verify the prover as long as (8.18) is satisfied:

$$v - G(t_2, r_1, r_2) + e_2 - f_2 - h_2 + F(r_1) + F(r_2) = G(t_0 + t_1, r_1, r_2) + f_0 + f_1 + h_0$$
$$+ h_1 + F(r_1 + r_2) - e_0 - e_1$$

$$(8.18)$$

**Theorem 1:** The identification scheme is statistically zero knowledge when the commitment scheme *Com* is statistically hiding.

**Proof.** *Let S be a simulator that will impersonate an honest prover against a cheating verifier without knowing the secret key. S selects the vectors* $s', r_0', t_0', t_1' \in_R \mathbb{F}_q^n$, $e_0', e_1', f_0, f_1, h_0, h_1 \in_R \mathbb{F}_q^m$ *and computes* $r_2' \leftarrow s' - r_0' - r_1'$, $t_2' \leftarrow r_0' - t_0' - t_1'$, $e_2' \leftarrow F(r_0') - e_0' - e_1'$. *In addition, S predicts a* $Ch' \in_R \{0, 1, 2, 3\}$

*that the cheating verifier will not choose. S computes the other parts needed to calculate the commitment values according to Ch' as follows:*

$$Ch^* = \begin{cases} 0, & h'_2 = v - F(s') + F(r'_0 + r'_2) - h'_0 - h'_1 \\ \text{others}, & h'_2 = F(r'_0 + r'_2) - h'_0 - h'_1 \end{cases}$$

$$Ch^* = \begin{cases} 1, & c'_0 = Com(r'_1, r'_2, v - G(t'_2, r'_1, r'_2) + e'_2 - f'_2 - h'_2 \\ & \qquad + F(r'_1) + F(r'_2)) \\ \text{others}, & c'_0 = Com(r'_1, r'_2, G(t'_0 + t'_1, r'_1, r'_2) + f'_0 + f'_1 + h'_0 + h'_1 \\ & \qquad + F(r'_1 + r'_2) - e'_0 - e'_1) \end{cases}$$

$$Ch^* = \begin{cases} 3, & f'_2 = v - F(s') + F(r'_0 + r'_1) - f'_0 - f'_1 \\ \text{others}, & f'_2 = F(r'_0 + r'_1) - f'_0 - f'_1 \end{cases}$$

*After all values are obtained, S computes commitment values*

$$c'_1 = Com(r'_1, t'_0, e'_0, f'_0), c'_2 = Com(r'_2, t'_0, e'_0, h'_0)$$
$$c'_3 = Com(r'_1, t'_1, e'_1, f'_1), c'_4 = Com(r'_2, t'_1, e'_1, h'_1)$$
$$c'_5 = Com(r'_1, t'_2, e'_2, f'_2), c'_6 = Com(r'_2, t'_2, e'_2, h'_2)$$

*and sends the cheating verifier. The cheating verifier responds with a challenge $Ch \in_R \{0, 1, 2, 3\}$ to the prover's commitment. The values of commitment, challenge and response in the proposed identification scheme are shown as follows:*

$$Ch = \begin{cases} 0, & ((c_0, c_1, c_2, c_3, c_4, c_5, c_6), 0, (r'_0, r'_2, t'_0, t'_2, e'_0, e'_2, h'_0, h'_2)) \\ 1, & ((c_0, c_1, c_2, c_3, c_4, c_5, c_6), 1, (r'_1, r'_2, t'_0, t'_2, e'_0, e'_2, f'_0, f'_1, h'_0, h'_1)) \\ 2, & ((c_0, c_1, c_2, c_3, c_4, c_5, c_6), 2, (r'_1, r'_2, t'_2, e'_2, f'_2, h'_2)) \\ 3, & ((c_0, c_1, c_2, c_3, c_4, c_5, c_6), 3, (r'_0, r'_1, t'_0, t'_2, e'_0, e'_2, f'_0, f'_2)) \end{cases}$$

*If $Ch^* = 0$ and $Ch = 2$, the communication values are $((c_0, c_1, c_2, c_3, c_4, c_5, c_6), 2, (r'_1, r'_2, t'_2, e'_2, f'_2, h'_2))$. Thus, $c'_5$ and $c'_6$ are verified. Then, one can verify $c_0$ from the following equation:*

$$c'_0 = Com(r'_1, r'_2, v - G(t_2, r_1, r_2) + e_2 - f_2 - h_2 + F(r_1) + F(r_2)) \qquad (8.19)$$

*When it is written $v - F(s') + F(r'_0 + r'_1) - f'_0 - f'_1$ instead of $f_2$, $c'_0 = Com(r_1, r_2, G(t_0 + t_1, r_1, r_2) + f_0 + f_1 + h_0 + h_1 + F(r_1 + r_2) - e_0 - e_1)$ is obtained. Thus, we verify $c'_0$. In the same way, we can verify $c'_1, c'_2, c'_3, c'_4$. S can impersonate with 3/4 probability. Consequently, someone using S can create a copy scheme that not be distinguished with 3/4 probability from the real communication. However, someone cannot get information about the identification scheme since the Com commitment scheme has statistically hiding. Thus, the identification scheme is a zero-knowledge scheme.* $\square$

**Theorem 2:** The identification scheme is proof zero knowledge with zero knowledge error 3/4 when commitment scheme *Com* is computationally binding.

**Proof.** *Let C be a cheating prover who response all challenges. C can compute the same output of* Com *with different values or find solution for* $(F, v)$. *Let*

$$((c_0, c_1, c_2, c_3, c_4, c_5, c_6), Ch_0, Rsp_0),$$
$$((c_0, c_1, c_2, c_3, c_4, c_5, c_6), Ch_1, Rsp_1),$$
$$((c_0, c_1, c_2, c_3, c_4, c_5, c_6), Ch_2, Rsp_2),$$
$$((c_0, c_1, c_2, c_3, c_4, c_5, c_6), Ch_3, Rsp_3)$$

*be four transcriptions of the proposed identification scheme such that* $Ch_i = i$ *and the decision function* $Dec(F, v, hc_i, Ch_i, Rsp_i) = 1$ *means that the verifier accepts the transcript with the honest prover. Let* $(c_0, c_1, c_2, c_3, c_4, c_5, c_6)$ *be commitment values and*

$$Rsp_0 = (r_0^{(0)}, r_2^{(0)}, t_0^{(0)}, t_2^{(0)}, e_0^{(0)}, e_2^{(0)}, h_0^{(0)}, h_2^{(0)})$$
$$Rsp_1 = (r_1^{(1)}, r_2^{(1)}, t_0^{(1)}, t_2^{(1)}, e_0^{(1)}, e_2^{(1)}, f_0^{(1)}, f_1^{(1)}, h_0^{(1)}, h_1^{(1)})$$
$$Rsp_2 = (r_1^{(2)}, r_2^{(2)}, t_2^{(2)}, e_2^{(2)}, f_2^{(2)}, h_2^{(2)})$$
$$Rsp_3 = (r_0^{(3)}, r_1^{(3)}, t_0^{(3)}, t_2^{(3)}, e_0^{(3)}, e_2^{(3)}, f_0^{(3)}, f_2^{(3)})$$

*be the responses of each challenge. We obtain:*

$$
\begin{aligned}
c_0 &= Com(r_1^{(1)}, r_2^{(1)}, G(t_0^{(1)} + t_1^{(1)}, r_1^{(1)}, r_2^{(1)}) + f_0^{(1)} + f_1^{(1)} + h_0^{(1)} + h_1^{(1)} \\
&\quad + F(r_1^{(1)} + r_2^{(1)}) - e_0^{(1)} - e_1^{(1)}) \\
&= Com(r_1^{(2)}, r_2^{(2)}, v - G(t_2^{(2)}, r_1^{(2)}, r_2^{(2)}) + e_2^{(2)} - f_2^{(2)} - h_2^{(2)} + F(r_1^{(2)}) + F(r_2^{(2)}))
\end{aligned}
$$
$$(8.20)$$

$$
\begin{aligned}
c_1 &= Com(r_1^{(1)}, t_0^{(1)}, e_0^{(1)}, f_0^{(1)}) \\
&= Com(r_1^{(3)}, t_0^{(3)}, e_0^{(3)}, f_0^{(3)}) \\
c_2 &= Com(r_2^{(0)}, t_0^{(0)}, e_0^{(0)}, h_0^{(0)}) \\
&= Com(r_2^{(1)}, t_0^{(1)}, e_0^{(1)}, h_0^{(1)}) \\
c_3 &= Com(r_1^{(1)}, t_1^{(1)}, e_1^{(1)}, f_1^{(1)}) \\
&= Com(r_1^{(3)}, r_0^{(3)} - t_0^{(3)} - t_2^{(3)}, F(r_0^{(3)}) - e_0^{(3)} - e_2^{(3)}, F(r_0^{(3)} + r_1^{(3)}) - f_0^{(3)} - f_2^{(3)}) \\
c_4 &= Com(r_2^{(0)}, r_0^{(0)} - t_0^{(0)} - t_2^{(0)}, F(r_0^{(0)}) - e_0^{(0)} - e_2^{(0)}, F(r_0^{(0)} + r_2^{(0)}) - h_0^{(0)} - h_2^{(0)}) \\
&= Com(r_2^{(1)}, t_1^{(1)}, e_1^{(1)}, h_1^{(1)}) \\
c_5 &= Com(r_1^{(2)}, t_2^{(2)}, e_2^{(2)}, f_2^{(2)}) \\
&= Com(r_1^{(3)}, t_2^{(3)}, e_2^{(3)}, f_2^{(3)}) \\
c_6 &= Com(r_2^{(0)}, t_2^{(0)}, e_2^{(0)}, h_2^{(0)}) \\
&= Com(r_2^{(2)}, t_2^{(2)}, e_2^{(2)}, h_2^{(2)})
\end{aligned}
$$

*Since* Com *has the binding property, we write the following equations:*

$$r_1^{(1)} = r_1^{(2)} = r_1^{(3)}, \qquad r_2^{(0)} = r_2^{(1)} = r_2^{(2)}, \qquad t_0^{(0)} = t_0^{(1)} = t_0^{(3)}, \qquad t_2^{(0)} = t_2^{(2)} = t_2^{(3)},$$

$$e_0^{(0)} = e_0^{(1)} = e_0^{(3)}, e_2^{(0)} = e_2^{(2)} = e_2^{(3)}, f_0^{(1)} = f_0^{(3)}, h_0^{(0)} = h_0^{(1)}, f_2^{(2)} = f_2^{(3)}, h_2^{(0)} = h_2^{(2)},$$

$$t_1^{(1)} = r_0^{(0)} - t_0^{(0)} - t_2^{(0)}, \quad e_1^{(1)} = F(r_0^{(0)}) - e_0^{(0)} - e_2^{(0)} = F(r_0^{(3)}) - e_0^{(3)} - e_2^{(3)}, \quad h_1^{(1)} =$$

$$F(r_0^{(0)} + r_2^{(0)}) - h_0^{(0)} - h_2^{(0)}, f_1^{(1)} = F(r_0^{(3)} + r_1^{(3)}) - f_0^{(3)} - f_2^{(3)}. \text{ From (8.20)},$$

$$v = G(t_0^{(1)} + t_1^{(1)}, r_1^{(1)}, r_2^{(1)}) + G(t_2^{(2)}, r_1^{(2)}, r_2^{(2)}) + f_0^{(1)} + f_1^{(1)} + f_2^{(2)} + h_0^{(1)}$$
$$+ h_1^{(1)} + h_2^{(2)} + F(r_1^{(1)} + r_2^{(1)}) - e_0^{(1)} - e_1^{(1)} - e_2^{(2)} - F(r_1^{(2)}) - F(r_2^{(2)})$$

(8.21)

*If we write* $t_0^{(0)}$, $r_0^{(0)} - t_0^{(0)} - t_2^{(0)}$, $t_2^{(0)}$, $r_1^{(1)}$, $F(r_0^{(2)}) - e_1^{(2)}$, $f_0^{(3)}$, $h_0^{(0)}$, $r_2^{(2)}$,
$F(r_0^{(3)} + r_1^{(3)}) - f_0^{(3)} - f_2^{(3)}$, $F(r_0^{(0)} + r_2^{(0)}) - h_0^{(0)} - h_2^{(0)}$, $F(r_0^{(0)}) - e_0^{(0)} - e_2^{(0)}$
$= F(r_0^{(3)}) - e_0^{(3)} - e_2^{(3)}$ *and* $e_2^{(0)}$ *instead of* $t_0^{(1)}$, $t_1^{(1)}$, $t_2^{(2)}$, $r_1^{(2)}$, $e_2^{(3)}$, $f_0^{(1)}$, $h_0^{(1)}$, $r_2^{(1)}$, $f_1^{(1)}$,
$h_1^{(1)}$, $e_1^{(1)}$ *and* $e_2^{(2)}$ *in (8.21), respectively, we get* $v = G(r_0^{(0)}, r_1^{(1)}, r_2^{(2)}) + F(r_1^{(1)} + r_2^{(2)})$
$+ F(r_0^{(0)} + r_2^{(2)}) + F(r_0^{(0)} + r_1^{(1)}) - F(r_0^{(0)}) - F(r_1^{(1)}) - F(r_2^{(2)})$. *Due to the used polar*
*form and its trilinear property, we obtain* $v = F(r_0^{(0)} + r_1^{(1)} + r_2^{(2)}) = F(s)$. *We con-*
*clude that a solution of* $r_0^{(0)} + r_1^{(1)} + r_2^{(2)}$ *for v is extracted. The proof indicates that*
*anyone must be able to response at least three out of the four challenges to reach the*
*secret key or solve the multivariate cubic polynomials system. Thus, the proposed*
*identification scheme is soundness.*□

Recall that the first study related to identification scheme based on multivariate polynomials is [11]. When evaluating efficiency of their scheme, they consider the 3-pass identification scheme applying $MQ(n, m, \mathbb{F}_q, k)$, where $n$ is the number of variables, $m$ is the number of equations, $q$ is the size of $\mathbb{F}$ finite field, and $k$ is the security level in [11]. These are the estimation of system parameters, public key, secret key, and communication length for 3-pass identification scheme. They use $MQ(84, 80, \mathbb{F}_2, 80)$ that satisfies 80-bit security. For the 5-pass identification scheme, they use $MQ(45, 30, \mathbb{F}_{2^4})$ and show efficiency of their scheme. In [13], they use $MC(84, 80, \mathbb{F}_2)$ and $MC(33, 22, \mathbb{F}_{2^4})$ for the 3-pass identification scheme and 5-pass identification scheme, respectively. In the following studies, $MQ(84, 80, \mathbb{F}_2, 80)$ and $MC(84, 80, \mathbb{F}_2, 80)$ security parameters are used for 3-pass identification schemes.

## 8.3.7 Comparison of all identification schemes based on multivariate polynomials

In this section, we compare all the identification schemes described in view of commitment length, memory requirements, and computation time. Now, we give the computation of the cost (commitment length, memory requirements, computation time) of the identification scheme for [25]. First, we choose the secret key over $\mathbb{F}_q^n$. Thus, each parts of the secret key is $n$–bit. The output of $F$ polynomial system is $m$–bit, whereas the outputs of Com commitment function and hash values are $2m$–bit.

*Table 8.2   The identification schemes comparison*

| | Pass | D[1] | Prover | Verifier | Commitment length | Total | CT[2] |
|---|---|---|---|---|---|---|---|
| [11] | 3 | $MQ$ | $9m + 2n$ | $4m$ | $5m + 2n + 2$ | $18m + 4n + 2$ | 4/3 |
| [12] | 3 | $MQ$ | $16m + 3n$ | $8m$ | $8m + 3n + 2$ | $32m + 6n + 2$ | 5/2 |
| [24] | 3 | $MQ$ | $14m + 3n$ | $4m$ | $13m + 3n + 3$ | $31m + 6n + 3$ | 4/3 |
| [13] | 3 | $MC$ | $11m + 3n$ | $4m$ | $11m + 2n + 2$ | $26m + 5n + 2$ | 3/2 |
| [14] | 3 | $MC$ | $13m + 2n$ | $6m$ | $13m + 3n + 2$ | $32m + 5n + 2$ | 9/4 |
| [25] | 3 | $MC$ | $17m + 2n$ | $10m$ | $20m + 4n + 2$ | $47m + 6n + 2$ | 9/4 |
| [11] | 5 | $MQ$ | $5m + 2n$ | $2m$ | $5m + 2n + 2$ | $12m + 4n + 2$ | 3/2 |
| [13] | 5 | $MC$ | $5m + 2n$ | $2m$ | $5m + 3n + 2$ | $12m + 5n + 2$ | 2 |

[1]D refers to the degree of the multivariate polynomials used in identification schemes.
[2]CT refers to computation time.

Now, we compute memory requirement for the prover. The prover calculates two parts of the secret key that are $2n$-bit, three outputs of $F$ that are $3m$-bit, seven commitment values that are $14m$-bit. Total memory requirement for the prover is $17m + 2n$-bit.

Memory requirement for the verifier is $10m$-bit in the worst case. Otherwise, the memory requirement is $6m$-bit since the verifier computes three commitment values.

The communication length is calculated by the received and sent values: commitment values are $14m$-bit, $Ch$ is 2-bit, and $Rsp$ is $6m + 4n$-bit. The total communication length is $20m + 4n + 2$. The total memory that includes the prover, verifier, and communication length is $47m + 6n + 2$-bit.

In the scheme, the most time consuming parts are the computing of the commitment value that include $F$ and $G$ functions. Therefore, $F$ and $G$ functions are crucial for computation time. The computation time is computed by dividing the number of the $F$ and $G$ functions into the number of the challenges [12]. The computation time of the proposed scheme is 9/4.

In Table 8.2, we give the comparison of all identification schemes based on multivariate polynomials. Recall that the parameters are $n = 84$, $m = 80$, $k = 80$. In Table 8.2, $MQ(84, 80, \mathbb{F}_2, 80)$ and $MC(84, 80, \mathbb{F}_2, 80)$ are used for 80-bit security.

From Table 8.2, the dividing technique, the number of passes in the scheme and the degree of the used multivariate polynomial systems are important in terms of efficiency of the schemes. The computation time is an important criteria when evaluating the identification schemes. When we compute the total memory for 80-bit security level, there is no significant difference between these systems in terms of memory requirements.

## 8.4   Cloud and IoT applications of quantum secure identification scheme

In this section, we explain the concepts of the Internet of Things (IoT) and cloud computing. Then, we introduce the use of the identification schemes in cloud and IoT areas.

There are many definitions for the IoT. The International Telecommunication Union (ITU) define IoT as a concept that anything can be connected Internet and communicate each other at any place at any time [26]. The IoT is a technology that enables all machines and devices to connect to each other and to communicate with various communication protocols.

In 1991, a group of academics who work in Cambridge University developed a camera system with the aim of seeing the coffee machine. This camera system take three photo of the coffee machine in one minute and send the photos to all academicians. Thus, all of them had an opportunity to see the coffee machine in real time. This system was assumed to be the first application of the IoT [27]. It is known that Kevin Ashton used first the term of IoT that was the title of his presentation in 1999. In 2005, the ITU published the first report about IoT [28]. In 2008, on the Foreign Relations Council, Samuel Palmisano, IBM CEO proposed the concept of "Smart Planet." With this, the concept of IoT has attracted more attention.

The number and types of devices connected to the Internet and each other have been increasing day by day. It is estimated that connected devices will be 50 billion by 2020, which shows that smart devices and environments will be in our lives more than they are now [29]. The IoT has many field of applications such as industrial automation, home and building automation, medical, transportation, energy management systems, environmental and infrastructure monitoring. Smart buildings, intelligent cars, intelligent farms, and intelligent environments can be given as an example of the IoT. In Table 8.3, the areas of the use of identification schemes are summarized [30].

The emergence of smart devices in all areas of our lives will lead to various security problems such as unauthorized and unpermissioned monitoring and even control of smart devices. Implementing identification schemes into these smart systems will overcome security problems. The importance of identification schemes is better understood when we think that all devices in a smart house are managed from a control center. In a system where there has no identification

*Table 8.3   The areas of use of identification schemes*

| Areas | Purpose |
|-------|---------|
| Agriculture, forestry, and fishing | To give a unique identification number for each farm animal |
| Manufacturing | To identify and control at all stages from production to consumption of products |
| Transportation | To manage transportation by giving id to all transportation means and stations, to manage safety of traffic and to use of roads in accordance with their capacity |
| Construction | To give an identity number all buildings and manage the building structure |
| Medical care | To identify patient and systems for safe drug distribution and to integrate hospitals these processes |

scheme, the control of all devices can be taken control by a third party. For this reason, identification schemes play an important role for IoT. However, there is no standardized identification scheme for the currently used smart devices [30]. Companies and countries use some identification schemes according to the structure to be created.

Cloud computing is a new technology that has become popular in recent years. Cloud computing can be considered as the combination of hosting and grid computing. It enables us to store hardware, software, and disk space we need on a server and when we want to reach the data, we can use them remotely via Internet only. In other words, the data is held in remote distributed computers, which can be accessed from anywhere in the world and with any hardware. According to the definition given by the NIST, cloud computing is a model that provides common, practical, and reachable network access to the shared pool of configurable computing resources that can be quickly priced and released with minimal management effort or service provider interaction [31].

A reliable cloud-computing system is obligated to provide security mechanisms such as protection against unauthorized access to information, authentication, encryption for sensitive data protection on devices that may be stolen or lost, and compatibility with hardware/software mechanisms [32]. In this content, the main components of cloud security are data privacy, data integrity, authentication, identity management, physical and personal security, accessibility, security of application services, and privacy. It is clear that identification is important in cloud computing. In cloud-computing services, user identities, passwords, and Kerberos are used to identify users' identities.

## 8.5    Challenges and future directions

There is no standard for identification schemes to be used in the post-quantum world. Recall that the NIST has announced to evaluate and then standardize quantum resistant public-key cryptosystems [7]. Therefore, there is a need to start a challenge for the standardization process of quantum secure identification schemes. As a future work, proposed identification scheme can be transformed to digital signature scheme by applying Fiat–Shamir transform. In addition, blind, ring, and threshold signature schemes can be designed by using the identification schemes as in [33–35].

## 8.6    Conclusion

We review all the identification schemes based on multivariate polynomials over a finite field. We also propose a novel identification scheme based on MC polynomials. Then, we compare all identification schemes in terms of memory requirements, commitment length, and computation time. We explain the use of the identification schemes into cloud and IoT areas. In brief, we emphasize the importance of quantum secure identification schemes.

# Acknowledgment

The authors are partially supported by TÜBİTAK under grant no. EEEAG-116E279.

# References

[1] Bone S, and Castro M. A brief history of quantum computing. Imperial College in London. 1997. Available from: http://www.doc.ic.ac.uk/~nd/surprise_97/journal/vol4/spb3.

[2] de Wolf R. Quantum computing: Lecture notes. 2018.

[3] Ajmare M, and Shute N, editors. Google moves toward quantum supremacy with 72-qubit computer. [homepage on the Internet]. Washington: Science News Magazine of The Society; 2018. Available from: http://sciencenews.org.

[4] Shor PW. Algorithms for quantum computation: Discrete logarithms and factoring. In Foundations of Computer Science, 1994 Proceedings, 35th Annual Symposium. 1994. p. 124–134.

[5] Buchmann JA, Butin D, Göpfert F, *et al.* Post-quantum cryptography: state of the art. In: Ryan PYA, Naccache D, Quisquater JJ, editors. The New Codebreakers. Berlin: Springer; 2016. p. 88–108.

[6] Bernstein DJ, Buchmann J, and Dahmen E. Post-quantum cryptography. Berlin, Heidelberg: Springer; 2009.

[7] Chen L, Jordan S, Liu YK, *et al.* Report on post-quantum cryptography. National Institute of Standards and Technology; 2016. Internal Report 8105.

[8] Takagi T. Recent developments in post-quantum cryptography. IEICE Transactions on Fundamentals of Electronics, Communications and Computer Sciences. 2018;101(1):3–11.

[9] Hashimoto Y. Multivariate public key cryptosystems. In: Mathematical Modelling for Next-Generation Cryptography. Singapore: Springer; 2018. p. 17–42.

[10] Ding J, and Petzoldt A. Current state of multivariate cryptography. IEEE Security & Privacy. 2017;15(4):28–36.

[11] Sakumoto K, Shirai T, and Hiwatari H. Public-key identification schemes based on multivariate quadratic polynomials. Annual Cryptology Conference. 2011;LNCS 6841:706–723.

[12] Monteiro FS, Goya DH, and Terada R. Improved identification protocol based on the MQ Problem. IEICE Transactions on Fundamentals of Electronics, Communications and Computer Sciences. 2015;E98-A:1255–1265.

[13] Sakumoto K. Public-key identification schemes based on multivariate cubic polynomials. International Workshop on Public Key Cryptography. 2012; LNCS 7293:172–189.

[14] Nachef V, Patarin J, and Volte E. Zero knowledge for multivariate polynomials. 2nd International Conference on Cryptology and Information Security in Latin America-LATINCRYPT 2012. 2012;LNCS 7533:194–213.

[15] Chen M, Hülsing A, Rijneveld J, *et al.* From 5-pass MQ-based identification to MQ-based signatures. International Conference on the Theory and Application

of Cryptology and Information Security Advances in Cryptology – ASIA-CRYPT 2016. 2016;LNCS 10032:135–165.

[16]   Cheng C, Lu R, Petzoldt A, *et al.* Securing the Internet of Things in a quantum world. IEEE Communications Magazine. 2017;55(2):116–120.

[17]   Liu Z, Raymond Choo K, and Grossschadl J. Securing edge devices in the post-quantum Internet of Things using lattice-based cryptography. IEEE Communications Magazine. 2018;56(2):158–162.

[18]   Fiat A, and Shamir A. How to prove yourself: Practical solutions to identification and signature problems. In: Odlyzko AM, editor, Advances in Cryptology — CRYPTO'86. 1987;LNCS 263:186–194.

[19]   Feige U, Fiat A, and Shamir A. Zero-knowledge proofs of identity. Journal of cryptology. 1988;1(2):77–94.

[20]   Simari GI. A primer on zero knowledge protocols. Universidad Nacional del Sur. 2002;6(27):1–12.

[21]   Goldreich O. *Foundations of cryptography*. Cambridge: Cambridge University Press; 2009.

[22]   Yasuda T, Dahan X, Huang YJ, *et al.* MQ challenge: Hardness evaluation of solving multivariate quadratic problems. NIST Workshop on Cybersecurity in a Post-Quantum World (2015): http://eprint.iacr.org/2015/275; 2015.

[23]   Massachusetts Institute of Technology [homepage on the Internet]. Cambridge: Eitan Reich; 2005 [cited 2018 May 8]. Available from: https://math.mit.edu/dav/bilinearforms.pdf.

[24]   Soysaldı M. Quantum secure new identification and signature schemes based on multivariate polynomials. [M.Sc.]. Ondokuz Mayıs University. Samsun, Turkey; 2018.

[25]   Akleylek S, and Soysaldı M. A new quantum secure identification scheme. The 9th Defense Technologies Congress (SAVTEK 2018). 2018; Proceedings(29 June):873–881.

[26]   ITU-T. Overview of the Internet of Things. International Telecommunication Union Y-2060; 2012.

[27]   Garcia Macias JA, and Pinedo-Farusto ED. An experimental analysis of Zigbee networks. IEEE. 2008; 33rd IEEE Conference:723–729.

[28]   ITU. The Internet of Things. International Telecommunication Union; 2005. ITU Internet Reports.

[29]   Evans D. The Internet of Things: How the next evolution of the internet is changing everything. Cisco Internet Business Solutions Group (IBSG); 2011. Available from: https://www.cisco.com/c/dam/en_us/about/ac79/docs/innov/IoT_IBSG_0411FINAL.pdf.

[30]   Kang MS, Jun HJ, and Kim TS. Necessity and expectation for an identification scheme in IoT service: Cases in South Korea. Indian Journal of Science and Technology. 2016;9(24):1–10.

[31]   Mell P, and Grance T. The NIST definition of cloud computing. National Institute of Standards and Technology; 2011. NIST SP 800–145.

[32]   Krutz RL, and Vines RD. *Cloud Security: A Comprehensive Guide to Secure Cloud Computing*. Wiley Publishing; 2010.

[33]  Mohamed MSE, and Petzoldt A. RingRainbow – an efficient multivariate ring signature scheme. In: International Conference on Cryptology in Africa. Cham: Springer; 2017. p. 3–20.

[34]  Petzoldt A, Szepieniec A, and Mohamed MSE. A practical multivariate blind signature scheme. In: International Conference on Financial Cryptography and Data Security. Cham: Springer; 2017. p. 437–454.

[35]  El Bansarkhani R, Mohamed MSE, and Petzoldt A. MQSAS – A multivariate sequential aggregate signature scheme. In: International Conference on Information Security. Cham: Springer; 2016. p. 426–439.

*Chapter 9*

# Authentication issues for cloud applications

*Bahram Rashidi[1]*

## 9.1 Introduction

Cloud computing is a technology for sharing of computing resources and other services to handle the cloud applications. In this technology, services are delivered through the Internet. The aim is to increase the computing power to execute millions of instructions per second. Therefore, cloud computing uses networks of a large group of servers or service providers to distribute data processing. There are different security issues for cloud applications as they include many systems and technologies such as networks, databases of information, operating systems, virtualization, resource scheduling, transaction management, load balancing, concurrency control, parallel computing, and memory management. Therefore, providing secure communications for many of these systems and technologies is applicable and necessary. The challenges of security in cloud computing can be categorized into network level (network protocols and network security such as distributed nodes, distributed data, Internode communication), user authentication level (encryption/decryption techniques, authentication methods), data level (data integrity and availability such as data protection and distributed data), and generic issues (traditional security tools, and the use of different technologies). Authentication, in the cloud applications, is the process of validating and guaranteeing the identity of cloud service subscribers or users. The reliability and security of the cloud computing environment especially are based on authentication. Therefore, this chapter discusses security issues for cloud applications and then focus on the authentication technologies in the cloud system.

The chapter is organized as follows. In Section 9.2, security issues in the cloud environment are discussed. Also, authentication technologies for cloud applications are presented in Section 9.3. In Section 9.4, advantages and disadvantages of authentication methods are presented. Research challenges and future perspectives are discussed in Section 9.5. Section 9.6 concludes the chapter.

[1]Department of Electrical Engineering, University of Ayatollah Ozma Borujerdi, Iran

## 9.2    Security issues in cloud applications

As cloud applications have been widely used, service providers and users enable to use resource and service easily without owning all the resource required. However, cloud computing has some security issues such as virtualization technology security, massive distributed processing technology, service availability, massive traffic handling, application security, access control, and authentication. The provision of user data security is extremely vital and remarkable because if data security is not provided, the cloud system will practically lose its concept. Therefore, security solutions and issues in this system are constantly updated. Cloud computing security is a sub-domain of computer security and network security. It refers to a wide range of technologies, applications, policies, infrastructure, and approaches used for data protection in the cloud computing. We can use various technologies such as intrusion detection systems, firewalls as well as separation of obligations on different networks and cloud layers for providing security. The works [1–10] review different security issues in the cloud systems. In [1], the authors firstly evaluate cloud security by identifying unique security requirements and secondly present a viable solution that eliminates these potential threats. This work proposed a trusted third party (TTP) for the establishment of specific security characteristics within a cloud environment. To provide security, user privacy, and preserve data integrity on the cloud, the service providers must first secure virtualized data (on resource centers) [5]. In [5], a trust-overlay network over multiple data centers to implement a valid system for providing trust between service providers and data owners is used. The works [4,6] focus on data security in mobile cloud computing. In [9] and [10], security issues to cloud computing are discussed, including privacy, trust, control, data ownership, availability, integrity, confidentiality, data location, audits and reviews, business continuity and disaster recovery, legal, regulatory and compliance, security policy, and emerging security threats and attacks. In [11], a method for multimedia data security in the cloud environment is reported. This method watermarks and compresses the data before its storage in the cloud and also reduces the storage requirement.

Figure 9.1 shows graphical representation of security issues in the cloud applications. In the following subsections, we briefly described these important security issues in more detail.

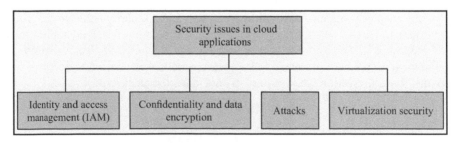

*Figure 9.1    Security issues in the cloud applications*

## 9.2.1 Identity and access management (IAM)

The biggest challenge for cloud services is the provision of identity. This includes safe and timely management when provisioning and de-provisioning of users in the cloud. Identity management refers to important security mechanisms for enabling data protection that creates and maintains the identity of the cloud user. Also, it de-provisions the user account when the user leaves the cloud service. It controls access to the resources by placing restrictions on the esta-blished identities [12]. Identity management in the cloud consists of three perspectives, namely, the identity provisioning model, the log-on model, and the service model. The access control unit provides management of access author-ized users to cloud services. In this case, parts of the system resources are allo-cated in terms of CPU, memory, storage and network bandwidth. There are three access control methods including *discretionary access control (DAC)*: It helps a user to establish the authority to the resources. *Media access control (MAC)*: It provides horizontal/vertical access rules in the security standards. *Role-based access control (RBAC)*: This method is widely used in commercial organizations, which gives an access authority to a user group based on their role in the organization.

IAM components are shown in Figure 9.2. In the following subsections, we briefly describe these components.

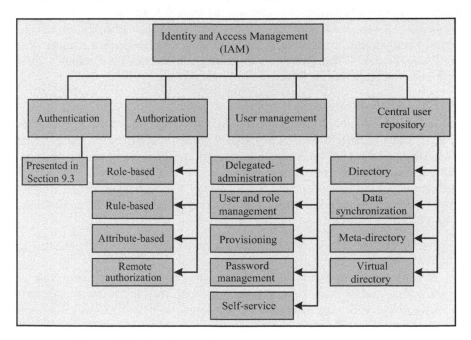

*Figure 9.2   Identity and access management components*

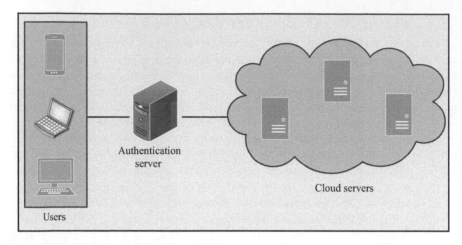

*Figure 9.3    General scheme of authentication in the cloud applications*

### 9.2.1.1    Authentication

Authentication is a mechanism for verifying the user's identity. Authentication in the cloud system guarantees that the proper user is getting access to the provided information from the cloud provider [13]. Authentication in the cloud computing is guaranteed when accessing the stored data in the cloud; in this case, the identity of the user is provided to the cloud service provider. The general scheme of authentication in the cloud applications is shown in Figure 9.3. The users for access to the cloud server for the use of services must be verified by the authentication server. It should be noted that its strength directly affects the reliability and security of the cloud environment. Therefore, in the following subsections, we specially focus on authentication technologies in cloud applications.

### 9.2.1.2    Authorization

Authorization is important for users in the cloud system when they access to some cloud services because it enables prove of their identities. Therefore, authorization is usually used after the authentication by checking the resource access request. In addition, the authorization can provide complicated access controls based on the data or policies including user attributes, user roles, actions taken, access channels, time, resources requested, external data, and business rules [14]. Figure 9.4 shows three authorization models, which are presented as follows:

- **User-push model:** The user conducts a handshake with the authority first and then with the resource site in a sequence.
- **Resource-pulling model:** In this model, the resource puts in the middle. The user first checks the resource at the first step. Then the resource contacts its authority to verify the request at the second step, and the authority authorizes at the third step. Finally, at the fourth step, the resource accepts or rejects the request from the user.
- **Authorization agent model:** This model puts the authority in the middle. The user checks with the authority at step 1 and the authority makes decisions

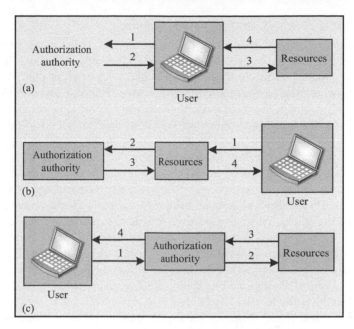

*Figure 9.4 Three authorization models: (a) user-push model; (b) resource-pulling model; and (c) authorization agent model*

on the access of the requested resources. Finally, the authorization process is complete.

### 9.2.1.3 User management

This part includes password management (it allows the user to change his (or her) password and unlock your account, even if the user has forgotten his (or her) password), role management (it helps user manage authorization, which enables user to specify the resources that users in his (or her) application are allowed to access), self-service, life-cycle management, and user provisioning. User management defines the set of administrative functions such as propagation, identity creation, and maintenance of the user identity [15]. One of user management components is the management of user life-cycle that enables an enterprise to manage the lifetime of an account, from the first stage of provisioning to the final stage of de-provisioning. Self-service is a key concept within user management such as self-password reset to handle password reset requests.

### 9.2.1.4 Central user repository

Central user repository (CUR) stores and delivers identity information to other services, and provides service to check credentials sent from users [12]. The CUR offers a logical view of the identities of an enterprise. Both meta-directory (provides an aggregate set of identity data) and virtual directory (delivers a unified Lightweight Directory Access Protocol (LDAP) view of consolidated identity information) can be used to manage disparate identity data from different user repositories of applications and systems.

## 9.2.2    *Confidentiality and data encryption*

Cloud outsource storage is one of the important services in the cloud applications. To reduce the cost of managing data and maintaining hardware and software, the cloud users upload data to cloud servers. The users can encrypt their data before uploading them to cloud servers to eliminate privacy risks and data confidentiality. Confidentiality is one of the most important security mechanisms for the protection of the user's data in the cloud applications. This mechanism includes encryption of the plaintext to ciphertext before the data is stored in the cloud. In this way, the user's data is protected even for cloud service providers, so that they cannot modify or read the content that is stored in the cloud. In order to provide secure communication over the cloud, encryption algorithms play an important and essential role. Encryption algorithms are valuable and fundamental tools for the protection of the data. One of the important encryption schemes is the symmetric key encryption. Symmetric key encryption converts the data into secret form by using "a key" called *main key*, this key is used to encryption and decryption the data. In this encryption algorithm, the most used algorithm is the advanced encryption standard (AES) [16]. Also, other lightweight symmetric key encryption algorithms such as HIGHT, SIMON, SPECK, PRESENT, and KATAN are used to improving security performance of the cloud systems. Figure 9.5 shows a general block diagram of data encryption and decryption in a cloud system. Data owner encrypts the plaintext by encryption function with shared secret key and sends the ciphertext to cloud service provider. A user with the shared secret key can achieve the plaintext.

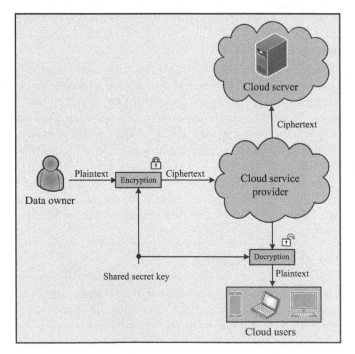

*Figure 9.5    General block diagram of data encryption and decryption in a cloud system*

### 9.2.2.1 Attribute-based encryption (ABE) for the cloud system

Some cryptographic algorithms which have been used for cloud system increase the protection of privacy. ABE is a type of public-key cryptography in which the user's secret key and the ciphertext are dependent on attributes [17–20]. In this cryptographic system, the decryption of a ciphertext is possible only if the set of attributes of the user-key matches the attributes of the ciphertext. Two main approaches for ABE are presented as follows [21–24]:

- **Ciphertext-policy ABE (CP-ABE):** This encryption scheme associates the set of attributes to the plaintext by encrypting it with the corresponding public-key components. An architecture of a CP-ABE scheme for cloud storage system is shown in Figure 9.6.
- **Key-policy ABE (KP-ABE):** KP-ABE is an important type of attribute-based encryption, which enables senders to encryption of plaintexts under a set of attributes. An architecture of a KP-ABE scheme for cloud storage system is shown in Figure 9.7. In the KP-ABE, attribute sets are used to describe the encrypted messages. Also, the private keys are associated with the specified policy that users will have.

In [20], an ABE structure with verifiable outsourced decryption is presented. It can simultaneously check the correctness for transformed ciphertext for the authorized users and unauthorized users. In this case, the authorized and unauthorized users can verify the correctness for the transformed ciphertext, but only the authorized user has the ability to decryption of the ciphertext to obtain the plaintext. In [24], the authors presented an expressive CP-ABE structure for supporting partially hidden access structures (where each attribute is divided into an attribute name and an attribute value, and the attribute value in an access structure is not given in the ciphertext) in the prime-order groups with improved efficiency.

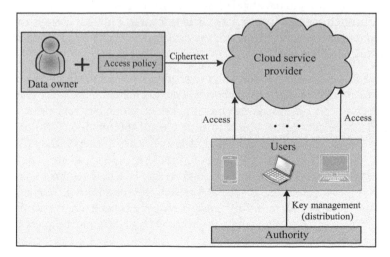

*Figure 9.6   An architecture of a CP-ABE scheme for a cloud storage system*

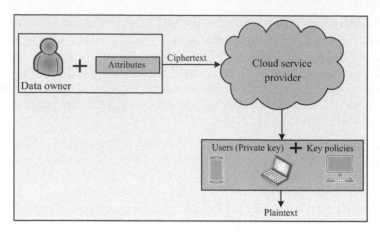

*Figure 9.7    An architecture of a KP-ABE scheme for cloud storage system*

## 9.2.2.2    Searchable encryption for cloud system

The data search service is often used in the cloud storage environment. Therefore, an important issue in outsourcing cloud storage is providing a searchable encryption (SE) approach. SE is a suitable approach for protection of users secret data, which offer secure search functions over encrypted data (while maintaining the server-side search capability without leaking information in plaintext data) [25–30]. In this approach, to improve the search efficiency, the capability to search the specific keywords (indexes) within the encrypted data is provided. In more detail, in the SE scheme, the data before uploading on the server by the user is encrypted. In this case, to efficiently search of the encrypted data, the data owner constructs and uploads an index of encrypted data is send to the server. The user must be authorized by the server to perform a search. The user enters keywords to generate a trapdoor when the search request to the cloud server. The server computes a score based on the index and then returns highly correlated data to the user [30]. The SE system can be categorized into two classes: SE based on symmetric-key cryptography and SE based on public-key cryptography.

- **SE based on symmetric-key cryptography:** This approach allows only private key owners to generate ciphertexts and to create trapdoors for search. The architecture of a SE based on symmetric-key cryptography scheme is shown in Figure 9.8. A data owner wants to store a set of information (files) on a cloud server. As the server is semi-trusted, data owner has to encrypt the information before outsourcing them. In addition, data owner send secure index (query keyword) as search token to the cloud server. If a user requires some information (files) containing a special keyword, he (or she) will require to send some information in terms of query keywords (search query) to the cloud server. Then, to determine which information (file) contains the query keyword the server will search the ciphertext.

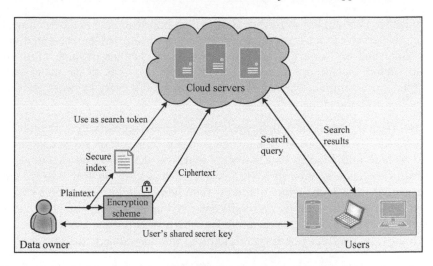

*Figure 9.8   Architecture of a SE based on symmetric-key cryptography scheme*

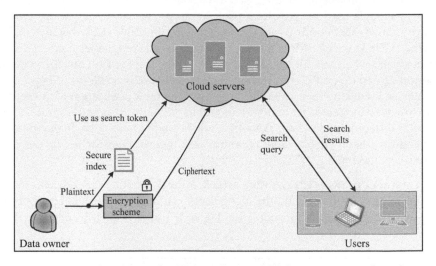

*Figure 9.9   Architecture of a SE based on public-key cryptography scheme*

- **SE based on public-key cryptography:** SE based on public-key cryptography enables a number of users who know the public-key to produce ciphertexts but allows only the private key owner to create trapdoors for search [25]. The architecture of a SE based on public-key cryptography scheme is shown in Figure 9.9. Data owner sends the information (file) with corresponding secure index (keyword) to user **A**. In order to protect the contents of the information (file) and keywords, both are encrypted with user **A** public key. However, in this case, the cloud server cannot make a routing decision according to the keywords. Therefore, it is required to give the cloud server the ability to decide whether a certain keyword is contained in an information or not. Meantime, the cloud server cannot learn anything about the contents of the encrypted information and keywords [26]. If user **A** (with private key) needs some information to submit the information in terms of query keywords to the cloud server. Then, to determine which information contains the query keyword the server will search the ciphertext.

In [27], a dynamic SE which is reliable and privacy-preserving with multi-user query capability is proposed. It is dedicated to protecting secret saved data files on cloud storage and enables data users to search on the encrypted files under the control of the data owners. In [28], a secure SE structure, applicable to the cloud environment, based on using multikey fully homomorphic encryption (MFHE) which is capable of operating on inputs encrypted under multiple unrelated keys is presented. In [29], a robust, fault-tolerance and SE structure for data outsourcing in the cloud system by considering both numeric and non-numeric data is proposed.

## 9.2.3 Attacks against information in the cloud environments

The threats to information in the cloud environments can change based on the cloud delivery models used by the cloud user organizations. There are various types of security threats that confirm cloud computing is vulnerable. Distributed denial-of-service (DDoS) attacks form the major threats faced by Internet users and cloud applications, where resources are shared by many users. DDoS attacks target the resources (memory, CPU processing space, or network bandwidth) of these applications, and reducing their capability to provide optimum utilization of the network infrastructure by heavy amounts of unreal traffic and consume resources. DDoS includes different types of attacks which are shown in Figure 9.10. In the following subsections, these attacks and recommended defense approaches in the cloud system are presented [31,32]:

- **Internet Protocol (IP) spoofing attack:** In the IP spoofing attack, packet transfer between the end user and the cloud server can be intercepted and their headers changed such that the IP source field in the IP packet is made by either an illegal

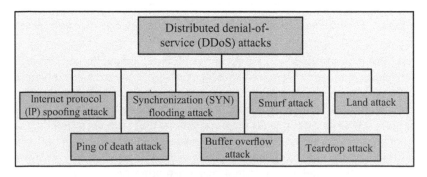

*Figure 9.10   Different types of DDoS attacks in the cloud system*

IP address or by an unreachable IP address. Tracking such an attack is hard due to the fake IP address of the IP source field in the IP packet. The methods for detecting an IP spoofing attack can be used in the network resources.

- **Synchronization (SYN) flooding attack:** A Transmission Control Protocol connection starts with a typical 3-way handshake. A 3-way handshake is performed between a legal user and the server begins by sending a connection request (in the form of an SYN message) from the user to the server. Then, the server by sending back (SYN-ACK) a request to the user acknowledges (SYN). Finally in the last step, to completion the connection, the user sends an ACK request to the server. SYN flooding attack occurs when the attacker sends a huge number of packets to the server. In this case, the process of the 3-way handshake does not complete.
- **Smurf attack:** In this attack, a large number of Internet Control Message Protocol (ICMP) echo requests send by the attacker. The attacker's requests are spoofed such that the IP destination address is the broadcast IP address and its source IP address is the victim's IP. Preventing this kind of attack is difficult, but it can be reduced by two different defense approaches. The first defense approach is configuration of the routers to disable the IP-directed broadcast command. Also, the second defense method is needed, which is the configuration of the operating systems. In this case, there is no response to the ICMP packets sent to the IP broadcast addresses.
- **Ping of death attack:** In this attack, an IP packet with a size larger than the limit of the IP protocol is sent by the attacker. Managing an oversized packet affects the victim's machine within the cloud system and it's resources. These attacks have not affected any cloud system layers. Because in recent network resources and operating systems disregard any oversized IP packets.
- **Land attack:** This attack uses a C-program file called "Land.c" to send forged Transmission Control Protocol SYN packets with the victim's IP address in the source and destination fields. In this case, the victim's machine will receive the request from itself and crash the system. Such an attack is prevented by dropping ICMP packets that contain the same IP address in the source and destination fields in recent networking devices and operating systems.
- **Teardrop attack:** This type of attack uses a C-program file called "Teardrop. c" to send invalid overlapping values of IP fragments in the header of Transmission Control Protocol packets. Therefore, the victim's machine within the cloud system will crash in the re-assembly process. These attacks can be handled in recent operating systems and network resources.

## 9.2.4   *Virtualization security in the cloud system*

Virtualization is a technology allows the development of an intelligent abstraction layer that hides the complexity of underlying software or hardware. In computing, virtualization is the development of a virtual version of a resource, an operating system, a storage device, or network. Therefore, it consists of storage virtualization, server virtualization, network virtualization, application virtualization, memory virtualization, platform or hardware virtualization, and desktop virtualization [33,34]. If virtualization technology is applied to the cloud system, it creates some security risk that may be exploited harmfully and cause a major security incident. Also, mapping of the virtual machines to the physical machines has to be performed very securely. There are different risks such as risk for access control, the risk of DDoS attack, the risk of virtualization platform building network, and the risk of virtualization platform security. Therefore, providing security for the virtualization technology in the cloud computing has been a popular research topic.

In [33], a secure architecture in a hypervisor-based virtualization technology in order to secure the cloud environment is proposed. In work [35], the authors presented the usage of assistive technology (AT) in the cloud computing based on the virtualization technology for providing software tools to people with disabilities. The proposed approach allows users to access remote virtual machines (VMs) through an HTML5 web interface.

## 9.3 Authentication architectures and strategies in the cloud applications

Authentication is the process for confirming the user's identity. In this case, unauthorized users will be forbidden to enter and only authorized users will be allowed to enter. In the traditional authentication process, the system identifies and validates the user through a username and a password, respectively. Authentication is one of the important security technologies of data security for the cloud applications. The important point in authentication is the protection of information from the access of unauthorized users. Therefore, the servers refuse to visit requests from unknown users and manage the access of the confirmed users. Privacy is a remarkable requirement in authentication approaches to ensure that the user is known only to legal entities. The authentication method should protect private data of users from eavesdropping during the authentication process [13]. Technologies commonly used to authenticate a user in the cloud applications are shown in Figure 9.11. These technologies are described in the following subsections.

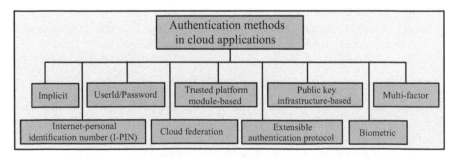

*Figure 9.11    Authentication methods in cloud applications*

### 9.3.1 UserId/Password authentication

UserId/Password authentication is simple and easy to use, and is a commonly used authentication technique, but it must have a certain level of complication and regular renewal to keep the security [3]. In this authentication method, the user should enter the username and password to login to the system and access the information in the cloud. The well-known weakness in the UserId/Password authentication technology is proving that the request is from the legal owner. Because even if the correct username and password are provided, it is still difficult to prove that the request is from the legal owner. In [36] and [37], the authors presented the authentication given to the cloud by using a graphical password (image password). The proposed scheme in work [37] is resistant to spyware and shoulder-surfing attacks. In [38], to achieve better security than the alphanumerical password, a scheme which allows improving the authentication mechanism in the cloud system using the password generator module is described.

### 9.3.2 Trusted platform module-based authentication

Trusted platform module (TPM) is a hardware-based security module that uses crypto-processor that can store secret keys that protect information [39]. Crypto-processor constructed by a random number generator, RSA key generator, SHA-1 hash generator, encryption-decryption signature generator. The Trusted Computing Platform (TCP) is based on TPM and provides some important security services in the cloud computing environment. It is used in authentication, confidentiality, integrity, role-based access, and data protection in cloud applications [40]. In [40], the authors proposed a new way that is conducive to improve the secure and dependable computing in the cloud. In this design, the authors integrate the TCP into the cloud computing system.

Figure 9.12 shows trusted platform support service architecture for cloud applications based on TCP. Trusted platform software stack (TSS) components are the main parts of the TCP cloud computing. TSS provides fundamental resources to support the TPM. Here, TSS is a bridge between the cloud applications and the hardware in the lowest layer. It is constructed based on two layers, the first layer is a TSS service provider (TSP) and the second layer is TSS core services (TCS). In this structure, the cloud applications call the function of TSP for providing some security modules. These security modules send calls to TCS. Then TSS converts these calls to according TPM instructions. The TCG Device Driver Library converts the calls from TCS to the TPM orders in hardware level. After the TPM perform the instructions, then the results are returned up forward. Each layer gets results from the low layer and converts them to suitable results that the up layer needs.

### 9.3.3 Public key infrastructure-based authentication

Public key infrastructure (PKI) authentication process is based on public-key cryptography. It enables the users to authenticate the other parties based on the certificate without shared secret information. The PKI together with TTP (to the establishment of the necessary trust level) provides a technically sound and legally acceptable means to the implementation of strong authentication and authorization

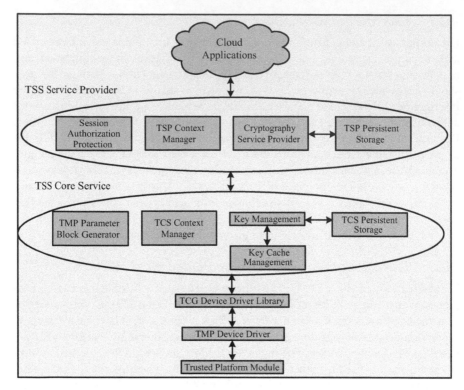

*Figure 9.12    Trusted platform support service architecture for the cloud applications based on TCP*

in the cloud applications. PKI has been used in the design of security protocols such as secure socket layer/transport layer security (SSL/TLS) and secure electronic transaction (SET) with the main aim is to provide authentication [3]. The success of PKI depends on the controlling access to private keys similar to other types of encryption systems. In [41], a secure elliptic curve cryptography-based mutual authentication protocol for secure communication of embedded devices and cloud servers using HTTP cookies has been proposed. In [42], an enhanced identity-based mutual authentication scheme using elliptic curve cryptography for client-server cloud architecture is proposed. In [43], a user authentication in the multi-server environment using elliptic curve cryptography as security foundation is proposed.

## 9.3.4    Multi-factor authentication

Multi-factor authentication (MFA) is a secure method for confirming (prove) a user's claimed identity. In this method, the user is granted access only after successfully presenting two or more factors to completion of the authentication mechanism. In an authentication process, if at least one of the steps is missing or supplied incorrectly, the user's identity is not established with sufficient certainty and access to the data is protected and blocked. Therefore, the aim of MFA is to create a layered defense and make it more difficult for an unauthorized person to gain access. The authentication factors for MFA can be divided into generally three categories as follows [4,13,44]:

- **Knowledge (something the user knows):** Such as a password/passphrase, PIN, or the answers to secret questions, etc.
- **Possession (something the user has):** Such as a one-time password (OTP) token device, smartcard, a USB stick with a secret token, a bank card, a key fob, a phone's SIM card, etc.
- **Inherence (something the user is or user's identifiable biometric characteristics):** Some physical characteristics of the user (biometrics), such as a fingerprint, eye iris, face, voice, typing speed, signature, hand geometry, earlobe geometry, and the pattern in keypress intervals.

Basically, MFA is the process of combining two authentication methods such as UserId/Password and biometrics. Figure 9.13 shows multi-factor authentication steps. These steps include knowledge, possession, inherence, and access. A 2-factor authentication process is shown in Figure 9.14. In this case, the first factor is something the user knows (knowledge) and the second factor is equal to something the user has (possession) or something the user is (inherence).

In Figure 9.15, a standard MFA process in a cloud-computing environment is presented. This process includes five steps: 1 – User tries to access cloud application. 2 – Request is processed by MFA solution. 3 – Additional factor authentication required. 4 – User successfully authenticates by the additional factor. 5 – Access granted.

In [45], the authors presented two-factor authentication scheme based on Schnorr digital signature and feature extraction from fingerprint to overcome the above aforementioned issues. In [46], a suitable authentication mechanism by using dual-factor authentication protocol (DFAP) along with the mobile token to refuse

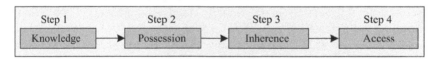

*Figure 9.13   Multi-factor authentication steps*

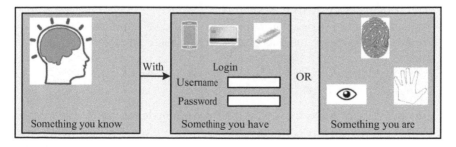

*Figure 9.14   2-factor authentication*

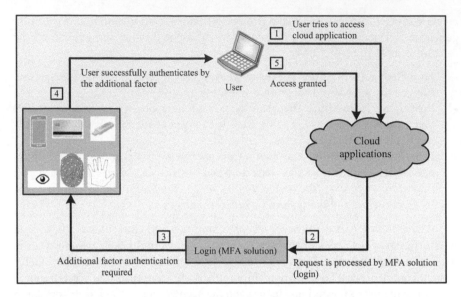

*Figure 9.15    A standard MFA process in a cloud-computing environment*

Malware is proposed. In the first step, the password is used to verify the user's profile and in the second step access to the cloud's services is provided.

## 9.3.5    Implicit authentication

Implicit authentication approach uses observations of user behavior for authentication and it is well suited for mobile devices. In this approach, user behavior is translated into the authentication score and thus allowing users to access cloud services clearly. A number of techniques have been studied to provide a suitable service for user profile information in the mobile cloud environment [47,48]. Implicit authentication can potentially use a wide range of data sources of behavioral to make authentication decisions. For example, modern smart phones provide rich sources of behavioral data such as [47]:

1. Location
2. Accelerometer measurements or motion
3. WiFi, Bluetooth, or USB connections
4. Application usage such as browsing patterns and software installations
5. Biometric-style measurements such as typing patterns, fingerprint, and voice data
6. Contextual data such as the content of calendar entries
7. Phone call patterns.

Figure 9.16 shows the framework of the machine-learning algorithm to compute the authentication score. In the first step, we learn a user model from a user's past behavior which characterizes an individual's behavioral patterns. Based on the user model and some recently observed behavior, we can compute the probability

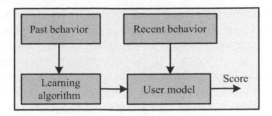

*Figure 9.16    Framework of the machine-learning algorithm for computing the authentication score*

that the device is in the legal user's hands. We use this probability as an authentication score, which is used to make an authentication decision.

In [47], the authors presented implicit authentication approach users based on behavior patterns. A flexible framework for supporting authentication decision based on a behavioral authentication approach is presented in [48]. In [49], an adaptive neuro-fuzzy inference system (ANFIS)-based implicit authentication system is proposed to improve mobile security. The authentication system is implemented in a continuous and transparent manner. In [50], an authentication method for implicit, continuous authentication of the smartphone user based on behavioral characteristics, by leveraging the sensors already built into smartphones is proposed.

### 9.3.6    Internet-personal identification number (I-PIN) authentication

I-PIN is an authentication technique used to confirm a user identity when the user uses the Internet in Korea now. This technique is currently used in Korea. It operates in a way that the organization which itself performed the identification of the user issues the assertion [51]. In [52], the authors proposed a technique to strengthen user authentications with the I-PIN when users sign up for memberships in the OpenID (is authentication exchange protocol for identity management in the Internet to safe, faster, and easier login to websites), and this technique compensates the phishing problem of relaying parties (RPs) which users could receive Internet service with the OpenID.

### 9.3.7    Context-aware cloud authentication

A context-aware cloud can assist in the dynamic and adaptive authentication method, while a complete user- and device-profiling is not possible. This authentication method is able to collect the user's personal information and preferences as well as to provide proper services for them. The design includes methods that interpret and infer the high-level context and resources management technique that manages distributed resources effectively. Therefore, context-aware cloud constantly retrieves structured information from users and through active classification and inference, in this case, can be built a model of the user who has legal access to systems and resources [3]. Authentication based on the context-aware cloud can be done dynamically depending on the variable conditions of the user's risk factor at a specific time. This type of risk-based authentication goes hand in hand with implicit authentication.

In [53], a context-awareness role-based access control (RBAC) model that provided efficiently access control to the user through active classification, inference, and judgment about the user who accesses to system and resource. The main contribution in [54] is the improvement of the user experience in the multi-factor authentication based on an enhanced multimodal biometrics (MFA-MB) process for cloud computing. Next, the authors develop an algorithm to authenticate cloud users with this new scheme and provide a solution to control/keep a low complexity while increasing the security level. In this work, the integration of class-association rules (CARs) in the cloud computing authentication process allows also to identify the actual context (time, place, device, etc.) which impacts the choice of biometrics used in multimodal biometric authentication (MBA) based on one user's status. In [55], a practical context-aware authentication system for mobile cloud computing is presented. The structure is cost-effective and easy to implement. The environmental data is only sent when the user makes an authentication request. In work [56], the authors proposed a platform for authentication using provisioning in the cloud computing applications. The authentication platform using provisioning first authenticates by using ID/Password, PKI, etc. which a user input. Second, it authenticates with the authentication manager through the user profile and patterns. Also, it stores the changes in the state via the monitor.

### 9.3.8    Cloud federation authentication

Federated identity is a useful feature for identity management. OpenID, Open Authorization (OAuth), and SAML are the main concepts for federated cloud service authentication [3,57]. In the OpenID, a user creates an account with the identity provider of his (or her) choice and can then use an agent to negotiate authentication. OAuth is an authentication standard for allowing users to share their private resources stored on a protected resource server without having to hand out their credentials [57]. OAuth specification is aimed to complement OpenID and let users delegate access to a protected resource through an authorization server that issues tokens that do not include user's credentials. OAuth has become a popular choice for cloud providers due to its simplicity. Figure 9.17 shows the architecture for OAuth with an independent authorization server. This process is presented by the following steps:

1.   The client requests authorization from the resource owner.
2.   The resource owner redirects the request to authorization server.
3.   The client requests the authorization grant from the authorization server by offering the client credentials.
4.   The authorization server validates the client credentials and the authorization grant, and if valid, sends an access token.
5.   The client requests the protected resource from the resource server and authenticates by offering the access token.
6.   The resource server validates the access token, and if valid, serves the request.

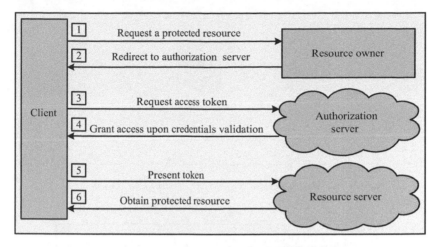

*Figure 9.17   Architecture for OAuth with an independent authorization server*

In [58], the authors described a structure for the Federation establishment, where clouds that need external resources ask to federated clouds the provision of extra physical resources. The structure consists of three phases: discovery of available external cloud resources, match-making selection between discovered cloud providers, and authentication for trust context establishment with selected clouds. In this work, the main focus is the authentication phase. In [59], the authors presented an approach to the cloud federation by considering a layered model where negotiation is constrained to well-defined sets of parameters. Additionally, user and site policies can be used to negotiate federation between partners, or translated to delegate tasks to other layers of a single site.

### 9.3.9   Extensible authentication protocol

Extensible Authentication Protocol (EAP) is implemented on the cloud environment for providing the authentication process. It is used for the transport and usage of keying material and parameters generated by the EAP approach. There are three major components to the authentication process as follows:

1. Supplicant (client and user)
2. Authenticator
3. Authentication server.

Architecture for extensible authentication protocol is shown in Figure 9.18. The authenticator (network access server (NAS)) sends requests for access to the system and the responses grant or deny access. In [60], a structure for EAP Challenge-Handshake Authentication Protocol (CHAP) for the authentication cloud computing environment is proposed. This method subjugates spoofing identity theft (SIT), data tampering threat (DTT), and DoS attack. In EAP-CHAP, when the client demands data or any service of the cloud computing, service provider authenticator (SPA) first

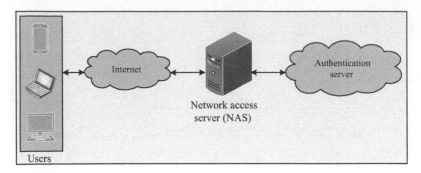

*Figure 9.18 Architecture for extensible authentication protocol*

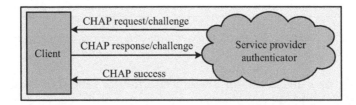

*Figure 9.19 Architecture for EAP-CHAP in the cloud environment*

requests for client identity. The process between client and SPA is presented in Figure 9.19. Authentication process of EAP-CHAP is performed in three steps.

1. When client demands a service, SPA sends a *challenge* message to the client.
2. Client responds with a value calculated by using one way has function on the challenge.
3. Authenticator checks the response value against its own calculated hash value. If values match, the cloud provider will give service, otherwise it should terminate the connection.

## 9.3.10 Biometric authentication

Physical biometric is a type of authentication based on the identification of physiological or behavioral characteristics of a human. In this case, the users are identified according to their physical biometric characteristics. In addition, it is a powerful authentication process providing the factors *what we are* and *what we know*. For the implementation of authentication process based on physiological characteristics, we have different approaches that include face recognition, hand geometry, iris recognition, retinal recognition, palm print recognition, ear recognition, and tongue recognition. Also, for behavioral characteristics, we have methods such as gait recognition, keystroke (dynamic and static), signature recognition, and voice recognition. Three factors of information security: authentication, identification, and non-repudiation are supported by biometric authentication [61–63]. The physical biometrics method

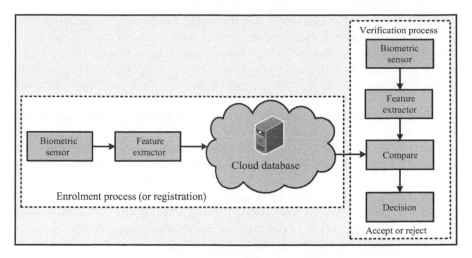

*Figure 9.20    General structure of the biometric authentication*

cannot support a great number of users need to be authenticated at the same time. In this case, it is time-consuming for the biometric authentication process. Figure 9.20 shows the general structure of the biometric authentication.

In [61], the authors proposed and implemented an authentication method of mobile cloud computing using fingerprint recognition system to enhance mobile cloud-computing resources. The total process of capturing (the fingerprint image is captured by existing mobile device camera) and matching fingerprint is hosted on the cloud server to take all benefits from cloud. In [64], the authors proposed a cloud platform designed to support basic web applications shared by small and medium companies. The platform is constructed using the OpenStack (is a collection of open source softwares that provides a framework for the cloud computing) architecture and the authentication mechanism is based on an original biometric approach that easily integrates fingerprint and face characteristics. The platform guarantees secure access of multiple users and completes the logical separation of computational and data resources related to different companies. In [65], a framework to provide the security from the mobile terminal based on biometric authentication is proposed. The biometric technique is implemented by fingerprint authentication and iris scan as a two-step verification. In [66], the authors proposed a bio-key generation algorithm called finger vein high-dimensional space self-stabilization (FVHS) for flexible cloud-computing authentication. This method combines the advantages of both biometrics authentication and user-key authentication. It directly generates stable strong bio-key sequences from finger vein biometrics. This method can extract a finger vein bio-key with a genuine accept rate (GAR) of more than 99.9%, while the false accept rate (FAR) is less than 0.8% and equal error rate (EER) is less than 0.5%. In [67], a keystroke dynamics-based authentication mechanism using Bayesian regularized feed-forward neural network is presented. Experimental results have shown that the Bayesian regularized neural network models have suitable results. In [68], a biometric-based authentication protocol, which can be used as the second factor for the cloud users to send their authentication requests, is proposed. In this method, the credential submitted by the users consists of the biometric feature vector and the verification code. For the user to successful authenticate, both vector and code must be combined, transformed, and shuffled correctly. In work [69], a behavioral biometric authentication method which enables identify users based on keystroke dynamic authentication (KDA) is presented. In addition, elliptic curve cryptography (ECC) is used as a cryptography technique to improve the security of the method. In [70], a secure authentication approach based on multiple biometric fingerprints during the registration for a cloud service is presented.

The tongue also provides both geometric shape and physiological texture information. These features are potentially useful in identity verification cloud applications. In work [71], an extraction and recognition algorithm of tongue-print images is proposed for biometrics authentication system.

## 9.3.11  Single sign-on (SSO)

Single sign-on (SSO) is an identity management system where a user may be validated in a single authentication and can then access other limited resources without a repeated authentication (without a need to log in again to a program). This authentication mechanism is a kind of passport that is provided during the first time authentication [72]. No further authentication is required to a user for other sites or process. One example of the TTP authentication in the cloud is the SSO.

This protocol defines multiple users (clients). These users want access to a service which can be data, an application, or a part of an application. Using SSO, the user retrieves a proof of identity and access, which is used to access the services. A workflow of SSO architecture in the cloud environment is shown in Figure 9.21. For SSO protocols, various terms are used for the systems involved. These terms consist of *identity provider* (IdP): It is responsible for the authentication process and handles the storing of user information as attributes in an identity token. When a user authenticates, the IdP creates an object that contains the information of the user, which can be used when a service provider requests user attributes. *Service provider* (SP): It offers a certain service and is in general protected by a kind of security guard. When a user wants to use the service, the guard requests identifying information from the user. *Authorization server* (or Trusted authority): The authorization server sends access tokens to the users after successful authentication.

There are different structures of SSO with the most common being enterprise single sign-on (ESSO) and web single sign-on (WSSO). Different technologies are used in each structure to reduce the number of times a user has to enter their username/password in order to get access to protected resources. In [73], implementation of the cloud for storage and virtual machines images to run the SSO on the top layer of the cloud is proposed. The work [74] discussed the risk of identity stealing when service access is provided through an SSO authentication.

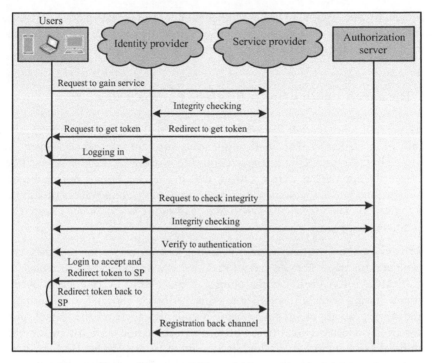

*Figure 9.21    Workflow of the SSO architecture in the cloud environment*

## 9.4    Advantages and disadvantages of authentication methods

In this section, we briefly investigate the advantages and disadvantages of authentication methods. The authentication method based on password cannot sufficiently provide information security against the various new attacks. The MFA method is a secure method. Because it requires a secondary factor in the authentication process such as biometric characteristics. The feasibility of the second factor is limited by complexity and cost. The context-based methods are more independent compared to the other methods because the authentication process is completed at least with user interaction (reducing the user involvement in the authentication process can be improved the usability of authentication). The accuracy of the context-based method is lower than UserId/Password, biometric, and multi-factor authentication methods (also the context-based authentication methods need more computation power compared to these methods) because the authentication process depends on the accuracy of the result of analyzing user pattern information [13]. Biometric-based authentication methods are highly vulnerable to privacy attacks. A major weakness of physical biometrics related to the situation where a great number of users need to be authenticated at the same time. In this case, it is time-consuming for the biometric authentication process. In the SSO approach, a user can be validated in a single authentication and can then access other limited resources without a repeated authentication. In this case, no further authentication or login again to a program is required to a user for other sites or process.

## 9.5   Research challenges and future perspectives

In this section, the overall research challenges and future perspectives about authentication issues in the cloud applications are summarized. However, new security techniques and solutions are required to work with cloud systems. Traditional security approaches may not work well in the cloud environments because these environments are complex and composed of a combination of different technologies [8]. Therefore, some challenges and future works in this research area are recommended below.

- **Privacy in the authentication strategies:** Privacy protection and outsourced computation need notable attention in the cloud application. Personal data must always remain under the control of the user. Also, the user's decision about sharing of data is another important subject. Especially, when implicit and context-aware cloud authentication strategies are used, the identity provider needs access to real-time information about the user. Biometric-based authentication methods are highly vulnerable to privacy attacks. The proper privacy protection techniques can be applied to these methods. Therefore, the privacy issues need to more attention.
- **Bring your own device (BYOD) challenge in the cloud:** The BYOD policy allows the workers to bring laptops, computers, tablets, and smartphones from home to work on (in small- and medium-sized businesses). In this case, the workers enhance their efficiency via familiarity with their equipment. However, there are security concerns. In the cloud system, one of the biggest challenges is the BYOD policy that does not facilitate the implementation of TPM devices in the enterprise network. BYOD also brings the true challenge to develop access control policies in enterprise and cloud environment.
- **Usability and scalability in the authentication mechanisms:** Usable and scalable, easy to learn, use, administer, the user logs in once and gain access to all services, and inexpensive to maintain authentication mechanisms in the cloud environments are attractive subjects in this research area. The implicit and adaptive type of authentication approach is trying to increase the usability by making authentication as transparent and seamless as possible. In [75], the authors proposed a query authentication scheme for the cloud-based storage system based on our recently proposed multi-trapdoor hash functions. In this method, the data is populated by multiple sources and retrieved by the clients is presented. The clients are allowed to verify the authenticity and integrity of the retrieved data in a scalable and an efficient way, without requiring implicit trust on the storage service provider. In [76], a context-aware scalable authentication (CASA) is proposed, which envisions using multiple passive factors to modulate active factors to authenticate users.

- **Elliptic curve cryptosystems (ECCs):** In the two last decades, the elliptic curves have been considered in many cryptographic applications such as banking transactions, mobile security, smart cards, Internet protocols (web transactions and secure document transfers) and network applications. Therefore, there is a need to conduct extra works related to ECC security solutions for cloud applications. In [43], an authentication scheme in multi-server environment using elliptic curve cryptosystem as security foundation is proposed.

- **Lightweight block ciphers:** New lightweight block ciphers such as HIGHT, SIMON, SPECK, PRESENT, and KATAN are attractive subjects for providing security in the cloud computing. Little research has been done in this area.

- **Authenticated encryption:** Message authenticity, message confidentiality, and integrity are desirable goals over a network. Authenticated encryption is a scheme which simultaneously achieves these properties. This type of encryption can be constructed based on a message authentication scheme (a message authentication code (MAC) is more commonly used to message authentication) combined with a symmetric block cipher (encryption scheme) as generic composition [77]. This encryption system can be considered in the authentication approaches in cloud applications.

- **Homomorphic encryption:** The encryption function can be a homomorphic encryption. Homomorphic encryption allows the server to do the operation on ciphertext without knowing the original plaintext. In other words, in this encryption scheme complex mathematical operations have to be performed on encrypted data without using the original data [78]. This encryption system can be applied for data protection in the cloud computing.

- **Security of mobile cloud computing:** Creating a safer, enhanced, and more secure user environment for mobile cloud computing is a very important issue in cloud applications. Therefore, there is a need to perform more continued researches on new threats and to create a solution to such threats in this area. For example, the context-based authentication methods need more computation power compared to the UserId/Password, biometric, and multi-factor authentication methods. In this case, context-based authentication methods are less appropriate in mobile cloud computing compared to identity cloud-based methods. Also, in mobile cloud computing, the authentication information are stored in the cloud servers, so the user privacy is highly important.

- **Hybrid, high-secure, and flexible cloud authentication:** Security level and authentication process in the cloud system can be provided in a suitable form by means of a combination of the different authentication and cryptographic algorithms methods. A combination of PKI, LDAP, and SSO presented in [1] can address most of the identified threats in the cloud computing dealing with the authenticity, confidentiality, integrity, and availability of data. In [37], to achieve better security than the alphanumerical password, an applicable authentication scheme in the cloud environment using the password generator module based on the combination of different techniques such as multi-factor authentication, one-time password, and SHA-1 is proposed. In [66], the authors proposed a bio-key generation algorithm called finger vein high-dimensional space self-stabilization (FVHS) for flexible cloud-computing authentication. This method combines the advantages of both biometrics authentication and user-key authentication. It directly generates stable strong bio-key sequences from finger vein biometrics. In [79], the authors proposed the combination of trusted computing, Federated Identity Management, and OpenID Web SSO to solve identity theft in the cloud. In [80], an authentication method called NemoAuth based on the mnemonic multimodal approach is proposed. In this method, the dynamic knowledge and biometric-based approaches are combined to improve the accuracy of the authentication method. The proposed method utilizes different capabilities of the mobile device (such as gyroscopic, gravity, orientation, proximity, pressure, ambient light, temperature, touch screen, and moisture sensors, microphone, and camera) to improve the usability of authentication by using mnemonic images.

## 9.6   Conclusion

This chapter has discussed the security issues and standard and traditional authentication methods for cloud applications. Furthermore, the other existing authentication methods in literature are presented. Cloud applications have various security issues because they include many technologies such as networks, databases, operating systems, virtualization, resources, system control, and memory management. Therefore, it is very important that data transactions and interconnects of the systems in the cloud environments to be secure. We classified the security issues in four sections according to the security mechanisms they provide: identity and access management (authentication, authorization, user management, and central user repository), confidentiality and data encryption, attacks against information in cloud environments, and virtualization security in the cloud system. The authentication is a very important part of data security in the cloud applications. Here, authentication methods are classified and presented into 11 sections. The described authentication technologies, for better security, can be used by combining them suitably or a secure authentication method for the effective authentication in the cloud system can be developed. The advantages and disadvantages of the authentication methods are described. However, new security solutions are required to work with cloud systems. Therefore, suitable and secure authentication approaches and protocols for the cloud system should be designed and developed as further researches.

## References

[1]   Zissis, D. and Lekkas, D., 'Addressing Cloud Computing Security Issues', *Future Generation Computer Systems*, 2012, Vol. 28, No. 3, pp. 583–592.

[2]   Pfarr, F., Buckel, T., and Winkelmann, A., Cloud Computing Data Protection A Literature Review and Analysis, *Proceedings of the 47th Hawaii International Conference on System Science*, 2014, pp. 5018–5027.

[3]   Yun Lim, S., Mat Kiah, M.L., and Fong Ang, T., 'Addressing Cloud Computing Security Issues', *Acta Polytechnica Hungarica*, 2017, Vol. 14, No. 2, pp. 69–89.

[4] Baqer Mollah, M., Abul Kalam Azad, M.D., and Vasilakos, A., 'Security and Privacy Challenges in Mobile Cloud Computing: Survey and Way Ahead', *Journal of Network and Computer Applications*, 2017, Vol. 84, pp. 38–54.

[5] Hwang, K. and Li, D., 'Trusted Cloud Computing with Secure Resources and Data Coloring', *IEEE Internet Computing*, 2010, Vol. 14, No. 5, pp. 14–22.

[6] Bhatia, T. and Verma, A.K., 'Data Security in Mobile Cloud Computing Paradigm: A Survey, Taxonomy and Open Research Issues', *The Journal of Supercomputing*, 2017, Vol. 73, No. 6, pp. 2558–2631.

[7] Hamlen, K., Kantarcioglu, M., Khan, L., and Thuraisingham, B., 'Security Issues for Cloud Computing', *International Journal of Information Security and Privacy*, 2010, Vol. 4, No. 2, pp. 39–51.

[8] Hashizume, K., Rosado, D.G., Fernandez-Medina, E., and Fernandez, E.B., 'An Analysis of Security Issues for Cloud Computing', *Journal of Internet Services and Applications*, 2013, Vol. 4, No. 5, pp. 1–13.

[9] Onwubiko, C., *Security Issues to Cloud Computing*. In *Cloud Computing: Principles, Systems & Applications*, First Edition, Springer-Verlag, New York, 2010.

[10] Tianfield, H., 'Security Issues in Cloud Computing', *Proceedings of the IEEE International Conference on Systems, Man, and Cybernetics*, October 14–17, 2012, COEX, Seoul, Korea, pp. 1082–1089.

[11] Deshpande, P., Sharma, S.C., and Peddoju, S.K., 'Data Storage Security in Cloud Paradigm', *Proceedings of the Fifth International Conference on Soft Computing for Problem Solving*, 2016, Singapore, pp. 247–259.

[12] Naik, N., Jenkins, P., and Peddoju, S.k., 'A Secure Mobile Cloud Identity: Criteria for Effective Identity and Access Management Standards', *Proceedings of the 4th IEEE International Conference on Mobile Cloud Computing, Services, and Engineering*, 2016, Oxford, UK, pp. 89–90.

[13] Alizadeh, M., Abolfazli, S., Zamani, M., Baharun, S., and Sakurai, K., 'Authentication in Mobile Cloud Computing: A Survey', *Journal of Network and Computer Applications*, 2016, Vol. 61, pp. 59–80.

[14] Mimura Gonzalez, N., Antonio Torrez Rojas, M., and Maciel da Silva, M.V., 'A Framework for Authentication and Authorization Credentials in Cloud Computing', *Proceedings of the 12th IEEE International Conference on Trust, Security and Privacy in Computing and Communications*, 2013, Melbourne, VIC, Australia, pp. 509–516.

[15] Indu, I., Rubesh Anand, P.M., and Bhaskar, V., 'Identity and Access Management in Cloud Environment: Mechanisms and Challenges', *Engineering Science and Technology: An International Journal*, 2018, Vol. 21, No. 4, pp. 574–588.

[16] Rezaeian Farashahi, R., Rashidi, B., and Sayedi, S.M., 'FPGA-Based Fast and High-Throughput 2-Slow Retiming 128-bit AES Encryption Algorithm', *Microelectronics Journal*, 2014, Vol. 45, No. 8, pp. 1014–1025.

[17] Wang, G., Liu, Q., Wu, J., and Guo, M., 'Hierarchical Attribute-Based Encryption and Scalable User Revocation for Sharing Data in Cloud Servers', *Computers & Security*, 2011, Vol. 30, No. 5, pp. 320–331.

[18]  Lai, J., Deng, R.H., Guan, C., and Weng, J., 'Attribute-Based Encryption With Verifiable Outsourced Decryption', *IEEE Transactions on Information Forensics and Security*, 2013, Vol. 8, No. 8, pp. 1343–1354.

[19]  Liu, Z., Jiang, Z.L., Wang, X., and Yiu, S.M., 'Practical Attribute-Based Encryption: Outsourcing Decryption, Attribute Revocation and Policy Updating', *Journal of Network and Computer Applications*, 2018, Vol. 105, pp. 112–123.

[20]  Li, J., Wang, Y., Zhang, Y., and Han, J., 'Full Verifiability for Outsourced Decryption in Attribute Based Encryption', *IEEE Transactions on Services Computing*, 2017, Vol. 11, No. 7, pp. 1–12.

[21]  Waters, B., 'Ciphertext-Policy Attribute-Based Encryption: An Expressive, Efficient, and Provably Secure Realization', *Proceedings of the International Workshop on Public Key Cryptography (PKC)*, 2011, Taormina, Italy, LNCS Vol 6571, Springer, pp. 53–70.

[22]  Cui, H., Deng, R.H., Lai, J., Yi, X. and Nepal, S., 'An Efficient and Expressive Ciphertext-Policy Attribute-Based Encryption Scheme with Partially Hidden Access Structures, Revisited', *Computer Networks*, 2018, Vol. 133, pp. 157–165.

[23]  Wang, C.J. and Luo, J.F., 'A Key-Policy Attribute-Based Encryption Scheme with Constant Size Ciphertext', *Proceedings of the Eighth International Conference on Computational Intelligence and Security*, 2012, Guangzhou, China, pp. 447–451.

[24]  Attrapadung, N., Libert, B., and Panafieu, E., 'Ciphertext-Policy Attribute-Based Encryption: An Expressive, Efficient, and Provably Secure Realization', *Proceedings of the International Workshop on Public Key Cryptography (PKC)*, 2011, Taormina, Italy, LNCS Vol. 6571, Springer, pp. 90–108.

[25]  Boneh, D., Crescenzo, G.D., Ostrovsky, R., and Persiano, G., 'Public Key Encryption with Keyword Search', *Proceedings of the International Conference on the Theory and Applications of Cryptographic Techniques*, 2004, Interlaken, Switzerland, pp. 506–522.

[26]  Yunling, W., Jianfeng, W., and Xiaofeng, C., 'Secure Searchable Encryption: A Survey', *Journal of Communications and Information Networks*, 2016, Vol. 1, No. 4, pp. 52–65.

[27]  Ocansey, S.K., Ametepe, W., Li, X.W., and Wang, C., 'Dynamic Searchable Encryption with Privacy Protection for Cloud Computing', *International Journal of Communication Systems*, 2018, Vol. 31, No. 1, pp. 1–8.

[28]  Liu, J., Han, J.L., and Wang, Z.L., 'Searchable Encryption Scheme on the Cloud Via Fully Homomorphic Encryption', *Proceedings of the Sixth International Conference on Instrumentation & Measurement, Computer, Communication and Control*, 2016, Harbin, China, pp. 108–111.

[29]  Huang, J.Y. and Liao, I.E., 'A Searchable Encryption Scheme for Outsourcing Cloud Storage', *Proceedings of the IEEE International Conference on Communication, Networks and Satellite (COMNETSAT)*, 2012, Bali, Indonesia, pp. 142–146.

[30] Hwang, R.J., Lu, C.C., and Wu, J.S., 'Searchable Encryption in Cloud Storage', *International Journal of Computer and Information Engineering*, 2014, Vol. 8, No. 7, pp. 1080–1083.

[31] Darwish, M., Ouda, A., and Capretz, L.F., 'Cloud-Based DDoS Attacks and Defenses', *Proceedings of the International Conference on Information Society*, 2013, Toronto, Canada, pp. 1–5.

[32] Carlin, A., Hammoudeh, M., and Aldabbas, O., 'Defence for Distributed Denial of Service Attacks in Cloud Computing', *Proceedings of the International Conference on Advanced Wireless, Information, and Communication Technologies*, 2015, Sousse, Tunisia, pp. 490–497.

[33] Sabahi, F., 'Secure Virtualization for Cloud Environment Using Hypervisor-Based Technology', *International Journal of Machine Learning and Computing*, 2012, Vol. 2, No. 1, pp. 39–45.

[34] Sabahi, F., 'An Importance of Using Virtualization Technology in Cloud Computing', *Journal of Computers & Technology*, 2015, Vol. 1, No. 2, pp. 56–60.

[35] Mulfari, D., Celesti, A., Villari, M., and Puliafito, A., 'Using Virtualization and noVNC to Support Assistive Technology in Cloud Computing', *Proceedings of the IEEE 3rd Symposium on Network Cloud Computing and Applications*, 2014, Rome, Italy, pp. 125–132.

[36] Gurav, S.M., Gawade, L.S., Rane, P.K., and Khochare, N.R., 'Graphical Password Authentication: Cloud Securing Scheme. *Proceedings of the International Conference on Electronic Systems, Signal Processing and Computing Technologies*, 2014, Nagpur, India, pp. 479–483.

[37] Darbanian, E. and Fard, G.D., 'A Graphical Password Against Spyware and Shoulder-Surfing Attacks', *Proceedings of the International Symposium on Computer Science and Software Engineering (CSSE)*, 2015, Tabriz, Iran, pp. 1–6.

[38] Darbanian, E. and Fard, G.D., 'A Novel Strong Password Generator for Improving Cloud Authentication', *Proceedings of the International Conference on Computational Modeling and Security*, 2016, Bengaluru, India, pp. 293–300.

[39] Rai, V.K. and Mishra, A., 'Authentication of Trusted Platform Module Using Processor Response', *Proceedings of the International Symposium on Security in Computing and Communication*, 2014, Delhi, India, pp. 325–334.

[40] Shen, Z., Li, L., Yan, F., and Wu, X., 'Cloud Computing System Based on Trusted Computing Platform', *Proceedings of the International Conference on Intelligent Computation Technology and Automation*, 2010, Changsha, China, pp. 942–945.

[41] Kalra, S. and Sood, S., 'Secure Authentication Scheme for IoT and Cloud Servers', *Pervasive and Mobile Computing*, 2015, Vol. 24, pp. 210–223.

[42] Mishra, D., Kumar, V., and Mukhopadhyay, S., 'A Pairing-Free Identity Based Authentication Framework for Cloud Computing', *Proceedings of the International Conference on Network and System Security*, 2013, Madrid, Spain, pp. 721–727.

[43]    Truong, T.T., Tran, M.T., Duong, A.D., and Echizen, I., 'Provable Identity Based User Authentication Scheme on ECC in Multi-Server Environment', *Wireless Personal Communications*, 2017, Vol. 95, No. 3, pp. 2785–2801.

[44]    Jeong, Y.S., Park, J.S., and Park, J.H., 'An Efficient Authentication System of Smart Device Using Multi Factors in Mobile Cloud Service Architecture', *International Journal of Communication Systems*, 2015, Vol. 28, No. 4, pp. 659–674.

[45]    Yassin, A., Jin, H., Ibrahim, A., and Zou, D., 'Anonymous Password Authentication Scheme by Using Digital Signature and Fingerprint in Cloud Computing', *Proceedings of the Second International Conference on Cloud and Green Computing*, 2012, Xiangtan, China, pp. 282–289.

[46]    Abdul, A.M., Jena, S., and Balraju, M., 'Dual Factor Authentication to Procure Cloud Services', *Proceedings of the Fourth International Conference on Parallel, Distributed and Grid Computing (PDGC)*, 2016, Waknaghat, India, pp. 533–537.

[47]    Shi, E., Niu, Y., Jakobsson, M., and Chow, R., 'Implicit Authentication through Learning User Behavior', *Proceedings of the 13th International Conference on Information security*, 2011, Boca Raton, FL, USA, pp. 99–113.

[48]    Chow, R., Jakobsson, M., Masuoka, R., *et al.*, 'Authentication in the Clouds: A Framework and Its Application to Mobile Users', *Proceedings of the ACM workshop on Cloud computing security workshop*, 2010, Chicago, Illinois, USA, pp. 1–6.

[49]    Yao, F., Yerima, S.Y., Kang, B., and Sezer, S., 'Continuous Implicit Authentication for Mobile Devices Based on Adaptive Neuro-Fuzzy Inference System', *Proceedings of the International Conference on Cyber Security and Protection of Digital Services (Cyber Security)*, 2017, London, UK, pp. 1–7.

[50]    Lee, W.H. and Lee, R.B.,, 'Sensor-Based Implicit Authentication of Smartphone Users', *Proceedings of the 47th Annual IEEE/IFIP International Conference on Dependable Systems and Networks (DSN)*, 2017, Denver, CO, USA, pp. 309–320.

[51]    Choi, Y.S., Lee, Y.H., Kim, S.J., and Won, D.H., 'Security Analysis on the Implementation Vulnerabilities of I-PIN', *Korea Institute of Information Security & Society*, 2007, Vol. 17, No. 2, pp. 145–148.

[52]    You, J.H. and Jun, M.S., 'A Mechanism to Prevent RP Phishing in OpenID System', *Proceedings of the 9th IEEE/ACIS International Conference on Computer and Information Science*, 2010, Yamagata, Japan, pp. 876–880.

[53]    Ahn H., Jang C., Chang H., and Choi E., 'User Authentication Using Context-Awareness RBAC Model on Cloud Computing', *Future Communication, Computing, Control and Management*, 2012, Lecture Notes in Electrical Engineering, Springer, Vol. 142, pp. 253–257.

[54]    Mansour, A., Sadik, M., Sabir, E., and Azmi, M., 'A Context-Aware Multimodal Biometric Authentication for Cloud-Empowered Systems', *Proceedings of the International Conference on Wireless Networks and Mobile Communications (WINCOM)*, 2016, Fez, Morocco, pp. 1–8.

[55] Benzekki, K., Fergougui, A.L., and ElAlaoui, A.E., 'A Context-Aware Authentication System for Mobile Cloud Computing', *Proceedings of the First International Conference on Intelligent Computing in Data Sciences*, 2018, Fez, Morocco, pp. 379–387.

[56] Ahn, H., Chang, H., Jang, C. and, Choi, E., 'A Context-Aware Authentication System for Mobile Cloud Computing', *Proceedings of the International Conference on Advanced Communication and Networking*, 2011, Brno, Czech Republic, pp. 132–138.

[57] Noureddine, M. and Bashroush, R., 'An Authentication Model towards Cloud Federation in the Enterprise', *Journal of Systems and Software*, 2013, Vol. 86, No. 9, pp. 2269–2275.

[58] Celesti, A., Tusa, F., Villari, M., and, Puliafito, A., 'Three-Phase Cross-Cloud Federation Model: The Cloud SSO Authentication', *Proceedings of the Second International Conference on Advances in Future Internet*, 2010, Venice, Italy, pp. 94–101.

[59] Villegas, D., Bobroff, N., Rodero, I., et al ., 'Cloud Federation in a Layered Service Model', *Journal of Computer and System Sciences*, 2012, Vol. 78, No. 5, pp. 1330–1344.

[60] Marium, S., Nazir, Q., Ahmed, A., Ahthasham, S., and Mehmood, M.A., 'Implementation of EAP with RSA for Enhancing the Security of Cloud Computing', *International Journal of Basic and Applied Sciences*, 2012, Vol. 1, No. 3, pp. 177–183.

[61] Rassan, I. and, Shaher, H., 'Securing Mobile Cloud Computing Using Biometric Authentication (SMCBA)', *Proceedings of the International Conference on Computational Science and Computational Intelligence*, 2014, Las Vegas, NV, USA, pp. 157–161.

[62] Yampolskiy, R.V. and Govindaraju, V., 'Behavioural Biometrics: A Survey and Classification', *International Journal of Biometrics*, 2008, Vol. 1, No. 1, pp. 81–113.

[63] Koong, C.S., Yang, T.I., and Tseng, C.C., 'A User Authentication Scheme Using Physiological and Behavioral Biometrics for Multitouch Devices', *The Scientific World Journal Hindawi Publishing Corporation*, 2014, Vol. 2014, pp. 1–12.

[64] Masala, G.L., Ruiu, P, Brunetti, A., Terzo, O., and, Grosso, E., 'Biometric Authentication and Data Security in Cloud Computing', *Proceedings of the International Conference on Security and Management*, 2015, Las Vegas, USA, pp. 9–15.

[65] Khatri, S.K. and Vadi, V.R., 'Biometric Based Authentication and Access Control Techniques to Secure Mobile Cloud Computing', *Proceedings of the 2nd International Conference on Telecommunication and Networks*, 2017, Noida, India, pp. 1–7.

[66] Wu, Z., Tian, L., Li, P., Wu, T., Jiang, M., and Wu, C., 'Generating Stable Biometric Keys for Flexible Cloud Computing Authentication Using Finger Vein', *Information Sciences*, 2018, Vol. 433, pp. 431–447.

[67]    Zareen, F.J., Matta, C., Arora, A., Singh, S., and Jabin, S., 'An Authentication System Using Keystroke Dynamics', *International Journal of Biometrics*, 2018, Vol. 10, No. 1, pp. 65–76.

[68]    Wong, S.K. and Kim, M.H., 'Towards Biometric-Based Authentication for Cloud Computing', *Proceedings of the 2nd International Conference on Cloud Computing and Services Science*, 2012, pp. 501–510.

[69]    Babaeizadeh, M., Bakhtiari, M., and Maarof, M.A., 'Authentication Method through Keystrokes Measurement of Mobile Users in Cloud Environment', *International Journal of Advances in Soft Computing and its Applications*, 2014, Vol. 6, No. 3, pp. 94–112.

[70]    Rajeswari, P., Raju, S.V., Ashour, A.S., and Dey, N., 'Multi-fingerprint Unimodel-Based Biometric Authentication Supporting Cloud Computing', *Proceedings of the 2nd International Conference on Telecommunication and Networks*, 2017, Noida, India, pp. 1–7.

[71]    Diwakar, M. and Maharshi, M., 'An Extraction and Recognition of Tongue-Print Images for Biometrics Authentication System', *International Journal of Computer Applications*, 2013, Vol. 61, No. 3, pp. 94–112.

[72]    Heijmink, N., *Secure Single Sign-On: A Comparison of Protocols*, Master thesis, Radboud University Nijmegen, 2015.

[73]    Revar, A.G. and Bhavsar, M.D., 'Securing User Authentication Using Single Sign-On in Cloud Computing', *Proceedings of the International Conference on Engineering Nirma University*, 2011, Ahmedabad, Gujarat, India, pp. 1–4.

[74]    Cusack, B. and Ghazizadeh, E., 'Evaluating Single Sign-On Security Failure in Cloud Services', *Business Horizons*, 2016, Vol. 59, No. 6, pp. 605–614.

[75]    Chandrasekhar, S. and Singhal, M., 'Efficient and Scalable Query Authentication for Cloud-Based Storage Systems with Multiple Data Sources', *IEEE Transactions on Services Computing*, 2016, Vol. 10, No. 4, pp. 520–533.

[76]    Hayashi, E., Das, S., Amini, S., and Oakley, I., 'CASA: Context-Aware Scalable Authentication', *Proceedings of the Ninth Symposium on Usable Privacy and Security*, 2011, Newcastle, UK, pp. 1–10.

[77]    Degabriele, J.P., *Authenticated Encryption in Theory and in Practice*, PhD dissertation, University of London, 2014.

[78]    Acar, A., Aksu, H., Uluagac, A.S., and Conti, M., 'A Survey on Homomorphic Encryption Schemes: Theory and Implementation', *arXiv preprint arXiv:1704.03578v2*, 2017.

[79]    Ghazizadeh, E., Zamani, M., Manan, J.I.A., and Alizadeh, M., 'Trusted Computing Strengthens Cloud Authentication', *The Scientific World Journal*, 2014, Vol. 2014, pp. 1–17.

[80]    Le, Z., Zhang, X., and Gao, Z., 'NemoAuth: A Mnemonic Multimodal Approach to Mobile User Authentication', *Proceedings of the IEEE International Conference of IEEE Region 10 (TENCON)*, 2013, Xi'an, China, pp. 1–6.

# Chapter 10

# The insider threat problem from a cloud computing perspective

## *Keshnee Padayachee*[1]

Cloud computing is viewed as a cost-effective and scalable way of providing computing resources for both large and small organizations. However, as cloud storage is outsourced it is highly susceptible to information security risks. The insider threat may become particularly insidious with the predilection towards cloud computing. Insiders have a significant advantage, as not only do they have knowledge about vulnerabilities in policies, networks or systems but they also have the requisite capability. An 'insider' is any individual who has legitimate access to an organization's information technology infrastructure whereas an 'insider threat' uses the authority granted to him/her for illegitimate gain. Fundamentally, the insider threat concern is a complex issue, as the problem domain intersects the social, technical, and socio-technical dimensions. From a cloud-computing perspective, the concept of the insider is multi-contextual and consequently propagates more opportunities for malfeasance. The definition of an insider changes from context to context; an insider is someone who works within an organization that uses a cloud-based system and it also includes a user that works for a cloud service provider. Clearly, the concept of the insider within the cloud-computing domain is amorphous. This chapter intends to define the insider threat and identify the various types of insider threats that exist within the cloud-computing domain. This chapter considers the challenges involved in managing the insider threat and possible mitigation strategies including authentication schemes within cloud-based systems. To this end, this chapter also considers the various mitigation strategies that exist within the technical, social and socio-technical domains in order to identify gaps for further research.

## 10.1 Introduction

Cloud computing is an Internet-based system where 'resources, software and information' are provisioned devices on demand to computers and other devices [1]. Cloud computing 'refers to both the applications delivered as services over the

[1]Institute for Science and Technology Education, University of South Africa, South Africa

Internet and the hardware and systems software in the data centres that provide those services' [2]. Cloud computing offers several benefits – lower costs, greater scalability, ease of accessibility via the web, lower risks [3] and increased storage [1]. Further, the attributes of multi-tenancy, elasticity (i.e. users can increase/decrease resources as required), 'pay as you go' plans (i.e. only pay for services used) and the self-provisioning of resources by users [4] make cloud computing an attractive option. However, there is a concern about security with respect to privacy and authorization particularly with the copious amount of data available in the cloud [4] which increases its susceptibility to data breaches [1] by insiders. The impact of insider threats in the cloud can be substantial causing brand damage, loss of productivity [1] and a breakdown of trust between the cloud service users (CSU) and cloud service providers (CSP) [5].

The result of an insider attack in a cloud infrastructure can 'vary from data leakage to severe corruption of the affected systems and data' [6]. Insiders can do a range of damages in the cloud which includes rebooting the physical machine, cloning the virtual machine (VM), copying from the VM, obtaining snapshots of the VM/data, the installation of a new guest VM and switching on any guest VM [7]. Insiders commit maleficence for a variety of reasons – to steal intellectual property or to exfiltrate (i.e. pilfer) data to a competitor [8]. Verizon's [9] 2017 Data Breach Investigations Report found that 25% of data breaches are committed by insiders. The recent report compiled by the Cloud Security Alliance [10] identified malicious insider threats as one of the 12 critical issues to cloud security, in addition to data breaches, weak identity, credential and access management, data loss, insufficient due diligence, abuse and nefarious use of cloud services and denial of service. Clearly, the insider threat is an issue of concern in the cloud and the multi-dimensionality of the insider threat problem further complicates the issue.

The complexity of the cloud offers many opportunities for an insider threat, which is a multilayered concept in the cloud. Cloud computing operates on four layers – hardware/data centre layer (i.e. physical resources such as routers and servers), infrastructure layer (i.e. the virtualization layer), platform layer (i.e. operating systems and application frameworks) and the application layer (i.e. actual cloud implementation) [3]. Every layer of the architecture that is physical infrastructure or platform and application is 'implemented as a service to the layer above' and 'every layer can be perceived as a customer of the layer below' [3]. The cloud service model can be grouped into three services – software as a service (SaaS), platform as a service (PaaS) and infrastructure as a service (IaaS) [4]. SaaS involves the provisioning of 'applications over the Internet' [3]. Typically SaaS is hosted by a provider that provisions an application to multiple clients (e.g. Netsuite) [1]. PaaS allows the development of applications without the client managing the underlying infrastructure which typically includes databases, middleware and development tools (e.g. Google App Engine) [1]. IaaS involves the 'provisioning of infrastructural resources' [3] such as hardware (i.e. server, storage and network) and associated software (operating systems virtualization technology and file systems) as a service [1]. IaaS providers simply maintain the data centre and CPUs and must manage the application software themselves [1]. The foundation of IaaS is native virtualization where a hypervisor 'provides an abstraction of the hardware resources to a set of VMs executing above it' [11] (e.g. Amazon Web Services [1]). All cloud services are affected by insider attacks [6].

There are four types of deployment models. The term *public cloud* refers to a cloud which is available to the general public [2] whereas the term *private cloud* refers to an 'internal cloud' which is for the exclusive use of a single organization [3]. Public clouds are less secure than other types of models and subject to privacy and security concerns [12]. Private clouds are more secure as they are deployed with an organization's internal data structure [12]. The term *hybrid cloud* refers to deploying a mix of private and public clouds. A hybrid cloud offers more security, however, the process must be carefully managed (i.e. choosing between the split of public or private cloud options) [3]. Hybrid clouds are hosted within a secure network and offer more control over security [13]. *Community* clouds are shared by a community with a common purpose (e.g. security requirements) [1]. Regardless of the deployment or service, insider threats are a major concern in cloud computing as there is a lack of transparency between the provider and the client [1].

Insider threats in the cloud loom large due to the lack of transparency and the lack of clearly defined procedures and processes. This murkiness allows an insider within a cloud-computing environment to affect a multitude of users simultaneously [14]. Cloud computing is risky as the storage is external, it is information which is shared over the Internet, therefore the client does not have control over the data, particularly within a multi-tenancy situation and CSPs and CPUs are spread across different geographical areas [14]. These factors embolden the insider to act maliciously as they can commit cybercrime in the cloud surreptitiously. Clearly managing the insider threat within the cloud is challenging due to its polymorphic nature within the cloud.

## 10.2    Challenges to insider threat mitigation in the cloud

This section discusses the various challenges in relation to dealing with the insider threat problem and commences with defining the insider threat. Cloud computing has 'inherited all the security issues from existing systems' plus additional features that are unique to cloud computing [15], hence it is sensible to consider the insider threat problem in non-cloud-based systems. Many of the current techniques and challenges for the insider threat solutions for the cloud originate from the insider threat solutions for legacy systems.

### 10.2.1   Defining the insider threat

An insider is any individual who has legitimate access to an organization's information technology infrastructure [16] whereas an insider threat uses the authority granted to him/her for illegitimate gain [17]. Insider threats range from a disgruntled employee or a terminated employee whose system credentials are still valid to a system developer who has in-depth knowledge of the system [18] (termed 'long view insiders' [19]). Gunasekhar *et al.* [20] categorize insiders by their levels of access privileges – pure insider, insider associate, insider affiliate, and the outside affiliate. A *pure insider* is the most dangerous as he/she has full access rights. An insider such as a system administrator or root administrator has more privileges than a typical user. An *insider associate* is not technically an employee; nonetheless, he/she has physical access (e.g. cleaners). Similarly, *insider affiliates* only have access by virtue of a spouse, friend or third party. An *outside affiliate* has no access. However, an outside affiliate may influence an insider via social engineering attacks. This is termed an *influencing threat source* by someone who is not an actual insider but who influences other insiders to commit a crime and becomes an insider by proxy [21].

The CERT division (a leader in information security) defines a malicious insider (or an insider threat) as a 'current or former employee, contractor or other business partner who has or had authorized access to an organization's network, system or data and intentionally exceeded or misused that access in a manner that negatively affected the confidentiality, integrity or availability of the organization's information or information systems' [22]. In cloud computing, the scope of the insider has expanded to include insiders from the following spheres – central processing units (CPUs), CSP, Internet service providers, 'cloud provisioning services (brokers)', other clients of the CSP and 'other clients of the third-party cloud-provider' [21]. A cloud-related insider may be viewed from three perspectives: (1) a rogue administrator employed by the cloud service provider, (2) an 'employee in the victim organization that exploits cloud weaknesses for unauthorized access' and (3) an 'insider who uses cloud resources to carry out attacks against the company's local IT infrastructure' [23]. In the first case, a rogue administrator uses his/her privileged access to cause mayhem. This may result in the loss of confidentially or integrity and may even damage the cloud provider's reputation [8]. In the second case, the insider exploits the vulnerabilities in the cloud to gain access either accidentally or intentionally while in the latter case 'the insider uses cloud services as a tool to attack his own organization' [8]. There is a fourth perspective of an insider namely the *acid cloud*, where CSP itself becomes a malicious player [24].

The original definition by the CERT is maintained when considering cloud-related insiders [23]. In the cloud context, the insider steals information from the cloud or uses the credentials from other users to destroy or steal information from cloud data centres [20]. Nikolai and Wang [25] indicate that there are three types of insiders – (1) malicious insiders who deliberately attempt to conduct theft, sabotage, fraud and espionage; (2) accidental insiders whose unintentional misuse of systems is performed without the intent of harm and (3) a non-malicious insider who intentionally attempts self-benefiting activities without malicious intent. There are two classes of insider threats: traitors and masqueraders. Traitors are legitimate users that abuse their privileges and masqueraders are insiders who impersonate other users for malicious purposes [26,27]. Insiders have a significant advantage over external threats as they not only have knowledge about vulnerabilities in policies, networks or systems [28] but also the requisite capability, however, within the cloud, the lines between insiders and outsiders have become blurred [29]. Probst and Hunker [27] indicate that the most important aspect of

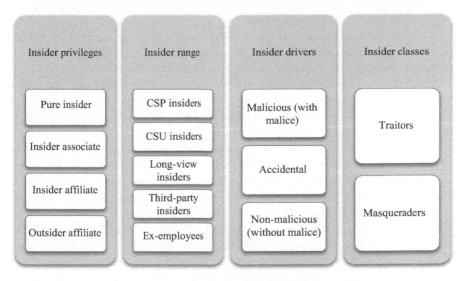

*Figure 10.1    Categories of insider threats*

defining insiders is determining their identity and their 'degrees of insiderness'. *Insiderness* implies the degree to which an insider can cause maleficence, which is dependent on the context. For example, a rogue administrator has a high degree of insiderness and therefore is capable of causing greater damage than an insider associate. Figure 10.1 recapitulates the categories of insiders discussed in this section.

## 10.2.2    Background of insider threat mitigation

Wood [30] describes the attributes of an insider threat as access, knowledge, privileges, skill, risk, tactics, motivation and process (which includes identification of the target through to launching the attack). The motivations of malicious insiders are varied which contribute to the complexity in moderating an insider threat – apathy, espionage, sabotage, terrorism, embezzlement, extortion, bribery, corruption, ignorance [31], revenge, disgruntlement, avarice, divided loyalty, delusion, stress and lack of rules while accidental misuse could be due to the inadequate system knowledge [32]. Understanding motivations can be complex as it is intrinsic to the insider while skills and knowledge are extrinsic and this can be used to identify potential insider threats. In understanding the challenges of dealing with an insider threat, it may be practical to map the capability of insiders, which also contributes to the difficulties in moderating an insider threat. For example, Bowen *et al.* [33] mapped the following capability characteristics to design honeypots to account for each competency level. An insider with a low competency level relies on cursory scans such as shoulder surfing to snoop. An insider with a medium competency level can perform verifications from other sources (e.g. a search engine) to check the authenticity of the information. An insider with a high competency level is able to use sophisticated tools (e.g. keystroke loggers), whereas a highly privileged insider usually knows how to overcome decoys or detection systems and knows how to disable or avoid these. Sophisticated users are more dangerous as they are more likely to cause detrimental attacks and are also able to cover their tracks more effectively [34]. It may be prudent to monitor those insiders with higher privileges more closely.

Mechanisms to undermine the insider threat include monitoring, detection, mitigation [33], deterrence and profiling. With respect to monitoring and detection, Zeadally *et al.* [35] list several techniques to detect insider threats which include intrusion detection systems, system calls, data-centric approaches, honeypot approaches, dynamical-system theory-based approaches, anti-indirect-exfiltration approaches and visualization approaches.

Intrusion detection mechanisms are plagued with false positives [33]. Anomalous behaviour may not be identified by intrusion detection systems [35] as insiders may be able to disable intrusion detection systems [17] or be able to perform malicious acts during the course of normal activities [36]. Similarly detecting system calls are also outdone by false positives [35] as it is difficult to discern normal activities from malicious activities. Furthermore, system administrators have to wade through copious amounts of data. The data-centric approach is a way of sifting through large amounts of data to find malicious insiders, however this technique is in its infancy [35]. Unlike intrusion detection systems and system calls, a honeypot (i.e. a decoy) is unlikely to be plagued by false positives as any interaction with a honeypot is bound to be illicit [37]. Honeypots succeed in containing the activities related to an insider threat [38] and help to trace further malicious activity in other places in the system [39]. However, using honeypots is a form of entrapment and there could be legal [40] and ethical concerns [41]. Dynamical-system theory-based approaches create a profile for a typical user and compare this against any deviations of insider behaviour to identify an attack, however, the profiling needs to be accurate in order for the approach to work [35]. Profiling has its drawbacks as it assumes that human behaviour is predictable [18].

Anti-indirect-exfiltration approaches are based on determining indirect exfiltration as opposed to direct data exfiltration which occurs after a software system has been developed and information is exfiltrated opportunistically [19]. This occurs when an insider exploits a vulnerability in the software system in development or maintenance causing disruptions of operations or corruption of data [19]. Young and Dahnert [19] developed a system called DevEyes that audits emails, chats and version controls of software development. There is little evaluation of this type of technique [35]. Visualization approaches involve visually representing unusual patterns of activity of insider threats, however, this technique is difficult to manage due to copious amounts of data and also that analyzing the visualizations can be difficult [35].

Monitoring can be cumbersome as there is a huge range of human characteristics that can be monitored [18]. Monitoring behaviour can also violate the privacy rights of an individual [18]. Data loss prevention tools which prevent the leakage of sensitive information may be used to monitor data usage so as to detect and mitigate insider threats [42]. Data loss prevention prevents the leakage of sensitive information and it involves managing, classifying, monitoring and protecting data according to its state (i.e. data at rest, data at the endpoint or data in motion) [43].

Data loss prevention mechanisms cannot intercept a message that is encrypted [44] or obfuscated using steganography [45].

There will always be a prerequisite for technical controls such as encryption, access control, minimum privilege, auditing, reporting [46] and sensitive system isolation. Instituting proper password policies [47] can also be useful, however, insiders may use masquerading techniques and use a peer's account rather than their own to commit maleficence [48]. Traditional access controls are susceptible to the insider threat as the system grants access as long as the access is authorized [49] whereas authentication mechanisms may only work for outsiders [46]. Choi and Zage [50] highlight that even multifactor authentication systems based on 'what you have' (i.e. smartcards), what you know (i.e. pin) and 'what you are' (i.e. biometrics) can be compromised once an insider has access and biometric systems can often be socially unacceptable and invasive. They recommend location as a fourth factor that may curb the insider threat, namely location as a preventive measure.

The practical enforcement of least privilege may be limited due to fluctuations in work responsibilities. Encryption mechanisms may be cracked by insiders due to the fact that insiders have privileged access [51] and they have knowledge of the decryption mechanisms. The isolation of a sensitive system may be a more susceptible information security practice, as storing all the sensitive and confidential data in one location makes it an easy target for insiders [52]. Periodic audits also assist in detecting suspicious users however audit trails and event logging must be tamperproof as insiders may well tamper with audit trails to conceal their maleficent behaviour [53].

While the above controls are necessary to prevent other types of threats to security, they have limitations specifically when considering the complexity of the insider threat. It has been suggested that an integrated approach might be more effective than relying on a single control or entity. For example, integrating profiling and honeypots [26] to reduce false positives or using a multi-faceted approach such as multi-factor authentication. In Section 10.2.3, we consider the machinations of cloud-based security that complicate the insider threat problem.

## 10.2.3   *Machinations of cloud-based security*

In a cloud-based system, several issues complicate security. Legal bindings can be difficult to administrate across different countries where diverse and conflicting legislations apply [6,29]. Perhaps, it might be useful to have service level agreements [54] to manage conflicts. Determining the origin of an attack can be challenging [6] particularly in a complex environment like the cloud where attacks can originate at the CSU, CSP or even from third parties. In the next elaboration, we consider the roles and responsibilities towards security in each cloud service model.

### 10.2.3.1   Security issues in the SaaS service model

The provider is responsible for security and privacy [54]. The CSU's data is housed in the data centre of the CSP which may be replicated to increase availability [55]. The following issues may concern the SaaS: network security, data security, data locality, data segregation, data authentication and authorization data integrity, data access, data breaches, data confidentiality, data availability, backup, virtualization and vulnerability, web application security, identification and sign-out processes [55]. With SaaS, insiders of the CSU do have direct access to databases whereas the CSP employees have more access to information and this could cause serious repercussions [56]. With SaaS, the CSP is responsible not only for the physical and environmental security but also for all services rendered, consequently, the responsibilities of the CSU with respect to security are reduced [57].

### 10.2.3.2 Security issues in the PaaS service model

The CSU is responsible for the security as 'they build their own applications' and the CSP is responsible for isolating their customers' 'applications and workstations from one another' [54]. However, the security that is below the application layer such as the service provider manages the host and network intrusion and they have to ensure that data is inaccessible between applications [55]. Cloud mismanagement is a major concern in that CSUs are often faced with a situation where CSP administrators have privileged access to nodes where the client's data is located and they can misuse their privileges by introducing security flaws [58].

### 10.2.3.3 Security issues in the IaaS service model

The IaaS service model is extensible and provides few application-like services, however, it is expected that the CSU will secure operating systems, applications and content [54]. Only basic services are provisioned such as perimeter firewalls and load balancing [13] by the CSP. With IaaS, the CSU's data is hosted in the CSP's VM, therefore the CSP can create copies and backups of the VM, or delete the VM, and can also login into the CSU's VM for administrative purposes [24]. The CSP must ensure environmental security, physical security and virtualization security whereas the CSU must manage data security, applications security and operating system security [55]. Encryption is problematic as the data is manipulated in the VM which is at the CSP's data centre [11]. Rocha and Correia [11] considered scenarios where the insider has root access to the VM of the services and no credentials for authentication. They found that it is possible for an insider to find passwords and decryption keys from memory snapshots of a VM. The insider can extract volumes of confidential information while doing backups and relocating VMs which helps an insider in thwarting protection mechanisms. Nguyen *et al.* [59] suggest that malicious insiders can download the default templates, which are used for the common operating system and poison the template making machines that are deployed from the poisoned template.

### 10.2.4 Security concerns in the cloud

According to Popović and Hocenski [60], there are ten security concerns that are complicated by cloud computing:

- *Lack of knowledge/transparency* – no knowledge or control of where the resources run
- *Legislative risks* – difficult to determine across countries and to determine liability

- *Incompatibility* – incompatibility when a user decides to use another provider
- *Encryption/Decryption* – determining where and how control over encryption/decryption keys should be managed
- *Integrity* – ensuring the integrity of the data where updates occur only in response to an authorized transaction
- *Availability of data logs* – data logs must be available for perusal by the client organization
- *Updates* – clients must ensure that updates are done to ensure security
- *Government regulations* – adhering to government regulations across geographical locations
- *Audits* – maintaining the consistency of security and ensuring the auditability of the data, which is difficult to achieve given the 'dynamic and fluid nature' of VMs
- *Privacy rights* – privacy of the user data is not assured as service providers may undergo external audits [61].

Ogigau-Neamtiu [57] lists several risks to adopting cloud computing. These issues include misunderstanding of responsibilities between the CSP and the CSU, data security and confidentially issues, lack of standards, interoperability issues, reliability and availability issues and malicious insiders. These issues are summarized in Table 10.1.

Theoharidou *et al.* [62] argue that there are a number of challenges specific to cloud computing such as:

- *Multi-tenancy* which involves the sharing of the same infrastructure by multiple CSUs, which complicates data isolation and the management of each CSU's concerns;
- *Dynamicity* of the cloud which is problematic as monitoring the continual and copious data flow is difficult;
- *Data duplication* which involves copying data across data locations, hence it is difficult to determine where it is stored and how to assign responsibility; and
- *Storage and access of data* across multiple locations, which can expose data to legal issues across geographical locations.

Malicious insiders use discrepancies such as the 'misunderstanding of the responsibilities' and lack of standards, poor security management and interoperability issues to their advantage. Insiders can also use the cloud attributes such as multi-tenancy, dynamicity, data duplication and the proliferation of data across multiple locations to conduct maleficence inconspicuously.

In Section 10.2.5, we consider the challenges of managing the insider threat in the cloud.

## 10.2.5 *Moderating the insider threat in cloud-based systems*

CSPs are often not transparent about their hiring process; they often react to the insider threat retrospectively and the monitoring of their employees are inadequate [14,15]. Solutions such as not allowing physical access to the servers do not work

*Table 10.1    Summary of the risks in adopting cloud computing (adapted from Ogigau-Neamtiu [57])*

| Risk | Details |
| --- | --- |
| Misunderstandings of responsibilities | As the responsibilities are shared, there could be misunderstandings. Each cloud service offers various scales of security between the CSP and the CSU. |
| Data security and confidentiality issues | Due to the lack of transparency, it is difficult for the CSU to be assured that the CSP manages their data properly. Issues that require introspection include:<br><br>– Who can create/access/modify the data?<br>– Where will the data be stored?<br>– What happens to the deleted data?<br>– How are backups managed?<br>– How is the data transfer managed? |
| Lack of standards | As the technology is immature, there is no comprehensive and commonly accepted set of standards. There are some organizations which have been established in order to research and develop the specifications (e.g. Cloud Security Alliance, European Network and Information Security Agency, Cloud Standards Customer Council, etc.) |
| Interoperability issues | As there may be incompatibility issues, it is a complex matter when a CSU decides to use another CSP. |
| Reliability and availability issues | Continuous and reliable access to data is essential as downtimes can severely influence the operations of the CSU. |
| Malicious insiders | The malicious activities of an insider could potentially have an impact on the confidentiality, integrity and the availability of client data and services. Insiders are at high risk due to the roles they play in the CSP. CSPs are often responsible for system administration, information security and auditing. The net effect of this state of affairs is that the CSU is highly vulnerable to insider maleficence. |

as attacks can be done remotely [11]. Instituting a zero tolerance policy for insiders is also a retrospective technique that does not work [11]. CSPs could use encryption mechanisms to prevent insiders from the CSP side from malicious acts, however, this is difficult to achieve if the insider has access to the encryption keys although it is possible to store the encryption keys on a different domain other than on the cloud [6]. A client should be able to encrypt and decrypt data to and from the cloud, however, the decryption keys are often available to the CSP [29]. In some cases insiders that work for the CSP can infer information such as the size, from the data without actually exposing the data; this is known as homomorphic encryption [29]. Using logging mechanisms does not work as maleficence is found retrospectively [11]. The CSP could set up an insider detection model to track logins, etc. [6]. Intrusion detection systems can be done in IaaS but not PaaS or SaaS unless the CSP supplies the service [6]. Given the virtualization of the cloud where information and data computer resources are stored virtually in data centres, the idea of perimeter protection is redundant against the insiders [63]. Lim *et al.* [64] suggested that authentication in the cloud is complicated by the fact that passwords and other authentication data have to be stored on the cloud and malicious insiders can exploit this approach. Password authentication [64] can easily be cracked especially if users apply weak password rules. The public-key infrastructure-based (PKI) authentication scheme is a core service in cloud-based computing. The scheme uses public-key cryptology which authenticates users based on a digital certificate [64]. The PKI authentication scheme which provides computational security-based asymmetric key cryptology is subject to eavesdropping, man-in-the-middle attack and masqueraders where the attacker can easily crack a private key [65].

Theoharidou *et al.* [62] argue that an insider in the cloud has more access to data especially if all the security mechanisms are managed by the CSP. They have more opportunities and increased capability to launch attacks on multiple clients. In the cloud, the insider has escalated system privileges and the insiders misuse these privileges to either provide information to outsiders that should not have access or to deny legitimate users from access [14]. Hence, proper mitigation requires implementation of security controls on both the CSU and CSP side. It is difficult to set up evolving policy enforcement on insiders such as system administrators on the CSP as they have to perform functions such as obtaining a 'back-up of the client data and migrating virtual machines of users to different nodes for load balancing' [66].

Theoharidou *et al.* [62] highlight several insufficiencies that show that the following failures increase the probability of an insider threat from the CSP in succeeding in maleficence. These insufficiencies are highlighted in Table 10.2.

It is evident that typical controls such as encryption, access controls, authentication and monitoring are ineffective for mitigating the insider threat in non-cloud-based systems. These controls are even more inadequate within the machinations of the cloud. In Section 10.3, specific mitigation strategies for the insider threat in the cloud are explored.

## 10.3   Cloud-based insider threat mitigation strategies

This section will unpack the various mitigation strategies for cloud-related insider threats. These strategies will be reviewed with respect to how well the dimensions of technical, social, and socio-technical solutions are covered, as mitigating with the insider threat requires a multilateral approach. The mitigation strategies available for cloud-related insider threats include intrusion detection systems, security information and event management, data loss prevention, access control systems and honeytokens [25]. Duncan *et al.* [21] suggest that insiders are often disgruntled and are motivated by money, hence it would be prudent to monitor aspects such as 'social media comments', visitors, changes in behaviour, challenging authority, emails and network traffic, record events, system logs and central recording of shell commands. However, Alhanahnah *et al.* [67] caution that monitoring techniques are not effective in public or community clouds.

Table 10.2    *Insufficiencies that increase the probability of an insider threat in the cloud (adapted from Theoharidou et al. [62])*

| Insufficiencies | Responsibility | |
| --- | --- | --- |
| | CSP | CSU |
| Failure to audit third parties | * | |
| Undocumented responsibilities for data stewardship | * | * |
| Weak data labelling, handling and security policies | * | * |
| Lack/weak data leakage mechanisms | * | |
| Unrestricted access | * | |
| Lack of policies for offsite access | * | |
| Lack of background checks | * | * |
| Weak user authentication and access policies | * | * |
| Lack of disciplinary actions | * | * |
| Weak user-access management | * | * |
| Unclear roles and responsibilities | * | * |
| Weak segregation of duties | * | * |
| 'Need to know principle' not applied | * | * |
| Weak per tenant encryption | * | |
| Weak key management | * | * |
| Unrestricted access to audit tools | * | |
| Irregular or poor risk assessment | * | * |
| Poor tenant segmentation | * | * |

Note: *indicates the entity (CSP/CSU) responsible for managing the insufficiency.

## 10.3.1    *Mitigating insider threats emanating from the CSP*

In this perspective, we consider what the *cloud service provider* can do to mitigate insider threats from the provider itself. Spring [68] suggests that the CSP subscribe to the best practices with respect to insider threat mitigation such as 'separation of privileges, least privilege, access control systems, alarm systems, administrator logging, two-factor authentication, codes of conduct, confidentiality agreements, background checks, and visitor access'. Logging and audit trails can be a way of deterring insiders as they can be traced [6]. Legal bindings can also be a deterrent to insiders [6].

There are various types of rogue administrators: 'hosting company administrators', 'virtual image administrators', 'system administrators' and 'application administrators' [8] that work for the CSP. Mandal and Chatterjee [69] view these four types of administrators along a continuum where each type of administrator has a different level of access, which contributes to the level of severity and risk of the damage caused. The administrators and their levels of access and the corresponding severity and risk of the damage caused are summarized in Table 10.3.

Mandal and Chatterjee [69] suggest that the following mitigation strategies be used – shared authentication among administrators, no manual communication among administrators, geographically isolated administrators, agreements, a specific insider threat mitigation strategy and log-based monitoring. The application of each technique is summarized in Table 10.4.

Table 10.3 *Hierarchical view of rogue administrators in cloud providers and their access privilege and harmfulness (adapted from Mandal and Chatterjee [69])*

|  | Types of administrators |
| --- | --- |
| ↑ Increased severity<br>Increased access<br>Increased risk | Hosting company administrators<br>Virtual image administrators<br>System administrators<br>Application administrators |

Table 10.4 *Techniques to contain the rogue administrator (adapted from Mandal and Chatterjee [69])*

| Techniques | Application |
| --- | --- |
| Shared authentication | A group of administrators must be appointed to apply the socio-technical approach where a shared authentication technique could be applied where all and sundry must submit their permissions in order for a security critical operation to be done; this must be also enforced by a balanced leave policy so that the administrators are able to accomplish the shared authentication technique. |
| No manual communication | No manual communication must be possible between co-administrators as this prevents a concept called 'Elucidating the insiders' where insiders are provoked to become rogue. Rogue administrators use sympathy or blackmail to engage other insiders. |
| Geographic isolation | Administrators should be geographically isolated to prevent collusion. |
| Agreements | Agreements should be in place not to share said information on the social networks or chat servers as this can result in the 'Elucidating insiders' problem. |
| Insider mitigation | All organizations should apply mitigation techniques, which can be achieved using the policies formulated by the CERT. |
| Log-based monitoring | A log-based monitoring system must be in place to monitor activities of the insiders for forensic purposes. |

Mahajan and Sharma [1] have provided mitigation strategies in response to three types of problems that may be committed by the rogue administrators in the cloud: (1) changing the content of user files without the knowledge or consent of the owner, (2) obtaining private keys of encrypted user files and (3) web template poisoning. They suggest that the first attack can be prevented if the owner of the information is presented with a pop-up window that shows that their information has been updated. For the latter two attacks, Mahajan and Sharma [1] suggest a one-time password (OTP). If a rogue administrator attempts to steal a user's data, the respective user will receive an OTP. A cloud-based rogue administrator should

*Table 10.5   A risk assessment from the CSP side to contain the insider threat (adapted from Duncan and Creese [21])*

| Property | Risk assessment query |
|---|---|
| Yield | What is the amount of customer or provider data that can be exfiltrated by the attacker? |
| Utility | What is the value of the yield to the insider threat? |
| Impact | What is the impact of the damage to the client or provider?, e.g. reputational damage |
| Probability | What is the likelihood of the organization being attacked by an insider? |
| Access requirements | What is the level/type of access required to perform an attack? |
| Payload duration | How long would it take an attacker to launch another attack? |
| Harvest duration | How long would it take an insider to harvest the data? |
| Knowledge and skills | What is the level of knowledge and skills required for an insider to carry out an attack? |

have access to the encrypted data and not private keys whereas a local rogue administrative may have the keys but not the encrypted data.

Duncan and Creese [21] suggest that providers should conduct a risk-based assessment of the insider threat as a mitigation strategy. They should consider the following elements: yield, utility, impact, probability, access requirements, payload duration, harvest duration, knowledge and skills. Each property together with a corresponding risk assessment determination query is summarized in Table 10.5.

Nkosi *et al.* [70] argue that a solution to detecting the insider threat on the CSP side should be a function of both technical and non-technical processes. Their model considers behavioural patterns that deviate from the norm. The model is based on the following processes. First, user identities must be managed. This involves pre-employment checks, credit reports, criminal checks, etc. prior to employment. The candidate is given access to the appropriate cloud resources. The roles must be decentralized where mapping is one role per specific account. A system administrator's privileges must be terminated when they leave. Second, users must receive training and the system must monitor their actions during the training for pattern matching. Third, all events must be logged and this information is used to generate pattern and to form a user profile of the usage. Fourth, sequential pattern mining is used to identify patterns to compare the current patterns against the generated user profile.

The mitigation strategies for the CSP appear to be socio-technical considering both the social and technical solutions towards containing the insider threat. In the next section, migration strategies for containing the insider threat from CSU is considered.

## 10.3.2   Mitigating insider threats emanating from the CSU and the CSP

In this perspective, we consider what the *Cloud Service User* can do to mitigate insider threats emanating from the provider side and from within. The CSU can

Table 10.6    *A comparison of techniques to mitigate insider threats (adapted from Kandias et al. [6])*

| Insider threat in the CSP | | Insider threat in the CSU | |
| --- | --- | --- | --- |
| **Technique** | **Responsible** | **Technique** | **Responsible** |
| Cryptographic techniques | Client | Identity and access management | Client and provider |
| Geo-redundant data centres | Client and provider | Multifactor authentication | Client and provider |
| Separation of duties | Provider | Log analysis and auditing | Client |
| Logging and auditing | Provider | Insider prediction/ detection models | Client |
| Legal contracts | Provider | | |
| Insider detection models | Provider | | |

ensure confidentially and integrity using encryption [6] to protect against insider threats from the CSP. The CSU can also ensure the availability of data by using multicentres that could provide backup should the primary centre fail [6]. To protect against insiders from within, the CSU should collect and audit all logs [6]. The CSP could host intrusion detection systems for IaaS clients to detect attacks [6]. In this perspective, we also consider what the CSP can do to mitigate insider threats from the CSU. The CSP can provide anomaly detection as they have access to the data and could inform the CSU of unusual activity [6]. The CSP can provide access control, identity management to enforce separation of duties and multifactor authentication [6]. Various techniques that could apply to each entity together with the corresponding responsible entity are summarized in Table 10.6.

Clearly, the roles of the CSP versus the CSU are blurred with respect to managing insider threats. Hence, we take the view that both CSUs and CSPs are equally responsible for mitigating insider threats.

## 10.3.3    Specific techniques towards containing cloud-related insider threats

We now consider the specific techniques proposed for cloud-related insiders. These techniques can be implemented by either the CSP or the CSU. In this section, encryption, detection, prevention, honeypots and authentication and the related concept of access control are all presented.

### 10.3.3.1    Encryption

Encryption techniques can easily be cracked by insiders due to their knowledge and privileged access. Ali *et al.* [71] proposed a 'secure data sharing in clouds methodology' which encrypts a file with a single encryption key and two different keys shared for each of the users, the other key shared is stored by a trusted third party which helps to counter insider threats. The trusted third-party manages the key management, encryption, decryption and the access control. The trusted third-party divides the key into two parts. One part of the key is transmitted to the user and another part is maintained by an access control list. A user is authenticated by the third-party and the key from the user and only then can the user gain access to the requested data. A user who has been terminated will not be able to decrypt the data as he/she only has a portion of the key.

AlZain *et al.* [72] propose a novel model involving multi-clouds databases, which provide a cloud with database storage in multi-clouds where the security and privacy is preserved by applying a multi-share technique and thereby avoiding the negative effects of a single cloud and also reducing the security risks from malicious insiders. Similar to AlZain *et al.* [72], Gunasekhar *et al.* [20] also argue against that the traditional model of encryption which does not work as the encryption and cryptology algorithm and the decryption keys are hosted in a single cloud and that offers no protection against CSP insiders. They suggest multiple clouds where encrypted information is stored in one cloud centre and the keys to decrypt the data are stored in another cloud. They suggest abiding by the following principles:

- Data must be encrypted with a strong cryptographic algorithm.
- Mutual agreement between CSP and the CSU should be formalized regarding encrypted data.
- Keys that are used while encrypting data are stored on another cloud by accounting security policies of cloud service providers.
- Provide digital certificates to the insiders of cloud providers as well as insiders of organizations to authorize the right persons.
- Establish network monitoring and auditing tools to detect the unintended behaviour of insiders.

Mandhare and Shende [73] suggest layers of protection and storing information disjointly to prevent both hackers and insiders from maliciousness: the first layer will contain a user authentication module, which defines the access rights; these access rights must also apply to file types and programs. The second layer will involve encryption of data. Unlike Ali *et al.* [71] and Gunasekhar *et al.* [20] who suggest disjoining the keys, they suggest storing the encrypted file disjointly across different locations. The user can access the file if they have the validation key, the encryption key and valid email identification; the system will then re-join the file and display it to the user.

Rizvi *et al.* [74] state that the problem with encryption is deciding who should hold the keys and who should perform the encryption. They suggest having a trusted third-party auditor. The problem, however, is the trusted third-party auditor could also become an insider threat in the cloud. Hence, the third party should be audited. They suggested a CSU should use service level agreements and the CSP should use a time-bound session key to check the integrity of the third party.

Mandal [69] suggests that CSPs may outsource resources to a third party if they require additional resources to save on space, cost and maintenance and to increase security. This arrangement can be problematic as the CSU may sue the provider if the third party is in breach due to an insider threat in the third party.

Mandal [69] recommends the following mitigation strategies – service-level agreements for the loss due to the insider, an insider threat free certificate from a recognized authority, regular audit response and a procedure for mitigating insider threats.

### 10.3.3.2   Detection

The problem with detection techniques for identifying insider threats is that they often give false positives. Nikolai and Wang's [25] methodology involves a three-step approach for IaaS cloud systems – training, monitoring and detection. In the training mode, the system is trained during normal activities on the IaaS considering the number of active users on nodes and the number of Transmission Control Protocol (TCP) bytes transmitted from these nodes to the network. These metrics are then used to create an anomalous score for each metric. The system is then placed in a monitor mode where the metrics gathered here are compared against the training mode. The detection of an insider attack involves detecting anomalies in the login and data transfers. This also involves gathering forensic evidence. The forensic evidence is gathered after finding anomalies in the login and data transfer detection. Nikolai and Wang [25] claim that this technique results in a 100% detection rate with no false positives.

Khorshed *et al.* [7] argue that remediation for an insider threat typically occurs post facto and that the CSP's lack of transparency is problematic. They propose a monitoring model of insider activities in the cloud with the following aim: to detect an insider attack while it is happening and to reveal patterns of the attack to the CSU even if the CSP is not being transparent about the attack. Their technique uses machine learning, to take proactive actions and at the same time notify the data owners/administrators of the attack. This increases transparency. It detects an attack by considering whether there is a variation of the norm in the log.

Gunasekhar *et al.* [75] suggest using the following detection mechanisms for insider threats in cloud-based systems: using host-based user profiling in order to detect anomalies; monitoring aspects such as compliance with policies and procedures, database access and modifications, unusual events and actions and system calls; and monitoring network-based activities such as search information, browsing, downloading to local drives and printing of sensitive documents. These may help thwart the insider threat.

The concept of extrusion detection differs from intrusion detection in that 'the target of the offending traffic is within the network with the traffic leaving the network' [21]. Duncan *et al.* [21] suggest using the following techniques towards extrusion detection in the cloud. Monitoring logs, key files, and directories may help but it must be done in real time to prevent extrusion. Honeytokens may also assist identifying insiders. An email filter may be used to identify suspicious transactions. Session data and forensics could be used to identify and prevent extrusions. Statistical data could be used to identify unusual patterns.

### 10.3.3.3   Prevention

Gunasekhar *et al.* [75] assert that a single solution to the insider threat problem is inadequate for cloud security. They recommend a combination of prevention

Table 10.7    *Prevention techniques to contain the insider threat in the cloud (adapted from Gunasekhar et al. [75])*

| Technique | Policies |
| --- | --- |
| Awareness of security | All insiders must have awareness of policies and procedures. |
| Classification of duties | In order to prevent and detect maliciousness, the duties should be classified or segregated. |
| Rotating of duties | Multiple people should be involved in a critical duty and it should be rotated. |
| Limited privileges | Limit access to information on a 'need to know' basis. |
| Encryption | Sensitive data must be encrypted and stored securely. |
| Defence in depth | Layered security for each layer. |
| Complete solution | All areas must be covered by data, technology and data centres. |

detection mechanisms to help thwart the insider threat. They endorse the following prevention policies as a possible resolution to the problem as shown in Table 10.7.

The prevention techniques of 'classification of duties', 'rotating duties', 'limiting privileges' and encryption have been used in the past in legacy systems. These techniques are effective; however, insiders may have the knowledge to overcome these techniques.

### 10.3.3.4    Honeypots

Honeypots can be a means of containing the insider threat in the cloud. Balamurugan and Poornima [61] suggest honeypots could be deployed as a service to cloud users. All malicious activities can be redirected to the honeypot. The client will receive logs on malicious attacks and will have to take the necessary action to prevent future attacks. However, this system was developed for hackers and not insiders.

Another suggestion is 'security by obscurity', which involves 'the principle of protecting things by hiding them' [76], for example, when sensitive information is placed in hidden files [77]. Stuttard [77] maintains that security by obscurity is a useful technique as it places obstacles in the way of would-be attackers. Stolfo *et al.* [78] indicate that user behaviour profiles and decoy technology such as honeypots can be used to detect illegitimate users masquerading as insiders. Stolfo *et al.* [78] have coined the term *Fog Computing* and it involves feeding the malicious user with disinformation. The correlation of abnormal behaviour coupled with the masquerader downloading the decoys can be a means of corroborating that the user is, in fact, a masquerader [78]. The aim is to flood the masquerader with disinformation diluting the real information that he/she may have accessed. This notion is similar to security by obscurity.

### 10.3.3.5    Authentication schemes and access control

Authentication may be a proactive approach to managing the masqueraders as a strong authentication scheme can prevent insiders from stealing credentials from other insiders. Taylor *et al.* [79] suggest that a secure authentication scheme in the cloud can prevent misuse and this can help identify suspects. Manzoor *et al.* [80]

suggest the following authentication strategies for cloud-based computing – OTP; risk-based authentication; sequence of activities, multilevel authentication, biometric authentication. Other schemes such as graphical passwords, smart cards, 3D passwords are most suitable towards preventing masqueraders.

An OTP is a password scheme that is only 'valid for a short time period and can be used just for one login session' [80]. Mahajan and Sharma [1] suggest a solution where a rogue administrator changes a user's file without their knowledge. While users can encrypt their files, the rogue administrator can gain access to the keys. Mahajan and Sharma [1] suggest that OTP may help with thwarting such a problem where the user will get an OTP to access the file to prevent the malicious insider from accessing it.

A risk-based authentication scheme is based on a risk score that is related to login information [81]. Babu and Bhanu [82] suggest an authentication technique that involves keystroke analysis based on past behaviour and risk-based access control where the risk of accessing a resource is calculated. Keystroke analysis is a biometric technique; it appears that biometrics work best for frustrating masqueraders [83]. Biometric authentication is based on 'physical, psychological or behavioural characteristics' [81].

Multifactor authentication combines a number of authentication methods, however it can be difficult to support [64]. Singh and Chatterjee [84] argue that typical authentication systems are easy for insiders to thwart and hence propose a multi-tier authentication scheme for cloud computing. The first tier is the simple username and password scheme; however, the second tier involves the user performing a predetermined activity sequence in order to gain access. Sarma *et al.* [85] suggest an authentication technique that involves recognizing facial features of the cloud user in addition to the username and password, which is essentially a two-factor authentication scheme using biometrics. This scheme is used to verify patterns of misuse. They also propose a monitoring model, which classifies users into legitimate users, possibly legitimate users, possibly not legitimate users and not legitimate users. A legitimate user is an authentic user operating within the bounds of information that they are entitled to access while an illegitimate user is identified by patterns of misuse. Sarma *et al.* [85] recommend that to prevent performance issues, the organizations may want to make use of facial recognition for illegitimate users and in exceptional cases for possibly legitimate users. This technique can prevent a malicious insider from doing further damage.

Braga and Santos [58] argue for a system to secure PaaS services against mismanagement. They set up a bipartite model between cloud administrators and an auditor (third party) who validates software configurations. Cloud administrations have limited privileges and if they require super user privileges then a request to privilege evaluation will be needed. The auditor must endorse commands to allow root privileges. The use of a trusted third party can become a bottleneck for the system [64].

Sundararajan *et al.* [66] suggest an access control that can generate immutable policies based on both the client and provider that propagates access control policies to the provider securely to prevent insider threats in the cloud.

This system will run within a trusted platform, which cannot be compromised by the CPS using mandatory access control. However, they concede that a major challenge is distinguishing between legitimate and malicious users.

In Section 10.3.4, all the techniques discussed are outlined within a framework.

### 10.3.4    Framework of techniques

Hunker and Probst's [18] approach to delineating the insider threat mitigation from three perspectives will be used in a theoretical framework. Insider threat mitigations strategies are delineated into technical, socio-technical and sociological approaches (including psychological and organizational approaches). It has been suggested that psychological and sociological tools are valuable in managing the insider threat [6] and technical controls alone are insufficient.

Hunker and Probst [18] argue that a solution to the insider threat should combine prevention, detection and response handling using technical, socio-technical and sociological approaches. *Technical* approaches include formal policy languages, access control, monitoring, integrated approaches, trusted systems and other system hardening and predictive modelling tools. *Socio-technical* approaches include policies, monitoring, profiling, prediction tools, forensics and the organization's response handling strategy to the insider. This approach involves integrating the technical and the sociological aspects of the insider. *Sociological* approaches (including psychological and organizational approaches) include understanding insider threat motivations, the role of organizational culture, policies, human factors, profiling, monitoring and predictive tools, privacy and legal considerations.

We now consider the tools discussed previously and categorize them according to the framework, which is demonstrated in Figure 10.2. Clearly, the concepts for socio-technical solutions are lacking except for the techniques presented for insider threat mitigation according to the CERT as suggested by Mandal and Chatterjee [69]. Risk Assessments are suggested by Duncan *et al.* [21] and insider threat detection models based on sequential pattern mining by Nkosi *et al.* [70]. Nkosi *et al.* [70] recommend employment checks, termination procedures, and sequential mining to generate user profiles. The solutions by the CERT [86] involve a range of solutions that are socio-technical such as 'know and protect your critical assets', 'beginning with the hiring process, monitor and respond to suspicious or disruptive behaviour', 'implement strict password and account management policies and practices' and 'close the doors to unauthorized data exfiltration'. There is a proliferation of technical solutions.

After conducting a coding analysis, it was found that 52% of the tools are technically oriented whereas 28% of the tools could be considered as being sociologically oriented. The remaining 21% of the tools could be considered socio-technical. The concepts of authentication [1,6,69,82,84,85], Anomaly detection [15,25], multi-clouds computing security [20,72], key-splitting [20,71,73], authentication schemes and using trusted third parties [58,66,69,71,74] are the most popular techniques proposed. The idea of a trusted third party appears to be very popular;

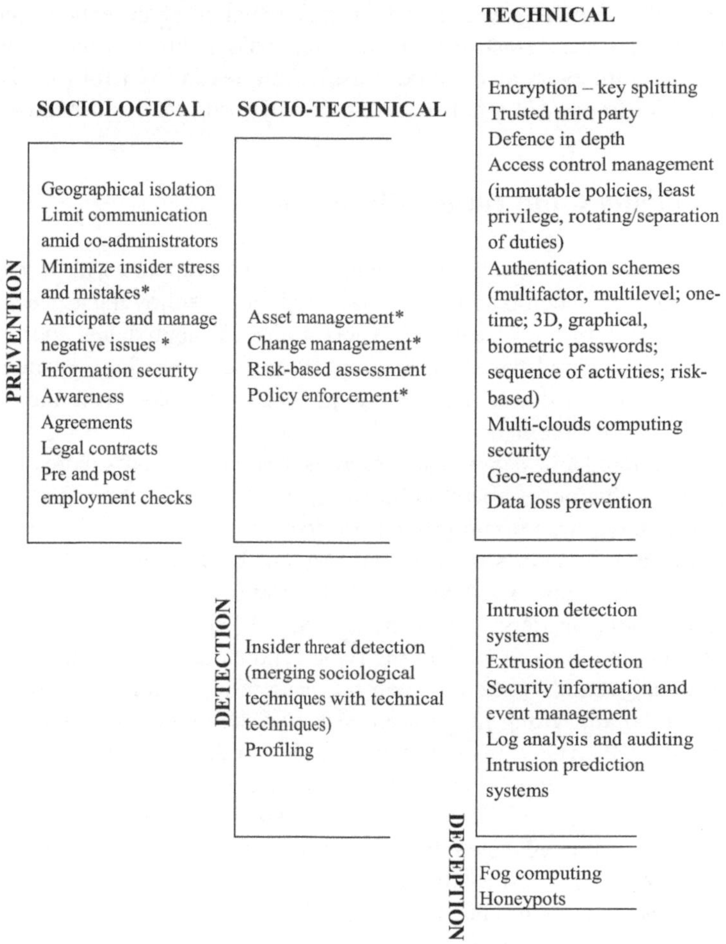

**TECHNICAL**

Encryption – key splitting
Trusted third party
Defence in depth
Access control management
(immutable policies, least
privilege, rotating/separation
of duties)
Authentication schemes
(multifactor, multilevel; one-
time; 3D, graphical,
biometric passwords;
sequence of activities; risk-
based)
Multi-clouds computing
security
Geo-redundancy
Data loss prevention

**SOCIOLOGICAL**     **SOCIO-TECHNICAL**

**PREVENTION**

Geographical isolation
Limit communication
amid co-administrators
Minimize insider stress
and mistakes*
Anticipate and manage
negative issues *
Information security
Awareness
Agreements
Legal contracts
Pre and post
employment checks

Asset management*
Change management*
Risk-based assessment
Policy enforcement*

**DETECTION**

Insider threat detection
(merging sociological
techniques with technical
techniques)
Profiling

Intrusion detection
systems
Extrusion detection
Security information and
event management
Log analysis and auditing
Intrusion prediction
systems

**DECEPTION**

Fog computing
Honeypots

*Figure 10.2    A framework of mitigation strategies for managing insider threats in the cloud*

however, issues of delegating security to a third party may open more opportunities for insiders. Authentication schemes towards mitigating the insider threat appear to be most common; perhaps, limiting the access can prevent further damage.

Figure 10.2 presents a framework of insider threat mitigation techniques for cloud computing based on the techniques revealed in the extant literature. This list of techniques is not exhaustive; however, it may assist organizations in managing the insider threat in the cloud. The framework is delineated into three components: technical, socio-technical and sociological. Each component is further subdivided into prevention versus detection techniques. Prevention techniques assist in averting the insider threat problem in the cloud whereas detection techniques help identify insider threats during the course of normal activities. A further component to the technical component was considered and that is of deception techniques, namely, techniques that assist in deflecting the insider threat, usually with disinformation. This framework also includes the techniques from CERT (denoted by an asterisk) in order to present a holistic view of mitigating the insider threat.

## 10.4    Challenges and future directions

This section will list the various gaps identified in the literature with respect to the previous sections. Claycomb and Nicoll [8] consider the following aspects as being important areas for future research – 'social-technical approaches and predictive models', 'specific cloud-based indicators', VM segmentation, awareness and reporting, publically available data sets on normal user behaviour in the cloud and automated policy enforcement.

As demonstrated in Section 10.3, there is a need for more studies to be conducted under the theme of socio-technical approaches. Claycomb and Nicoll [8] suggest thorough research on improving pre-screening techniques. It is evident that merely checking an insider's background may not be sufficient, perhaps an automated psychological analysis, which includes aptitude tests, may be a means of identifying potential insiders. Claycomb and Nicoll [8] suggest that more research should be done to uncover more than the typical indicators such as unusual working hours, abnormal search patterns such as behavioural indicators for anomaly detection. Nikolai and Wang [25] have considered the number of active nodes and the number of TCP bytes transmitted from nodes to the network in order to compare against normal behaviour in the cloud. However, gathering cloud-based indicators may involve copious data and the analysis of such copious data must be automated. It has been suggested that the techniques applied to managing Big Data could be used to control insider threats [87].

Further research on monitoring should involve reducing false positives, as insiders who are falsely accused, is a libellous issue. It is clear that awareness plays a crucial role in mitigating the insider threat. Hence, it is vital to create an awareness strategy that is more structured and which involves more than mere training strategies. Situational awareness works on three levels: perception (i.e. sensitivity to environmental cues), comprehension (i.e. sense-making of the information by combining, storing, interpreting and retaining) and projection (i.e. forecasting about future incidents) [88]. This concept appears to be a core component that is absent from cloud-based insider threat management. Therefore, it would be 'interesting to measure to what extent a human decision-maker is aware of the situation, i.e. has reached a certain level of situational awareness; and how well he/she manages to maintain and develop this awareness as time progresses' [89]. Having full situational awareness can prevent insiders from rationalizing their crime by claiming ignorance. Situational awareness can also help incident response teams identify and respond to insider threats more effectively.

VM Segmentation is an under-researched area, the possible reason being that the boundaries between VMs are not distinct as they are with physical servers [90].

Segmentation of the VM which involves the isolation of VMs to protect data [91] is an approach to reducing the opportunities for malicious insiders.

Claycomb and Nicoll [8] suggest that publically available data sets that show normal behaviour in the cloud could be used to identify anomalous behaviour in the cloud. Gaining access to such information would be difficult as this information is confidential and the key to protecting organizational assets. Perhaps developing a database of anonymous behavioural sets that can be shared among trusted third parties might be a way to resolve this issue based on a community of practice.

Claycomb and Nicoll [8] suggest better management of discrepancies in policies with a consideration toward automated verifiable policies in the cloud. Automated Policy Enforcement can be applied throughout a cloud service provider's infrastructure and technical mechanisms can be developed for non-cloud based systems such as sticky policies which can be extendable to cloud computing [92]. There should be mechanisms for automatically detecting compliance problems, data protection laws, industry regulations, standards and best practices, service-level agreements and policy enforcement [92]. Automating the process of determining compliance to security policies [93] can be a useful approach towards preventing the insider threat.

In addition to the areas identified by Claycomb and Nicoll [8], we now consider the themes of authentication, Internet of Things (IoT) and Big Data also being identified as emergent areas with respect to insider threat research. Authentication schemes are based on the following factors – knowledge (what the user knows, e.g. password), possession (what the user owns, e.g. smartcards), inherence (who the user is, e.g. biometrics), dynamic (dependent on the environment) and sometimes it can be based on social networks or location [94]. According to Velásquez *et al.* [94], systematic reviews of most cloud-based authentication schemes are based on knowledge and possession. Clearly, there needs to be a deeper inspection with regard to dynamic and inherence type authentication schemes. For example, implicit authentication which uses 'observations of user behaviour for authentication' is more suitable to mobile devices, however, this methodology which uses location, motion, communication and usage of applications is not well established in cloud computing [64] but may have relevancy for IoT research. While risk-based authentication and implicit authentication work in tandem and determine the profile of the user with the risk profile of the transaction [64], this can impact the insider threat problem within the cloud and requires further research. A context-aware authentication mechanism is dynamic and adaptive, and responds to current conditions depending on a user's risk factor [64]. These schemes are both inherent and dynamic, and they require more research with respect to the insider threat. A summary of potential techniques is presented in Table 10.8.

The areas of cloud-based computing, IoT and Big Data systems share a similarity as they manage copious data sets with which will conflate the insider threat problem in the future. Consequently the problem of the insider threat in Big Data systems which deals with organizing and managing large sets of data [95] needs further investigation. There are traitors who can easily circumvent security mechanisms, as the 'sensitivity of customer information stored in the system is

*Table 10.8    Potential techniques for cloud-related insider threats*

| Domain | Potential techniques |
| --- | --- |
| Socio-technical approaches and predictive models | Automated psychological analysis |
| Specific cloud-based indicators | Using Big Data analytics to analyse copious insider threat data |
| VM segmentation | Isolation of VMs |
| Awareness and reporting | Situational awareness |
| Publicly available data sets of anomalous behaviour | Database of anonymous insider threat behaviour as a community of practice. |
| Policy | Automated policy enforcement |
| Authentication | Implicit and dynamic authentication schemes |

increasing by day' and crucially there is no well-defined security standard within the big data community [95]. The problem of the insider threat appears to grow with the Big Data context as insiders can alter the data without being detected [96]. Clearly, there is a need to establish standards in this field particularly with respect to the insider threat.

The IoT is a source of big data and 'comprises billions of devices that can sense, communicate, compute and potentially actuate' which connects 'real world objects to the internet' [97]. Generally, IoT architecture has four main key levels: perception layer, network layer, middle-layer and application layer [98]. The middle layer consists of data storage technologies like the cloud, as discussed in this chapter and the insider can easily tamper with this data storage for personal benefit [98]. Most of the research in IoT has focused on external threats, but it can be perceived that all devices are 'insiders' which have access [99]. Nurse *et al.* [99] emphasize that IoT devices such as smart watches, smart-glasses, activity trackers and smartphones are unexplored areas with respect to the insider threat problem.

## 10.5    Conclusion

As discussed in this chapter, the insider threat is a multifaceted and multi-layered concept in the cloud and a highly complex issue to resolve. The problem is difficult to contain as insiders have authorized access and the requisite knowledge and capability to commit maleficence. The current solutions such as detection systems, intrusion detection systems and firewalls are more effective for detecting external threats. Insiders are hard to detect as they have the capability of bypassing detection mechanisms. The idea of delegating security to another third party that is trusted may either ease the burden of the insider threat in the cloud or it may complicate the management of the insider threat. The question of liability will be of great concern. Clearly, there is no single solution that can address the insider threat problem in the cloud. The answer may lie in an integrated solution that combines technical, socio-technical and sociological techniques. Alternatively proactive authentication techniques that can deny access based on the risk potential of the insider either pre-access or during the access may be an effective means of curbing the insider threat.

# References

[1] Mahajan A., and Sharma S. 'The malicious insiders threat in the cloud'. *International Journal of Engineering Research and General Science*. 2015;**3**(2): 245–56.

[2] Armbrust M., Fox A., Griffith R., *et al.* 'A view of cloud computing'. *Communications of the ACM*. 2010;**53**(4):50–8.

[3] Zhang Q., Cheng L., and Boutaba R. 'Cloud computing: State-of-the-art and research challenges'. *Journal of Internet Services and Applications*. 2010; **1**(1):7–18.

[4] Carlin S., and Curran K. 'Cloud computing security'. *International Journal of Ambient Computing and Intelligence*. 2011;**3**(1):14–9.

[5] Bamiah M. A., and Brohi S. N. 'Seven deadly threats and vulnerabilities in cloud computing'. *International Journal of Advanced Engineering Sciences and Technologies*. 2011;**9**(1):87–90.

[6] Kandias M., Virvilis N., and Gritzalis D. 'The insider threat in cloud computing'. In: Bologna S., Hämmerli B., Gritzalis D., and Wolthusen S., (eds.). *6th International Workshop on Critical Information Infrastructures Security*; Lucerne, Switzerland, Sep 2011. Berlin, Heidelberg: Springer; 2011. pp. 93–103.

[7] Khorshed M. T., Ali A. S., and Wasimi S. A. 'A survey on gaps, threat remediation challenges and some thoughts for proactive attack detection in cloud computing'. *Future Generation Computer Systems*. 2012;**28**(6):833–51.

[8] Claycomb W. R., and Nicoll A. 'Insider threats to cloud computing: Directions for new research challenges'. In: Bai X., Belli F., Bertino E., Chang C. K., Elçi A., Seceleanu C., *et al.*, (eds.). *IEEE 36th Annual Computer Software and Applications Conference*; Izmir, Turkey, Jul 2012. Los Alamitos, CA: IEEE; 2012. pp. 387–94.

[9] Verizon. *2017 Data Breach Investigations Report* [online]. 2017. Available from http://www.verizonenterprise.com/verizon-insights-lab/dbir/2017/ [Accessed 12 May 2018].

[10] Cloud Security Alliance. *The Treacherous 12 Cloud Computing Top Threats in 2016* [online]. 2016. Available from https://downloads.cloudsecurityalliance.org/assets/research/top-threats/Treacherous-12_Cloud-Computing_Top-Threats.pdf [Accessed 20 Mar 2018].

[11] Rocha F., and Correia M. 'Lucy in the sky without diamonds: Stealing confidential data in the cloud'. *IEEE/IFIP 41st International Conference on Dependable Systems and Networks Workshops (DSN-W)*; Hong Kong, China, Jun 2011. Los Alamitos, CA: IEEE; 2011. pp. 129–34.

[12]    Ramgovind S., Eloff M. M., and Smith E. 'The management of security in cloud computing'. In: Venter H. S., Coetzee M., Loock M., (eds.). *Information Security for South Africa (ISSA), 2010*; Sandton, Johannesburg, South Africa, Aug 2010. Danvers, MA: IEEE; 2010. pp. 1–7.

[13]    So K. 'Cloud computing security issues and challenges'. *International Journal of Computer Networks*. 2011;**3**(5):247–55.

[14]    Yusop Z. M., and Abawajy J. H. 'Analysis of insiders attack mitigation strategies'. *Procedia-Social and Behavioral Sciences*. 2014;**129**:611–18.

[15]    Khorshed M. T., Ali A. B. M. S., and Wasimi S. A. 'Monitoring insiders activities in cloud computing using rule based learning'. In: Wang G., Tate S. R., Chen J.-J., and Kouichi Sakurai K., (eds.). *10th International Conference on Trust, Security and Privacy in Computing and Communications*; Changsha, Hunan Province, and P. R. China, Nov 2011. Los Alamitos, CA: IEEE; 2011. pp. 757–64.

[16]    Magklaras G. B., and Furnell S. M. 'A preliminary model of end user sophistication for insider threat prediction in IT systems'. *Computers & Security*. 2005;**24**(5):371–80.

[17]    Schultz E. E. 'A framework for understanding and predicting insider attacks'. *Computers & Security*. 2002;**21**(6):526–31.

[18]    Hunker J., and Probst C. W. 'Insiders and insider threats – an overview of definitions and mitigation techniques'. *Journal of Wireless Mobile Networks, Ubiquitous Computing, and Dependable Applications*. 2011;**2**(1):4–27.

[19]    Young S., and Dahnert A. 'DevEyes insider threat detection'. *Second Worldwide Cybersecurity Summit (WCS)*; London, United Kingdom, Jun 2011. New York: IEEE; 2011. pp. 1–3.

[20]    Gunasekhar T., Rao K. T., Reddy V. K., Kiran P. S., and Rao B. T. 'Mitigation of insider attacks through multi-cloud'. *International Journal of Electrical and Computer Engineering*. 2015;**5**(1):136.

[21]    Duncan A., Creese S., and Goldsmith M. 'An overview of insider attacks in cloud computing'. *Concurrency and Computation: Practice and Experience*. 2015;**27**(12):2964–81.

[22]    Cappelli D. M., Moore A. P., and Trzeciak R. F. *The CERT guide to insider threats: How to prevent, detect, and respond to information technology crimes (theft, sabotage, fraud)* (Boston, MA: Addison-Wesley Professional; 2012).

[23]    CERT INSIDER THREAT CENTER. *Insider Threats Related to Cloud Computing – Installment 2: The Rogue Administrator* [online]. 2012. Available from    https://insights.sei.cmu.edu/insider-threat/2012/08/-insider-threats-related-to-cloud-computing–installment-2-the-rogue-administrator.html [Accessed 3 Mar 2018].

[24]    Duncan A., Creese S., Goldsmith M., and Quinton J. S. 'Cloud computing: Insider attacks on virtual machines during migration'. *12th IEEE International Conference on Trust, Security and Privacy in Computing and Communications (TrustCom)*; Melbourne, Australia, Jul 2013. Los Alamitos, CA: IEEE; 2013. pp. 493–500.

[25] Nikolai J., and Wang Y. 'A system for detecting malicious insider data theft in IaaS cloud environments'. *IEEE Global Communications Conference (GLO-BECOM)*; Washington, DC, Dec 2016. Los Alamitos, CA: IEEE; 2016. pp. 1–6.

[26] Salem M. B., and Stolfo S. J. 'Combining baiting and user search profiling techniques for masquerade detection'. *Journal of Wireless Mobile Networks, Ubiquitous Computing, and Dependable Applications (JoWUA)*. 2012;3(1/2): 13–29.

[27] Probst C. W., Hunker J., Gollmann D., and Bishop M. 'Aspects of insider threats'. In: Probst C., Hunker J., Gollmann D., Bishop M., (eds). *Insider Threats in Cyber Security*. **49**. Boston, MA: Springer; 2010. pp. 1–15.

[28] Cappelli M., Moore A. P., and Shimeall T. J. *Common sense guide to prevention/detection of insider threats* [online]. 2006. Available from http://www.cert.org/archive/pdf/CommonSenseInsiderThreatsV2.11070118.pdf (Carnegie Mellon University, CyLab and the Internet Security Alliance, Tech. Rep.) [Accessed 17 July 2018].

[29] Hay B., Nance K., and Bishop M. 'Storm clouds rising: Security challenges for IaaS cloud computing'. In: Sprague R. H., (ed.). *44th Hawaii International Conference on System Sciences (HICSS)*; Kauai, HI, USA, Jan 2011. Los Alamitos, CA: IEEE; 2011. pp. 1–7.

[30] Wood B. J. 'An insider threat model for adversary simulation'. *SRI International, Research on Mitigating the Insider Threat to Information Systems*. 2000;**2**:1–3.

[31] Nance K., and Marty R. 'Identifying and visualizing the malicious insider threat using bipartite graphs'. In: Sprague R. H., (ed.). *44th Hawaii International Conference on System Sciences (HICSS)*; Koloa, Kauai, HI, USA, Jan 2011. Los Alamitos, CA: IEEE; 2011. pp. 1–9.

[32] Magklaras G. B., and Furnell S. M. 'Insider threat prediction tool: Evaluating the probability of IT misuse'. *Computers & Security*. 2001;**21**(1):62–73.

[33] Bowen B. M., Salem M. B., Hershkop S., Keromytis A. D., and Stolfo S. J. 'Designing host and network sensors to mitigate the insider threat'. *IEEE Security & Privacy*. 2009;**7**(6):22–9.

[34] Anderson D. F., Cappelli D., Gonzalez J. J., *et al.* 'Preliminary system dynamics maps of the insider cyber-threat problem'. In: Kennedy M., Winch G. W., Langer R. S., Rowe J. I., Yanni J. M., (eds.). *22nd International Conference of the System Dynamics Society*; Oxford, England, Jul 2004: Wiley; 2004. pp. 25–9.

[35] Zeadally S., Byunggu Y., Dong H. J., and Liang L. 'Detecting insider threats: Solutions and trends'. *Information Security Journal: A Global Perspective*. 2012;**21**(4):183–92.

[36] Pfleeger C. P. 'Reflections on the insider threat' in Stolfo S. J., Bellovin S. M., Keromytis A. D., Hershkop S., Smith S. W., and Sinclair S., (eds). *Insider Attack and Cyber Security*. US: Springer; 2008. pp. 5–16.

[37] Spitzner L. 'Honeypots: Catching the insider threat'. *19th Annual Computer Security Applications Conference (ACSAC 2003)*; Las Vegas, USA, Dec 2003. Los Alamitos, CA: IEEE,; 2003. pp. 170–9.

[38]    McGrew R., Rayford B., and Vaughn J. R. 'Experiences with honeypot systems: Development, deployment, and analysis'. *39th Annual Hawaii International Conference on System Sciences (HICSS'06)*; Maui, HI, USA, Jan 2006. Los Alamitos, CA: IEEE Computer Society 2006. pp. 220a-a.

[39]    Padayachee K. 'A conceptual opportunity-based framework to mitigate the insider threat'. In: Venter H. S., Loock M., and Coetzee M., (eds.). *Information Security for South Africa*; Johannesburg, South Africa, Aug 2013. Los Alamitos, CA: IEEE; 2013. pp. 1–8.

[40]    Spitzner L. *Honeypots: Are They Illegal?* [online]. 2010. Available from http://www.symantec.com/connect/articles/honeypots-are-they-illegal [Accessed 17 July 2018].

[41]    Kabay M. E. *Honeypots, Part 4: Liability and ethics of honeypots* [online]. 2003. Available from http://www.networkworld.com/newsletters/2003/0519sec2.html [Accessed 17 July 2018].

[42]    Silowash G. J., and King C. *Insider threat control: Understanding data loss prevention (DLP) and detection by correlating events from multiple sources* [online]. 2013. Available from http://www.dtic.mil/docs/citations/ADA610587 [Accessed 17 July 2018].

[43]    Liu S., and Kuhn R. 'Data loss prevention'. *IT Professional*. 2010;**12**(2):10–13.

[44]    Joch A. *Why you can't stop insider threats: You can only hope to contain them* [online]. 2011. Available from http://fcw.com/articles/2011/02/28/feat-cybersecurity-insider-threats.aspx [Accessed 17 July 2018].

[45]    Cole E., and Ring S. *Insider threat: Protecting the enterprise from sabotage, spying, and theft* 1st ed (Rockland, Maine: Syngress; 2006). pp. 49–100.

[46]    Colwill C. 'Human factors in information security: The insider threat–Who can you trust these days?'. *Information Security Technical Report*. 2009;**14**(4):186–96.

[47]    Hinduja S., and Kooi B. 'Curtailing cyber and information security vulnerabilities through situational crime prevention'. *Security Journal*. 2013;**26**(4):383–402.

[48]    Cappelli M., Moore A. P., Shimeall T. J., and Trzeciak R. *Common Sense Guide to Prevention/Detection of Insider Threats* [online]. 2006. Available from https://www.cylab.cmu.edu/files/pdfs/CERT/CommonSenseInsiderThreatsV2.1-1-070118-1.pdf [Accessed 17 July 2018].

[49]    Baracaldo N., and Joshi J. 'An adaptive risk management and access control framework to mitigate insider threats'. *Computers & Security*. 2013;**39**, Part B:237–54.

[50]    Choi S., and Zage D. 'Addressing insider threat using "where you are" as fourth factor authentication'. *2012 IEEE International Carnahan Conference on Security Technology (ICCST)*; Boston, MA, USA, Oct 2012. Los Alamitos, CA: IEEE; 2012. pp. 147–53.

[51]    Walton R., and Limited W.-M. 'Balancing the insider and outsider threat'. *Computer fraud & security* 2006;**2006**(11):8–11.

[52]    Cappelli M., Moore A. P., Shimeall T. J., and Trzeciak R. *Common Sense Guide to Prevention/Detection of Insider Threats* [online]. 2006. Available

from      https://www.cylab.cmu.edu/files/pdfs/CERT/CommonSenseInsider-ThreatsV2.1-1-070118-1.pdf [Accessed 10 May 2014].

[53]  Insider Threat Integrated Process Team (DoD-IPT). *Insider Threat Mitigation*. U.S. Department of Defense; 2000.

[54]  Takabi H., Joshi J. B., and Ahn G.-J. 'Security and privacy challenges in cloud computing environments'. *IEEE Security & Privacy*. 2010;**8**(6):24–31.

[55]  Shoro S., Rajper S., and Baloch B. 'Cloud computing security'. *Sindh University Research Journal-SURJ (Science Series)*. 2017;**49**(4):831–4.

[56]  Subashini S., and Kavitha V. 'A survey on security issues in service delivery models of cloud computing'. *Journal of Network and Computer Applications*. 2011;**34**(1):1–11.

[57]  Ogigau-Neamtiu F. 'Cloud computing security issues'. *Journal of Defense Resources Management*. 2012;**3**(2):141–8.

[58]  Braga B., and Santos N. 'P-Cop: A cloud administration proxy to enforce bipartite maintenance of PaaS services'. In: Foster I., Radia N., (eds.). *9th International Conference on Cloud Computing (CLOUD)*; San Francisco, Jun–Jul 2016. Los Alamitos, CA: IEEE; 2016. pp. 888–93.

[59]  Nguyen M.-D., Chau N.-T., Jung S., and Jung S. 'A demonstration of malicious insider attacks inside cloud iaas vendor'. *International Journal of Information and Education Technology*. 2014;**4**(6):483.

[60]  Popović K., and Hocenski Ž. 'Cloud computing security issues and challenges'. *Proceedings of the 33rd international convention (MIPRO)*; Opatija, Croatia, May 2010. Rijeka, Croatia: Croatian Society for Information and Communication Technology; 2010. pp. 344–9.

[61]  Balamurugan M., and Poornima B. S. C. 'Honeypot as a service in cloud'. *IJCA Proceedings on International Conference on Web Services Computing (ICWSC) ICWSC (1)*, Nov 2011. New York, USA: Foundation of Computer Science; 2011. pp. 39–43.

[62]  Theoharidou M., Papanikolaou N., Pearson S., and Gritzalis D. 'Privacy risk, security, accountability in the cloud'. *5th International Conference on Cloud Computing Technology and Science*; Bristol, United Kingdom, Dec. 2013. Los Alamitos, CA: IEEE; 2013. pp. 177–84.

[63]  Hori Y., Nishide T., and Sakurai K. 'Towards countermeasure of insider threat in network security'. *2011 Third International Conference on Intelligent Networking and Collaborative Systems*; Fukuoka, Japan, Nov–Dec 2011. Washington, DC, USA: IEEE Computer Society; 2011. pp. 634–6.

[64]  Lim S. Y., Kiah M. M., and Ang T. F. 'Security issues and future challenges of cloud service authentication'. *Acta Polytechnica Hungarica*. 2017;**14**(2):69–89.

[65]  Khalid R., Zukarnain Z. A., Hanapi Z. M., and Mohamed M. A. 'Authentication mechanism for cloud network and its fitness with quantum key distribution protocol: A survey'. *Journal of Theoretical and Applied Information Technology*. 2015;**81**(1):51–64.

[66]  Sundararajan S., Narayanan H., Pavithran V., Vorungati K., and Achuthan K. 'Preventing insider attacks in the cloud'. In: Abraham A., Mauri J. L., Buford J. F., Suzuki J., and Thampi S. M., (eds.). *International Conference*

*on Advances in Computing and Communications*; Kochi, Kerala, India, Jul 2011. Verlag Berlin Heidelberg: Springer; 2011. pp. 488–500.

[67]    Alhanahnah M. J., Jhumka A., and Alouneh S. 'A multidimension taxonomy of insider threats in cloud computing'. *The Computer Journal*. 2016;**59**(11): 1612–22.

[68]    Spring J. 'Monitoring cloud computing by layer, Part 1'. *IEEE Security & Privacy*. 2011;**9**(2):66–8.

[69]    Mandal K. K., and Chatterjee D. 'Insider threat mitigation in cloud computing'. *International Journal of Computer Applications*. 2015;**120**(20).

[70]    Nkosi L., Tarwireyi P., and Adigun M. O. 'Insider threat detection model for the cloud'. In: Venter H. S., Loock M., and Coetzee M., (eds.). *2013 Information Security for South Africa*; Johannesburg, South Africa, Aug 2013. Piscataway, NJ: IEEE; 2013. pp. 1–8.

[71]    Ali M., Dhamotharan R., Khan E., *et al.* 'SeDaSC: Secure data sharing in clouds'. *IEEE Systems Journal*. 2017;**11**(2):395–404.

[72]    AlZain M. A., Pardede E., Soh B., and Thom J. A. 'Cloud computing security: From single to multi-clouds'. *45th Hawaii International Conference on System Science (HICSS)*, ; Kuala Lumpur, Malaysia, Jun 2012. Los Alamitos, CA: IEEE; 2012. pp. 5490–9.

[73]    Mandhare S., and Shende R. 'An intelligent approach for data fortification in cloud computing'. *International Conference on Advances in Communication and Computing Technologies (ICACACT 2014)*; Mumbai, India, Aug 2014. Piscataway,NJ: IEEE; 2014. pp. 1–6.

[74]    Rizvi S., Razaque A., and Cover K. 'Third-party auditor (TPA): A potential solution for securing a cloud environment'. *2nd International Conference on Cyber Security and Cloud Computing*; New York, Nov 2015. Los Alamitos, CA: IEEE; 2015. pp. 31–6.

[75]    Gunasekhar T., Rao K. T., and Basu M. T. 'Understanding insider attack problem and scope in cloud'. *2015 International Conference on Circuits, Power and Computing Technologies [ICCPCT-2015]*; Nagercoil, India, Mar 2015. Piscataway, NJ: IEEE; 2015. pp. 1–6.

[76]    Zwicky E. D., Cooper S., and Chapman D. B. *Building internet firewalls* (California, CA: O'Reilly Media, Inc.; 2000).

[77]    Stuttard D. 'Security & obscurity'. *Network Security*. 2005;**2005**(7):10–12.

[78]    Stolfo S. J., Salem M. B., and Keromytis A. D. 'Fog computing: Mitigating insider data theft attacks in the cloud'. *Security and Privacy Workshops (SPW), 2012 IEEE Symposium on*; San Francisco, CA, USA, May 2012. Los Alamitos, CA: IEEE; 2012. pp. 125–8.

[79]    Taylor M., Haggerty J., Gresty D., and Lamb D. 'Forensic investigation of cloud computing systems'. *Network Security*. 2011;**2011**(3):4–10.

[80]    Manzoor A., Tahir M. A.-u.-H., Wahid A., Shah M. A., and Akhunzada A. 'Secure login using multi-tier authentication schemes in fog computing'. *EAI Endorsed Transactions on Internet of Things*. 2018;**3**(11):1–6.

[81]    Sepczuk M., and Kotulski Z. 'A new risk-based authentication management model oriented on user's experience'. *Computers & Security*. 2018;**73**: 17–33.

[82]    Babu B. M., and Bhanu M. S. 'Prevention of insider attacks by integrating behavior analysis with risk based access control model to protect cloud'. *Procedia Computer Science*. 2015;**54**:157–66.

[83]    Liu L., De Vel O., Han Q.-L., Zhang J., and Xiang Y. 'Detecting and preventing cyber insider threats: A survey'. *IEEE Communications Surveys & Tutorials*. 2018. Available from: 10.1109/COMST.2018.2800740.

[84]    Singh A., and Chatterjee K. 'A secure multi-tier authentication scheme in cloud computing environment'. *2015 International Conference on Circuits, Power and Computing Technologies [ICCPCT-2015]*; Nāgercoil, India, Mar 2015. Piscataway, NJ: IEEE; 2015. pp. 1–7.

[85]    Sarma M. S., Srinivas Y., Abhiram M., Ullala L., Prasanthi M. S., and Rao J. R. 'Insider threat detection with face recognition and KNN user classification'. *International Conference on Cloud Computing in Emerging Markets (CCEM)*; Bangalore, India, Nov 2017. Los Alamitos, CA: IEEE; 2017. pp. 39–44.

[86]    CERT INSIDER THREAT CENTER. *Common Sense Guide to Mitigating Insider Threats, Fifth Edition*. 2016. Report No.: CMU/SEI-2015-TR-010 CERT Division.

[87]    Huth C. L., Chadwick D. W., Claycomb W. R., and You I. 'Guest editorial: A brief overview of data leakage and insider threats'. *Information Systems Frontiers*. 2013;**15**(1):1–4.

[88]    Endsley M. R., and Garland D. 'Theoretical underpinnings of situation awareness: A critical review', in Endsley M. R., and Garland D. J., (eds). *Situation Awareness Analysis and Measurement*. Mahwah, NJ: Lawrence Erlbaum Associates; 2000. pp. 3–32.

[89]    Franke U., and Brynielsson J. 'Cyber situational awareness – A systematic review of the literature'. *Computers & Security*. 2014;**46**:18–31.

[90]    ProSecure. *Virtual Machines – Real Vulnerabilities* [online]. 2009. Available from https://smedia3.webcollage.net/d6c60b4741298145a81f7016044 b90f9a25f7a05?Signature=zx5XWnDax8LtdzwwG3HiqGdGqhw%3D& AWSAccessKeyId=AKIAIIE5CHZ4PRWSLYKQ&Expires=1893529478 &response-content-type=application/pdf [Accessed 28 Mar 2018].

[91]    Raj P., and Raman A. C. *The Internet of Things: Enabling Technologies, Platforms, and Use Cases* (Boca Raton, FL: CRC Press; 2017).

[92]    Papanikolaou N., Pearson S., Mont M. C., and Ko R. K. 'A toolkit for automating compliance in cloud computing services'. *International Journal of Cloud Computing 2*. 2014;**3**(1):45–68.

[93]    Ranise S., and Siswantoro H. 'Automated legal compliance checking by security policy analysis'. In: Tonetta S. S. E., and Bitsch F, (ed.). International Conference on Computer Safety, Reliability, and Security. Lecture Notes in Computer Science. Cham, Switzerland: Springer; 2017. pp. 361–72.

[94]   Velásquez I., Caro A., and Rodríguez A. 'Authentication schemes and methods: A systematic literature review'. *Information and Software Technology*. 2018;**94**:30–7.

[95]   Aditham S., and Ranganathan N. 'A system architecture for the detection of insider attacks in big data systems'. *IEEE Transactions on Dependable and Secure Computing*. 2017. Available from: doi:10.1109/TDSC.2017.2768533.

[96]   Smyth G. 'Using data virtualisation to detect an insider breach'. *Computer Fraud & Security*. 2017;**2017**(8):5–7.

[97]   Rao A. P. 'Adaptive control strategies for task scheduler using internet of things'. In: Krishna P. A. V., (ed.). *Exploring the Convergence of Big Data and the Internet of Things*. Hershey, PA: IGI Global; 2017. pp. 129–40.

[98]   Farooq M. U., Waseem M., Khairi A., and Mazhar S. 'A critical analysis on the security concerns of internet of things (IoT)'. *International Journal of Computer Applications*. 2015;**111**(7).

[99]   Nurse J. R., Erola A., Agrafiotis I., Goldsmith M., and Creese S. 'Smart insiders: Exploring the threat from insiders using the internet-of-things'. *International Workshop on Secure Internet of Things (SIoT)*; Vienna, Austria, Sep 2015. Los Alamitos, CA: IEEE; 2015. pp. 5–14.

## Chapter 11

# Cryptographic engines for cloud based on FPGA

*Ramasubramanian Natarajan[1] and Manjith Baby Chellam[2]*

Cryptographic operations are being performed in all security critical applications and devices. Encryption/Decryption and authentication operations are used in the cloud server for full virtual machine encryption, protection of data at rest, data in motion, etc. Execution of cryptographic operations on the processor reduces the efficiency and increases heat production. Integration of field-programmable gate array (FPGA) devices to cloud data centers opens up the opportunity to implement critical tasks in hardware, thereby improving the efficiency. Security being a critical application on cloud can be implemented on hardware to improve performance and reduce heat production. This chapter presents hardware implementation of four cryptographic engines—AES, DES, SHA, and MD5 on FPGA. Finally, an adaptive reconfigurable security system with the four cryptographic engines using partial reconfiguration is discussed. Depending on the dynamic need, only the necessary algorithm can be loaded which saves power and area.

## 11.1 Introduction

### 11.1.1 Field-programmable gate array (FPGA)

Computations in the digital world can be performed by software and hardware. Software is highly flexible, but cannot be pushed beyond a limit for high performance. Hardware like application-specific integrated circuit (ASIC) on the other hand has huge amount of resources for optimized performance. But ASIC circuits are permanently fused to the chip and cannot be reconfigured. FPGAs overcome this limitation by reconfiguration feature. FPGAs provide software flexibility to hardware. They can be customized to any hardware circuit according to the need. The configured hardware can be modified to create new circuit at a

[1]Department of Computer Science and Engineering, National Institute of Technology, Tiruchirappalli, India
[2]Department of Computer Science and Engineering, National Institute of Technology, Puducherry, India

later time. FPGAs contain logic elements—look up tables (LUTs), flip-flops, multiplexors for implementing combinational and sequential logic, various programmable I/O blocks, programmable interconnects, and memories like BRAM and DRAM. FPGAs are used in data centers, servers, aerospace, video/image processing, ASIC prototyping, etc. One of the major fields that adopted FPGAs recently is the cloud server where FPGAs are used as accelerators. FPGAs can reduce the processor load, thereby improving performance and reducing power production [1,2].

## 11.1.2   *Cryptographic algorithms for encryption and authentication*

Encryption is the process of hiding data or information from unauthorized users. It is done by a series of operations to make the data unreadable. Authentication ensures about the identity of an entity, authenticate that a message has not been altered and protects against denial of an entity in a communication process. Modern cryptography has adopted mathematical theories to make the encryption and authentication process unbreakable.

Depending on the amount of data needed to be encrypted, there are two types of encryption techniques. Symmetric encryption deals with huge amount of data, whereas asymmetric encryption can be used for encrypting small amount of data like authentication code, encryption keys, etc. Two symmetric encryption algorithms—advanced encryption standard (AES), data encryption standard (DES) and two hash code generation algorithms—secure hash algorithm (SHA), message digest 5 (MD5) along with their hardware implementation on FPGA are discussed in this chapter.

## 11.1.3   *Need of hardware cryptographic engines for cloud servers*

Encryption is being used in the cloud for encrypting user virtual machines, encrypting data at rest and data in motion, encryption as a service, etc. [3,4]. Hash code algorithms are used to provide authentication and integrity of user and data, respectively. Allocation of processor resources for costly cryptographic process not only reduces the overall speed of the cloud server but also increases the heat production. In order to accelerate cryptographic process, algorithms can be implemented as a hardware on FPGA which is called an accelerator. An accelerator can be loaded into FPGA to create dedicated hardware for encryption process whenever it is needed [5,6].

The chapter describes the implementations of AES, DES, SHA, and MD5 on FPGA with proper pipelining. Multistage pipelining for the necessary operations has been done to reduce the path delay and thereby improving high throughput. After describing the implementation details, a security system containing all four cryptographic engines is proposed. The security system is designed to load the necessary accelerator based on the dynamic need. The system will reduce the area and static power consumption since only the accelerators that are currently needed will be online.

The chapter is organized as follows. Section 11.2 presents the basic working of AES, hardware implementation of AES on FPGA, and discusses the efficiency of the system. Section 11.3 explains the working of DES, corresponding hardware implementation, and the efficiency. Sections 11.4 and 11.5 present SHA and MD5 implementations, respectively, with their efficiencies. Partial reconfiguration feature is explained in Section 11.6. Section 11.7 presents an adaptive security system based on cryptographic algorithms and partial reconfiguration.

## 11.2    Advanced encryption standard

AES is a symmetric encryption algorithm that has a fixed input length of 128 bits and key length of 128/192/256 bits, which operates in 10/12/14 rounds depending on the key length. The 128-bit AES algorithm steps are depicted in Figure 11.1.

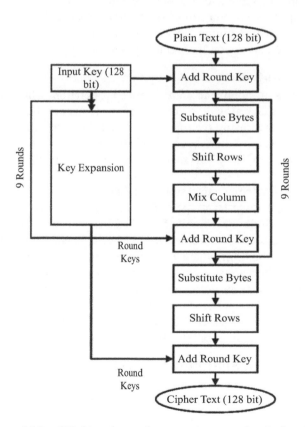

*Figure 11.1    128-bit advanced encryption standard algorithm*

The input is divided into 4 × 4 state array. The algorithm has four basic operations, namely, Substitute Byte, Shift Rows, Mix Column, and Add Round Key. The four operations are carried out repeatedly on the input state array. Byte Substitution replaces each element in state array with a corresponding element in S-box. The S-box was constructed from Galois Field, GF (8), which was designed to secure all attacks. After the substitution operation, elements are left circular shifted in Shift Rows operation. Add Round Key performs the XOR operation of each state array element with the round key produced from the Expansion Key operation. AES has been used widely for all security application since its introduction [7,8]. The following sections discuss how each operation in AES can be implemented on hardware with multistage pipeline.

## 11.2.1   Hardware realization of AES on FPGA

Implementation of AES on hardware includes mapping each operation of the algorithm to LUTs, multiplexors, memory units, etc. of FPGA to create the corresponding logic. The mapping should be done for efficient resource utilization and pipeline. The input text and S-box values are stored in LUTs and keys are stored in registers. The operations—Substitute Byte, Shift Rows, and Mix Column—work on the input text. Mix Column operates on the input text and input key. Key Expansion operation works on the input key alone.

### 11.2.1.1   Substitute Byte

Substitute Byte is a nonlinear transformation operation which replaces each element in input state array with a corresponding element in the S-box. The S-box elements are calculated using two operations— GF inversion over binary field GF (28) and affine transformation over GF (2) [9]. S-box values can be calculated using combinational logic for GF inversion and AT, or directly storing the values inside the algorithm.

The hardware implementation stores the values of S-box in FPGA memory and retrieved during Substitute Byte operation. The S-box memory contains 256 bytes (16 × 16) which include the combination of all hexadecimal values. Let $x$ be the input state array whose S-box values are to be calculated. Then, output $y$ can be calculated as $y_i = $ S-box$(x_i)$, where $i = 0$ to 15. Here, S-box is a set of LUTs in FPGA where the values are stored. The state array contains 16 hexadecimal values and hence the retrieval from S-box has to be carried out 16 times. Since the values are stored in LUTs, 16 operations can be unrolled and can be done in parallel. Figure 11.2 shows the schematic of the proposed unrolled operation of S-box accesses which are done in parallel [10].

### 11.2.1.2   Merging of Substitute Byte and Shift Rows

Shift Rows operation carries out left circular shift of the input state array. While doing hardware implementation of Shift Rows, the content of state array memory is exchanged to do the shifting operation. In order to reduce the number of clock cycles for doing Substitute Byte and Shift Rows operation, the S-box values that are retrieved during Substitute Byte operation are shifted or updated in registers

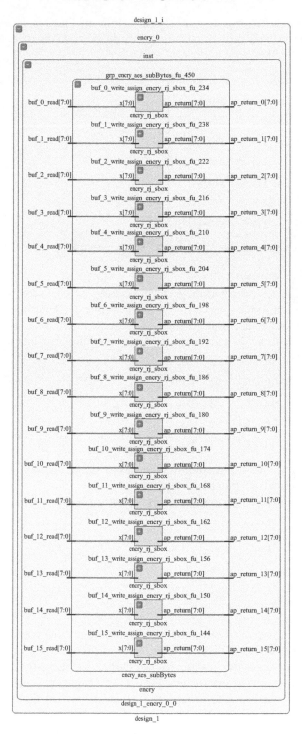

*Figure 11.2   Schematic of unrolled Substitute Byte*

corresponding to shifted registers. In short, the intermediate results after Substitute Byte are not stored and directly shifting is carried out. Mathematically, it can be shown in (11.1) [10].

$$
\left.
\begin{aligned}
y_0 &= s\_box[x_0] y_8 = s\_box[x_{10}] \\
y_1 &= s\_box[x_1] y_9 = s\_box[x_{11}] \\
y_2 &= s\_box[x_2] y_{10} = s\_box[x_8] \\
y_3 &= s\_box[x_3] y_{11} = s\_box[x_9] \\
y_4 &= s\_box[x_5] y_{12} = s\_box[x_{15}] \\
y_5 &= s\_box[x_6] y_{13} = s\_box[x_{12}] \\
y_6 &= s\_box[x_7] y_{14} = s\_box[x_{13}] \\
y_7 &= s\_box[x_4] y_{15} = s\_box[x_{14}]
\end{aligned}
\right\}
\tag{11.1}
$$

where $x_i$ is the input and $y_i$ is the output. The schematic is shown in Figure 11.3.

### 11.2.1.3   Mix Column

The Mix Column transformation performs mixing of each column of the state array. Each column in the state array is considered as the coefficient of vectors in GF (28). These values are multiplied by a constant matrix of dimension $4 \times 4$ in which each element is a hexadecimal value representing elements of GF (28). It is represented in (11.2).

$$
\begin{bmatrix} y_0 \\ y_1 \\ y_2 \\ y_3 \end{bmatrix} \times
\begin{bmatrix} 02 & 03 & 01 & 01 \\ 01 & 02 & 03 & 01 \\ 01 & 01 & 02 & 03 \\ 03 & 01 & 01 & 02 \end{bmatrix} =
\begin{bmatrix} x_0 \\ x_1 \\ x_2 \\ x_3 \end{bmatrix}
\tag{11.2}
$$

$x_0$, $x_1$, $x_2$, and $x_3$ are the input column elements of the state array. $y_0$, $y_1$, $y_2$, and $y_3$ are the output column elements.

$y_0$, $y_1$, $y_2$, and $y_3$ can be computed as shown in (11.3).

$$
\begin{aligned}
y_0 &= \propto \oplus x_0 \oplus \delta(x_0 \oplus x_1) \\
y_1 &= \propto \oplus x_1 \oplus \delta(x_1 \oplus x_2) \\
y_2 &= \propto \oplus x_2 \oplus \delta(x_2 \oplus x_3) \\
y_3 &= \propto \oplus x_3 \oplus \delta(x_3 \oplus x_0)
\end{aligned}
\tag{11.3}
$$

where $\propto = x_0 \oplus x_1 \oplus x_2 \oplus x_3$

The hardware implementation of Mix Column has to be pipelined to improve throughput. The latency of Mix Column, when executed at 1.23 ns path delay, is found to be three. Hence, the initiation interval of Mix Column is four. This reduces the pipeline efficiency since it creates stalls [11]. It cannot execute a new input for four clock cycles. In order to reduce the initiation interval of Mix Column, the design has to be sub-pipelined. The sub-pipelining has been carried by inserting registers between sub-operations to make the initiation interval to one. Since the

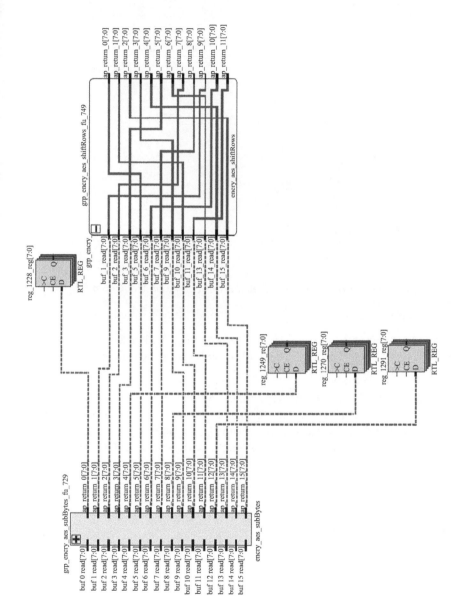

*Figure 11.3  Merging of Substitute Byte and Shift Row*

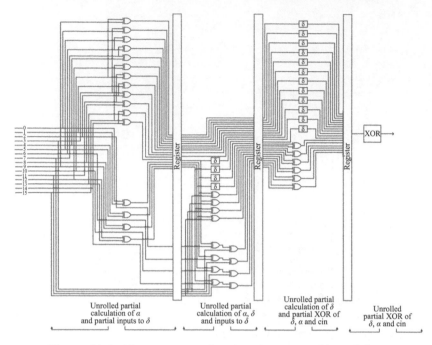

*Figure 11.4    Four-stage pipelined architecture of Mix Column*

latency of Mix Column is three, a four-stage pipelining will reduce the initiation interval from four to one. The hardware implementation is shown in Figure 11.4 [10].

### 11.2.1.4    Key Expansion

The Key Expansion provides round keys for the AES algorithm. It receives 128-bit key, expands it, and provides to Add Round Key operation at each round of the algorithm [10]. The Key Expansion operation is shown in Figure 11.5.

The input is divided into four blocks—Kb0, Kb1, Kb2, and Kb3. The operations carried out on four blocks are given in (11.4).

$$Kbnew0 = Kb0 \oplus [\text{ShiftRows}(\text{s\_box}(Kb3)) \oplus \text{Rcon}]$$
$$Kbnew1 = Kb1 \oplus \text{Kbnew0}$$
$$Kbnew2 = Kb2 \oplus \text{Kbnew1}$$
$$Kbnew3 = Kb3 \oplus \text{Kbnew2}$$

$$(11.4)$$

The latency for carrying out the operations on the key is found to be four for a path delay of 1.23 ns. Hence, the initiation interval of Key Expansion is five. To reduce the stalls caused by this, the Key Expansion operation has been pipelined to make the initiation interval to one. A five-stage pipelining would reduce the initiation interval to one by placing registers between sub-operations of Key Expansion. A five-stage pipelined design of Key Expansion is shown in Figure 11.6. S-box

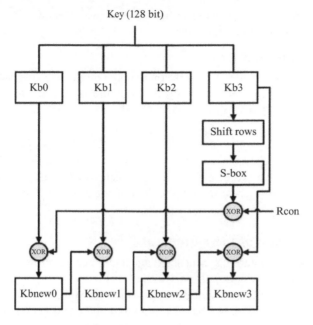

*Figure 11.5   Key Expansion*

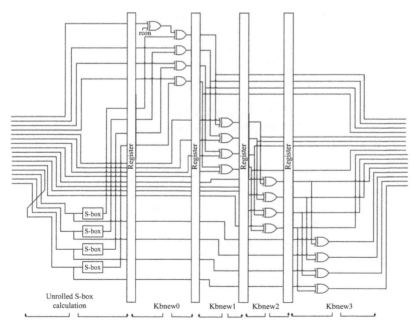

*Figure 11.6   Five-stage pipelined architecture of Key Expansion for 1.23 ns path delay*

calculation is done on first stage. Kbnew0, Kbnew1, Kbnew2, and Kbnew3 are calculated in subsequent clock cycles.

### 11.2.1.5    Add Round Key

Add Round Key performs XOR operation between input state array and the sub key received from Key Expansion module. Let $x$ be the input state array and $k$ be the sub key, then the output $y$ is given as in (11.5).

$$y_i = x_i \oplus k_i \tag{11.5}$$

where $y_i$ is the $i$th output bit, $x_i$ is the $i$th input bit , and $k_i$ is the $i$th key bit.

The latency of Add Round Key for a path delay of 1.23 ns is found to be zero. Hence, the initiation interval is one which does not cause any stalls in the system. Hence, there is no need for further sub-pipeline.

## 11.2.2    Efficiency of the system

The accelerator is simulated, synthesized and implemented on XC7VX690T device using Xilinx Vivado System edition 16.2 [12–14].

The efficiency of the system depends on the throughput and resource utilization. The values are calculated based on (11.6), (11.7), and (11.8) [11]:

$$\text{Throughput} = \frac{\text{Number of output bits}}{\text{Critical path delay}} \tag{11.6}$$

$$\text{Throughput} = \frac{\text{Number of input blocks} \times \text{Number of processed bits}}{\text{Clock period} \times \text{Number of cycles}} \tag{11.7}$$

$$\text{Efficiency} = \frac{\text{Throughput}}{\text{Area(slices)}} \tag{11.8}$$

The number of output bits produced by AES algorithm is 128 bits. Critical path delay in the system is 1.23 ns. Hence, the throughput produced by the system is 104.06 Gbps. The overall latency of the system is 58 clock cycle. Since the initiation interval of the system is one, the latency does not affect the throughput of the system. The resource utilization is found to be 2,617 slices. Hence, the efficiency of the system is 39.7 Mbps.

Some of the related works for AES hardware implementation are described here. Authors in [15] proposed the implementation for pipelined S-box using composite field arithmetic. It could achieve an efficiency of 17.08 Mbps on XC6VLX240T device. Lee *et al.* [16] employed constant binary matrix-vector multiplications along with a four-stage pipelined AES design. The system could achieve a throughput of 3.8 Gbps. Farashahi *et al.* [17] proposed 2-slow retiming technique that extends the c-slow retiming technique by replacing every register with two in appropriate positions to reduce the delay in pipelined AES design. Dependency errors in previous methods were avoided by data forwarding. The method achieved a throughput of 86 Gbps at 671.524 MHz.

## 11.3    Data encryption standard (DES) hardware accelerator

### 11.3.1    DES

DES is a symmetric block cipher encryption algorithm published in 1975. The algorithm has 64-bit input/output and 56-bit key. The operations of the algorithm are permutation of input, 16 Feistel rounds, and a final inverse permutation. A round key generator generates sub keys for each Feistel round. DES uses confusion and diffusion property for security strength. Permutation operations achieve diffusion property in DES and XOR operations involved in Feistel rounds achieves confusion property. Figure 11.7 shows the steps involved in the DES algorithm [8]. Initial permutation (IP) step performs permutation of 64-bit input according to the permutation table. After IP, 16 rounds of function (F) that contains expansion, permutation and substitution are performed. Afterward, a 32-bit swap and final permutation are performed. Each operation along with their hardware implementations is discussed below.

### 11.3.2    Hardware realization of DES

DES has been implemented on FPGA by mapping the operations of DES on to the resources on FPGA for creating logic and for storing data values. The plain text (input) and key (input) are stored in FPGA register.

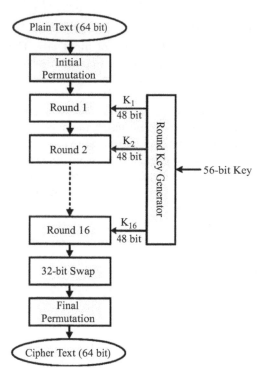

*Figure 11.7    Data encryption standard*

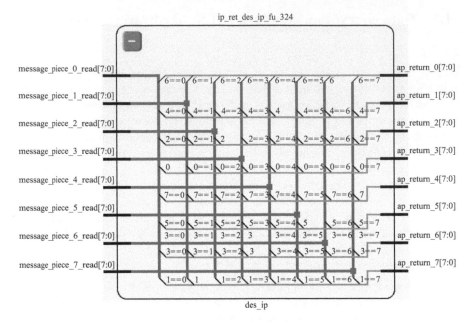

*Figure 11.8    Schematic of initial permutation*

### 11.3.2.1    Initial permutation

Initial permutation performs transformation of input bits. The order of transformation is specified in permutation table. Permutation table contains 64 entries for each bit in the input text. Transformation is performed on each input bit by referring to the permutation table.

The permutation in hardware is performed by exchanging the register values through proper interconnection based on the permutation table. Instead of storing values of permutation table on memory and referring each time, the interconnection between the input and output registers is changed to get the permuted output. Figure 11.8 shows the schematic of the hardware implementation of Initial Permutation. message_piece connection gets the input to permutation table and ap_returns gives the output after permutation.

The latency observed for Initial Permutation is zero for a path delay of 4 ns. Hence, the initiation interval is one which does not cause any stalls in the pipeline.

### 11.3.2.2    Feistel round

The Feistel round in DES can be described as shown in (11.9).

$$Left_i = Right_{i-1}$$
$$Right_i = Left_{i-1} \oplus F(Right_{i-1}, Key_i)$$

(11.9)

The function F in Feistel round of DES divides the 64-bit input into two halves, and then performs Expansion, XOR with the round key, S-box substitution, and permutation. The process is shown in Figure 11.9.

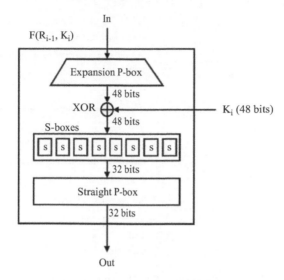

*Figure 11.9   Function F in the Feistel round of DES*

### 11.3.2.3   Expansion P-box

The expansion function in F is a combination of permutation and expansion of input. It converts 32-bit data to 48 bit with permutation. The expansion is carried out using redundant input values. The expansion table contains 48 entries. Expansion permutation is performed on input by referring to the expansion table.

Hardware realization of Expansion Permutation is done by interchanging the input connections to output for performing permutation and creating additional connections for performing expansion. The process is shown in the screenshot of the schematic in Figure 11.10. r_read gives the input to the block, and ap_return gives output from the block. There are four r_read (8 bits) lines and six ap_return (8 bits) lines.

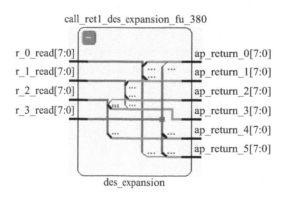

*Figure 11.10   Schematic of expansion permutation*

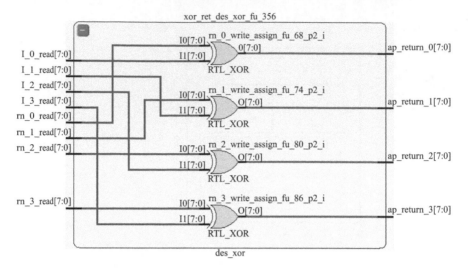

*Figure 11.11    Schematic of XOR between the input and key*

The expansion permutation takes a latency of zero at 4 ns path delay. The output will be available on the same clock cycle itself.

### 11.3.2.4   XOR key

The 48-bit output from Expansion Permutation is XORed with the 48-bit round key $K_i$. The schematic of the operation is shown in Figure 11.11. m_read pins gives the message input and l_read gives the key input to the block. XOR gates are used to realize XOR operations. The process takes a latency of zero at 4 ns path delay which gives the output at the same clock cycle.

### 11.3.2.5   Substitution boxes

The function F contains eight S-boxes which reduce and the 48-bit input to 32-bit. Each S-box contains six inputs and four outputs. Four bits from six input bits will be selected based on the S-box table and gives as output from each S-box. S-box creates the real confusion property in the DES.

S-box function is implemented in hardware using ROM for storing input values. The selected four bits are transferred to register and are given to output pins. The schematic of a single S-box function is shown in Figure 11.12. The S-box value is stored in ROM q00_i. From there, depending on the input, the value is selected to the register qo_reg. The overall implementation of the S-box function is shown in Figure 11.13. Eight S-box units are seen from s1_U to s8_U.

The S-box function takes a latency of one clock cycle at 4 ns path delay. The output will be made available after one clock cycle.

### 11.3.2.6   Permutation box P

The 32-bit output from the S-box function is permuted based on the permutation table, P, and produces 32-bit output.

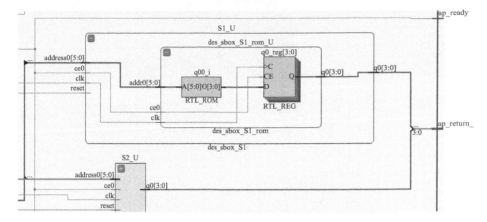

*Figure 11.12   Schematic of the details of a single S-box*

Implementation of P is done by interchanging the input connection from input to output. The schematic is shown in Figure 11.14. ser_read and ap_return are the input and output pins, respectively. The latency of P function is zero for 4 ns path delay. It does not cause any stalls in the pipeline and the output is made available in the same clock cycle.

The pipelined design for function F is shown in Figure 11.15. Registers are inserted between functions to store the intermediate results during pipeline execution. The expansion function, XOR and a part of S-box function form the first stage of the pipeline. It takes 3 clock cycles for execution. The rest of S-box function and Permutation function forms the second stage of the pipeline. It takes 2 clock cycles for the completion of the second stage pipeline.

### 11.3.2.7   32-bit Swap

Swapping is being carried out by dividing the 64 bit output from Feistel rounds into two 32 bit halves and interchanging the two halves as shown in Equation (11.10).

$$Left_{i(1...32)} = Right_{i-1(33...64)}$$
$$Right_{i(33...64)} = Left_{i-1(1...32)}$$

(11.10)

Hardware realization of swap function is done by interchanging the internal connection between input and output ports as shown in Figure 11.16. The output pins are connected to the corresponding input pins to get a swapped output.

### 11.3.2.8   Inverse initial permutation

Inverse initial permutation is performed by rearranging the message bits according to the inverse permutation table. The hardware realization can be done by changing the interconnections of the input and output pins depending on the table as shown in Figure 11.17. The permutation rules will not change with changes in the input message.

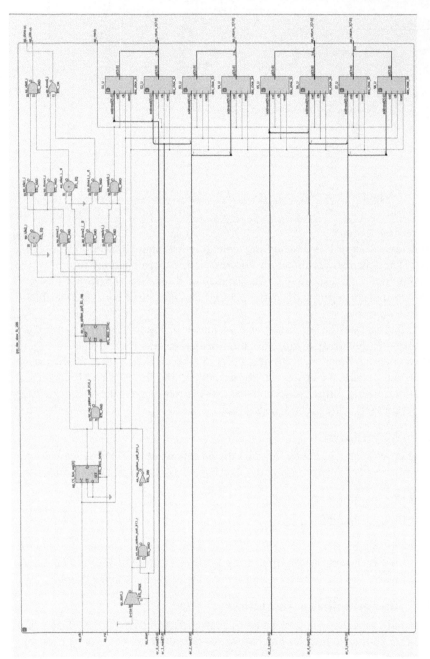

*Figure 11.13 Overall schematic view of the S-box function*

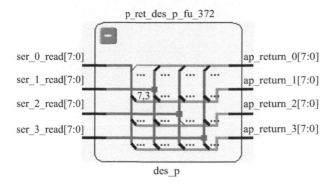

*Figure 11.14    Schematic of permutation, P*

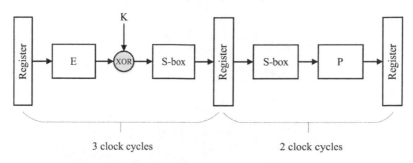

*Figure 11.15    Pipelined design of function, F*

### 11.3.2.9    Efficiency of the system

The efficiency of AES accelerator on XC7VX690T device can be calculated by (11.6)–(11.8). The latency of the overall system is 68 clock cycles. The system is executed with a clock frequency of 250 MHz. The throughput obtained for the pipelined design is 235 Mbps and the resource utilization is 873 slices. Hence, the efficiency of the system is 0.269 Mbps.

Neelam *et al.* [18] have proposed FPGA implementation of triple DES. Authors in [19] have implemented DES based on time variable permutation.

## 11.4    Secure hash algorithm (SHA-256)

SHA was developed by the NIST in 1993 used for generating hash code. SHA-256 was released in 2002 with increased security. SHA is a message digest algorithm for providing authentication of messages. The algorithm operates on 512-bit input block and produces a fixed length output of 256 bits [8].

The algorithm consists of basic steps—appending padding bits, append length, initialize hash buffer, and process message in 512-bit blocks. Padding is done by adding a bit value 1 and then followed by *n* number of zeros, where *n* is the smallest

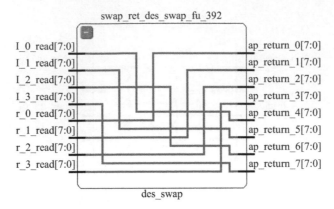

*Figure 11.16    Schematic of swap function*

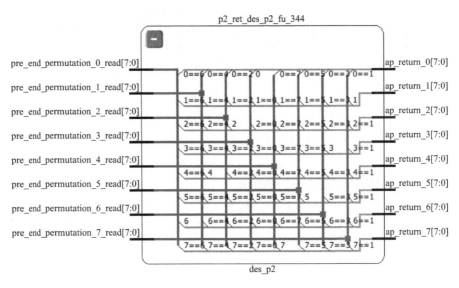

*Figure 11.17    Schematic of inverse initial permutation*

positive integer such that $m + 1 + n \equiv 448$, where $m$ is the message length. The length of the initial message is appended in the next field [8].

### 11.4.1    Block decomposition

For each 512-bit input block M, 64 words of 32 bits are to be created.

First 16 words are obtained by dividing M into 32-bit blocks as shown in (11.11).

$$M \rightarrow W_1 || W_2 || \ldots || W_{16} \tag{11.11}$$

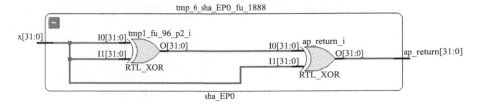

*Figure 11.18   Schematic of $\sigma_0(W)$ hardware implementation*

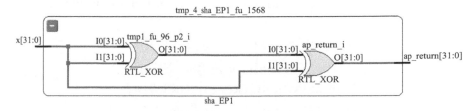

*Figure 11.19   Schematic of $\sigma_1(W)$ hardware implementation*

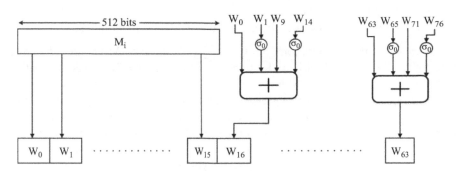

*Figure 11.20    Calculation of $W_0$ to $W_{63}$ from $M_i$*

The rest of the words are obtained as given in (11.12).

$$W_i = \sigma_1(W_{i-2}) + W_{i-7} + \sigma_0(W_{i-15}) + W_{i-16} \tag{11.12}$$

where

$$\sigma_0(W) = ROTR(w, 1)XOR\ ROTR(w, 8)XOR\ SHR(w, 7)$$
$$\sigma_1(W) = ROTR(w, 19)XOR\ ROTR(w, 61)XOR\ SHR(w, 6)$$

The schematic for the hardware implementation of $\sigma_0(W)$ and $\sigma_1(W)$ is shown in Figures 11.18 and 11.19, respectively. XOR gates are used to realize the corresponding function. x is the input pin and ap_return is the output pin.

Figure 11.20 shows the process of obtaining $W_t$ from $M_i$. $W_0, W_1 \ldots W_{15}$ are obtained by dividing the 512-bit input into 16 parts, each with 32 bits. The rest of

$W_i$ are calculated from these $W_i$ values using rotate right, shift right and XOR as shown in (11.12).

## 11.4.2   Round function

The round function of SHA is shown in Figure 11.19. The round function is repeated 64 times. A, B, C, D, E, F, G, and H are initialized with 64-bit constant values. The process of round function is shown in Figure 11.21.

Round function does shuffling of each 64-bit hash codes and series of logical functions (ANDs, NOTs, ORs, XORs, ROTates) with $W_t$ and $K_t$. The process provides avalanche and completeness properties. The elements in Figure 11.21 are given in (11.13).

$$CH(e, f, g) = (e \text{ AND } f) \text{ XOR} (\text{NOT } e \text{ AND } g)$$
$$MAJ(a, b, c) = (a \text{ AND } b) \text{ XOR } (a \text{ AND } c) \text{XOR} (b \text{ AND } c)$$
$$\sum 1(a) = \text{ROTR}(a, 28) \text{XOR ROTR}(a, 34) \text{XOR ROTR}(a, 39)$$
$$\sum 0(e) = \text{ROTR}(e, 14) \text{XOR ROTR}(e, 18) \text{XOR ROTR}(e, 41)$$

$$(11.13)$$

$\boxed{+}$ = addition modulo 2^64
$K_t$ = an additive constant
$W_t$ = a 32-bit word derived from the current 512-bit input block.

Hardware implementation of CH, $\sum 1$, $\sum 0$, and MAJ are shown in Figures 11.22, 11.23, 11.24, and 11.25, respectively. The functions are realized using AND and XOR gates along with rotation operation as shown in (11.13).

The pipelined hardware implementation of round function and $W_t$ calculation is shown in Figure 11.26. The calculation of $W_0$ to $W_{16}$ is being done in one clock cycle. Calculation of $W_{17}$ to $W_{58}$ needs 10 clock cycles. The stages are sub-pipelined so that all stages require one clock cycle for completion. Finally, the values $W_{59}$ to $W_{63}$ and the functions CH, $\sum 1$, MJ, and $\sum 0$ are completed in the last pipeline stage in one clock cycle. The functions CH, $\sum 1$, MJ, and $\sum 0$ for 64 rounds are unrolled and executed within one clock cycle. Hence, the entire

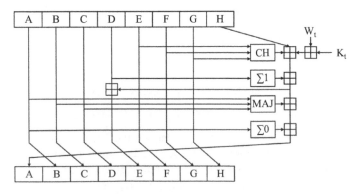

*Figure 11.21   Round function of SHA-256*

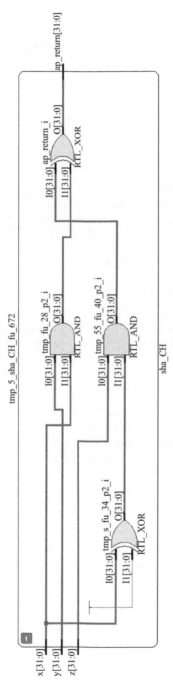

*Figure 11.22  Schematic of CH hardware implementation*

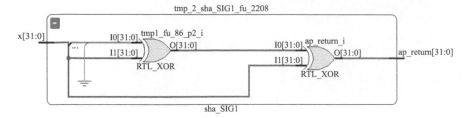

Figure 11.23    Schematic of $\sum1$ hardware implementation

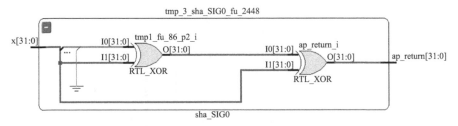

Figure 11.24    Schematic of $\sum0$ hardware implementation

round function takes one 12 clock cycles for the execution of 64 rounds. The initiation interval of the pipelined design is one since each pipeline stage can be reused after each clock cycle.

### 11.4.3    Efficiency of the system

The accelerator on XC7VX690T device has an initiation interval of one for the given pipelined design for a clock frequency of 250 MHz. Hence, the throughput does not depend on the latency of the system. The throughput of the accelerator is 64 Gbps. The number of slice utilization is 2,873. Hence, the efficiency of the system is 22.2 Mbps.

## 11.5    MD5

MD5 is a message digest algorithm developed by Professor Ronald Rivest of MIT. The algorithm produces 128-bit hash value for variable length input. MD5 algorithm divides the message into 512-bit blocks. Padding is added to the last block so that length of the message is 448 mod 512. The length of the message is inserted at the end. The algorithm contains mainly four functions, with each operation being repeated 16 times. The functions are called compression functions [8].

### 11.5.1    Processing of message block

Four buffers—A, B, C, and D, each of 32 bits are used for the calculation of hash code. It is initialized with a predefined constant. Each 512-bit input message block

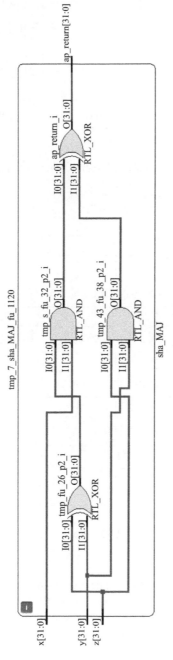

Figure 11.25   Schematic of MAJ hardware implementation

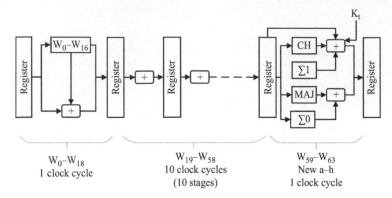

*Figure 11.26    Multistage pipelined architecture of round function and $W_t$ calculation*

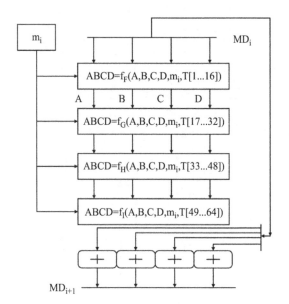

*Figure 11.27    MD5 processing steps*

is divided into 16 words of 32 bit each. The processing of message consists of four rounds as shown in Figure 11.27. Each round mixes the contents of four buffers with input blocks using four functions—F, G, H, I. These functions contain 16 operations. The function f, which performs each one of the four functions—F, G, H, I, is called a compression function [8].

## 11.5.2 Compression function

Each round of MD5 has 16 operations of the form as shown in Figure 11.28. X[k] denotes 32-bit input message and T[i] denotes 32-bit constant calculated based on (11.14). A, B, C, and D are initialized with predefined constants. Function g is performed on these inputs as shown in (11.12) and (11.13) [8]:

$$A = B + ((A + g(B, C, D) + X[k] + T[i]) <<< s) \qquad (11.14)$$

A, B, C, and D are message digest buffers, g denotes any one of the functions—F, G, H, I defined, as in (11.15).

$$\begin{aligned} F(B,C,D) &= (B \wedge C) \vee (\sim B \wedge D) \\ G(B,C,D) &= (B \wedge D) \vee (C \wedge \sim D) \\ H(B,C,D) &= B \oplus C \oplus D \\ I(B,C,D) &= C \oplus (B \wedge \sim D) \end{aligned} \qquad (11.15)$$

X[k] denotes the *k*th 32-bit word of the message block.
T[i] is a function of sine that can be calculated based on (11.16).

$$2^{32} \times abs(\sin(i)), \quad 0 < i < 65 \qquad (11.16)$$

Hardware implementation of functions—F, G, H, I, and shifting function are shown in Figures 11.29, 11.30, 11.31, 11.32, and 11.33, respectively. The basic logic operations are implemented using basic gates. The input and output sizes are 32 bits as seen in the schematic.

The pipeline design of MD5 compression function is shown in Figure 11.34. The calculation of $A + g(B, C, D) + X[k] + T[i]$ is being done in the first stage of the pipeline which takes one clock cycle at 4 ns path delay. The shifting operation of the above result is done in the next pipeline stage with one clock cycle. Finally,

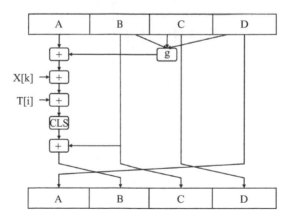

*Figure 11.28   MD5 compression function*

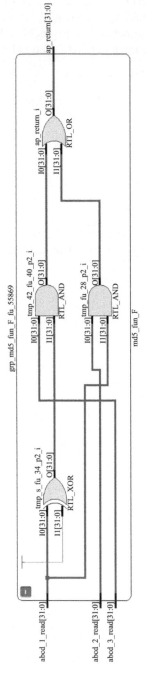

*Figure 11.29  Schematic of F hardware implementation*

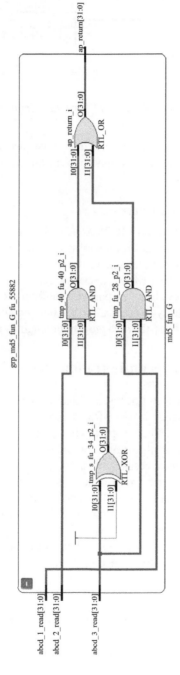

*Figure 11.30  Schematic of G hardware implementation*

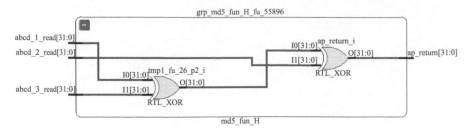

*Figure 11.31    Schematic of H hardware implementation*

the addition of shifted result and B is done in the last pipeline stage in one clock cycle. The initial values of message digest buffers and values of T are stored in FPGA registers.

### 11.5.3   *Efficiency of the system*

The latency of the accelerator on XC7VX690T device is 235 clock cycles at 250 MHz frequency and the initiation interval is one for the pipelined design. The resource utilization is 1,984 slices. Hence, the throughput and efficiency of the accelerator are 32 Gbps and 16.1 Mbps, respectively.

The next section describes about the partial reconfiguration feature of FPGA and developing an adaptive security system using partial reconfiguration feature. The security system makes use of the four cryptographic engines as building blocks.

## 11.6   Dynamic partial reconfiguration (DPR)

In AISC, the hardware circuit cannot be modified after it is manufactured. DPR is the property of FPGA to change a part of hardware circuit without disturbing the execution of rest of the circuit. This property saves space, power and allows change of circuit due to the change of algorithms parameters or faults. Space and power are saved by loading only the necessary modules to the hardware at a time. Static power can be reduced by loading only the needed module. Keeping unused accelerator on hardware consumes a lot of static power [20].

Figure 11.35 shows the overview of the DPR. The part in FPGA device where reconfiguration has to be carried out is called reconfigurable partition (RP). The module or accelerator which is to be loaded into RP is called reconfiguration module (RM). More than one RM can be mapped to a RP. Only the necessary module can be loaded at a time.

## 11.7   Security system with AES, DES, SHA, and MD5 using DPR

The security system consists of two encryption and two authentication accelerators which can be configured to FPGA device anytime when they are needed. The system can be used to provide real-time data security for IoTs, embedded systems, electronic

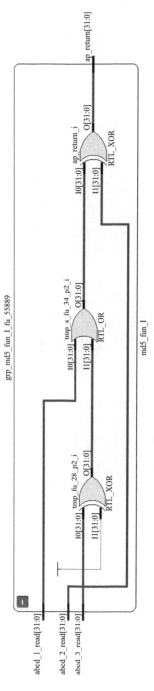

*Figure 11.32   Schematic of I hardware implementation*

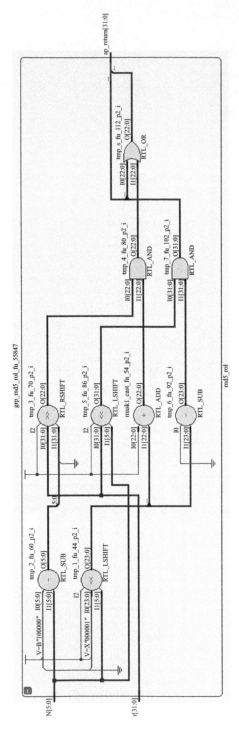

Figure 11.33   Schematic of shifting hardware implementation

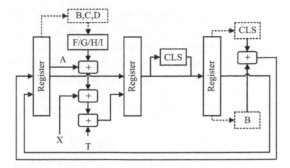

*Figure 11.34   Pipeline design of compression function*

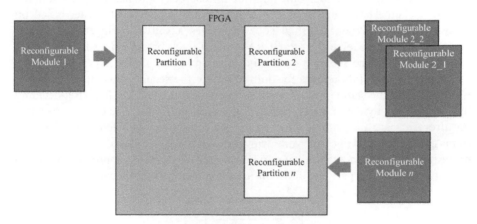

*Figure 11.35   Overview of DPR*

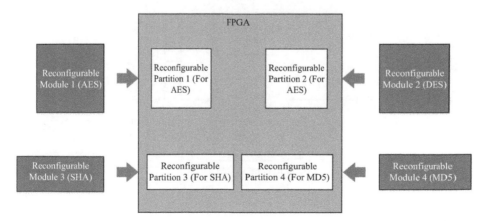

*Figure 11.36   Proposed security system using DPR*

commerce applications, network processor, etc. Building IPSec security system for the above-mentioned area is a main application of the proposed security system.

The security system is created using two encryption accelerators—AES and DES and two authentication accelerators—SHA and MD5. The system uses DPR feature to load or create the accelerator on demand in FPGA. Figure 11.36 shows the proposed security system that loads the encryption/authentication accelerator on demand. AES is loaded into RP1, DES into RP2, SHA into RP3, and MD5 into RP4.

### 11.7.1    Partial reconfiguration controller (PRC)

The PRC is responsible for swapping in and swapping out the RMs into and out of RPs. PRC can be configured to receive the software as well as hardware triggers. For the security system, the PRC was configured to receive software triggers. The reconfigurable partition and some additional resources (optional) are present in the virtual socket. The virtual socket manager controls the virtual socket based on software trigger. When a virtual socket receives a software trigger, it activates the fetch path to receive the stored RM to load into corresponding RP. The PRC configuration for the security system is shown in Figure 11.37 [20].

The implementation steps for doing DPR for the security system are shown in Figure 11.38. The static module contains interfaces and ports for IO. After deciding the static and dynamic parts, IPs for dynamic parts are created and resource requirements are noted. The PRC has to be configured with four virtual socket managers for receiving software triggers. After the synthesis of design, floor planning and implementation have to be carried out. Blanking configuration which contains only static part and full configuration has to be implemented separately.

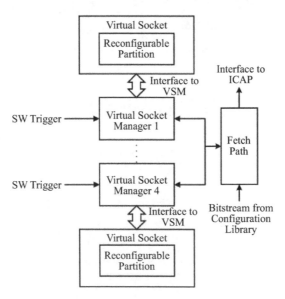

*Figure 11.37    Partial reconfiguration controller configuration for the security system*

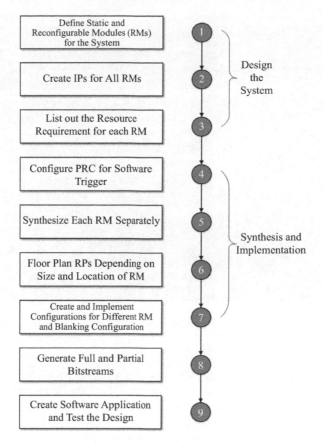

*Figure 11.38   Steps for implementing the DPR system*

After generating full bitstream and partial bitstream, testing with a software can be performed [21].

The chip layout of the security system on XC7VX690T device is shown in Figure 11.39. Four RPs for AES, DES, SHA, and MD5 are seen as blocks. The RMs are loaded into the RPs dynamically when the need arises.

The security system can be used in embedded systems, IoTs, cloud server, network security processor, etc. One of the applications where the system found useful is creating the IPSec security system. Nguyen *et al.* [22] and Wang *et al.* [23] have proposed PR systems for IPSec using AES/3DES and SHA. The systems has used partial reconfiguration feature to develop the system.

## 11.8   Future direction

The cryptographic engines for FPGA are stored and dumped into the device as bitstream. Researches show that these bitstreams are prone to many attacks such

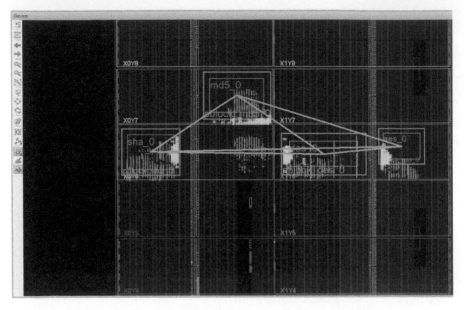

*Figure 11.39    Chip layout of security system on XC7VX690T device*

as reverse engineering, cloning, insertion of Trojans. The security measure provided by the manufacturers is encrypting the bitstream. Many researchers have successfully cracked that encryption since the bitstream gives clues of the design and the existing encryption techniques were developed not for hardware protection [24–27]. The future direction can be directed toward the ways to encrypt a hardware design, not the bitstream. Logic encryption is a promising and an evolving field where encryption of hardware is performed using the insertion of logic gates or multiplexors. Encrypted hardware circuits cannot be reverse engineered or insert Trojans without the key. Cloning of encrypted circuit results in malfunctioned hardware. Not only FPGA designs but all electronic devices also can be protected from the threats that are pointed out at the beginning of this section.

## References

[1]    Hauck, S and DeHon, A. *Reconfigurable computing: the theory and practice of FPGA-based computation*. Vol. 1. Burlington, MA: Elsevier, 2010.

[2]    Kilts, S. *Advanced FPGA design: architecture, implementation, and optimization*. Hoboken, NJ: John Wiley & Sons, Hoboken, NJ, 2007.

[3]    Google (2016). Encryption at Rest in Google Cloud Platform Google Cloud Platform Encryption Whitepaper.

[4]    HP (2013). HP Atalla Cloud Encryption Securing Data in the Cloud, Technical White Paper.

[5] Tarafdar N, Eskandari N, Lin T, and Chow P. Designing for FPGAs in the Cloud. IEEE Design & Test. 2018;35(1):23–9.

[6] Asiatici M, George N, Vipin K, Fahmy SA, and Ienne P. Virtualized execution runtime for FPGA accelerators in the cloud. IEEE Access. 2017;5:1900–10.

[7] Daemen, J and Rijmen, V. *The design of Rijndael: AES-the advanced encryption standard.* Springer Science & Business Media, Berlin, Heidelberg, 2013.

[8] William, S. *Cryptography and network security: principles and practices.* Pearson Education India, 2006.

[9] Heron S. Advanced encryption standard (AES). Network Security. 2009;2009(12):8–12.

[10] Chellam MB, and Natarajan R. AES hardware accelerator on FPGA with improved throughput and resource efficiency. Arabian Journal for Science and Engineering. 2018;43(12):6873–6890.

[11] Hennessy, John L., and David A. Patterson. *Computer architecture: A quantitative approach.* Waltham, MA: Elsevier, 2011.

[12] Xilinx(UG871) (2013) Vivado Design Suite Tutorial: High-Level Synthesis. https://www.xilinx.com/support/documentation/sw_manuals/xilinx2014_1/ug871-vivado-high-level-synthesistutorial.pdf.

[13] Xilinx(UG892) (2014). Vivado Design Suite User Guide: Design Flows Overview (UG892). https://www.xilinx.com/support/documentation/sw_manuals/xilinx2013_3/ug892-vivado-design-flows-overview.pdf.

[14] Xilinx(UG903) (2013). Vivado Design Suite User Guide: Using Constraints (UG903). https://www.xilinx.com/support/documentation/sw_manuals/xilinx2013_1/ug903-vivado-using-constraints.pdf.

[15] Oukili S, and Bri S. High throughput FPGA implementation of advanced encryption standard algorithm. Telkomnika. 2017 1;15(1):494.

[16] Lee H, Paik Y, Jun J, Han Y, and Kim SW. High-throughput low-area design of AES using constant binary matrix-vector multiplication. Microprocessors and Microsystems. 2016 1;47:360–8.

[17] Farashahi RR, Rashidi B, and Sayedi SM. FPGA based fast and high-throughput 2-slow retiming 128-bit AES encryption algorithm. Microelectronics Journal. 2014;45(8):1014–25.

[18] Neelam R, and Soni D. FPGA implementation of high speed triple data encryption standard. InICT in Business Industry & Government (ICTBIG), International Conference on 2016. pp. 1–5. IEEE.

[19] Oukili S, and Bri S. FPGA implementation of Data Encryption Standard using time variable permutations. In 2015 27th International Conference on Microelectronics (ICM), 2015 Dec 20. pp. 126–29. IEEE.

[20] Koch, Dirk. *Partial reconfiguration on FPGAs: architectures, tools and applications.* Vol. 153. Springer Science & Business Media, New York, 2012.

[21] Xilinx(UG909) (2016). Vivado Design Suite User Guide Partial Reconfiguration, UG909 (v2016.1). https://www.xilinx.com/support/documentation/sw_manuals/xilinx2015_4/ug909-vivado-partial-reconfiguration.pdf.

[22]    Nguyen TT, Nguyen VC, Huynh TV, Luong QY, and Dang TH. Performance enhancement of encryption and authentication IP cores for IPSec based on multiple-core architecture and dynamic partial reconfiguration on FPGA. In 2018 2nd International Conference on Recent Advances in Signal Processing, Telecommunications & Computing (SigTelCom), 2018 Jan 29. pp. 126–131. IEEE.

[23]    Wang H, Bai G, and Chen H. A GBPS IPSEC SSL security processor design and implementation in an FPGA prototyping platform. Journal of Signal Processing Systems. 2010 1;58(3):311–24.

[24]    Soni, Ritesh K. Open-Source Bitstream Generation for FPGAs. Diss. Virginia Tech, 2013.

[25]    Swierczynski P, Fyrbiak M, Koppe P, and Paar C. FPGA Trojans through detecting and weakening of cryptographic primitives. IEEE Transactions on Computer-Aided Design of Integrated Circuits and Systems. 2015;34(8): 1236–49.

[26]    San I, Fern N, Koc CK, and Cheng KT. Trojans modifying soft-processor instruction sequences embedded in FPGA bitstreams. In 2016 26th International Conference on Field Programmable Logic and Applications (FPL), 2016 Aug 29. pp. 1–4. IEEE.

[27]    Beckhoff C, Koch D, and Torresen J. The xilinx design language (xdl): Tutorial and use cases. In 2011 6th International Workshop on Reconfigurable Communication-centric Systems-on-Chip (ReCoSoC), 2011 Jun 20. pp. 1–8. IEEE.

*Chapter 12*

# Data protection laws

*Hiba Alginahi[1], Yasser M. Alginahi[2]*
*and Muhammad Nomani Kabir[3]*

Data protection, data privacy, and information privacy are all terms defined as the process of protecting important data/information from corruption, scam, fraud, loss, or compromise. This includes the relationship between the data collection and technology, the public perception and expectation of privacy, and the political as well as legal roots surrounding that data. Therefore, data protection laws aim to provide a balance between the individual's privacy rights and the proper use of data.

Data protection is a concern for individuals and organizations who collect, analyze, store, and transmit data; such data could be written on paper or stored on a computer system or network. Both ways of handling information may be prune to loss, damage, or errors. Documents handled as hardcopies may be copied easily, stolen, lost, destroyed, etc. Therefore, it is very difficult to protect such information available in hardcopy format and, in reality, there is no secure method that would safeguard such documents. One may propose to store them in vaults which are secure and protect documents from humidity, light, and fire; however, many questions would be raised in the process of applying/handling such securing strategy before and after storage. On the other hand, electronic information stored on electronic devices and networks needs to be handled very carefully so that these physical systems and the information stored in them do not fall in the hands of those who may use it in fraud, abuse, scam, etc., in addition to policies which should be in place to secure information during the process of transmission and storage. In this chapter, issues related to data protection laws are discussed.

## 12.1 Introduction

In this era of technology, personal, private, or public systems or devices require protection of information which are encountered in daily dealings. The types of information processed may include but not limited to systems used in credit

[1]Department of Forensic Science, University of Windsor, Canada
[2]Department of Electrical and Computer Engineering, University of Windsor, Canada
[3]Faculty of Computer Systems & Software Engineering, Universiti Malaysia Pahang, Malaysia

bureaus, banks, law enforcement, health services, education, and government services. Hence, these systems need to have laws and policies that govern the use, transmission, storage, and processing of information on their premises, computer systems, and networks. Therefore, legislations, policies, guidelines, rules, laws, or directives must be available to guarantee the protection of information for organizations and individuals. For organizations, any digitally stored information must be properly protected, and this includes personal, social, medical, education, marketing, products, and financial information for the organization, employees, partners, and clients. For individuals, it is important that personal information is not exposed, shared, or used without prior consent. Therefore, data protection is not just a legal necessity, nevertheless it is crucial to protecting and maintaining organizations.

The importance of creating and using data protection laws increases as the amount of data created, processed, and stored continues to grow at record rates, i.e., information explosion. Data is exponentially growing presenting many challenges to organizations and researchers [1]. Some of the main challenges include management complexity; data centers power, cooling, and space limitations; data movement; storage; shortage of skills to manage and integrate big data systems, and development/implementation of Data Protection Laws (DPLs). Such challenges alerted organizations to invest in big data solutions and cloud technology.

Some interesting statistics/facts presented in an article written by Bernard Marr, in 2015, show that data volumes are exponentially exploding; for example, data created between 2013 and 2015 is more than that created in the entire previous history of humanity. It is also predicted that by 2020 approximately 1.7 MB of information on the Internet will be created every second for every person on this earth reaching a total of approximately 44 trillion GB [2]. In August 2015, the number of people who used Facebook exceeded one billion in a single day and the numbers are increasing [3]. In addition, there is a massive growth in video and image data used especially when using social media, such as, Facebook, LinkedIn, WhatsApp, Twitter, YouTube, Instagram, and Snapchat. It is predicted that, in November 2015, every minute up to 500 h of video was uploaded to YouTube [4]. The Internet is reaching all parts of the world and more data is being collected every second and as a result the Internet of Things (IoT) has exploded with the billions of devices being connected to the Internet, meaning that more data is being collected, transferred, and stored. IoT-connected devices installed worldwide are estimated to increase from 20.35 billion in 2017 to 70.44 billion in 2025 [5].

The need to protect personal and sensitive data collected from individuals or businesses by government organizations and other businesses is to prevent data from being misused by other parties for fraud schemes, identity thefts, etc. Information that businesses usually store includes but not limited to names, addresses, e-mails, phone numbers, bank accounts, credit card details, and health and tax information. DPLs exist to provide the balance between the ability of businesses/ organizations to use data for the purposes they are intended for and the rights of individuals to privacy. Therefore, the purpose of DPLs should guarantee that individual's information is not processed without their consent. The rapid growth of IT and the increase use of Internet in our daily activities and interactions make

DPLs a crucial requirement for businesses to follow. By using the Internet, information is transferred, shared, collected, and stored immediately; therefore, organizations must follow DPLs to process and use personal data, so that it does not fall in the wrong hands. Undoubtedly, it is upon the shoulders of the organizations to follow strict security and DPLs to avoid any consequences which may result from not applying or implementing such polices.

The 2016 data breach investigations report by Verizon showed that in 93 percent of the cases where data was stolen, it took few minutes for the systems to be compromised; however, most of the time the organizations were not aware of the breach and typically customers or law-enforcement are the ones who sound the alarms [6]. This shows that the system was exposed to hackers for an undefined period during which more data could be exposed. Another recent example is the Equifax breach reported on September 7, 2017, which impacted approximately 143 million US consumers as well as some Canadian consumers [7]. However, on the same day Equifax announced the breach, it notified the public that it was a victim to a massive cyberattack from May 13 to July 30. Equifax's security team noticed the hack on 29 July; however, it did not inform its customers until September 2018. On 8 May, the executive managers of Equifax submitted a "statement for the record" to the Securities and Exchange Commission (SEC) detailing the extent of the consumer data breach it first reported on 7 September. In this report, approximately 146.6 million consumers records were exposed; such data include Social Security Numbers, date of births, drivers' licenses, phone numbers, e-mails, thousands of ID images, and credit card numbers, thus, allowing identity theft by thieves and fraudsters [7]. Even though such incidents occur on a daily basis, in the case of Equifax, according to fortune.com, over 10,000 other companies continued to download the software that was hacked permitting for more data to be vulnerable to more attacks [8]. Unfortunately, these companies keep using vulnerable systems due to the fact that they may not have alternate systems to use in order to run their businesses and as a result customer's information is at more risk of being exposed to intruders who may take advantage of unsecure systems. In some cases, it may take businesses years to discover the detail of a breach; for example, the case of Yahoo where it took the company few years to present the total number of users affected by a breach which happened in 2013 and 2014. Initially, Yahoo reported an incident in 2016 that around a billion users' accounts were exposed and in 2017 the number of users was updated to be around 3 billion users [9].

The advancements in technology allowed the increase in more devices as well as smart devices being connected to the Internet causing an exponential increase in data being produced, transmitted, processed, and stored. With this technological prosperity, more challenges evolved in terms of infrastructure, as well as information security. Therefore, the need for tougher data protection laws is inevitable in view of the recent breaching incidents which call for strict measures to protect personal data. Thus, there should be immediate discovery and announcement of hacking occurrences to limit the vulnerability of data being exposed, also immediate communication with those whose data were hacked, so that they can take some measures to avoid any inconvenience that may affect them such as, suffering or distress from identity theft. In taking such measures, organizations can avoid any unpredictable consequences.

The objective of this chapter is to provide an overview on understanding data protection laws and policies. In this chapter, the following topics are discussed: reasons for DPLs, principles of DPLs, data classification, global cyberlaws, DPLs and social media, EU General Data Protection Regulation (GDPR), challenges of DPLs and cybersecurity, data privacy and cyber security checklist, recommendations and future direction in this area, and finally concluding remarks.

## 12.2   Why data protection policies?

Data vulnerability due to hacking, breaching, theft, loss, etc. and the afflictions due to the consequences of breaching are the main reasons why data protection policies are needed. Therefore, in this technological era, governments are imposing the implementation of data protection policies upon them and requiring organizations to implement DPLs to govern the usage, flow, and storage of information. The data exposure statistics are overwhelmingly alarming making it a large responsibility upon governments and businesses to take measures to protect personal and sensitive information. According to [10], as of August 20, 2018, at the time this book is being written, the total number of data records lost or stolen since 2013 is approximately 9,728,017,988 and only 4 percent of the breaches were "secure breaches." This shows that "secure breaches" contain encrypted data and when stolen are rendered useless. The breach level index shows that the frequency of records being stolen or lost is approximately 4.7 million/day, which is approximately 55 records every second [10].

In data protection, organizations usually provide comprehensive suite of policies that govern their operations with individuals from the public, the collection of information and internally governing the dealing with information. Such internal and external legislations/policies/guidelines/rules/laws/directives are also used to limit negative activities, encourage certain behaviors, or drive good practices, thus providing the employees with the support they need to perform their jobs with knowledge and confidence. The polices can be a guide to achieve and deliver these objectives. Therefore, some of the reasons for developing data protection policies include but not limited to [11,12]:

- Considering the law: DPLs place legal responsibility upon the shoulders of the data controller who oversees how and why personal data is processed in accordance to the principles and comprising enforceable standards over the way individual's data is collected, managed, processed, used, and stored. These principles are interpreted by the controller to be applied to specific circumstances in order to comply with the law.
- Limiting liability: by applying adequate policies, businesses and organizations could have limited liability in cases of breach or fraud.
- Maintaining compliance with complex regulations: nowadays, it is the intention of each organization to comply with data privacy regulations, as penalties for noncompliance continue to rise.

- Improving business processes: implementing data protection policies has a positive and practical commercial impact on organizations, and this includes consistency in decision-making, increasing awareness, making personal data management and infrastructure more resilient, instilling trust and confidence in individuals when they are deciding to share their data.
- Avoiding fines, lost revenue, and loss of customers: "data breaches can wreak havoc on an organization's bottom line through bad publicity, [12]" fines, legal action, and loss of strategic customers.
- Avoiding bad publicity and legal action: not having policies in place could cause practical and commercial risks. For example, an organization's reputation could be damaged, and this would be more serious than receiving a fine. Therefore, data breaches making headlines can inflict devastation on an organization. Table 12.1 shows some recent publicized breaches.
- Protect against theft, breach, fraud, and accidental disclosure of personal information by clients, partners, and employees, as well as monitor unacceptable employee's conduct.
- Data protection in cloud applications and storage: it is very critical to have policies in place to govern the protection of information in virtual and cloud models.

Finally, the goal of each business/organization is to provide security policies which will eliminate any breaching that could cause harm to its employees, partners, and clients. Therefore, secure and automated quality control methods to monitor the

*Table 12.1    Examples of publicized breaches and the number of users impacted*

| No. | Year | Organization | No. of users impacted |
|---|---|---|---|
| 1 | 2018 | My Heritage | 92 million |
| 2 | 2017 | Equifax | 147.9 million users |
| 3 | 2016 | Adult Friend Finder | 412.2 million accounts |
| 4 | 2016 | Uber | 57 million Uber users, 600,000 drivers exposed |
| 5 | 2014 | Facebook (Cambridge Analytica was responsible) | Over 50 million |
| 6 | 2015 | Anthem | 78.8 million |
| 7 | 2014 | JP Morgan Chase | 7 million small businesses, 76 million households |
| 8 | 2014 | eBay | 145 million users |
| 9 | 2014 | Home Depot | 56 million customers |
| 10 | 2013 | Target Stores | 110 million |
| 11 | 2013 | Adobe | 38 million users |
| 12 | 2012–2014 | US Office of Personnel Management | 22 million employees |
| 13 | 2013–2014 | Yahoo | 3 billion users |
| 14 | 2011 | Sony's PlayStation Network | 77 million |
| 15 | 2011 | RSA Security | 40 million employee records |
| 17 | 2008 | Heartland Payment Systems | 134 million |
| 18 | 2006 | TJX Companies, Inc. | 94 million |

compliance of organization with DPLs could help improve organizational and technical efficiencies, provide methods for more comprehensive information governance, and promote compliance. Hence, ensuring that organizations adhere to data protection policies is crucial as the effects of noncompliance can be devastating for individuals and organizations. Table 12.1 shows some of the biggest breaches in the twenty-first century and the number of customers/users impacted [9,13].

## 12.2.1  *Principles of data protection laws*

Protecting personal and sensitive information, in accordance with the DPLs requires businesses to adhere to specific principles in order to keep individual's data accurate, safe, secure, and lawful. The basic principles of DPLs which are presented in many available laws may include but not limited to the following articles [14,15]:

- Data shall be collected and handled in a lawful and fair way for specified and stated purpose.
- Data collected should be adequate, relevant, and not excessive.
- Information collected cannot be disclosed to third parties unless specifically authorized by the individual or as stated by law.
- Individuals' records should be kept accurate, up to date and for no longer than intended.
- Procedures and periodic reporting mechanisms shall be available for individuals to check and ensure the accuracy of their data.
- Transmission of personal information to locations where "equivalent" DPLs cannot guarantee the data protection is prohibited.
- Data should be prepared and processed keeping in mind the rights of the individual.
- Some data is sensitive/classified and must not be collected unless under extreme circumstances.
- Data should continuously be kept secure and protected.

## 12.3  Data classification

Data classification is the method of organizing data by related categories/classes, so that it may be prepared, utilized, processed, and secured more proficiently and efficiently. The classification of data includes tagging and labeling, which makes the data effectively searchable and trackable; it removes data repetitions, resulting in faster search, less storage, and backup costs. Thus, data classification is important when it comes to compliance, security, and risk management. In brief, data classification is a valuable approach that empowers appropriate security reactions according to the data type being copied, retrieved, stored, or transmitted [16].

## 12.3.1  *Types of data classification*

Data classification includes a multitude of tags, defining the type of data, confidentiality, integrity, and availability. Confidentiality is the preserving of authorized restrictions on information access and disclosure [17]. Integrity is guarding against inappropriate information alteration or destruction. Availability is ensuring timely and reliable access to and use of information. Therefore, the unauthorized information disclosure and alteration or disruption of access to information could have a disastrous adverse impact on the individuals, and organizations' operations and resources. The data's sensitivity level is frequently classified based on different levels of significance and confidentiality, in accordance to the security procedures in place to ensure the protection of each classification level. For example, the common sensitivity classification types for a commercial organization may classify data as confidential, private, sensitive or public, and for military organizations into top secret, secret, confidential, sensitive, but not classified and unclassified. Therefore, such type of data classification is considered a starting point for many organizations in the process of data classification, and then additional identification and tagging strategies and measures that label/classify data based on its relevance to the organization, quality, importance, and other classifications.

## 12.3.2  The data classification process

Data strategies differ depending on the organization, which generates different volumes and types of data. Therefore, classification can support an organization to meet the conditions for retrieving information, it is a complex process, unless it is automated by organizations according to certain criteria and categories which will help classify data, recognize and state its objectives, outline the roles, and implement security procedures that correspond with data categories and tags. Thus, proper implementation of this process will provide people involved with a system within which to operate. Guidelines/procedures/policies/laws should be well defined, straightforward, considerate of the security requirements of data types, and are easily understood by employees to achieve compliance. The data classification process does not only make information easy to find, it also makes sense of the huge data available at any given time. In other words, it presents the data in an organized way within the organization's control, where it is saved, retrieved, and protected. Therefore, the implementation of this process offers a framework that facilitates acceptable data protection procedures and promotes employee compliance with privacy and security policies [17–19].

It is very expensive to classify and tag all the data in a database. Usually organizations do not implement this, and full-data classification may only be carried out by governments. Therefore, organizations need to be selective on the type of data to classify. So, it is a good idea to classify data in line with the company's confidentiality requirements in addition to considering the integrity and availability of the data. Moreover, "A plan must be put in place, by an organization or data architecture team, to first source the desired data, standardizing the path to it, documenting the data's structure and general content along with any known business rules, and then ultimately communicating this initial set of information to relevant constituencies [20]."

Once the strategies for "metadata" collection are established and realized, the organization can execute a "classification taxonomy" to tag the assets/resources of different types according to the significance level of the business, "This set of tags can range from its quality classification, to its encryption/security level, to its volatility." The continuous monitoring of the data classification system is vital to the success of any organization. As a result, information needs to be categorized and stored in specific storage tier to reduce cost as well as maintain compliance. Therefore, cost could be reduced by saving less important and outdated information to low performance cheaper storage archives and readily available data kept on high performance storage. "This way the system can be kept running at peak efficiency for users while still maintaining data for any compliance requirements and keeping costs at a manageable level [20]." This helps rank the data based on its sensitivity, importance, store it according to prearranged procedures, and manage its retention for compliance. No doubt that technology has been integrated in many areas, and data classification and protection is one of these areas; therefore, there are many tools which perform metadata analysis, discovery, repository management and data movement to track, identify and classify data. The success of a data classification system is a result of implementation strategy in accordance to the organization's objective.

In conclusion, the data classification process that comes with data security and compliance is very crucial since it is part of complying with the DPLs. Consequently, for an organization to apply data classification process, it must study the implications and costs before attempting to implement such process. Before implementing a classification system, organizations must consider the confidentiality, integrity, and availability of the data. In addition, it needs to receive the support of the executive management, as well as its employees who will work on the system, use effective metadata strategy to tag data, perform data cleansing to eliminate data redundancy, perform information audit to understand the type of data, implement the classification design, and finally test, monitor, and maintain the system [17–21].

## 12.4    Global cyberlaws

More than one-hundred countries including almost all European countries and most of the countries in the Caribbean and Latin America, Africa, and Asia have implemented comprehensive DPLs or in the process of drafting such laws. However, the US is notable for not adopting a comprehensive DPL but implemented limited legislation/policies in some areas. These legislation/policies are based on the Fair Information Practice developed in the 1970s by the Department for Health, Education and Welfare [22].

The United Nations Conference on Trade and Development (UNCTAD), a permanent intergovernmental body, was established by the UN General Assembly in 1964. The UNCTAD Global Cyberlaw Tracker which tracks the state of the following categories of cyberlaws legislations worldwide:

● Data protection and privacy
● Online consumer protection
● E-transactions
● Cybercrime

The statistics presented in Tables 12.2–12.6 were calculated and analyzed based on the data available from the UNCTAD, cyberlaws.net, and DLP piper, which is true as of May 2018. Table 12.2 shows the worldwide statistics of the state of cyberlaws legislations [23–26].

The different cyberlaws legislation categories are explained in detail.

*Table 12.2   The worldwide statistics of the state of cyberlaws legislations*

| Type of legislation | Legislation (%) | Draft legislation (%) | No legislation (%) | No data (%) |
|---|---|---|---|---|
| Data protection and privacy | 57.7 | 9.8 | 20.6 | 11.9 |
| Online consumer protection | 57.7 | 9.8 | 20.6 | 11.9 |
| E-transaction laws | 77.8 | 9.8 | 4.6 | 7.7 |
| Cybercrime laws | 72.2 | 9.3 | 18.0 | 0.5 |

*Table 12.3   The data protection and privacy legislation worldwide statistics*

| Continent | Legislation | Draft legislation | No legislation | No data | Total |
|---|---|---|---|---|---|
| Africa | 23 | 7 | 12 | 12 | 54 |
| Americas | 18 | 8 | 9 | 0 | 35 |
| Asia-Pacifica | 27 | 4 | 19 | 10 | 60 |
| Europe | 44 | 0 | 0 | 1 | 45 |
| Total | 112 | 19 | 40 | 23 | 194 |

*Table 12.4   The online consumer protection legislation worldwide statistics*

| Continent | Legislation | Draft legislation | No legislation | No data | Total |
|---|---|---|---|---|---|
| Africa | 23 | 7 | 12 | 12 | 54 |
| Americas | 18 | 8 | 9 | 0 | 35 |
| Asia-Pacifica | 27 | 4 | 19 | 10 | 60 |
| Europe | 44 | 0 | 0 | 1 | 45 |
| Total | 112 | 19 | 40 | 23 | 194 |

*Table 12.5   The e-transaction legislation worldwide statistics for each continent*

| Continent | Legislation | Draft legislation | No legislation | No data | Total |
|---|---|---|---|---|---|
| Africa | 29 | 12 | 4 | 9 | 54 |
| Americas | 31 | 3 | 1 | 0 | 35 |
| Asia-Pacifica | 47 | 4 | 4 | 5 | 60 |
| Europe | 44 | 0 | 0 | 1 | 45 |
| Total | 151 | 19 | 9 | 15 | 194 |

*Table 12.6    The cybercrime legislation worldwide statistics for each continent*

| Continent | Legislation | Draft legislation | No legislation | No data | Total |
|---|---|---|---|---|---|
| Africa | 28 | 11 | 15 | 0 | 54 |
| Americas | 26 | 3 | 6 | 0 | 35 |
| Asia-Pacifica | 42 | 4 | 14 | 0 | 60 |
| Europe | 44 | 0 | 0 | 1 | 45 |
| Total | 140 | 18 | 35 | 1 | 194 |

## 12.4.1    Data protection and privacy legislation

Based on the collected data from the UNCTAD, 112 countries have laid in place legislations to secure data and 19 more countries have drafted legislations. In data privacy, Africa and Asia show a relatively similar level of adoption, where more than 50 percent of their countries having a legislation in place. From Table 12.3, the overall 57.7 percent of the countries have legislations, 9.8 percent have drafted a legislation, 20.6 percent have no legislation, and no data available for 11.6 percent of the countries. This shows that more awareness is seen in this area. The European continent is considered ahead of other continents in this area, where almost all countries, 98 percent of its countries have legislations in all the four categories. Latin American countries, while following the European model of having comprehensive DPLs, tend to fall behind. The main reason for this limitation is that most DPLs were designed following the norms set by the 1995 European Data Protection Directive, which does not address the relatively new issues. This is considered a challenge for developing countries.

## 12.4.2    Online consumer protection legislation

The online consumer protection legislation statistics is shown in Table 12.4 and is shown to have exactly the same statistics as that for the data protection and privacy legislation. Overall 57.7 percent of the countries have legislations, 9.8 percent have drafted a legislation, 20.6 percent have no legislation, and no data is available for 11.6 percent of the countries.

## 12.4.3    E-transactions legislation

The statistics of e-transactions legislation worldwide are shown in Table 12.5. The adoption of this legislation shows more countries adapting e-transactions legislation compared to other legislations. The reason is that it is a prerequisite to have legislations for conducting online commercial transactions hence, e-transaction laws identify the legal comparability between electronic forms and paper-based of exchange, these laws have been implemented by 151 countries, i.e., 77.8 percent of the world countries, and 9.8 percent have drafted legislation. According to the UNCTAD, "while four out of five countries in Asia and Latin America have such laws in place, Eastern and Middle Africa lag behind."

## *12.4.4 Cybercrime legislation*

Table 12.6 shows that 140 countries had decreed cybercrime legislations; however, 35 countries had no cybercrime legislation in place. This shows that more countries are adopting cybercrime laws compared to DPLs and online consumer protection laws. Such laws are considered very important to governments to address the increase in cybercrime due to the wide use of the Internet and social media. Table 12.6 shows that over 80 percent of the countries have adopted or are acting on adopting legislations in this area.

Table 12.7 provides the overall statistics on the number of countries which have adapted or acting on adopting legislation in the four categories related to data protection, online consumer protection, e-transactions, and cybercrime laws. In Table 12.7, "Legislation" refers to the countries which have legislation or draft legislation. On the other hand, "No Legislation" refers to the total number of countries with "no legislation" and "no data available" for those countries. The statistics show that e-transactions legislation is the most widely adopted, with Africa having the least number of countries, 75 percent of its countries, adopted or drafted legislation in this area and in contrast, the Americas and Europe having the highest number of countries, 97 percent of their countries, adopting or drafted legislation in this area. In addition, Asia-Pacifica region shows that 85 percent of its countries have legislation or are acting on legislation in this area. This shows that more countries are becoming aware of the importance of such laws and more countries are working in updating, developing, and implementing such laws.

A list of the data protection legislation and draft legislation currently available is given in Table 12.8. This list reflects the data protection legislation/draft legislation compiled from [23–26] and is not, in anyway or form complete as countries are continuously legislating and/or updating their laws. In addition, the constitutions of most of these countries contain articles or clauses related to individual rights and privacy. It is clearly seen from Table 12.8 that many of the legislation are in need for an update especially after the publication of the European Union (EU) GDPR. Therefore, this list is accurate as on date this chapter is written.

The list in Table 12.8 clearly shows that most of the laws are old and do not address the relatively new issues evolved as a result of new technologies, such as cloud computing, IoT, and Big Data.

## 12.5 DPLs and social media

Social media (Facebook, Instagram, Snapchat, Twitter, LinkedIn, WhatsApp, etc.) has taken over our lives; people spend many hours a day using social media and many companies are recruiting and advertising on such platforms. People tend to post a lot more than necessary on their social media profiles from names, age, residence location, what they do and so much more. But how much of that information is protected by laws against the use of personal information online for the benefit of companies? Privacy is a concern that is faced globally; and many countries have laws protecting personal data and information from being unlawfully used.

*Table 12.7 Overall statistics on adopting legislation worldwide*

| | Africa (%) | | Americas (%) | | Asia-Pacifica (%) | | Europe (%) | |
|---|---|---|---|---|---|---|---|---|
| | Legislation | No legislation | Legislation | No legislation | Legislation | No legislation | Legislation | No legislation |
| Data protection and privacy | 55.6 | 44.4 | 74.3 | 25.7 | 51.7 | 48.3 | 97.8 | 2.2 |
| Online consumer protection | 55.6 | 44.4 | 74.3 | 25.7 | 51.7 | 48.3 | 97.8 | 2.2 |
| E-transaction | 75.9 | 24.1 | 97.1 | 2.9 | 85.0 | 15.0 | 97.8 | 2.2 |
| Cybercrime | 72.2 | 27.8 | 82.9 | 17.1 | 76.7 | 23.3 | 97.8 | 2.2 |

*Table 12.8   List of countries and the title of data protection legislation/draft legislation*

| No. | Country | Title of legislation/draft legislation |
|-----|---------|----------------------------------------|
| 1 | Albania | Law no. 9887 on the Protection of Personal Data |
| 2 | Andorra | Qualified Law 15/2003 of 18 December on the protection of personal data |
| 3 | Angola | Law No. 22/11 of the Protection of Personal Data of 17 June 2011 |
| 4 | Antigua and Barbuda | Data Protection Act 2013 |
| 5 | Argentina | Law 25.326 on the Protection of Personal Data |
| 6 | Armenia | Law of the Republic of Armenia on the Protection of Personal Data (draft) |
| 7 | Australia | The Federal Privacy Act 1988 |
| 8 | Austria | Data Protection Act 2000 |
| 9 | Azerbaijan | Law on Personal Data 2010 |
| 10 | Bahamas | Data Protection (Privacy of Personal Information) Act 2003 |
| 11 | Barbados | Data Protection Bill 2005 |
| 12 | Belarus | Law of the Republic of Belarus on Information, Informa- tization and Protection of information - Law no. 8517 |
| 13 | Belgium | Law on Privacy Protection in relation to the Processing of Personal Data C28 |
| 14 | Benin | Law no. 2009-09 of 22 May 2009 on the organization of the protection of personal data |
| 15 | Bhutan | Bhutan Information Communications and Media Act 2006 |
| 16 | Bolivia | General Law on Telecommunications, Information and Communication Technologies - Law 167 of 08 August 2011 |
| 17 | Bosnia and Herzegovina | Law on the Protection of Personal Data |
| 18 | Brazil | Protection of Personal Data Bill 2011 |
| 19 | Bulgaria | Law for Protection of Personal Data |
| 20 | Burkina Faso | Law no. 010-2004 / AN Holding Data Protection at Personal Character |
| 21 | Cape Verde | Law no. 133 / V / 2001 of 22 January 2001 |
| 22 | Canada | Personal Information Protection and Electronic Documents Act |
| 23 | Chad | Law 007/PR/2015 on the Protection of Personal Data |
| 24 | Chile | Law 19.628 of 1999 |
| 25 | China | The Decision of the Standing Committee of the National People's Congress on Strengthening the Network Information Protection (2012). |
| 26 | Colombia | Law no. 1581 of 2012 |
| 27 | Costa Rica | Political Constitution of the Republic of Costa Rica, consolidated version to 5 October 2005 |
| 28 | Côte d'Ivoire | Law no. 2013-450 of 19 June 2013 on the Protection of Personal Data |
| 29 | Croatia | Act on Personal Data Protection |
| 30 | Cyprus | The Processing of Personal Data (Protection of the Individual) Law |

*(Continues)*

*Table 12.8*    (*Continued*)

| No. | Country | Title of legislation/draft legislation |
|-----|---------|----------------------------------------|
| 31 | Czech Republic | Law on Personal Data Protection |
| 32 | Denmark | Act on Processing of Personal Data |
| 33 | Dominica | Privacy and Data Protection Bill 2007 |
| 34 | Dominican Republic | Law no. 172-13, on Protection of Personal Data of 13 December 2013 |
| 35 | Ecuador | Protection of Privacy and Personal Data Bill 2016 |
| 36 | El Salvador | Decree no. 695, Official Journal no. 141. Last modified 20 April 2012 |
| 37 | Equatorial Guinea | Law 1/2016 (Data protection law) |
| 38 | Estonia | Data Protection Act |
| 39 | Finland | Personal Data Act |
| 40 | France | Law relating to the protection of individuals against the processing of personal data |
| 41 | Gabon | Law no. 001/2011 on the protection of personal data personal character |
| 42 | Gambia | Information and Communications Act no. 2 of 2009 |
| 43 | Georgia | Law of Georgia on Personal Data Protection |
| 44 | Germany | Federal Data Protection Act<br>Federal Data Protection Act – BDSG |
| 45 | Ghana | Data Protection Act (Act no. 843) 2012—DPA |
| 46 | Greece | Law on the Protection of individuals with regard to the processing of personal data |
| 47 | Honduras | Draft Law on Protection of Personal Data and Habeas Data of Honduras |
| 48 | Hungary | Act on Informational Self-Determination and Freedom of Information |
| 49 | Iceland | Law on the Protection and Processing of Personal Data 1989 |
| 50 | India | Information Technology Act 2000 |
| 51 | Indonesia | Law of the Republic of Indonesia Number 11 of 2008 Concerning Electronic Information and Transactions |
| 52 | Iran | Law on Electronic Commerce<br>Law 71063 on Computer Crimes |
| 53 | Iraq | Draft Data Protection and Privacy Law |
| 54 | Ireland | Data Protection Act, 1988 |
| 55 | Italy | Legislative Decree 30 June 2003, n. 196 - Code regarding the protection of personal data |
| 56 | Jamaica | Data Protection Bill 2012 |
| 57 | Japan | Act on the Protection of Personal Information |
| 58 | Jordan | Data Protection Bill |
| 59 | Kazakhstan | Law on personal data and their protection, 21 May 2013 |
| 60 | Kenya | Data Protection Bill 2012 |
| 61 | Republic of Korea | Korea's Personal Information Protection Act was promulgated in 2011 as amended |
| 62 | Kuwait | Law No. 20 of 2014 |
| 63 | Kyrgyzstan | Law on Personal Data 2008 |
| 64 | Latvia | Law on Protection of Personal Data of Natural Persons |
| 65 | Lesotho | Data Protection Act 2012 |
| 66 | Liechtenstein | Act amending the Data Protection Act, 2002 |
| 67 | Lithuania | Law on Legal Protection of Personal Data |
| 68 | Luxembourg | Data Protection Law |
| 69 | Madagascar | Law No. 2014-38 |

*Table 12.8    (Continued)*

| No. | Country | Title of legislation/draft legislation |
|-----|---------|----------------------------------------|
| 70 | Malawi | Electronic Transactions and Cybersecurity Act 2016 |
| 71 | Malaysia | Personal Data Protection Act 2010 |
| 72 | Mali | Law no. 2013-015 of 21 May 2013 |
| 73 | Malta | Data Protection Act 2001 |
| 74 | Mauritius | Data Protection Act 2004 |
| 75 | Mexico | Federal Law on Protection of Personal Data Held by Individuals 2010 |
| 76 | Monaco | Act controlling personal data processing 1993 |
| 77 | Montenegro | Law on Personal Data Protection 2008 |
| 78 | Morocco | Law no. 09-08/2009 on the protection of people toward data protection of a personal nature |
| 79 | Nepal | Right to Information Act, 2064 (2007) |
| 80 | Netherlands | Personal Data Protection Act 1998<br>Personal Data Protection Act |
| 81 | New Zealand | Privacy Act 1993 |
| 82 | Nicaragua | Law no. 787 Law on Protection of Personal Data |
| 83 | Niger | Draft law on the protection of personal data |
| 84 | Nigeria | Data Protection Bill 2011 |
| 85 | Norway | Personal Data Act 2000 |
| 86 | Oman | Royal Decree no. 69 of 2008 - Electronic Transactions Law |
| 87 | Pakistan | Electronic Data Protection Act 2005 – Draft |
| 88 | Panama | Personal Data Protection Bill 2016 |
| 89 | Paraguay | Law 4868/2013 on Electronic Commerce<br>Law 1682/2001 Regulates the Private Character Information |
| 90 | Peru | Law no. 29733—Personal Data Protection Law |
| 91 | Philippines | Data Privacy Act of 2012 |
| 92 | Poland | Act on the Protection of Personal Data 1997 |
| 93 | Portugal | Law of protection of personal data 1991 |
| 94 | Qatar | Law no. 13 of 2016 Concerning Privacy and Protection of Personal Data |
| 95 | Republic of Moldova | Law on Personal Data Protection 2007 |
| 96 | Romania | Law on the protection of individuals with regard to the processing of personal data, etc. (2001) |
| 97 | Russian Federation | Federal Law Regarding Personal Data 2006 |
| 98 | Saint Kitts and Nevis | Privacy and Data Protection Bill 2012 |
| 99 | Saint Lucia | Data Protection Act 2011 |
| 100 | Saint Vincent and the Grenadines | Privacy Act 2003 |
| 101 | San Marino | Law regulating the Computerized Collection of Personal Data 1983 |
| 102 | Sao Tome and Principe | Data Protection Law 2016 |
| 103 | Senegal | Law no. 2008–12 of 25 January 2008 on the Protection of Personal Data |
| 104 | Serbia | Law on Personal Data Protection 2008 |
| 105 | Seychelles | Data Protection Act 2003 |
| 106 | Singapore | Personal Data Protection Act 2012 |
| 107 | Slovakia | Act on the Protection of Personal Data 1992 |

*(Continues)*

*Table 12.8    (Continued)*

| No. | Country | Title of legislation/draft legislation |
|-----|---------|----------------------------------------|
| 108 | Slovenia | Personal Data Protection Act 1990 |
| 109 | South Africa | Protection of Personal Information Act 4 of 2013 |
| 110 | Spain | Organic Law 15/1999 on Personal Data Protection |
| 111 | Suriname | The Constitution of the Republic of Suriname, Article 17 |
| 112 | Swaziland | Data Protection Bill |
| 113 | Sweden | Personal Data Act 1998 |
| 114 | Switzerland | Federal Act on Data Protection, 1992 |
| 115 | Tajikistan | Law on Protection of Information (2 December 2002, No 71) |
| 116 | Thailand | Personal Data Protection Bill 2011 |
| 117 | Republic of Macedonia | Law on Personal Data Protection |
| 118 | Trinidad and Tobago | Data Protection Act 2011 |
| 119 | Tunisia | Law 63/2004 |
| 120 | Turkey | Data Protection Law 2016 |
| 121 | Uganda | The Data Protection and Privacy Bill, 2015 |
| 122 | Ukraine | Law on Personal Data Protection 2011 |
| 123 | United Arab Emirates | Dubai International Financial Centre (DIFC) Data Protection Law |
| 124 | UK of Great Britain and Northern Ireland | Data Protection Act 1998 |
| 125 | Tanzania | Data Protection Bill 2013 |
| 126 | United States of America | Privacy Act of 1974 |
| 127 | Uruguay | Law 18331 Protection of Personal Data, Habeas Data Action of 11 August 2008 and Regulatory Decree 414/2009 |
| 128 | Vietnam | Law on Protection of Consumers' Rights 2010 |
| 129 | Yemen | Law of the Right of Access to Information 2012 |
| 130 | Zambia | The Electronic Communications and Transactions Act, Act Number 21 of 2009—the Electronic Communications Act |
| 131 | Zimbabwe | Draft Data Protection Bill 2016 |

Facebook and Cambridge Analytica serve as a good recent example of firms that have used users' information without their permission. A lawsuit was filed against the firms by both American and British lawyers. The lawsuit claimed that the companies used private personal information from their users without their consent for the purpose of developing political propaganda campaigns in both the US and UK. Cambridge Analytica is a company that monitors and uses personal data to change audience behavior, both commercially and politically. The company has worked in support of many republican campaigns in the US elections, including Donald trump's campaign. Steve Bannon, who was Trumps campaign manager, served on the firm's board. Cambridge Analytica has denied allegations against them claiming they used Facebook data to help Donald Trump win the presidency in the 2016 elections. However, it is believed that both firms obtained private and personal information from 70 million Facebook users without their permission regardless of whether the data obtained was used in influencing elections [27]. So what laws are placed to protect users in such situations?

Unlawfully obtaining personal data is when a person purposely and knowingly discloses personal data without consent of the individual. The law however does not apply to personal data necessary to prevent or help investigate a crime. It is also against the law to sell or use personal data for the purpose of advertisements without consent. A person who does break the DPLs in the UK is guilty of an offence. European countries are known to have the strictest DPLs. The maximum fine a firm can face in the UK for the breaking of DPLs is €500,000, and those that commit criminal offences under the Data Protection Act are prosecuted and reported to the Parliament [26–28].

As for the US, they are known to have less strict and more complex DPLs. The USA has few federal DPLs, as well as state privacy laws, which differ from state to state. The federal laws mainly prohibit unfair and deceiving practices and ensure the protection of children's data. As for states they focus on data privacy in relation to healthcare companies and financial organizations. For example, the state of California has its own Data Protection Act protecting personal information online—California Government Code section 11015.5—this law prohibits agencies from sharing of an individual's information without the written consent of the individual [29].

As a result of the Facebook sharing user's information with a third party such as Cambridge Analytica, some companies began to take precautions for the protection of personal data of their users. Apple, for example, has been working on removing, from its App Store, apps which share location data of their users with third parties without the clear consent from the users (Sections 5.1.1 and 5.1.2 of the company's guidelines). The company clarifies to those app developers that the information they provided to their users as to what occurs to their data after its collection was not clear. Apple does notify the affected app developers informing them about the reasons for their Apps removal from the Apple Store. The developers can then choose whether or not they would change their data protection and resubmit their app to be reviewed by Apple [30].

In 2012, the Canadian House of Commons Standing Committee on Access to Information, Privacy and Ethics conducted a study on the efforts and measures taken by social media companies to protect the personal information of Canadians [31]. The committee presented the current situation and discussed the main issues of concern related to social media and individual's privacy protection, which include consent, accountability, usage, and retention. In Canada, the Personal Information Protection and Electronic Documents Act (PIPEDA) is the principal piece of legislation for protecting individuals' privacy in their dealings with social media companies and other organizations in the private sector. After their investigation, "The Committee" came up with a list of recommendations based on hearing witnesses representing different groups such as government, public interest groups, academia, etc., in addition to meeting with US privacy officials and law makers.

The study provided a list of recommendations for the Canadian government in order to establish guidelines directed at social media and data management companies [31]. These recommendations are also applicable to be implemented by any country to protect personal information online. The list of recommendation directed at social media companies emphasized that social media companies should

- help develop guidelines and practices that fully comply with PIPEDA.
- help develop agreements, contracts, and policies that are drafted in accessible, understandable language that clearly facilitates continuous consent.
- develop guidelines and polices to ensure individual's rights in the process of consent and access to their personal information.
- provide support to organizations offering training and education on digital activities and privacy.
- promote safe and active online activities, particularly to vulnerable groups such as children.
- provide support to organizations devoted to training, educating and promoting awareness to teachers, children, and their parents.
- provide support to digital literacy programs.

As the number of pages on the Internet exponentially grow, privacy statements and terms are used to govern the way information is being collected, used, and transmitted. Everyone is familiar with privacy statements which usually appear when we create social media or other types of accounts online such as e-mail accounts. Usually a privacy statement contains detailed information on how information will be collected and used; the list below provides most of the issues/ sections that may be available in a privacy statement [32].

- Collection, use, and sharing of personal information
- Notification of changes
- Links to third-party applications/websites
- Information security and accuracy
- Cookies, web beacons, and other technologies
- Retention
- Online advertising
- Privacy questions and access.

Compliance with such policies is very crucial as it affects billions of individuals and usually businesses and governments rely on security and privacy firms to confirm that their websites are operating according to national and international laws and regulations. Online privacy certification programs or seal programs issue certificates which appear as a seal or logo on the website to state that the website is following laws that govern data protection. Examples of online privacy seal programs include BBBOnline, Truste, and Webtrust [33,34]. Therefore, keeping up with technology changes and continuous updates to privacy policies will certainly help protect governments' and individuals' data from any vulnerability.

## 12.6    The EU general data protection regulation

The EU's DPLs are regarded as a gold standard which is used as reference by many countries. The European Data Protection Directive (Directive 95/46/EC) was adopted on October 24, 1995, and this directive includes policies on the processing of personal information and how it is used. This directive is considered the significant element of the EU privacy and human rights law. The Directive 95/46/EC was developed during the Internet infancy years and since then the technology has excelled rapidly raising many issues and challenges related to data protection forcing the EU commission to implement updated measures to strengthen the individual's rights of data protection to be in line with the current demands caused by the advancements in technology. Therefore, in 2016, the EU adopted the EU General Data Protection Regulation (GDPR), which is considered one of its greatest achievements in recent years. The GDPR is now recognized as law across the EU. The EU gave its member states two years to comply fully and implement the GDPR in their countries by May 2018 [26,35,36].

The new changes to the EU GDPR came to effect on May 25, 2018, at the time this book is being written. The purpose of the GDPR is to protect individuals from privacy and data breaches. The previous EU GDPR was available in 1995 and it took 23 years for it to be updated as a result of continuous and advancements in technology which created a data-driven world. The main updates to the regulatory policies witnessed an increase in territorial scope, an increase in penalties, and strengthening in consent conditions and data subject rights thus providing a positive impact on conducting business worldwide.

In the previous GDPR, the regional geographical applicability was ambiguous and referred to data process in the context of an establishment, as a result, this was challenged in several high-profile court cases and lead to the principal change to laws of data privacy which comes with the extended jurisdiction of GDPR to be applied to all organizations processing individual's information residing in the EU, irrespective of the location of the organization. This includes the activities relate to offering goods, services, monitoring of behavior taking place within the EU, in addition, non-EU businesses must appoint a representative in the EU in cases where data of EU citizens are being processed [26,35,36].

The penalties for organizations in breach of the GDPR could exceed either €20 million or fined up to 4 percent of the annual global turnover whichever is greater, for serious violations such as, violating the core of privacy by design concepts or not having customer consent to process data. The GDPR have implemented a tiered-based approach to fines. These penalties apply to both the controllers and processes which means that clouds are not exempt from this enforcement. The consent conditions have been strengthened and companies must provide their request for consent in a straightforwardly and clear accessible form using simple and clear language. This should be provided together with the reasons for data processing. In addition, the consent withdrawal by the individual should be carried out as easy as it is given [36].

The individual's rights include rights related to breach notification, rights of access, privacy by design, data probability, data to be forgotten, and data protection officers. The GDPR mandates that in case of a data breach organizations in all member states must notify their customers and controllers within 72 h of first being informed of the data breach. The rights of access include the right to obtain confirmation regarding whether personal data is processed, where, and for what reasons. Furthermore, an electronic copy of the personal data shall be provided free of charge. The Privacy by design concept ensures that technical and organizational procedures should be implemented during the system design to protect the rights of individuals. The guidelines call for the processing of the most needed data by the required persons. The GDPR policies related to data probability guarantees the right for an individual to receive he/her own personal data in an electronic format and provide the right to send the data to another controller. The GDPR gives individuals the control over their personal data and entitles them to have the data controller erase the personal data, stop the distribution of data, and ask third parties to halt the processing of data. Some of the conditions to erase data include the data is no longer needed for the purpose it was initially used for and in case the consent was withdrawn by the individual. This requires the controllers to compare the request by the individual against the public interest in the availability of data. The appointment of data protection officers (DPOs) is required for processors and controllers whose responsibilities involve processing procedures and systematic monitoring of individual's data [36]. The main requirements for appointing DPO are:

- The officer must be an expert and familiar with the DPLs and policies.
- May be an internal or external member service provider.
- The DPO must receive the contract details.
- The DPO must operate in a proper environment which provides the appropriate resources to carry the tasks of the job.
- The DPO must report the highest level of management.
- The DPO needs to keep out of tasks that may result in conflict of interest.

Recently, many organizations which collect information such as e-mail providers and social media companies are requesting their clients to agree to the updated privacy policy. These changes are a result of the EU data privacy laws which came into effect on May 25, 2018. Therefore, it is not a surprise that clients worldwide have been receiving these privacy agreements updates due to the fact that EU regulations influence data privacy legislations worldwide.

## 12.7 DPLs and cybersecurity challenges

A study by UNCTAD [37] identified several challenge areas in the development and implementation of DPLs where improvements are needed in, these are as:

- Gaps in coverage:
  The number of countries with DPL or drafted legislation are 112 and 19, respectively, and increasing; however, still nearly 32 percent of countries or less are with no laws in place. Therefore, having no laws in place usually leads to no trust and reduced confidence in a wide range of commercial activities. As a result, the countries with no legislations in place are at risk of losing international trade opportunities and these gaps in coverage make it very difficult to promote global interoperability.

- Addressing new technologies
  The current advancements in technology include cloud services, IoT, and big data analytics, in addition to the future technological innovations and increased connectivity with 5G networks. These technologies can deliver enormous benefits and at the same time create challenges in the areas of personal data protection and management of cross-border transfers of data. Hence, with IoT, the use of cloud services and the huge amount of data being collected, big data analytics is evolving as a solution used by many businesses to manage and analyze data from different sources using cloud services; however, causing major challenges for governments and businesses in providing comprehensive laws that governs the privacy of the data of subjects.
- Managing cross-border data
  The laws for transferring of personal data to different jurisdiction in a country or to other countries usually provide no restriction or restrictions with some exceptions. These are either one-off or ongoing exceptions. For the "one-off exception," it is noted that there is a broad agreement to allow a cross-border data transfer. However, for the ongoing exceptions there is no global agreement or consistency in their use. There are several approaches these are: "adequacy" assesses whether an entire target jurisdiction provides sufficient protection for the transfer of personal data, "consent" examines whether individuals can agree to the transfer of their personal data to other countries, "binding rules" reflects whether a specific company has set processes, guidelines, and review mechanisms for sufficient protection for the transfer of personal data, and "model contracts" assesses whether the contract wording provide sufficient protection of data. The implementation of these exceptions provides limitations, for example, in the "adequacy" approach this may present a challenge for countries that do not provide sufficient protection for personal data transfer, in addition to the lengthy process, the "consent" approach is prone to complaints and disputes, the "binding rules" approach is a lengthy and expensive approval process, and the "model contracts" provides challenges to develop appropriate model clauses and keeping it up-to-date.
- Balancing surveillance and data protection
  The topic of surveillance and data protection has not been addressed in detail in many laws and "many national laws included broad exceptions for law enforcement and national security surveillance. Even the European Data Protection Directive does not apply to law enforcement or national security"; however, this restriction is now removed in the new EU GDPR. Due to the growth in cloud computing, more interest in surveillance is becoming evident especially after Edward Snowden, a former US intelligence officer, exposed detail about the surveillance actions supported by the US intelligence services and their allies such as Germany and the UK [38]. Due to this exposure, legal cases were initiated by civil organizations and individuals challenging the extent of surveillance. The most significant case is the Schrems vs. Facebook case [39]. Maximillian Schrems, an Austrian national privacy advocate,

submitted a complaint against Facebook to ban Facebook from moving his personal data from Europe to the US. This case resulted in the revising of the Safe Harbor Agreement, which is renamed as the EU–US Privacy Shield and includes a commitment to more monitoring and tougher enforcement, in addition to new restrictions and conditions on surveillance. Therefore, since June of 2013, the US has initiated policy reforms to improve governance, identify restrictions on mass surveillance and intelligence agencies, as well as extension of some legal rights to foreign citizens.

- Strengthening enforcement
  The strengthening enforcement powers and sanctions have increased as a result of high-profile breaches seen in the last decade; however, proved to be inadequate to face these breaches. As a result, to the strengthening enforcement, continuous updates and amendments to these laws are noticed.
- Determining jurisdiction
  In the unavailability of an international agreement, the jurisdiction law is considered complex and recently, some governments have made some reforms to their laws. For example, now, the US Child Online Privacy Protection Act (COPPA) includes international service providers. In Japan, a recent law reform requires foreign data controllers to comply with key sections of the Japanese Act in cases data is being collected on Japanese citizens. Similarly, the EU GDPR now contains a clause that addresses the jurisdiction issue. These reforms are essential as they extend the data protection laws that target local residents to include any business regardless of its location.
- Managing the compliance burden
  "Data protection requirements risk limiting the opportunities for innovation or creating unrealistic compliance burdens on business [37]." Some of these requirements may overstrain businesses, such as appointment of DPO and establishment of local offices or data centers.

In general, the above challenges are a result of unavailable single global model for managing data privacy and protection. Therefore, in the absence of international DPLs, such challenges will continue to play a role in the development and implementation of these laws.

## 12.8   Data privacy and cybersecurity checklist

In preparing data protection guidelines and procedures, the first step an organization needs to do is to study the current situation of its network to prioritize cybersecurity and data protection procedures which could be initialized by making a checklist that could include, but not limited to, the following items [21,40–44]:

- Identify the security team, as well as legal and consultants who have experience with privacy laws, cybersecurity, and crisis management.
- Confirm that all pertinent regulatory requirements are encompassed into company guidelines and procedures.

- Confirm that the company has sufficient compliance testing techniques/ procedures set up to establish planned periodic testing and checking.
- Review available information security procedures, guidelines, and policies with the IT security team to ensure they reflect current regulatory requirements governing data security, privacy, and contractual obligations.
- Assign and document roles and responsibilities for compliance. Determine if your policies align with the company's business goals and practices. Link to your business continuity plan.
- Identify the information assets of each department, the information storage location, its importance and sensitivity, how it is used and what are the processes needed to access it.
- Regularly evaluate the business information security training, implementation, procedures, and policies.
- Develop a detailed incident response plan. So, you can use to conduct breach incidents drills and simulations to test the network/process and use the observations/ results to improve the incident response plan by focusing on cybersecurity and establishing attractive governance structures and internal controls.
- Develop risk management principles apply to information security. Conduct periodic risk assessments to identify cybersecurity threats, vulnerabilities, and business consequences.
- Consider operation strategies in circumstances where access to data is denied or data is lost.
- Consider joining an industry-centered cybersecurity information sharing initiative.
- Occasionally review the compliance of all employees and consultants who have access to data resources with the policies to affirm that continual access is pertinent and remove access for those who no longer need it. Document controls to avoid unauthorized or unlicensed access to the organization devices and networks.
- Update third-party vendor contracts to require warranties and representations regarding acceptable cybersecurity controls and conduct routine security documentations and compliance reviews.
- Verify that third-party vendors have adequate cybersecurity insurance protection coverage and identify practices that may invalidate the terms of their insurance protection.
- Assess with the business leaders the company's insurance coverage and exclusion terms for cybersecurity threats to ensure that the cyber insurance protection coverage terms are acceptable and suitable for the business and the risks which may be encountered.

## 12.9 Recommendations and future research directions in data privacy

Data privacy and security is a continuous process that is essential for any organization. Its purpose is to protect against any risks which may render data as vulnerable. From the view point of the authors, the recommendations below are needed to control any problems which may arise from not abiding by the data protection laws; therefore, organizations need to

- Develop a customized cyber security framework similar to the National Institute of Standards and Technology (NIST), presented in Chapter 2, which provides the following functions: identify, detect, protect, respond, and recover in order to manage the risks of a business/organization.
- Data classification is a high-cost process and organizations must do their homework to implement a secured classification system, so as to avoid any implications that may result from any errors.
- Confidential information should not be accessed by external drives, personal e-mails should not be used, personal smart devices should not be allowed in areas where highly sensitive information is used or stored, and the encryption of data should be in real time to response to breaching events.
- Develop a custom cybersecurity checklist to assistant businesses in their plans and procedures. This checklist must include best business practices, incident response plan, risk management principles and provide guidelines for the management, employees, and IT staff.
- Access to specific end-points in the network could be blocked in any cases of a slight breaching suspicion. Multi-authentication methods should be applied to access databases and secured information. Multiple secure real-time external and remote backup systems should be regularly used and available to backup information in case a breach caused the shutdown of the system or network by the security monitor.
- Since most countries have legislation or draft legislation in e-transactions, i.e., trade-related laws, then it may be appropriate to attach data privacy laws to such laws and by these countries would give this a higher priority. Therefore, this must be a prerequisite for conducting e-commerce or online services.
- An international body, such as the United Nations, should aim at setting grounds to establish an international "data privacy and security committee" consisting of members representing all countries or unions such as the Association of Southeastern Asian Nations (ASEN), the African Union (AU), the EU, and the Gulf Cooperation Council (GCC). The first step would be to have an international global conference sponsored by all countries to present the status, challenges and recommend solutions. As a result, this will eliminate separate laws for countries as well as any continual updates by countries since a global solution would make this uniform globally. Continual updates may be suggested every five or ten years if needed. This in turn will limit many of the challenges faced by countries in developing such polices. At least the number of experts available worldwide will be enough to tackle all the related issues of these polices and other resources could be distributed for other aspects related to implementation and compliance.
- Most of DPLs were designed following the norms set by the 1995 European Data Protection Directive which does not address the relatively new issues. This is considered a challenge for developing countries as the new EU GDPR is published and countries must tweak their laws to this new regulation.

- Provide support to organizations devoted to training, education and promoting awareness on data privacy and protection laws.

As a result of the recommendation listed above, the following future research directions are identified, which could help in promoting awareness and involve all countries of the world in the creation of data protection policies [44].

- Researchers should study the process for data privacy and cybersecurity for different sizes of establishments in order to propose a comprehensive checklist to follow in the protection of data from any risk it may encounter during system breaches keeping in mind the implementation of tiered level access and protection of information.
- Researchers need to be ahead of hackers in finding and fixing any system vulnerabilities that could risk sensitive data. Therefore, investigating different types of breaches which were publicized would serve as pivotal step in understanding how to create better strong and secure systems.
- Development of a uniform global data protection polices which can be used by any country without the need for policies developed by individual countries. This can also be applied to e-consumer and cybersecurity laws.

Therefore, the cooperation between researchers, law enforcement officers, and government consultants is essential to the development, monitoring, and continual improvement of data protection laws and policies.

## 12.10  Conclusion

The concept of privacy is reinterpreted by "social media users" living in this era of advanced technology engaging in social networking with unlimited Internet access. Young individuals are more familiar with the development of invasive technologies which offer convenience and productivity. So, people are not prune from reputational damage given the day and age we are living in. The years ahead are likely to bring increased attention to data collection, processing and transmission due to the advancements in technology in many areas such as IoT, big data, and cloud technology. These novel areas hold serious implications for security (as in hacking vehicles), as well as uncertain impacts on personal autonomy, privacy, and profiling. Data localization trends, data transfer disputes, aggressive government demands for decoding and access to underlying software code and algorithms, fake news, and election hacking will continue to shake the digital trade and affect political stability. The intersection of privacy, cybersecurity, human rights, and counter-terrorism remains fraught and subject to balanced governance in different jurisdictions. The field of privacy, data protection, and cybersecurity will hence keep on eschewing harmony for long time to come.

Data protection privacy laws bring positive benefits to the management of information; it is not a barrier to the effective business practice in either the public or the private sector. Security procedures or policies can help isolate or encode data in real time during situations where data may be at risk from hackers. Therefore, the implementation of a comprehensive data loss prevention approach should not be an afterthought; it can help organizations avoid making the negative disastrous headlines. A data breach can be very costly and could affect organizations and individuals. This could cost millions of dollars as individuals may seek compensation and governments impose penalties on organizations for failing to comply with DPLs. Therefore, following proper data protection procedures help prevent cybercrimes by ensuring personal information is protected.

Finally, everyone has a role in cybersecurity: as an individual you need to know your rights and responsibilities, as a staff member in any organization you need to receive proper training and ensure that you keep all information secure and protected, as an IT manager you need to secure, protect, and monitor the cybersecurity framework and as a management team for an organization you need to provide the proper support for the data privacy framework, provide the infrastructure needed for its proper implementation as well as oversee the whole process with the organization's security team. Hence, continual increase in awareness of the importance of data privacy laws and proper implementation and continual updates of cybersecurity framework processes will certainly help avoid any breaches that could have devastating effects on the individuals and organizations.

## Acknowledgment

This work was partially supported by RDU project number RDU1603102 from Universiti Malaysia Pahang.

## References

[1]   Sivarajah, U., Kamal, M. M., Irani, Z., and Weerakkody, V. 'Critical analysis of Big Data challenges and analytical methods'. *Journal of Business Research*. 2017; 70: 263–286.

[2]   Attaran M., Stark, J., and Stotler, D. 'Opportunities and challenges for big data analytics in US higher education, A conceptual model for implementation'. *Journal of Industry and Higher Education*. 2018; 32(3):169–182.

[3]   Murphy, M. More than 1 billion people now use Facebook every day [online], 2015. Available from https://qz.com/541609/more-than-1-billion-people-now-use-facebook-every-day/ [Accessed 26 Feb 2018].

[4]   Robertson, M. R. 500 hours of video uploaded to YouTube every minute (Forecast) [online], 2015. Available from http://tubularinsights.com/hours-minute-uploaded-youtube/ [Accessed 1 Mar 2018].

[5]   Marr, B. Big Data: 20 mind-boggling facts everyone must read [online], 2015. Available from https://www.forbes.com/sites/bernardmarr/2015/09/30/big-data-20-mind-boggling-facts-everyone-must-read/#5569979c17b1 [Accessed 1 Mar 2018].

[6]   Verizon's 2016 Data Breach Investigations Report finds cybercriminals are exploiting human nature [online], 2016. Available from https://www.

prnewswire.com/news-releases/verizons-2016-data-breach-investigations-report-finds-cybercriminals-are-exploiting-human-nature-300258134.html [Accessed 3 Mar 2018].

[7] O'Brien, S A. Giant Equifax data breach: 143 million people could be affected [online], 2017. Available from https://money.cnn.com/2017/09/07/technology/business/equifax-data-breach/index.html [Accessed 3 Mar 2018].

[8] Satter, M. Over 10,000 companies downloading software vulnerable to Equifax hack [online], 2018. Available from https://www.cyberscoop.com/apache-struts-downloads-sonatype-equifax/ [Accessed 13 May 2018].

[9] The most infamous data breaches [online], 2018. Available from https://www.techworld.com/security/uks-most-infamous-data-breaches-3604586/ [Accessed 13 August 2018].

[10] Data Breach Statistics – data records lost or stolen since 2013 – [online], 2018. Available from https://breachlevelindex.com/ [Accessed 20 Aug 2018].

[11] Lambert, P. Understanding the New European Data Protection Rules. New York, Auerbach Publications; 2017.

[12] Ferreira, J. Hegarty, C. and Grahn, A. 10 reasons why your organization needs data loss prevention [online], 2018. Available from https://focus.forsythe.com/articles/19/10-Reasons-Why-Your-Organization-Needs-Data-Loss-Prevention [Accessed 23 Jul 2018].

[13] Burgess M. Reddit hit by data breach after hackers hijack SMS login system [online], 2018. Available from http://www.wired.co.uk/article/hacks-data-breaches-in-2018 [Accessed 20 Aug 2018].

[14] Grentzenberg V., and Kirchner J. 'Data Protection and Monitoring' in Kirchner J., Kremp P., Magotsch M. (eds.) *Key Aspects of German Employment and Labour Law*. Berlin: Springer; 2018, pp. 135–151.

[15] Chua, H.N., Herbland, A., Wong, S.F., and Chang, Y. 'Compliance to personal data protection principles: A study of how organizations frame privacy policy notices'. *Telematics and Informatics*. 2017;34(4):157–70.

[16] Tawalbeh, L., Darwazeh, N. S., Al-Qassas, R. S., and AlDosari F. 'A secure cloud computing model based on data classification'. *Procedia Computer Science*. 2015;52:1153–1158.

[17] National Academies of Sciences, Engineering, and Medicine. *Protection of Transportation Infrastructure from Cyber Attacks: A Primer*. Chapter 7 Security Programs and Support Frameworks. Washington, DC: The National Academies Press; 2016. pp. 118–127.

[18] Rowley, J.E., and Farrow, J. Organizing Knowledge: Introduction to Access to Information: Introduction to Access to Information. London: Routledge; 2018.

[19] Pomerantz, J. R. 'Perceptual organization in information processing' in Kubovy, M., and Pomerantz, J. R. (eds.) *Perceptual organization*. London: Routledge; 2017, pp. 141–180.

[20] Mohamed, A. Data classification: why it is important and how to do it [online], 2018. Available from https://www.computerweekly.com/feature/Data-classification-why-it-is-important-and-how-to-do-it [Accessed 13 Apr 2018].

[21]    Department of Finance, Ireland. Protecting the confidentiality of personal Data Guidance Note [online], 2008. Available from https://www.dataprotection.ie/documents/guidance/GuidanceFinance.pdf [Accessed 24 Jan 2018].

[22]    U.S. Department of Health and Human Services. Studies of welfare populations: data collection and research issues. Fair information practice [online], 2002. Available from https://aspe.hhs.gov/report/studies-welfare-populations-data-collection-and-research-issues/fair-information-practices [Accessed 13 May 2018].

[23]    United Nations Conference on Trade and Development. *Data protection and privacy legislation worldwide.* [online], 2018. Available from http://unctad.org/en/Pages/DTL/STI_and_ICTs/ICT4D-Legislation/eCom-Data-Protection-Laws.aspx [Accessed on 15 May 2018].

[24]    Cyberlaws.net. Cyber laws of different countries [online], 2018. Available from http://cyberlaws.net/cyber-laws-different-countries/ [Accessed 17 Mar 2018].

[25]    Dyson, A., Halpert, J., Ramos, D. *et al.* Data protection laws of the world handbook [online]. 3rd edn, 2014, DLA Piper, Available from https://www.dlapiperdataprotection.com/index.html [Accessed 18 May 2018].

[26]    Corporate authors Council of Europe, European Court of Human Rights, European Data Protection Supervisor, European Union Agency for Fundamental Rights (EU body or agency), Handbook on European data protection law [online]. 2018. Available from http://fra.europa.eu/en/publication/2018/handbook-european-data-protection-law [Accessed 20 May 2018].

[27]    Cadwalladr, C. and Graham-Harrison, E. Revealed: 50 million Facebook profiles harvested for Cambridge Analytica in major data breach. [online]. 2018. Accessed from https://www.theguardian.com/news/series/cambridge-analytica-files [Accessed 23 Mar 2018].

[28]    Custers, B., Dechesne, F., Sears, A. M., Tani, T., and van der Hof, S. 'A comparison of data protection legislation and policies across the EU'. *Computer Law & Security Review*, 2018;34(2): 234–243.

[29]    California Legislative Information. *ARTICLE 1. General [11000 - 11019.11]* [online]. 1999. Available from http://leginfo.legislature.ca.gov/faces/codes_displaySection.xhtml?sectionNum=11015.5.&lawCode=GOV [Accessed 1 Jun 2018].

[30]    App Store. App Store Review Guidelines [online], 2018. Available from https://developer.apple.com/app-store/review/guidelines/ [Accessed 24 May 2018].

[31]    House of Commons, Canada. Chair: Dusseault, P. Privacy and social media in the age of big data report on the standing committee on access to information, privacy and ethics [online] 2013. https://www.ourcommons.ca/Content/Committee/411/ETHI/Reports/RP6094136/ethirp05/ethirp05-e.pdf [Accessed 16 Mar 2018].

[32]    Microsoft. Microsoft privacy statement [online]. 2018. Available from https://privacy.microsoft.com/en-ca/privacystatement [Accessed 25 May 2018].

[33]    Cavoukian, A., and Crompton, M. Web seals: a review of online privacy programs [online]. Venice: 22nd International Conference on Privacy and Personal Data Protection; 2000. Available from https://www.ipc.on.ca/wp-content/uploads/Resources/up-seals.pdf [Accessed 25 May 2018].

[34]    SANS Institute. Comparison of three online privacy seal programs [online]. 2002. Available from https://www.sans.org/reading-room/white-papers/privacy/comparison-online-privacy-seal-programs-685 [Accessed 3 June 2018].

[35]    European Data Protection Supervisor. The history of the general data protection regulation [online]. 2018. Available from https://edps.europa.eu/data-protection/data-protection/legislation/history-general-data-protection-regulation_en [Accessed 2 Jun 2018].

[36]    EU General Data Protection Regulation. GDPR key changes, an overview of the main changes under GDPR and how they differ from the previous directive [online]. 2018. https://www.eugdpr.org/key-changes.html [Accessed 2 Jun 2018].

[37]    United Nations. Data protection regulations and international data flows: Implications for trade and development [online]. 2016. Available from http://unctad.org/en/PublicationsLibrary/dtlstict2016d1_en.pdf    [Accessed 19 Apr 2018].

[38]    Walsh, P. F., and Miller, S. 'Rethinking 'Five Eyes' security intelligence collection policies and practice post Snowden'. *Intelligence and National Security*. 2016;31(3):345–368.

[39]    Schulz, T.J. 'Schrems v. Data Protection Commissioner (CJEU)'. *International Legal Materials*. 2017;56(2):245–272.

[40]    Stallings, W. *Effective Cybersecurity: A Guide to Using Best Practices and Standards*. Boston: Addison-Wesley Professional; 2018.

[41]    Dion, M., 2018. *Intelligence and Cyber Threat Management*. In Cybersecurity Best Practices. Wiesbaden: Springer Vieweg; 2018. pp. 363–392.

[42]    Sabillon, R. A Practical Model to Perform Comprehensive Cybersecurity Audits. *Enfoque UTE*. 2018;9(1):127–137.

[43]    Eversheds Sutherland, Cybersecurity preparedness checklist [online]. 2018. Available from https://www.aegislink.com/content/dam/aegislink/resources/presentations/public/2015/2015_07-2_07-23/Cyber_Claims_Tabletop_1.pdf [Accessed 23 May 2018].

[44]    Yuan, T. 'Towards the Development of Best Data Security for Big Data'. *Communication Network, University of Embu*. 2017;9(4):291–301.

## Chapter 13

# Conclusion

*Yasser Alginahi[1] and Muhammad Nomani Kabir[2]*

This book is a result of hard work of many researchers around the globe. The book contains theoretical and practical knowledge of state-of-the-art authentication technologies and their applications in big data, IoT, and cloud computing with this technologically connected world. The first six chapters of the book provide the fundamental details of the authentication technologies. Specifically, the role of each chapter can be summarized as follows:

- Chapter 1 provides the basic terminologies, motivation, recent history of data breaches, and overview of the remaining chapters.
- In Chapter 2, the authors discuss the fundamental principles and standards of the information technologies, classification of threats, IoT frameworks from different companies, NIST framework for critical infrastructure cybersecurity, and future research challenges in IoT.
- Chapter 3 presents different categories of authentication algorithms, in particular, hashing functions, symmetric and asymmetric authentication techniques with algorithms and examples. The chapter also provides how the algorithms can be used in IoT, cloud computing, and big data to maintain security. The chapter ends with research trends and future research challenges.
- Chapter 4 is concentrated on cryptographic algorithms which are the backbone of authentication technologies. The symmetric cryptographic algorithms e.g., data encryption standard (DES) and advanced encryption standard (AES) and asymmetric cryptographic algorithms, e.g., RSA, ElGamal public-key encryption and elliptic curve cryptosystems (ECC) are discussed in detail with examples. Finally, the chapter concludes with research challenges and future direction of research.
- Chapter 5 deals with the watermarking algorithms for multimedia to perform copyright protection, ownership verification, or content authentication. In this chapter, the authors classify different watermarking schemes, and describe the principles and algorithms of the fundamental schemes, e.g., robust, fragile and semi-fragile watermarking techniques. In addition, research challenges such as

[1]Department of Electrical and Computer Engineering, University of Windsor, Canada
[2]Faculty of Computer Systems & Software Engineering, University Malaysia Pahang, Malaysia

balancing among the imperceptibility, robustness and embedding capacity of the watermark schemes are presented.

- Chapter 6 is related to biometric authentication which has become challenging in the present era with the modern gadgets that are vulnerable to cyber-physical attacks. The authors in this chapter explain different types of attacks on biometric systems and their possible countermeasures such as biometric cryptosystem, fuzzy commitment scheme, fuzzy vault scheme, and cancellable biometrics. The authors conclude the chapter with research challenges of security issues in biometric cloud.

The first two chapters introduce the readers to the basic knowledge in authentication technologies. Chapters 3 and 4 build the foundation of authentication methods for them. Chapters 5 and 6 further develop the knowledge and skill on authentication techniques of multimedia content itself, and authentication techniques for biometric systems using cryptography. In light of big data, IoT, and cloud computing, Chapters 7 to 12 include some advanced topics which can be briefly described as follows:

- Chapter 7 presents authentication techniques for resource-constrained IoT systems using lightweight block ciphers to maintain secure communication. Ten recent lightweight block ciphers are evaluated in terms of power and energy consumption, latency, security level, throughput, and efficiency on 8-bit, 16-bit, and 32-bit microcontrollers. Finally, a guideline is provided to develop light-weight block ciphers for the low-cost Wi-Fi module in IoT systems.

- In Chapter 8, the authors discuss the secure identity management schemes using multivariate polynomials over a finite field for post-quantum era. The authors also propose a new identification scheme based on multivariate quadratic poly-nomials and the comparison with other schemes demonstrates that the proposed scheme achieves a lower computational complexity. The chapter is concluded with the discussion on quantum-secure identification schemes for cloud, IoT, and big data applications, as well as their research challenges.

- In Chapter 9, the author focuses on authentication schemes for cloud applica-tions. The security aspects of the cloud environment, e.g., identity and access management, confidentiality and data encryption, attacks against information in cloud environments and virtualization security are described. Different authen-tication schemes for cloud applications are presented.

- Chapter 10 presents the security risks in cloud storage due to insider threats. The author of the chapter discusses different insider threats in cloud computing, and the challenges involved in managing the insider threats. Potential solutions for insider threats, e.g., encryption, detection, prevention, honeypots, authentication, and the related concept of access control are presented.

- Chapter 11 provides the implementation techniques of four cryptographic algorithms—AES, DES, SHA, and MD5 on field-programmable gate array (FPGA) for applications in cloud computing. Efficiency for each algorithm is computed in terms of throughput, latency, and resource utilization. The implemented security system can be used in embedded systems, IoTs, cloud servers, and network security processors.

- Chapter 12 presents the principles of data protection laws (DPLs) available in different countries and organizations, data classification, global cyberlaws, DPLs for social media, EU General Data Protection Regulation (GDPR), data privacy, and cyber security checklist. The authors of the chapter include some recommendations, e.g., developing and updating a cybersecurity checklist, developing a uniform global data protection policies, training and educating the people on up-to-date security policies.

The objective of Chapters 7 to 11 is to develop fast and secure algorithms for resource-constrained IoT and cloud computing, while the aim of Chapter 12 is to protect the data by laws and policies. All these chapters include research challenges and future research directions with the evolution of technologies. The advanced topics of these chapters will be interesting for security experts, academic, and industrial researchers. Thus, the book will be a good reference for researchers in information security. Furthermore, Chapters 1 to 6 containing fundamental knowledge of authentication technologies can be an excellent reference for students, teaching staff, and practitioners.

# Index